ALSO BY RICHARD J. BARNET

THE YOUNGEST MINDS

PARENTING AND GENES
IN THE DEVELOPMENT OF
INTELLECT AND EMOTION

Ann B. Barnet, M.D.,
AND
Richard J. Barnet

A Touchstone Book
Published by Simon & Schuster

TOUCHSTONE
Rockefeller Center
1230 Avenue of the Americas
New York, NY 10020

First Touchstone Edition 1999
TOUCHSTONE and colophon are registered trademarks
of Simon & Schuster Inc.

Designed by Sam Potts
Manufactured in the United States of America
1   3   5   7   9   10   8   6   4   2

The Library of Congress has cataloged the hardcover edition as
follows:
Barnet, Ann B.
The youngest minds: parenting and genes in the development
of intellect and emotion / Ann B. Barnet and Richard J. Barnet
p. cm.
Includes bibliographical references and index. 1. Children—
Intelligence levels. 2. Infants—Intelligence levels. 3. Emotions
in children. 4. Emotions in infants. 5. Language acquisition.
6. Child rearing. 7. Child rearing—Social aspects. 8. Nature
and nurture. I. Barnet, Richard J. II. Title.
BF432.C48B37 1998
155.4'13—dc21   98-13450   CIP

ISBN 0-684-81537-0
0-684-85440-6 (Pbk)

The authors and publisher gratefully acknowledge permission to
reprint material from the following works:

Fig. 1-2: Reprinted from *Principles of Neural Science,* 3rd ed., E. R. Kandel, J. H.
Schwartz, and T. M. Jessell, eds., New York: Elsevier, 1991, Copyright © 1991 by
Appleton & Lange.

Fig. 1-3: Reprinted by permission of the publisher from *Postnatal Development of
the Human Cerebral Cortex,* by J. L. Conel, Cambridge, Mass.: Harvard University
Press, Copyright © 1939, 1959 by the President and Fellows of Harvard College.

Fig. 3-3: Reprinted from *Principles of Neural Science,* 3rd ed., E. R. Kandel, J. H.
Schwartz, and T. M. Jessell, eds., New York: Elsevier, 1991, Copyright © 1991 by
Appleton & Lange, courtesy of Marcus Raichle.

Fig. 3-4: Reprinted by permission of the publisher from *Human Behavior and the
Developing Brain,* Geraldine Dawson and Kurt W. Fisher, eds., New York: Guilford
Press, 1994.

Fig. 6-1: Reprinted by permission of the publisher from *Textbook of Medical Physiology,* 9th ed., by Arthur C. Guyton and John E. Hall, Philadelphia: W. B. Saunders,
1996.

For Julian, Joey, and Johanna

and

the children of the Family Place

CONTENTS

INTRODUCTION

This book grows out of our forty-five-year collaboration. The delights and tensions of being parents and the total pleasure of being grandparents are reflected in these pages. Our first daughter was born when one of us was in medical school and the other in law school. Our third grandchild arrived a few months ago. Like all parents, we have been more than witnesses to the miraculous transformations of childhood; for better or worse, every parent plays an important role in the development of a child's mind.

Recent advances in neuroscience and psychology are making it possible to understand more clearly how parents help to shape their children's brains. Our primary purpose in writing this book is to explain what is becoming known about how young children acquire language, develop emotional ties, gain control of their own emotions, become able to experience the joy and pain of others, and embrace moral values.

We bring a range of professional experiences and interests to this joint effort. Ann, a pediatric neurologist who has spent her adult life observing and caring for children, has developed research tools for studying children's brains, and diagnostic tests to detect abnormalities in infants' hearing, vision, and tactile sensation. For many years she directed electroencephalographic (brain wave) research at Children's

Hospital in Washington, D.C. She is also the founder of the Family Place, a community center for young children and their parents that offers poor families a variety of services, such as referrals to medical care, counseling, and parent education. Her interest in the role genes play in development dates from the two summers she spent studying the brains and behavior of mice at the Jackson Laboratory in Bar Harbor, Maine, just before she entered Harvard Medical School. Children, especially young children, have been at the center of her medical practice, neurological research, and volunteer work in the community.

Richard has spent most of his professional life as a writer and teacher. He is the author of twelve books and numerous articles on political and socioeconomic issues. In studying the social changes that accompany global economic integration, he was struck by how much the experience of childhood is changing around the world, and he became concerned about how this rapid transformation was affecting children. This sparked his interest in learning about the remarkable advances in the neurosciences in understanding some of the biological processes of early development. Precisely how environmental influences affect the expression of genes in the shaping of a child's brain is still a mystery, but it is becoming less of one year by year.

That human beings are social animals is a very old idea. From the moment of birth we need the nurture and love of other people. Over the last few years it has become clearer that the quality and character of interactions with others—parents, family members, and caregivers outside the family—actually influence brain development. At the same time, breakthroughs in genetics are providing new insights into the power of inborn factors to shape our lives.

The ancient nature-nurture dichotomy is not helpful in describing the development process. Even in an unborn baby, genes and environment interact almost from the moment of conception. Development is a lifelong dialogue between inherited tendencies and our life history. Children's brains are neither blank slates waiting for a story to be written nor immutable hard-wired circuits controlled by implacable genes. Whether and how a gene is expressed in an individual—that is, whether it ever speaks and what it says—depends on the dynamic interaction of genetic inheritance and the person's experiences. The notion that experience plays a role in development is not controversial, but differing understandings of how early interactions cast their shadows over later life have generated heated controversy throughout the twentieth century.

Our hope is to make the reader more aware of the continuous interplay of biological and environmental factors in specific areas of human development. We have looked at development from the perspective of both neurobiology and psychology, connecting islands of knowledge where we can. Science is telling us a great deal more than we used to know about what children need and when they need it. Although the combined efforts of neuroscientists, educators, psychologists, and pediatricians still fall far short of a comprehensive theory of brain development, a wide range of studies in many fields is yielding new knowledge of great promise.

We have tried to lay before the reader conflicting evidence and opposing views about what children need for healthy development. As alternative hypotheses are tested, a clearer picture will emerge. But clashes over conclusions supported by scientific evidence are virtually inevitable when the findings indicate a need to change personal behavior or social policy. Controversies over global warming and the dangers of tobacco are famous examples. Debates over scientific evidence about what children need and who should provide it are full of passion because the contending views carry with them implicit recommendations about how parents should act and how public money should be spent.

The book focuses on issues that seem especially important to us and on research that we find particularly compelling or intriguing. We cannot claim to be disinterested observers. We start with a concern that a large minority of children in the United States are facing considerable risks in growing up, and we believe that failure to meet their developmental needs is having serious consequences for our whole society. But we also start with the hope that better understanding of the interplay of genetic and environmental factors in children's development can lead to personal decisions and public policies that will reduce these risks. We undertook this project to deepen our own understanding of the space within each child between what is biologically determined and what can be changed; it would please us if what we have found is of use to others.

Three intertwined sets of connections define the process of development. The first set is the wiring of the brain itself. As nerve cells carry their trillions of electrochemical messages from one part of the brain to another, and from the brain to the body and back, the physical structure of the brain takes shape. Each person's set of brain connections is unique; it cannot be cloned. There is a basic reason for this. Even though fundamental features are shared, critical connections in the human brain are shaped and reshaped by ongoing experiences unique to the individual.

A second set of connections, the links between infants and their environment, powerfully affect the connection-making processes within the brain. Among these environmental influences, interactions with caregivers are especially important. Human connections are as important to the development of brain connections as having food to eat, sounds to hear, and light by which to see. Broadly speaking, all children require similar care. But the experience is different for each child because caregivers are not all the same, because each child is born with a distinct combination of traits, and because the character and quality of the interactions between caregivers and children are subject to many different influences.

A third set of connections establishes the social context within which the relationships between caregivers and children develop. The culture in which a family is embedded—and, more specifically, economic and social circumstances, habits, and values—influences the physical surroundings, the daily routines, and the emotional climate of the household. Financial worries, family insecurities, personal uncertainties, job-related stress, and a host of other factors rooted in the social order affect relationships within the family, notably the amount of time mothers and fathers have for their children and how that time is spent. Although we include some research findings from other countries and comparative data to illustrate the role culture plays in child development, our focus is on children in the United States. The explosion in scientific knowledge concerning the processes of brain development is giving us a clearer understanding of the experiences babies need to become healthy adults. But a whirlwind of social change is creating a climate in which it is becoming harder for great numbers of parents to provide these experiences for their children.

Most of this book deals with the first two sets of connections, those within the brain that organize a child's mental capacities and character and those that link children and caregivers. After a brief chapter on the basics of brain organization, we discuss in three chapters the interplay of biological and social links in language acquisition. Four subsequent chapters examine similar processes in the development of a child's capacity for emotional expression and self-control. While the third set of connections—the cultural, political, and economic factors that affect the care of children—are the background for the entire book, they are emphasized in the two final chapters.

In this book we raise many questions. How much does childhood experience influence development of specific human capabilities and character traits? In what ways? Why do things sometimes go wrong? What kinds of childhood experience improve a child's prospects? Why do some children do very well despite their wretched childhoods? What sorts of help increase the possibility of a good life for people who were neglected or otherwise deprived in early childhood?

Some of these questions can be approached with growing assurance. But information is accumulating so fast that theories and beliefs constantly require rethinking and revision. Some of the most intriguing ideas currently being advanced in the neurosciences are hotly debated. In presenting the scientific data we will make an effort to distinguish what we believe to be true because the evidence is convincing, what we find to be interesting and plausible, and what are no more than the informed guesses that have always spurred progress in science even when they turn out to be wrong.

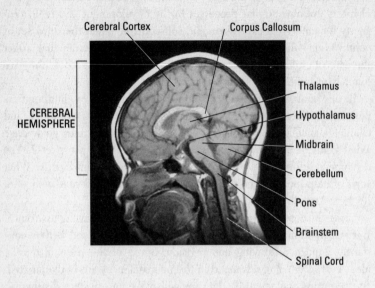

Cerebral Cortex Corpus Callosum

CEREBRAL
HEMISPHERE

Thalamus

Hypothalamus

Midbrain

Cerebellum

Pons

Brainstem

Spinal Cord

FIGURE 1-1. MRI FROM A NORMAL FIVE-YEAR-OLD CHILD.

This image shows the brain "cut" between the two cerebral hemispheres down the midline from nose to occiput (a midsagittal section); thus we are looking at the right side of the brain. The cerebral hemispheres consist of the cerebral cortex and several structures lying deep within it: the hippocampus, the amygdala, and the basal ganglia, which are not visible in the image. The broad white band, the corpus callosum, consists of nerve axon fibers that unite the hemispheres. (*Source:* Children's National Medical Center.)

Chapter One

HOW THE BRAIN
TAKES SHAPE

A baby lying in a crib gazing at her mother may strike us as the very picture of repose, but the little one is actually engaged in the most important work of her life. To an extent we are only just beginning to comprehend, human development is the story of the extraordinary changes that take place inside the head of a young child. Neuroscientists are beginning to tease out some of the secrets of the brain that enable us to think, to speak, to love, to control our impulses, to understand the notion of right and wrong, and to share the feelings of others—in short, the capacities of the mind.[1]

The physical substance of the human brain is quite ordinary. It is composed of the familiar elements found in all animals—carbon, hydrogen, oxygen, sodium, nitrogen, phosphorus, iron, calcium, potassium, and, in trace amounts, a few others. The genetic material of the human brain has no obviously unique properties. It shares with other cells of the body and with the bodies of other vertebrates the basic building-block molecules of the double helix—adenine, thymine, guanine, and cytosine. As in the rest of the human body, 98 percent of the DNA in our brain cells is indistinguishable from that in the brains of other mammals. The uniqueness of the human brain lies not only in its size and complexity but in the properties that make it extraordinarily open to experience.

Advances in neuroscience over the last two decades have confirmed the perceptive intuition of the American psychologist William James: the brain is not so much a thing as a process; its development begins shortly after conception and continues into old age.[2] The process is marked by the formation and orderly movement of billions of neurons, the cells that are the basic units of brain function, to the locations in the head that specify their role. Toward the end of their journey, neurons send out shoots and tendrils from their bodies that seek out and connect with other neurons, and with organs and muscles. The connection-making process greatly speeds up after birth, creating sets of active neural connections that coordinate and control every function of the body.

The process begins when the embryo is a few weeks old. Dense clumps of cells, the precursors of nerve cells, form at the top end of the tube that will become the brain and the spinal cord. Each of these cells divides, doubling their number. Then they double again several times, creating successive generations of cells. Those destined to become the cerebral cortex, the largest structure in the human brain and the one responsible for our distinctively human capabilities, move radially along spokelike scaffolds of supporting cells. Each new wave of doubled cells travels past its older relatives to the outermost layer. Although both cells in each doubled pair may migrate along the radial scaffold, more typically only one of the pair migrates, leaving the other to be the progenitor in the next round of doubling.[3] As each migrating neuron reaches its final destination, it becomes part of one of the brain's functional systems. On their way, neurons come into contact with other cells and with chemical substances released by cells; the contacts activate various genes that define each neuron's identity and purpose. Under the influence of nerve fibers projecting from a distant neuron in another part of the brain, some young nerve cells wander away from their radial path.[4] A neuron might end its migration in the motor area and become part of the system that regulates movement, or it might wind up in the auditory cortex and participate in hearing.

During this process of migration, neuropeptides and other specialized molecules are released by the tissue into which a neuron is starting to grow. These neurotrophic factors, as they are called, transmit chemical signals that either stimulate the neuron to extend its projections to a particular target or discourage a move in that direction. Neurons start out with the potential to perform many functions—they are not genetically programmed for a given role—but during development they become specialists. What any individual nerve cell will do in life, whether it helps enable hearing or imagination, or exerts control on breathing or sleep, depends on where the cell ends its journey. This mass migration is nearly complete by birth.

Neurons come in many more varieties than any other cell type found in the body. Each begins its life looking more or less like a sphere, but as it sets off on its journey and finally settles in its place, it alters its shape, sprouting branches called dendrites and axons. Seen through a microscope, dendrites look like profuse, bushy fibers dividing and subdividing into tiny twigs covered with knobby spines. Dendrites collect information and conduct it toward nerve cell bodies. Axons deliver the brain's commands. They are fewer in number than dendrites, and they usually have longer projections, with branchlike tips. A single neuron can send out and receive thousands of connections or only a few.

Nerve cells send and receive information. They communicate principally by means of electrical impulses flowing through their projecting fibers. Axons and dendrites "fire"—that is, become electrically active at certain thresholds of stimulation—and the impulse is propagated along the fiber. The end of each fiber that is transmitting information contains tiny bulbs housing molecules called neurotransmitters, chemical vehicles for conveying information between the axon of one neuron and the dendrite of another. Electrical stimulation causes neurotransmitter molecules to be released from their bulb and cross a gap to waiting receptor molecules of the neuron on the other side. By this means, information is transferred from one cell to the next. The junctions that link one neuron to another are called synapses. A neuron that has a branched axon can synapse with as many neurons as it has branches. Likewise, synaptic twigs from many neurons can converge on a single neuron. Dozens of neurotransmitters are busily at work in the brain. But in order to deliver their messages they must encounter specific receptor molecules. Receptors are like keyholes. They allow a neurotransmitter to key a cell's function only if it fits into and turns the receptor cell's locking mechanism.

Throughout life, under both genetic and environmental influences, neuronal connections are constantly being made, refined, and reorganized. Brain architecture takes shape and is constantly remodeled, par-

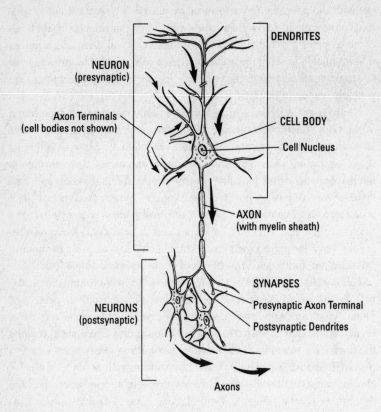

FIGURE 1-2. NERVE CELLS ARE THE BASIC UNITS
OF BRAIN FUNCTION.

This simplified drawing depicts three nerve cells (neurons). Axon projections from
nerve cells send information by means of electrical impulses. Dendrite projections receive information. Transmission from one cell to the next occurs at junction points
called synapses. (Direction of transmission is indicated by the arrows.) In the central
nervous system, information transfer is most often accomplished by means of chemical substances that are released at the ends of axons. These neurotransmitters diffuse
across the synaptic gap between two cells and attach to specialized receptors on the
dendrites of the postsynaptic (receiving) cell. One neuron can make many thousands
of synaptic connections or only a few. (*Source:* Adapted from Kandel, Schwartz, and
Jessell, *Principles of Neural Science*, 3rd ed., p. 19.)

ticularly in early life. For example, inputs to the brain from the right and left eye overlap in a fetus. But once the baby is born and is having normal visual experiences, the axons from each eye segregate themselves into the orderly alternating columns that support normal binocular vision. At first neurons only approximate their adult form and function; precision is attained as they respond to stimulation. Neurons that are potentially able to respond to visual patterns acquire their specific and precise function only if they receive appropriate visual stimulation. Practice shapes brain architecture. The motor cortex of professional violinists who began their careers as children has an unusually large area for control of the fingers of the left hand, because of the years of repetitive use of those fingers.[5]

Groups of neurons, and even smaller units such as groups of dendrites in the same neighborhood, respond to repeated patterns of stimulation by assembling into microcircuits that fire simultaneously or exhibit closely coordinated patterns of electrical activity. As the neurobiologist Carla Shatz puts it, "[Nerve] cells that fire together wire together."[6] Neural assemblies are reinforced, rearranged, or broken through use. In this manner, ever more complex, reliable, and finely tuned circuitry takes shape. Learning results from changes in synaptic connections generated by the patterns of nerve cell activity during a learning experience.

The connections that neurons make are not permanent physical bonds; the "wires" are not soldered together. Rather, every time a brain connection is made, information in the form of chemical molecules flows across a gap. At least forty different molecules, among them serotonin, dopamine, and glutamate, serve as neurotransmitters. Each is adapted for different information-processing functions and is at work in various neural pathways. Some neurotransmitters increase excitation or facilitate activity in a circuit, while others inhibit activity; some function swiftly, others more gradually; most are susceptible to feedback or other interactions with related cells and synapses. There are many fast, tight, and genetically preprogrammed connections; others are slower, and still others are subject to subtle modification each time they are made.

Groups of microcircuits become assembled into larger functional systems—for example, those coordinating the complex set of movements involved in sitting down in a chair or swallowing a mouthful of water, or those used in remembering today's date. Many circuits in the central nervous system contain neurons that modify information transfer or make it possible to carry bits of information along several divergent pathways simultaneously. Through repeated use, neural connections undergo structural modifications, becoming smoother, surer, and more automatic. Brain regions develop rich connections among themselves via projection pathways and feedback loops. At all levels of organization, from a single synapse to the complex and widely distributed systems involving the many billions of connections underlying thought and feeling, genetic and experiential influences are at play or have left their trace. These mechanisms make possible immensely variable and versatile thought and behavior, and, in fact, are the basis of adaptation and learning. "No matter how complex a neural circuit may appear," the Yale neurobiologist Gordon M. Shepherd writes, "we can be confident that it is designed to mediate specific naturally occurring behaviors."[7]

Systems of neurons acting in concert make it possible for our brains to receive, perceive, store, and use the sense information that bombards us from the world beyond our skin: what we hear, see, smell, taste, and touch; what we sense as hot and cold; what we feel as pain; and our awareness of the position and orientation of our body in space. Other neuron systems control and coordinate voluntary muscles as well as the involuntary processes involved in heartbeat, digestion, regulation of blood flow, and the release of hormones. Still other systems underlie memory, emotion, and language.

The most precise and most encompassing regulation of intellect and emotion, and sensory and motor processes as well, takes place in the cerebral cortex (Fig. 1). There are more neurons and synapses in the cerebral cortex, the rumpled gray mantle that covers the brain, than in any other region. The human cortex is huge compared to that of most other mammals. In a cat, for example, the cortex is less than one-quarter the size of the page you are reading; the human cortex is over six times the size of this page. A special feature of the human brain is the presence of vast numbers of neurons, most of them in the frontal cortex behind the forehead, that connect only with other neurons and share information only with other neurons. On this "neural chatter," as the developmental neurobiologist Phillip Nelson calls it, the subtle modulations of consciousness, memory, imagination, and awareness depend. Recent advances in neuroscience are enabling us to listen in more closely to this neural buzz.[8]

What happens in a neuron that receives information depends on the type of synapse involved. Synaptic receptors are highly specialized and can permit a wide range of effects. Sometimes the main effect is rapid excitation or inhibition. But sometimes there are instead (or in addition) more complex and longer-lasting modulations, both in the nerve cells themselves and in the neural networks of which they are a part. For example, stimulated neurons in certain brain regions make new proteins that may be the basis of long-term memories. Neurotransmitter molecules serve as "first messengers." The changes they cause in receptors on the other side of the synaptic gap activate second and subsequent messengers, molecules that initiate chains of reactions within the neuron receiving the information. Second messenger systems influence the neuron's metabolic processes, the readout of its genes, its manufacture of neuroactive substances such as peptides and hormones, and its reception, retention, and transmission of information.

During prenatal development many more neurons are made than are ultimately found in an adult. The dying off of surplus cells is part of the normal process that sculpts the brain before birth and throughout life. Pruning, which begins long before birth, clears away unused, abnormal, redundant, or temporary structures, as nerve cells that start with many potential functions become dedicated to specific tasks. By the time a baby comes into the world he or she possesses roughly a trillion nerve cells.[9] Unlike the cells that make up other organs such as the liver and stomach, neurons do not continually reproduce themselves. We are born with all the nerve cells we will ever have. How each individual's brain is formed and functions depends upon where these cells are, how they become interconnected, and which ones die.

The fate of an individual nerve cell is unpredictable but not random. Chance, error, and competition play a role in deciding which cells survive. Survival is influenced by the cell's location, its own activity, signals from other cells, and neurotrophic factors. One theory has it that every cell contains genes that enable it to self-destruct. Signals from other cells are needed to suppress the cell suicide program. This "social control" of cell survival maintains appropriate numbers of various cell types in a particular tissue.

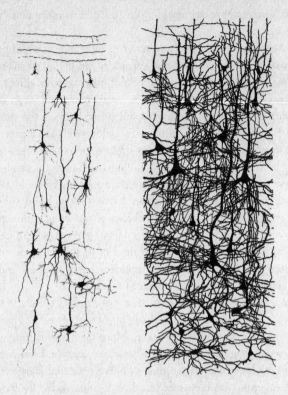

FIGURE 1-3. MOST NERVE CELL CONNECTIONS
DEVELOP AFTER BIRTH.

Neurons from the brain of a newborn, on the left, and from a twenty-four-month-old
child, on the right. Both drawings depict frontal cortical tissue prepared using the
same method. The major difference is the greater abundance of dendrites in the
older child's brain. (*Source:* Conel, *Postnatal Development,* Vol. I, Plate XX, and Vol.
VI, Plate XX.)

Another theory holds that programmed cell death is related to the inability of a neuron to find a target with which to connect. For example,
each mature muscle fiber is controlled by only one axon fiber from a
spinal cord motor neuron, but an immature muscle fiber has several
nerve fibers synapsing with it. All but one of the nerve fibers are elimi-

nated during development, resulting in efficient, well-tuned neuromuscular function.[10] The motor nerve cells that are unsuccessful in the competition to connect with muscle fibers die.

A newborn's brain has many more neurons than an adult's, but it has relatively few synapses. At birth, a firestorm of synapse creation begins. By the time a child is two, her brain has twice as many synapses as her mother's or father's. The period when brain connections proliferate explosively coincides with the period when a child is discovering new things for the first time in virtually every waking moment. Children are biologically primed for learning during this time. At the end of the child's first decade there is still a lush overgrowth of synapses, but by late adolescence, some neuroscientists estimate, half of all synapses in the brain have been eliminated.

Although the whole story is not yet written, current experimental data indicate that early experience plays a critical role in determining which synapses survive. Neural electrical activity resulting from stimulation seems to determine both synapse elimination and synapse stabilization. Each experience, whether it is a sight, a sound, or a touch, causes activity in a neural pathway. Repeated activation increases the strength of the signal in the pathway. This activity may give rise to chemical changes that stabilize the synapse, exempting it from elimination. Unused or inappropriately targeted synapses may be selectively eliminated by chemical substances released during neural activity.[11]

The schedules for making and breaking neural connections do not proceed at the same rate in all parts of the brain. Those governing functions such as breathing, temperature control, digestion, and blood pressure, although immature at birth, are relatively more mature than those that will be devoted to cognition. The least mature sets of connections—and therefore those most open to environmental influences—are those of the cerebral cortex. "The cortex develops as a whole rather than regionally," according to Pasko Rakic and his colleagues, who counted over 500,000 synapses in various cortical areas of monkeys at different ages and found that the rate of development in different areas was similar. This suggests that primary sensory and motor processes are not the only ones to have begun to function in infancy; so have "higher" thought processes that depend on the frontal cortex. These latter include categorizing, interpreting information, and controlling attention.[12]

In the first few years of life, the processes of synapse creation and elimination operate at full speed. The brain's energy requirements during this period are enormous. According to Harry Chugani, who measures the brain's utilization of energy-supplying glucose, a toddler's brain is as metabolically active as an adult's. The metabolic rate of a child's brain keeps rising; at age three it is two and a half times that of an adult. After that, it slowly decreases to adult level.[13]

Neurons and synapses in the young brain are extraordinarily sensitive to environmental influences. Nobel Prize–winning experiments by David Hubel and Torsten Wiesel showed extreme abnormalities in the brains of kittens when they were raised in the dark or denied normal visual experiences. When a kitten had one eye covered with a translucent shield for a few weeks, thereby depriving it of the experience of seeing visual forms, neurons in the pathway to the brain from the eye degenerated and the architecture of the brain's visual areas was distorted. When the shield was removed, the animals did not regain vision in the eye that had been occluded. This sort of deprivation had no effect whatsoever on adult animals.

Moreover, a number of studies in many species support the idea that challenging environments stimulate brain growth. Animals raised in experimentally enriched environments with lots of toys, mazes, wheels, nesting materials, and interesting and varied food had thicker cortexes and bigger and more intricate synaptic contacts than animals raised in barren cages. In one recent experiment, "enriched" adult mice formed more new neurons than mice housed in a standard laboratory environment.[14]

Special sensitivity to experience is the defining characteristic of early childhood. There are critical time periods when certain experiences must be available to the child so that normal development of connections can take place. This is easiest to grasp in extreme cases of deprivation. An infant born with a cataract and thus deprived of patterned visual stimulation will not be able to see even after the cataract is removed, unless the operation is performed promptly; a child born with a severe hearing loss will not learn to talk if hearing aids are not provided in time. A baby raised in an institution without a loving caregiver is stunted physically, cognitively, and emotionally. If nature's timetable is overridden or subverted—for example, by chronic neglect or abuse—

physiological processes may well be distorted, neural pathways altered, and developmental outcomes changed.[15] The "use it or lose it" feature of brain development also underscores the critical nature of early experience. The acquisition of information, whether a language, a memory, or the steps of a complex motor act such as eating with a spoon, has a lasting impact on brain development by determining which connections become stabilized and which are eliminated.

Since we are born with all the neurons we will ever have, the exuberant growth of synaptic projections accounts for a large part of the increase in size of a baby's brain. (The size of the brain is also augmented by growth in nerve cell bodies and in the brain structures that undergird the work of neurons—for example, blood vessels, supporting tissues, and myelin. The latter is a substance that coats axons, thereby insulating them and increasing their speed and efficiency.) Most of this postnatal growth occurs in the brain regions that are dedicated to cognitive processes.

Through their intricate, dynamic sprouts and spines, neurons transmit trillions of electrochemical messages. Each of us is born with the capacity for making an astronomical number of brain connections. There is no word for this number; it is written as 10 followed by 65 zeroes and is said to approximate the number of stars in the sky.[16] The growth of connections is triggered by the individual's genetic program interacting at many points with many different environmental influences. Yet even the most abundant neural network does not provide enough capacity in our brains to wire in every thought we think, every phrase we utter, or every move we make. Rather, our brains contain the mechanisms that allow for unbounded use. According to one line of current speculation, we somehow assemble from the bountiful stores of information in our brains the elements we need for the task at hand. The ways in which the circuits of the brain are elaborated, assembled, and interconnected determine what we can do, what we wish to do, how we think—indeed, who we are.

Learning takes place all through life; the landscape of the brain keeps changing under the influence of a continuing stream of experiences. But there are periods when one or another brain system is especially open to new experiences and especially able to take advantage of them. If these sensitive periods pass by without the stimulation for which the system is primed, opportunities for various kinds of learning may be substantially reduced. An adult's difficulty in correctly pronouncing words of a second language comes to mind. Being emotionally well attuned to other persons may be another instance.

Some innate developmental tendencies appear to be more open to experience than others. Human intelligence has invented myriad ways to mold, educate, and civilize the basic material of which we are made. Although there is now wide agreement among neuroscientists that there are periods when brain processes are especially sensitive to environmental input, there is no consensus on the extent to which experience can change the brain. Nor is there agreement on how long sensitive periods last, nor on the consequences if they should pass without the stimulation for which they are ready. "Do windows of opportunity . . . slam shut? Or are they merely lowered?"[17]

New discoveries are providing insights into how genes determine both the features of the body common to all living creatures and those that make each species, whether fruit fly, mouse, or human, unique. Of the 70,000 to 100,000 genes in the human genome (the usual estimates given), about half are expressed in the brain and a third are dedicated solely to brain function, a far greater number than for other organs.[18] The Human Genome Project will most likely construct a genetic map for humans within a decade. This means that we will know the location and lineup of each gene on our twenty-three pairs of chromosomes. We will understand how, where, and when some genes function.

But biologists face many challenges as they strive to discover how genes express themselves in cells singly and in combination, how they switch on and off during normal and abnormal development and during regulation of body functions, how the proteins they make determine both normal and abnormal functioning, and how they are influenced by their environment. Understanding the genetic contributions to individual differences in behavior among animals of a given species, including humans, is a distant goal.

New technologies for imaging and for detecting signals from brain structures while they are doing their work are opening windows into the living brain. We are beginning to understand more about how and when the brain's connections are made and unmade, and what these connections mean for the development of thought, feeling, and memory. Clearer comprehension of these processes holds out the possibility that, on some still far distant day, we may even understand the basis of consciousness itself.

New research findings, theories, and insights are emerging from psychology, linguistics, and computer science as well as neurobiology. Advanced experimental and statistical methodologies are adding new analytic power. The more we learn about what is happening inside the heads of children, the clearer it becomes that development is a continuous process that intertwines a baby's unique genetic endowment with his or her unique history. How genes play their role in brain development cannot be explained without understanding how experiences influence their expression at every stage. The most critical factor in the development of an infant's brain, assuming that he or she is neither seriously malformed nor malnourished nor subjected to dangerous levels of heat or cold, sensory isolation, infective agents, toxic chemicals, or radiation, is human interaction.

At birth the human brain is much less "finished" than the brains of other primates. A newborn human baby's brain will quadruple in weight by the time he becomes an adult; a baby chimpanzee's brain develops also, but only to about double its newborn weight. Human babies are born helpless, and they stay helpless a long time. They arrive expecting to be cared for and protected. They are also born to learn, and their ability to learn—to make adaptive changes in their behavior on the basis of experience—is at its peak in the early years of life, when they are making the brain connections on which learning and living depend. To be sure, as we will see, the brain has remarkable capacities for self-protection and recovery. But the loving care and nurture children receive in their first years—or the lack of these critical experiences—leaves lasting imprints on young minds.

Chapter Two

THE HOUSE OF MEANING

In this chapter we discuss the unique specialization of the human brain for language. The power to use language is part of the genetic endowment of all human beings. All of the world's languages share underlying principles of grammatical organization. Many linguists explain this observation by postulating an innate brain system for language that assumes different states as it matures and is exposed to experience. Young children rapidly acquire any language to which they are exposed. Because the brain is especially primed for language development in the earliest years of life, an infant who is born into a language-rich environment has a great advantage. Although children can acquire the basic elements of their native language without an adult to teach them, their language facility is enhanced by the support and encouragement of caregiving adults.

The Power of Language

When children acquire the ability to communicate with others through language, they have made the social connection uniquely important to human beings. The primary tool we use to make up our own minds and reach other people's minds is language—whether spoken, written, signed, sung, translated, or word-processed. We use arbitrary symbols—words—to convey meaning, putting them together in infinite combinations employing rules of grammar found in all languages. This unique capacity for stringing words together according to rules makes it possible to communicate meanings that cannot possibly be expressed in single words or words combined with gestures. We also use unvoiced words as we think. Our inner narratives thread the past to the present and help create and define our sense of self.

Most of our ability to convey what we think and to act in concert with other people depends on speech and its offspring, the written word. Language enables human beings to share dreams, desires, and intentions and to mobilize our energies on a vast scale. Our common understanding of verbal and written symbols has given us great power and a tremendous adaptive advantage over other species. We store billions of words in print and in electronic libraries, thereby extending their life across space and across generations. Satellite technology now makes it possible for a political figure, entertainer, or advertiser to speak to the whole world. All these developments give language great cumulative power to shape a civilization that increasingly depends upon the communication of information.

Language is a powerful tool for organizing human energy on a vast scale. The imprint of human beings on the natural order in our time is unprecedented, not only because of the sheer proliferation of our numbers, but because people are increasingly able to use technology to bring about sweeping changes. Far from being limited to the social realm, these changes affect the natural order itself. The sun still rises and the seasons change. Volcanoes still erupt and hurricanes chart their deadly path without human assistance. But increasingly, such natural phenomena as the weather, the kinds and the numbers of species inhabiting our planet, and the shifting boundaries between the oceans and the continents are profoundly affected by what billions of people do together.[1] And what people do is much influenced by what they hear, read, and say to one another.

Because so much more of our world is created and re-created through language than in earlier times, proficiency in language is becoming more crucial in all aspects of our lives—as students, teachers, producers, sellers, advocates, therapists, consumers, business negotiators, conflict mediators, lovers, marriage partners, family members, and users of print, video, voice mail, e-mail, and the Internet. In the twenty-first century there will be even less room for strong, silent types. Although we spend considerable time talking past one another or deceiving one another with words, intentionally and unintentionally, our yearning to be heard is very nearly our strongest desire. In Lewis Thomas's words, "language is at the core of our social existence, holding us together, housing us in meaning."[2]

A Language Organ?

Humans, avid social beings that we are, are born with the need for connection—to be touched, recognized, talked to, and heard by others of our kind. We use language to make connections with other people, on whom our very lives depend. Newborns arrive equipped with a brain built to acquire a language while that brain is young and growing. We learn our mother tongue because we are endowed with the dynamic capacity to fashion the billions of neural connections on which language depends. This capacity decreases with age. Facility and fluency in language are shaped—and, to a significant extent, determined—in childhood. The capacity to acquire language and the desire to communicate through language depend critically on biological endowment, but the development of verbal expressiveness and skill depends as much on human interaction as on innate potential. Sometimes, as we will show, language capacity fails to develop properly; amazingly, these instances are rare. As complex and delicately balanced as the biological and social systems underpinning language acquisition are, they are also sturdy, resilient, and self-mending.

Whether a child's first language is Portuguese, !Kung, or something else depends on who is talking to the infant. This point was not clear to Huck Finn's friend Jim, who wondered why French people speak French when English is so much easier. Nor was it obvious to King Psamtik I of Egypt. According to Herodotus, the fifth-century-B.C.

Greek historian, King Psamtik believed in the existence of an original world language, and so he devised an experiment to find out what language children would start speaking if they were simply left alone. The king commanded that two infants be separated from their mothers at birth and raised together by a silent caretaker. The infants would not be permitted to hear any human utterances other than their own. Psamtik's hypothesis was that the children would learn to talk without hearing any adult speech; they would intuitively speak the world's original language. After two years in isolation the children did communicate vocally with each other. No one could understand them; but the king's linguists concluded that they were speaking the world's original language, and the king was satisfied.

Today some linguistic theorists would agree with their ancient peers that hearing adult speech is not absolutely essential for children to acquire language. They would presume that the two children in Herodotus' story, never hearing their mother tongue, would nonetheless learn to communicate with each other by inventing some arbitrary referential communicative utterances—in other words, words. They would also invent rules to bind their utterances together—in other words, syntax. Their discourse would take place in a language they invented for themselves. In the 1970s the linguist Susan Goldin-Meadow studied children in a family so deaf that they could make no use of oral language. Although they had never been exposed to conventional sign language, they developed a system of gestures with many of the properties of language.[3] Human beings, it seems, even in sets as small as two, cannot help talking to one another.

A baby's first speech partner is usually her mother. Almost from the moment of birth an infant expects to find reciprocity. The locked gaze of mother and newborn is the first sign of the special relationship that develops between the baby and her most intimate caregivers.[4] Communication through language emerges from this early communication of love. The window of opportunity to learn our first language is wide open for about two years, partially open for another ten or twelve, and still open a crack for a while longer.

There are many examples of how the absence of appropriate stimulation blocks or distorts development of brain systems. Babies in bare, cheerless orphanages who are neither touched nor held by their caretakers, except for businesslike feeding and diaper changes, literally waste away because of sensory and emotional deprivation, even though they are fed and their physical needs are met.[5] The dire effects of abnormal sensory, cognitive, and social stimulation on the behavior of young animals such as kittens and monkeys have been demonstrated in many experiments. Abnormalities in brain anatomy and physiology due to deprivation of appropriate input are fairly well understood now, especially for vision.[6] Seeing only blankness, having no one to touch, or hearing only silence during critical periods of development can cause irreparable neurological damage.

Susan Curtiss, a linguist at the University of California, describes a woman she calls Chelsea, who was born with a severe hearing loss that somehow went unrecognized until she was over thirty years old.[7] When at age thirty-two Chelsea was finally fitted with hearing aids and began receiving language instruction, she rapidly learned to speak and understand many words. But Chelsea's ability to combine words into appropriate and well-formed sentences and phrases was pitifully limited, as evidenced by the examples Curtiss gives:

> The small a the hat.
> Orange Tim car in.
> I Wanda be drive come.
> Breakfast eating girl.
> The woman is bus the going.

Curtiss reports that Chelsea's conversation reflects her accurate assessment of social situations and that her gestures are useful in conveying her meaning. But, apparently, the critical period for assembling the structural principles of language came and went and could not be revisited.

The once-controversial idea that the human brain is programmed to acquire language according to an innate maturational timetable is now widely (but by no means universally) accepted.[8] There is much evidence to support Noam Chomsky's revolutionary hypothesis that human beings are born with a language-acquisition capability, which enables us to grasp basic word-combining rules common to all languages. Infants all over the world who are exposed to human language spoken by live human beings—neither TV nor "interactive" robots will do—will learn their mother tongue when the necessary brain connections have matured. This normally happens whether caregivers are taciturn or talkative, well-schooled or illiterate. Across the world the character and strategies of child care vary widely with respect to what is said to infants and toddlers, who says it, what tone of voice is employed, whether much attention is paid to babies' coos and cries, and how babies' vocalizations are interpreted. Yet with rare exceptions, we all learn language.

Many biologists and most linguists now believe that language capability is "embedded in the network of structures, processes, and connections of the human brain." Language comes naturally to children. As the linguist Steven Pinker remarks, *"children actually reinvent it,* generation after generation." Speaking is not something babies do because they are taught to do it. They cannot help doing it, because of the way their brains are constructed.[9]

What is the biological capability that makes language acquisition possible—in fact, virtually inevitable—for human children, and that determines its particular characteristics? The answer to this question is still unknown. Learning our mother tongue, so Chomskian linguistic theory has it, depends on an inborn language faculty that specifies and requires certain forms of word combinations in all languages and disallows others. These biologically determined linguistic principles are what Chomsky calls the "universal grammar."[10]

The related claims of universality and innateness are supported by empirical observation. All of the world's 4,000 to 6,000 languages share certain rules and principles governing sequences and combinations of words. And all normal children—indeed, most abnormal children as well—acquire language basics without much instruction. Constraints on word order and on the way clauses and phrases are put together give all languages from Albanian to Zuni certain shared properties. One apparently universal constraint is that you can move certain parts of speech but not others. "Who and George did they give birthday presents to?" is an impossible construction in any language, even though the meaning of the sentence is clear and parseable. "To whom and George . . ." only makes things worse. Slang, dialects, so-called primitive languages, "nonstandard English," even mixtures and between-languages like patois and creoles are not exempt from these universal rules.

Small children can make perfectly sensible sentences they have never heard before. Show some object to a three-year-old and say, "Here is a wug." Then show him another one and say, "Now there are two of them. There are two _____?" The child has never before heard anyone say "wugs." But he does have a mental rule for generating plurals, so he gives the right answer.[11] Very young children also exhibit their knowledge of rules for constructing sentences out of phrases and for switching word order to achieve the meaning they intend. Although young children make many errors as they experiment with language, they can distinguish between a sentence that follows rules they have never been taught and one that breaks these rules.

Linguists track these abilities with the help of games. The object of one such game is to encourage children to rephrase what they hear. For example, they are asked to change a declarative sentence into a question:

1. A unicorn is in the garden.
   Is a unicorn in the garden?
2. A unicorn that is eating a flower is in the garden.
   Is a unicorn that is eating a flower in the garden?
3. There is a unicorn that is eating a flower in the garden.
   Is there a unicorn that is eating a flower in the garden?

Children of nursery school age have no trouble consistently following rules for question making. In example 1 the auxiliary verb "is" is switched to the beginning of the sentence, followed by the subject "a unicorn." In example 2 the "is" that is the main verb of the sentence is likewise switched, while the "is" in the subject phrase "a unicorn that is eating a flower" does not move. Even a two-year-old would never say, "Is a unicorn that eating a flower is in the garden?" Nor would he be confused, in the third example, by the dummy subject "there," which is required by English syntax. (In fact, he might well use it in the first example.) The child might choose to get rid of part of the noun phrase, as in "Is a unicorn eating a flower in the garden?" but he always correctly preserves and places the main verb.

Why can't you move the first "is" that comes along? Because, as Pinker explains Chomsky's insight, the "basic design of language" forbids it. Though sentences are strings of words, our mental algorithms for grammar do not pick out words by their linear positions, such as "first word," "second word," and so on. Rather, the algorithms group words into phrases, and phrases into even bigger phrases, and give each one a mental label, like "subject noun phrase" or "verb phrase." The subject phrase in our second and third examples, "a unicorn that is eating a flower," is treated as a single unit, and the "is" buried in the phrase is ignored by the brain apparatus that enforces the question-forming rule. If this rule is wired into human brains, Chomsky reasoned, then children should get it right without going through a trial-and-error learning process. They should not have to hear examples of the form from their parents. Pinker reminds us that questions with a second auxiliary embedded within the subject phrase are so rare as to be nonexistent in "motherese" or "parentese," the simplified speech parents customarily (and unconsciously for the most part) use to communicate with toddlers. This kind of reasoning, which Chomsky calls "the argument from the poverty of input," is, in Pinker's words, "the primary justification for saying that the basic design of language is innate."[12]

Nonetheless, as developmental psycholinguists Elizabeth Bates and Virginia Marchman point out, children are "active and creative participants in the acquisition process."[13] They invent clever approximations to express their meaning, and they overgeneralize grammatical rules: "I eated up my crackers, Mommy, and then I broomed the floor clean!" Until she learns the past-tense form of an irregular verb, a child can employ her handy rules for regular verbs:

> Child: My teacher holded the baby rabbits and we petted them.
> Mother: Did you say your teacher held the baby rabbits?
> Child: Yes.
> Mother: What did you say she did?
> Child: She holded the baby rabbits and we petted them.
> Mother: Did you say she held them tightly?
> Child: No, she holded them loosely.[14]

At age three the child holds her rule more tightly than her mother's correction. By age five she will have memorized irregular forms of most common verbs. By eight or ten she has mastered most of the grammatical constructions of her language.

The linguist Virginia Fromkin offers a helpful summary of the reasons for believing that human language facility is inborn. A child acquires any language to which he or she is exposed. No language, spoken or signed, used in the community in which the child is born and raised is too difficult for the child to learn. No special talent or skill is needed. Geniuses do not acquire language and its basic rules of grammar any earlier than do normal or even dull children. Children do not need to be taught the basics of language. They only need to be exposed to it.[15]

Further evidence for the presence of a special biological predisposition for language is the speed and accuracy with which children get hold of the extraordinary complexities of any language. Children seem to arrive primed and eager to embark on the approximately three-year journey it takes to acquire their mother tongue. A baby goes from speaking no words at birth, to 50 or 100 words and two-word phrases at eighteen months or thereabouts, to nearly 600 words by age two and a half, to intricate and wordy constructions by three or four. A first-grader can understand about 13,000 words and expertly deploys tenses, embedded clauses, compounds, and combinations using rules only a grammarian could explicate. A middle school student can identify a spoken word in less than a third of a second by reviewing the more than 50,000 words, word meanings, word associations, connotations, and shadings stored in his or her mental dictionary. Any adult can understand a complex set of words, phrases, and sentences directed at him, and in little more time than it takes to process the sounds themselves can assemble appropriate words, phrases, and sentences in reply.[16]

Perhaps the most startling characteristic of language is how much we make from so little. The human vocal apparatus can make several hundred sounds, and each language uses only a small proportion of them. English, for example, uses about forty phonemes (speech sounds). These sounds are combined to make syllables, then words. (There are approximately 45,000 words in English.) Then, with inflections to create plurals, tenses, case and gender changes, and compound words like steamship and airplane, the numbers of words begin to get really large.[17] But when we combine words, the possibilities are staggering. George Miller, a Princeton linguist, calculated that the number of permissible English sentences consisting of twenty words or less is about 100,000,000,000,000,000,000; and, as Pinker points out, you can easily double or triple the length of a sentence or change its meaning with an "if," "and," or "but," or by switching a clause. Everyone uses clichés on occasion, and some of us cannot help saying "Have a nice day." But people do not normally "parrot" language. When someone does, we recognize that something is wrong.

Although the capacity for language may be built into our brains, the ways it unfolds are wonderfully varied. The number of languages in the world is the most obvious example of this, and differences among individuals speaking the same language is another. A recent study documents the wide differences in the rate at which children learn their language, a point Charles Darwin also noted.[18] The parents of 1,800 healthy children between eight months and thirty months old were asked to check off items on standardized lists that described their child's current level of linguistic accomplishment, including comprehended and spoken vocabulary, use of communicative gestures, understanding of grammatical constructions, and length of sentences and phrases the child could produce. The results for each measure of language competence were used to chart age norms similar to the height and weight percentile charts pediatricians use to follow the course of a child's physical growth.[19]

None of the babies could say words at eight months, but by sixteen months the median number of words they produced was about 40. By two years the median was about 300, and by two and a half nearly 600 words. But, as in a height chart, averages tell only part of the story. Big ranges were observed at every age for all the language measurements. In sixteen-month-old children, for example, the range for the group was from 0 to over 100 words; similarly, at two years, when the median spoken vocabulary was 300 words, the 10 percent of the children with the smallest vocabularies used about 50 words, while the 10 percent with the largest vocabulary averaged about 550 words.

The variation in children's language development was evident not only in their rate of acquisition of the various competencies involved but also in how, and in what order, they came to use their skills. These observations led Elizabeth Bates, one of the leaders in this study, to conclude that "the child's predispositions for language are not realized in universal sequences of development." The early lexicon of some children, for example, is heavily weighted toward naming persons ("Mommy"), other living creatures ("dog"), and things ("milk"). Other children seem to prefer action and function words, such as "up," "gimme," "uh-oh." Children may use several strategies to learn their language, depending on their temperament and cognitive style and on the kinds of language interactions that are reinforced by their caregivers.

The grammatical characteristics of a language also determine the order in which its features are learned. In English, word order is quite rigid and regular, and English-speaking children acquire word order rules (such as "subject first, then verb, then object") quite early. Turkish words are much more likely than English words to be inflected—that is, to change their form to make plurals, datives, possessives, and so on; Turkish children master grammatical inflections by about age two, when English-speaking children are just beginning this task. According to Bates, children seem to begin at a very early age to identify and utilize those clues to meaning that are most informative for their own language. They also pick up clear, frequent, and regular structures before they incorporate irregular and arbitrary forms into their speech. Children readily adapt to the peculiarities of their own language.[20]

To take into account the innateness and universality of grammatic principles is in no way to deny the influences of a given language environment. Universal underlying principles of syntax constrain the various rules and parameters for any particular language. When children are exposed to their native language, their linguistic experience acts upon the basic grammatical principles to establish the settings and rules that characterize their particular language. In this way, a child's language emerges in all its richness and complexity. How the capacity for grammar, basically the same for every human being, is realized in a given individual is subject to many interacting influences, some within the individual and others gleaned from the social environment. The neural processes through which maturation and experience act on the human faculty for language to produce differences among individuals are still unknown. Also at issue is the question whether language performance involves neural mechanisms used exclusively for language. Some theorists contend that language mechanisms are not unique but are similar to those used in other cognitive processing.

Language Circuits

No one has seen the "language organ." Indeed, there is accumulating evidence that the many cell assemblies, systems, and circuits serving language functions are not contained in a discrete region of the brain. With the help of new techniques for deciphering the activities of the living brain, we are beginning to get a clearer picture of the locations and specific functions of the components of the language apparatus. We are learning how these distributed systems contribute to language comprehension and production, and how they develop in children's brains.

Critical to acquiring language are sense organs to register incoming information. For most of us, those organs are our ears. A deaf person uses sight, or sensitivity to vibration. We depend upon a central nervous system specially adapted to receive, perceive, decode, integrate, and represent linguistic information and complex symbolic messages. Without it we would neither be able to take in the eddying streams of sound flowing toward our ears from several sources all at once—more often than not slurred, mumbled, and run together—nor could we almost instantly dissect and reconfigure them into syllables, words, phrases, sentences, and larger units of meaning.

To acquire and use language we need a short-term memory that is exquisitely sensitive to temporal sequences so that we can keep moment-by-moment track of information entering our ears and exiting our mouths. We depend also on the short-term memory systems through which we make coherent, connected, and dynamic mental representations of spatial and temporal information—not only sounds and words but also visual images, smells, and tactile perceptions. We need to sense the location of our body with respect to all this incoming information. We slot language information into categories that make linguistic, cognitive, *and* emotional sense to us, and we incorporate these symbolic representations into networks of associations, feelings, and memories, summoning them as needed. We store most of this information outside of conscious awareness, but in such a way as to summon and use it with almost infinite variety over a lifetime and with thousands of partners.

Without the superbly tuned neuromuscular system that coordinates breathing, vocal cords, palate, tongue, and lips, we could not produce the many combinations of sounds and silences that make up a language. To convey our meaning, we utilize modulation and feedback circuits that allow moment-by-moment adjustments in the intensity and emphasis of our speech as we assess its effects on our audience, whether it be a huge crowd or a single conversational partner. Our ability to communicate also depends on our using and understanding, in differing ways in various cultures and circumstances, the raised eyebrow, the pregnant pause, the shrugged shoulder, the inclined head, the raised hand.

We depend upon the concept of symbolic utterance, and on our ability to make use of symbolic utterances, to connect the idea in our heads with the object out there, or to an action, an intention, or a stream of ideas and feelings. To make socially adequate communicative connections we incorporate, often unconsciously, the emotional signals of speech. Even when we silently talk to ourselves, we often do so as if to a partner. A child's emerging sense of his or her self as unique and private seems to depend in part on the inner narrative that connects past to present, and self to others. There is speculation that each of these requirements for language is met by a uniquely human biological endowment.

Listening to Babies

At exactly the age of a year, he made the great step of inventing a word for food, namely, **mum** . . . , and now instead of beginning to cry when he was hungry, he used this word in a demonstrative manner or as a verb implying "Give me food." . . .

When a little over a year old, he used gestures to explain his wishes; to give a simple instance, he picked up a piece of paper and giving it to me pointed to the fire, as he had often seen and liked to see paper burnt. . . .

—from the diary Charles Darwin
kept on one of his ten children[21]

The little girl, as she came to ten months old, was a greater chatterer than ever, pouring out strings of meaningless syllables in joy and sorrow, with marvelous inflections and changes . . . and certain favored syllables over and over. . . . Week by week the notebook showed . . . [a vocalization] which developed through many variations (such as "M-ga," "Ga," "Gong," "A-gong"). [It] was used as loosely as it was pronounced: the baby murmured "Ng-gng!" pensively when someone left the room; when she dropped something; when she looked for something she could not find; when she swallowed a mouthful of food; when she heard a door close. She wounded her father's feelings by commenting "M-ga!" as her little hands wandered about the unoccupied top of his head.
—Millicent Washburn Shinn,
Biography of a Baby [her niece], 1900[22]

   Longitudinal observation of a child's progress continues to be a favorite method for studying language acquisition. Fond relatives who, like Darwin and Shinn, are also close observers can combine the natural enjoyment of their beloved's accomplishments with the rather more detached perspective of the scientist. Now audio- and videotape recorders and computer analyses facilitate the task for researchers in child development.[23] One of the founders of developmental psycholinguistics, Roger Brown, concluded from studies of this sort that the way children learn language is "approximately invariant across children learning the same language, and . . . across children learning any language."[24] He found, for example, that children learn grammatical forms in a certain order—for example, the present progressive ("jumping," "eating") before the past tense; the prepositions "in" and "on" before articles, such as "the" and "a."

   Studies of children's language development based on diaries, whether kept by parents or by outside experts, necessarily involve only a few children, and they cannot give us a picture of the variability we are likely to find among large groups. Giving a child a standard test in a laboratory setting can provide no more than a snapshot influenced by the focus of the experimenter and that child's particular reactions. Recording speech samples at home, on the playground, or in school gives yet another picture. Providing parents with checklists to record what their child can say and understand yields information conveniently and relatively inexpensively, thus allowing large numbers of children to be studied, but parents' views may be biased, and not every parent has the time and inclination to keep a diary. Despite their limitations, all these methods, applied appropriately, are useful for broadening our knowledge, for cross-checking, and for validation.

By using the physiological changes that occur when babies are presented with a sensory stimulus such as a sound, a touch, or a flash of light, scientists can study language development in infants far too young to speak or to show by their voluntary responses that they understand. Heart rate, skin conductance, motor movements (for example, turning the head toward a sound), or electroencephalographic (brain wave) activity can be monitored for the changes that regularly occur when a sensory stimulus is received and processed by the baby's nervous system. Experimenters also can take advantage of the fact that even very young infants respond more strongly to novel than to familiar stimuli. Suppose the experimenter allows a baby to hear a train of syllables— "Da, da, da, da . . ."—and then inserts a different stimulus—say, "ma"—into the train. The baby will show by his response, for example, a change in his heart rate, that he has discriminated between the two stimuli. Young infants can also be taught to control the production of stimuli that they enjoy. For example, Hanus Papousek, a Czech pediatrician, taught infants as young as six weeks to turn their head in order to activate flashing lights that fascinated them. Responses to sounds can be tested even in fetuses, by heart-rate monitoring and other techniques.[25]

Babies start listening before they are born. Experiments show that fetuses in the third trimester respond to a variety of sounds. The infant in utero can hear the rise and fall of its mother's voice, and probably can capture some of its prosodic qualities, such as intonation, cadence, stress, and length of phrase. Thus infants are exposed to some of the rhythms and patterns of their own language many months before they are ready for its words.

In one study, pregnant women recited a nursery rhyme out loud every day for four weeks during their third trimester. At the end of the four weeks, a tape recording of two rhymes (read by a female experimenter) was played. One rhyme was the one the mothers had recited over and over; the other was one that the mothers had never recited. The fetuses' responses were gauged by their heart rates. (To insulate the fetuses from their mothers' reaction, the mothers wore earphones that kept them from hearing the tape.) During the recitation of the rhyme that had been a daily part of their routine for four weeks, the fetuses' heart rates changed in a manner that did not occur when they heard the unfamiliar rhyme.[26]

Since a young child is likely to fall asleep, get cranky, "respond" correctly or incorrectly by chance, or ignore what the researcher wants him to attend to, experimenters trying to figure out what is on a baby's mind must be very patient as well as ingenious. One or another of the child's usual behaviors, such as sucking, can be pressed into service to analyze his responsiveness to varying types of stimuli. Usually, of course, a baby sucks to satisfy his hunger or to soothe himself. However, sucking patterns have also been found to change with the baby's state of arousal and attention. In one quite successful experimental method, a baby is given a pacifier connected to a sound-generating system. When the baby sucks, a pleasant sound ensues. Even an infant of one or two months quickly learns that his sucking controls the sound. At first he will suck vigorously to make the sound, but when the novelty wears off, he slows down or quits. If the experimenter then changes the sound, the baby will renew a fast and strong sucking pattern to make the new sound come on. This is taken to mean that the baby distinguishes the new sound from the old and that its novelty sparks new interest.

Obviously one cannot ask a toddler to produce nominals, gerunds, or a sample sentence with an embedded clause, so researchers have invented games to ascertain what a child this age is capable of saying and comprehending and to determine the rules he is using. In one experiment, the child sits on his mother's lap equidistant from two video monitors simultaneously showing different cartoon sequences. A voice from a centrally placed loudspeaker directs the child's attention to one or the other cartoon. For example, on one of the displays Cookie Monster is shown tickling Big Bird. On the other Big Bird is tickling Cookie Monster. The loudspeaker voice says either, "Cookie Monster is tickling Big Bird" or "Big Bird is tickling Cookie Monster." Nine-month-old children look with about equal pleasure at both sequences, suggesting that they do not understand who is who or who is doing what. But a toddler of seventeen months looks longer at the display that illustrates the sentence he has heard. The older child appears to comprehend not just the individual words but the difference in meaning signaled by the word order.[27]

Communication between baby and caregiver begins long before words pass between them. The child psychiatrist John Bowlby, struck by the capacity of tiny infants to behave in ways that cause adults to take care of them, became convinced that both newborns' capacity to signal for help and the normal nurturing responses of adults are biologically programmed.[28] A baby's cry moves adults to do what it takes to make her stop. The most typical, and usually the most effective, response is to pick the baby up, hold her close, and murmur comforting endearments. Even though she is still hungry, the baby stops crying, at least for a while. She stops because her hunger for closeness is met and because she is made to feel that her hunger for food will be met. Caregivers take pleasure in figuring out the meaning of a baby's cries. They are deciphering an ancient code. Experiments have demonstrated that there are distinctive cries associated with hunger, discomfort, and loneliness.[29] The baby teaches a willing listener the language of her cries.

Long before her first word, a baby is already an active participant in her own culture. She enters the world with a readiness to discover workable strategies for coping with social expectations. If all goes well, she soon discovers that her smile and coos, as well as her cries, have a powerful effect on her caregivers, evoking pleasurable responses from them and causing them to stay near. Parents and grandparents will work very hard for the reward of a smile.

Experimental psychologists have observed that how caregivers respond to an infant is a powerful environmental factor in promoting or retarding learning. Infants tune their actions to the acts of others, even in the early weeks of life. They reflect their mothers' smiles, responding with attentive and open gaze even before they can manage a voluntary smile. They can also break off communication by averting their gaze or turning their head away. An infant shows his preference for his mother by looking more at her than at anyone else in the room, and he relaxes more in her arms. A very young infant recognizes his mother's smell and voice. A three-month-old can initiate communication when he catches his mother's eye, but if the mother's face betrays disapproval of her infant's initiatives or if she makes no response, the baby's face becomes sober and he may whimper or cry.[30]

The first rule of discourse is mutual attentiveness. Thousands of hours of film and videotape have captured the engagement of mothers and newborn babies with each other. Each mother-and-infant pair interacts in its own subtly different way, but the choreography is essentially the same: the meeting of eyes, the movements toward each other, the facial expressions and postures of the head and body changing ever so slightly to mirror the other. Child psychiatrists sometimes call this delicate and lovely expressiveness "attunement."

Well before the age of six months, babies show that they know the second rule of successful conversation, taking turns; if they have a willing partner, they can initiate a communicative exchange and sustain it for a time, to the mutual delight of the pair.[31] The infant's system of communication expands to include joint attention with another to an object of mutual interest, another prerequisite for normal discourse. Thus, a baby will follow the mother's glance as she exclaims, "There's the ball!"

Purposeful gestures such as pointing are now added to the baby's repertoire, and sometimes these signals are accompanied by emphatic vocalizations such as "uh, uh, uh." Very early on the baby learns that her acts have the power to affect what happens next. She opens her mouth for the next bite of applesauce, complains if it doesn't arrive fast enough, and shakes her head vigorously (or purses her lips or drools down her chin) when she's had enough. When a baby is old enough to be conscious of her own intentions and experienced enough to expect that she will be understood by her partner, she begins to engage in truly intentional communication:

> Marta [a precocious nine-month-old] is unable to open a small purse, and places it in front of her father's hand. . . . Father does nothing, so Marta puts the purse in his hand and utters a series of small sounds, looking at him. Father still does not react, and Marta insists, pointing to the purse and whining. . . . Finally [her] father touches the purse clasp and simultaneously says, "Should I open it?" Marta nods sharply.[32]

Typically, a baby's comprehension is several months ahead of his ability to shape sounds into understandable words. Gradually the neuromuscular apparatus that coordinates the movements of breathing and the shape of the vocal tract becomes more finely tuned, enabling the child to reproduce words he hears. Long before baby's first real word is articulated, he is practicing his mother tongue as he plays with sounds. His musical inflection and range expands, as does the variety of syllabic combinations. The jargon of a sixteen-month-old can sound quite conversational, even though he employs few words in the adult lexicon.

Emotive utterances, the baby's first form of vocal communication, are increasingly brought under the control of higher brain centers, and their expression is regulated by social context and feedback. A baby will jabber less loudly and less often in the presence of a stranger than when he is alone with his parents. Urged to perform his standard repertoire, such as "Hi!" or "Bye-bye!" the toddler will wait until the moment the stranger closes the door behind him.

Here is one linguist's description of a child who is beginning to learn the magical power of language in a social situation:

> Sheila, who is almost 3 years old, was visiting me late one warm Saturday afternoon while her parents were shopping. An ice-cream van, loudspeaker jangling . . . stopped nearby. "Every night I get an ice cream," declared Sheila. Nonplussed, I used my stock response: "That's very nice, Sheila." "Yes, even when there is a baby-sitter, I get an ice cream," Sheila explained patiently. I had been backed into a corner by a 3 year old's grasp of the use of language as a social tool.[33]

Learning Our Mother Tongue

Although specialization in one's own language occurs early in life, we do not come into the world wired for French, Chinese, or Serbian. Newborns have been shown to be able to tell the difference between all the possible phonemes of human language. (Phonemes are the basic distinctive vocal units of speech. They may appear in one language but not another—like, for example, the English "o," the German "ö," and the Danish "ø"). However, by the time they are about a year old, children can recognize only the sound combinations and contrasts that occur in their mother tongue (unless they have been exposed to another language). Japanese newborns can distinguish between the sounds "ra" and "la," but a year later, they have lost this ability. Linguistic experience alters phonetic perceptions.[34]

By the time they are five months old, babies react to a switch in language. Infants who had been raised in households where either English or Spanish was spoken were presented with a tape recording of a woman's voice repeating a sentence over and over in one of the two languages. Soon the babies stopped showing any interest. When the sentence was replaced with a new one of the same length, in the same language as before, their attention did not revive; however, when the switch was made to a sentence of similar length in the *other* language, they became noticeably more engaged.[35]

How do infants tell one language from another before they can understand its words? Some of the cues babies have been shown to use are the unique prosodic qualities of a language, its intonations and rhythms. They also begin early to recognize the linguistic units that characterize their own language; they may be able to segment the speech stream into syllable-sized units that differ from one language to another. Characteristic clause and phrase structures and patterns of stress are other cues infants may use.

In the process of learning language, babies are seldom presented with neatly packeted words. Instead they face what would seem to be the monumental problem of segmenting the continuous speech stream into units that enable them to grasp meaning. "Parentese" probably helps a little. Adults tend to speak slowly, brightly, simply, and repetitively to babies. They unconsciously exaggerate the common vowel sounds of their language; by the time infants are twenty weeks old their babble contains the same vowel sounds (at higher pitch) as their parents' speech.[36] Experiments also show that infants are sensitive to some word boundaries, that they show preferences for speech marked by clauses, and that they take note of the temporal and frequency cues marking phrases (for example, a fall in pitch and a lengthening of the last segments of the clause). Infants may perceive sentences as strings of clauses, and they prefer their own language's patterns of stress. Around seven to nine months of age, infants of English-speaking parents begin to listen preferentially to words that exhibit the most common English-language pattern of prosody, i.e., stress on the first syllable. It has been reported that four-day-old French babies can distinguish French from other languages![37]

Recent work indicates that by about six months of age infants categorize the sounds of their own language. A perceptual requirement for readily understanding speech is the ability to ignore the myriad differences in pronunciation due to regional accents, intonation patterns, or voice timbre, differences that do not change the meaning of a word. Adults automatically adjust for variations in pronunciation from the "prototype" sounds of their language as exemplified in BBC English, for example, or the Middle American speech of television newscasters. (We easily grasp what Edward Kennedy and Henry Kissinger are saying, although each would have a hard time landing a job reading the news on national television.) Apparently, six-month-old babies also recognize their own language even when it is spoken in unfamiliar ways, and even before they can understand the meaning of words.

Linguists from the University of Washington and the University of Stockholm tested thirty-two American and thirty-two Swedish babies six months old. Each baby sat in his or her mother's lap and watched an assistant seated on the infant's right quietly play with toys that intrigued the infant. As this was going on, a tape playing through a loudspeaker on the infant's left was slowly repeating either a synthesized English vowel "ee" (as in "fee"), or the Swedish sound "y" (pronounced by forming the lips into an "o" and saying the sound "ee"). Sixteen American and sixteen Swedish babies were presented with the English "ee," and a like number of American and Swedish babies were presented with the Swedish "y."

After the prototype vowel had been played for a time, a variant pronunciation was introduced, different enough to catch the attention of all the babies. The infants were trained to turn their heads and look toward the loudspeaker when they heard the change. (Activation of a toy dancing bear pounding a drum rewarded the baby for turns made at the right moment.) After the baby demonstrated that she was turning her head in response to the highly distinguishable pronunciation variant, she was presented with many lesser variants. The researchers found that the American babies ignored minor variants in the sound "ee" most of the time—that is, they treated the variants exactly like the prototype— but *did* respond to minor variants in the Swedish sound. The Swedish babies behaved in exactly the opposite fashion: they responded more to variants in the unfamiliar English "ee" sound than to variants in their native-language "y." These six-month-old babies have already learned to organize speech sounds into categories important for their native language. They have assimilated the prototypes so well that variants in pronunciation are no longer perceived.

Parents often are convinced that their children remember and recognize words by the time they are seven or eight months old, and a recent experiment supports this belief. Peter Jusczyk and Elisabeth Hohne visited fifteen eight-month-old infants at home over a two-week period and played the same recorded stories to them each time. (The stories, written for older children, contained many words with which the babies had had no prior experience.) Two weeks after the last of the visits the children were brought to the laboratory, where they heard recorded word lists that contained content words that appeared in the stories (for example, "elephant," "peccaries," "jungle") as well as content words that did not ("apricot," "caribous," "camel"). The infants attended to previously heard words significantly longer than to previously unheard words. Since the infants remembered test words read from a *list* instead of hearing them as part of a story, the researchers took their results to mean that the infants had not only remembered sound patterns of individual words but were also able to segment individual words from fluent speech.[38]

The components of a language are affected in different ways by experience during the formative early months and years of life. Pronunciation is an obvious example. The syntax of a second language learned as an adult may be flawless and one's vocabulary as large as a dictionary, but the perfect accent of any eight-year-old speaking a language with which he is familiar is beyond reach for late learners. Most young children can simultaneously acquire two or three different languages with ease; most adults find simultaneous study of two foreign languages demanding to say the least.[39] Adult stroke victims who have lost language abilities usually recover only very limited function. In contrast, a pre-adolescent child with a similar brain injury has excellent prospects for recovering language, while very young victims are found to have nearly normal language ability within a few months of their stroke. It is likely that in normal children the brain plasticity of early life shapes all aspects of language—accent, size and content of one's mental dictionary, and one's social uses of language.

This shaping of language by experience was observed by Betty Hart and Todd Risley of the University of Kansas as they made monthly hour-long observations and tape recordings in the homes of forty-two normal infants from "ordinary," well-functioning families. The experiment began when the children were seven months old and continued until they were three. The researchers found that the families "differ[ed] immensely in the amount of experience with language and interaction they regularly provide[d] their children," although within a given family the amount of interaction was quite consistent from month to month. The researchers also found that the number of verbal interactions the parent had with the child, as well as the sheer number of words the parent used in these interactions, were highly correlated with the child's vocabulary both at three years of age and again at eight years of age.[40]

A huge leap is made when a baby uses words and then combinations of words to code intent and meaning. Around eighteen months of age the child makes the discovery that sounds are used referentially, that they are symbols.[41] Helen Keller, who was left blind and deaf by a devastating infection when she was nineteen months old, tells us in her autobiography of the brilliance of this moment of discovery (perhaps a rediscovery), when she was seven years old:

> One day, while I was playing with my new doll, Miss Sullivan [Helen's tutor] put my big rag doll into my lap also, spelled "d-o-l-l" [into Helen's hand] and tried to make me understand that "d-o-l-l" applied to both. . . . I became impatient at her repeated attempts and, seizing the new doll, I dashed it upon the floor. I was keenly delighted when I felt the fragments of the broken doll at my feet. . . . [Miss Sullivan] brought me my hat and I knew I was going out into the warm sunshine. We walked down the path to the well-house.

Someone was drawing water and my teacher placed my hand under the spout. As the cool stream gushed over one hand she spelled into the other the word *water,* first slowly, then rapidly. I stood still, my whole attention fixed upon the motions of her fingers. Suddenly I felt a misty consciousness as of something forgotten—a thrill of returning thought; and somehow the mystery of language was revealed to me. I knew then that "w-a-t-e-r" meant the wonderful cool something that was flowing over my hand. That living word awakened my soul, gave it light, hope, joy, set it free! . . . I left the well-house eager to learn. Everything had a name, and each name gave birth to a new thought . . . every object which I touched seemed to quiver with life.[42]

Words come to stand alone as conveyors of thoughts. This epiphany normally comes to us before we can retain the sharp memory of it that Helen Keller carried with her the rest of her life, and without her heartbreaking, brave struggle. But it is nonetheless a miracle. A rule system comes to govern meaning in spoken or signed, then written communication. A common way station on the road to language may be a private system of meanings between mother and child. Sometimes twins share a private language. We know a set of adult twins who sometimes still use "words" that they made up when they were toddlers playing together. But language is not private. It is a shared system of arbitrary symbols bound together by shared grammatical rules. The urge to participate in the system is one of the strongest human drives.

When I (Ann) was seven years old, Helen Keller came to speak at my school assembly. I can still hear Miss Keller's strange voice, clear, piercing, inflectionless, and feel the unseeing gaze of her bright sightless blue eyes. My mother says that I described Miss Keller as a big old statue that talked. I remember trying not to shrink away from her fingers on my lips and throat as she "listened" to my shy words of welcome from the Washington School second grade. The child Helen's desire to communicate her thoughts, to possess the ability "to speak in winged words that need no interpretation,"[43] drove her across seemingly insurmountable barriers of deafness and blindness to the world of speech. I could feel her reaching across the barrier to me.

Building the House of Meaning

Speech is continuous, but meaning is compiled word by word and phrase by phrase, and as we listen to phrases and sentences strung together we must constantly correct our interpretation until the whole thought is finished. (For example: "Ernie kissed Marcie and her sister . . . laughed.") Various grammatical elements such as nouns, verbs, prepositions, verb phrases, and so on have defined relationships to one another, but scientists who study the structure of language do not fully understand how the brain relates syntax, the grammatical structures that serve to relate words, to semantics, the organization of meaning.

Many linguists influenced by Noam Chomsky believe that syntactic structures are represented in the brain as autonomous neural processing mechanisms, or modules, whose function is relatively independent of semantics. How language processing is tied to meaning, reference, and relevant real-world context is an open question. How syntactic processes actually work, where in the brain their structures are located or their subroutines are assembled, and at what points in sentence comprehension they operate are matters of current debate and research.[44] Noninvasive neuroimaging and neurophysiological techniques are evolving to the point that experimental tests of various hypotheses can be made.

In one such recent study, researchers tracked the eye movements of their subjects as they listened to sentences that directed them to manipulate various objects placed on a table in front of them. In one test the objects on the table were an apple on a towel, another towel with nothing on it, and a box. One or the other of the following instructions was given:

1. "Put the apple on the towel [a] in the box."
2. "Put the apple that's on the towel in the box."

Upon hearing either instruction the subjects' eyes move promptly to the apple. At point [a] in sentence 1, most people assume that "on the towel" denotes the destination of the instruction "put" and they look from apple to empty towel.[45] Then, as they hear the instruction completed, they glance at the box and move the apple to it. If they hear instruction 2, they ignore the empty towel: they are immediately aware that the phrase "on the towel" modifies "apple" instead of "put," so they wait for the destination "in the box" before moving their eyes and completing the requested task.

The test was repeated using a different visual context: two apples, instead of one, were on the table, one on a towel and the other on a napkin. The same instructions were used:

1. Put the apple on the towel in the box.
2. Put the apple that's on the towel in the box.

In this visual context people *always* assumed that "on the towel" was information modifying "apple"; they *never* took it for the destination. Their eyes moved briefly between the incorrect choice, the apple on the napkin, to the correct choice, the apple on the towel, and they completely bypassed the irrelevant empty towel. Even though the sentences in the two tests were exactly the same, the brain processed them differently.

These results are taken to mean that people do not use syntactic processes independently of real-world context. Instead, from the earliest moments in linguistic processing, grammatical constraints are integrated in neural systems that coordinate both linguistic and nonlinguistic (in this case visual) information.[46]

Silent Talk

A first language need not be a spoken language. Deaf infants whose parents are prepared for the likelihood that their baby will be deaf (because they themselves or close family members were born deaf) use sign language with their infants right away. These children become fluent signers on approximately the same timetable as their hearing peers become speakers. They even babble in hand gestures.[47]

Of the approximately 4 million babies born each year in the United States, roughly 10,000 have a hearing impairment so severe that they will not develop any spontaneous spoken language. An additional 8,000 to 12,000 children born each year have hearing losses that will interfere with normal spoken language development unless they are treated promptly with hearing aids and speech therapy.[48] Most deaf children, indeed about 90 percent, have parents who hear. These parents face the unwelcome dilemma of having to choose their child's first language. Should it be one of the several sign languages that are used in the United States, or the oral language of the child's parents? Each path has its difficulties.

Some deaf people, especially those who have an inherited form of deafness and are born deaf, do not see deafness as a disability but as a way of life with its own culture. However, those who depend on sign language are often sorely disadvantaged, surrounded as they are by a large society that speaks another language. Furthermore, although American Sign Language is a language in its own right, it has no written form. Learning to read and write well in English is difficult for many deaf students.[49]

The controversy over which first language deaf children should be taught has been fanned by the development of the cochlear implant, a prosthetic device that mimics the function of the inner ear. Unlike hearing aids, which are removable devices that amplify sounds so that the biological inner ear can process them, the cochlear implant is an electronic substitute for the nonfunctioning inner ear. After being surgically implanted, the device transduces sound waves into small electrical impulses that stimulate the auditory nerve.

The results of implants in adults and older children are variable, but most users improve their oral and aural communication skills.[50] The problems a deaf baby will encounter in using a prosthetic device that imperfectly opens a sense channel with which he has had no experience are more daunting. But if it is true that there is a critical period for language learning, then maximum benefit from a cochlear implant will be attained if a child receives it as close as possible to the time when speech input is occurring in children who hear normally, which is to say as young as possible. A decision often must be made before the child is old enough to be part of the decision-making process.[51]

As of the mid-1990s the youngest child to have received an implant was two years old. The preliminary evidence available at this point suggests that children who received their implants at a younger age improved their scores on speech and language tests faster than older children did. This lends support to the critical-period hypothesis.[52]

Most children with moderate, severe, or even profound hearing loss can benefit from properly fitted hearing aids and a good educational program. Prompt diagnosis is essential, but is not so easy in a baby, since there may be nothing obviously wrong. In recent decades new technologies have made early diagnosis of hearing impairment extremely reliable. Computer-aided analyses of the electroencephalogram (the electrical activity of the brain, recorded from the scalp) can be used to discover "evoked responses," the electrical activity that occurs as the brain processes auditory and other sensory stimuli. Investigators can examine evoked responses to find out if a baby's brain has registered a sound. By varying the pitch and intensity of the sounds presented to the baby, a neurologist or audiologist uses evoked responses as a test of hearing.[53]

In his authoritative text, the neurobiologist Gordon Shepherd observes: "In humans, there can be little doubt that hearing has been the key to development of language, and through it, much of our culture."[54] This has been true over the history of our species, and it is true for each new baby who comes into the world. The brain needs to learn its first language, whether spoken or signed, in early childhood; problems with hearing must be diagnosed and treated promptly.

Chapter Three

PATHWAYS OF LANGUAGE

This chapter is about language disorders in children and what they tell us about normal brain development. As we have seen, some children have impaired language because they cannot hear well. But 3 to 6 percent of seemingly healthy and normal children who are not hard of hearing or otherwise deprived of stimulation have extreme difficulty in producing and understanding language. A genetic basis for certain of these developmental language disorders is likely. Current research suggests that some of the children have an abnormality in their perception of both language and nonlanguage sounds. Others may have a defect in part of the brain's specialized system for acquiring language. We briefly describe the neuroanatomical structures that support language abilities and consider the left brain's increasing specialization for language as a child matures. We will also review some technological and experimental advances, such as functional magnetic resonance imaging (fMRI), evoked-response tests, and new tests of behavior, that now make it possible to study the normal brain as it processes information.

Genes and Language Development

Most neuroscientists believe that we carry genetic instructions for language, but these genes have not yet been located or identified. There is agreement that the language-acquisition system is much too complex to operate under the influence of a few "language genes," or "grammar genes," or "symbolic-representation genes." If language genes are ever found, it is much more likely that each one of them will turn out to be a member of a construction crew carrying out a specific operation at one of the many work sites where the house of language is being built. At these sites gene products (proteins and enzymes) would be involved in cellular processes, synapse formation, computational activities, and circuit building at a level of organization far removed from the levels of behaviors we are able to recognize as speech and language.

Certain of the genes that make language possible might also participate in other brain functions. They might contribute to the ability to process data that change rapidly, or to working memory, or to the capacity to grasp a complex pattern with only a bare minimum of information, or to detect signals masked by background noise. Genetic abnormalities might disrupt normal operations in one or another of the many components of language capability. An abnormality during development might leave a certain genetic switch on too long, or turn an activity off too soon. A mutation in even a single gene that is active during some critical moment in the development of a neural pathway could conceivably interfere with the construction or regulation of a whole system. It is, in fact, amazing that this happens so seldom. Neuroscientists speculate that in the process of evolutionary adaptation backup systems emerged that protect critical functions.

Certain language disorders that run in families provide opportunities for clearer understanding of how genes work. Identical twins, who have identical genes, often exhibit the same disability. Fraternal twins, who share about half of their genetic endowment with their twin, often do not. In some families, inheritance patterns suggest the action of a dominant gene, a recessive gene, or a sex-linked gene. (In the last instance, boys are affected but not girls, or vice versa.) Language abnormality may be just one of a distinctive cluster of abnormalities that includes other problems such as epilepsy or attention deficit, but it need not be.[1]

It is often difficult to distinguish genetic and prenatal factors from environmental influences on language development. Did Johnny acquire greater language skills or acquire them earlier than George because his mother talked to him in a bright, simple baby-focused speech and faithfully read him bedtime stories? Or was it because he was genetically endowed with a golden tongue? One study of fifty normal adopted children and fifty normal children brought up by their biological parents was designed to help answer these questions. In their IQ scores and general cognitive ability, the adopted children resembled their biological parents more closely than their adoptive parents. But the influence of the adoptive mothers' speaking styles, types of sentences used, and the average length of their phrases or sentences was reflected in the children's speech patterns. Two environmental effects, in addition to the obvious one that determined which language was spoken and with what regional variations, proved especially significant whether the child was living with his biological or adoptive parents. There was a positive correlation between time spent reading books to the children and the children's language facility. And mothers' echoing of their infants' vocalizations also seemed to help the children develop their language skills.[2]

Genes and experience interact at all points, but the nature of the interactions and the relative weights of various factors at various times during development are puzzles as yet unsolved. Is it a gene defect or some unknown abnormality in the intrauterine environment that causes the profound communication disorder called autism? Is stuttering due to some genetic susceptibility that reveals itself under specific environmental conditions? A few presumably genetic disorders and a few instances where there is a radically abnormal environment allow study in humans of so-called pure gene or pure environmental effects on language development, but even at the extremes both genes and environment are at work. Systematic manipulations of genes and environmental conditions can be done only with laboratory animals, and animal research leaves important questions about human language unanswered. Therefore, study of the dozen or so gene-based language disorders thus far reported is especially valuable for gaining an understanding of how the human language system is put together.

Scientists in Canada and Britain have been following a thirty-person Canadian family in which half the members over three generations have a language disorder. The evidence is persuasive that the disorder is inherited.[3] Until they are about seven years old, the speech of affected family members is unintelligible; when they do finally make themselves understood, their speech is full of errors in grammar and articulation. Each family member was given a number of standard linguistic-competence tests, and the investigators also made use of writing samples and teachers' reports. With respect to some aspects of language, the affected and unaffected family members were about the same. They could all point correctly to objects, follow complex commands, understand passive sentence constructions ("The truck is not pulled by the car" versus "The truck does not pull the car"), and grasp reflexives (distinguishing "He washes himself" from "He washes him"). But the affected family members consistently produced sentences such as "The boy eat three cookie" and "Yesterday the girl pet a dog," and they could not recognize where they had gone wrong. From the types of errors made, similar in all the relatives with the disorder, the investigators concluded that their capacity for grammatical language was selectively impaired. They lacked a rule for making plurals and for marking tenses and gender. The words themselves are stored in their mental dictionaries, but affected individuals are unable to use them appropriately in constructing sentences. They lack the ability to change the form of the words to match the role the word plays in a particular sentence.

With intensive instruction the affected family members do learn plurals and tenses, but they learn them one by one. They do not, and apparently cannot, find the right word by using the right rule. With instruction they correct a sentence such as "The little girls is play with his brother" and then continue to form it correctly. However, a different but similarly constructed sentence would be riddled with errors. This family has linguistic abnormalities so specific that they allow researchers to focus on an essential component of normal language, the inflectional gadgetry that most of us automatically use as an essential indicator of meaning in every sentence we utter or write.

Growth and development always occur within a "genetic envelope of possibilities."[4] The linguistic capabilities of the Canadian family just described are bounded in this manner. However, growth and development are influenced not only by genes but by prenatal and postnatal events that enhance or further limit genetic potential. Children with Down syndrome, a disorder in which many genes are expressed abnormally, are inevitably retarded in motor, cognitive, and language development. They often have abnormalities in their hearts, ears, and other organs. For most of human history these children were classified as idiots, given minimal care, or institutionalized, and they died young. But as parents rebelled at abandoning their "failed" offspring and demanded educational opportunity and state-of-the-art medical care, the range of possibilities within the genetic envelope of Down syndrome became clearer. In 1955 only 40 percent of babies with Down syndrome lived to their fifth birthday; now over 90 percent do, and by the time they are adults many people with Down syndrome exhibit mental and social capabilities that make it possible for them to do productive work and enjoy a measure of independent living.[5] Although achievement of ultimate goals in prevention and treatment will depend on advances in basic understanding of genes and their expression at the molecular level, we are often able to intervene effectively on the basis of what is already known. The Canadian family described above has had the benefit of modifications in their environment that enable them to "push the envelope": clear delineation of their specific difficulties with speech and language; the devoted collaboration of teachers, therapists, and family members; and excellent educational and medical resources.

Now a clearer comprehension of their disorder's genetic basis and the brain locations and neurophysiology involved seems also to be at hand. Scientists at the University of Oxford and the Institute of Child Health in London have recently located a small region of Chromosome 7 that is abnormal only in affected family members. Moreover, researchers who are studying the family report that they have conducted brain imaging studies showing that affected family members have functional and possibly anatomical abnormalities in their frontal cortex and certain underlying structures. The actual gene mutation (or mutations) in the abnormal family members is not yet identified, and the gene's function is not characterized; however, if the new research is successfully extended, new insights into the molecular genetics of processes vital to normal speech and language development will result.[6]

Another distinct impairment of language learning, also inborn and possibly genetic, is described in a group studied by Paula Tallal of Rutgers University and her colleagues. Again, as with the Canadian family, the first step was to determine the precise nature of their language problems. These children, who are otherwise normal, have a great deal of trouble in comprehending speech. They are late in learning to talk, and they articulate words poorly. In almost all of them, reading problems show up when they start school and they are classified as dyslexic.

Even though their hearing of tones and other nonspeech sounds is normal, the children often mix up such words as "bet" and "pet" or "tattle" and "cattle," and they act as if they cannot hear the difference.

On the basis of her observations of the kinds of errors they make, Tallal formulated the hypothesis that the children in fact cannot hear the difference between syllables such as "da," "ta," and "ka," (or "de," "te," and "ke," and so forth). These syllables begin with the English speech sounds (phonemes) that are called stop-consonants; they are articulated quickly and are characterized by a staccato transition from the consonant to the vowel. (Because of the time it takes to move lip and tongue muscles, the consonant sounds in the syllables "ma" and "la" last about three times as long as the stop-consonant sound in "ka.") Tallal's studies over the past two decades, and those of other researchers as well, indicated that this group's problem was an inability to distinguish rapid transitions in the stream of speech. They surmise that this inability to process oncoming speech quickly and accurately garbles the children's perceptions and gives them incomplete and incorrect information.[7]

More precise understanding of what has gone wrong, coupled with technical advances in sound recording, have paved the way for a trial of a specific treatment. Tallal and her collaborator Michael Merzenich, who does research on how the brain is altered by various experiences, are teaching the children to hear the sounds they miss. The children listen to speech generated by a computer that stretches out stop-consonants and slows down their transition to the vowel that follows. Instead of the natural forty-millisecond transition from "b" to "a" in the syllable "ba," the computer stretches the "b" out to as long as half a second. The computer is also programmed to emphasize hard-to-distinguish sounds such as "b" and "v" by making them louder as well as longer. To train the children, the experimenters use video games whose level of difficulty is set by each pupil's own progress. After a child learns to hear a slow transition—for example, choosing correctly between "cccccccow" and "bbbbbbough," the consonant sounds are gradually speeded up. He listens to books like *The Cat in the Hat* recorded in slow computer-processed speech, then gradually learns to recognize the words in the book presented at a normal speed.

Initial results were promising. The five- to nine-year-old children who were the subjects of study had been at least two years behind in their language skills. After one month of daily therapy, they showed, on average, a gain of two years in speech comprehension. Then for three months they were not exposed to computer-processed speech and were tested again. It was found that they had maintained their earlier gains. The researchers speculate that the gradual speedup of processing requirements induces permanent changes in auditory timing cells and circuits; thus, more accurate information is delivered to the brain's language centers. The changes are possible, they believe, because of the plasticity—the ability to respond to experience—that especially characterizes the immature brain.

Although researchers agree that certain children are born with a phonological defect, its nature is still disputed. Speech scientists point out that affected children who cannot distinguish syllables which are similar—for example, "ba," "da," and "va"—have no trouble with "ba-sa" or "da-sha." This difference suggests that the problem is in distinguishing *similar* sounds, rather than in an inability to identify the correct *sequence* of rapidly presented and overlapping sounds of speech.[8]

Tallal's group is also working on methods for diagnosing deficits in processing auditory sequences in younger children using a behavioral test. (Babies are trained to look at a visual display when they perceive a change in an auditory stimulus sequence.)[9] Pilot studies suggest that infants from families with developmental language disorders are more likely to perform poorly on the test—that is, they do not pick up alterations in sequence as well as infants from families without the disorder. If early diagnosis proves feasible, it may be possible to begin therapy at an earlier age.

The relation of a postulated auditory timing impairment to dyslexia, the reading disorder that affects millions of people, is as yet unclear. The two may be distinct conditions affecting different elements of language function. Different genetic or prenatal developmental factors may be at work. Some dyslexic children may have impaired visual perception. Dyslexia, like auditory timing impairment, runs in families and there are probably several types.[10]

But accumulating evidence suggests that an abnormality in brain language processes underlies most forms of dyslexia. Most dyslexic children, and adults as well, usually use spoken language quite normally, but they have little awareness of the sounds that make up the words they speak and hear. Because of this anomaly they have great trouble, for example, in grasping the notion that "hen" can be grouped with "pen" and "men" because the words rhyme, or that "hen" can be grouped with "hill" and "hat" because they share an initial consonant. They cannot segment a word into its constituent sounds, the task of any beginning reader of a language such as English that uses an alphabetic code. As a consequence they are unable to make the connections between speech sounds and the printed word. They cannot adequately decode single words, and their efforts to do so are slow, labored, and inaccurate. When they read aloud, they hesitate and mispronounce as they try with great effort to decipher words. Their reading comprehension is poor, apparently because they must put so much attention and effort into word-by-word decoding that they do not have the mental resources left over to assimilate the information fast enough.

During the past decade there has been impressive progress in sorting out the problems faced by dyslexic readers and in devising specific educational programs to meet their needs. The insight that dyslexia is primarily a language disorder rather than a visual disorder or a sign of immature cognition has made it possible to develop therapies targeted to the special difficulties dyslexics face in learning to read. A dyslexic child's phonologic deficit can be identified in kindergarten or even earlier and she can be provided with carefully designed instructional games to heighten her phonologic awareness. She then can be helped to link the sound segments in words to the print that represents them.

Several trials of such educational interventions have had promising results. In one study, kindergarten children received special training that helped them to increase their phonologic awareness and connect sound segments to letters. They became better readers and spellers than comparable children in the same class who did not receive the training, and they maintained their gains through the two-year period they were followed.[11] Tailored educational programs for dyslexic children provide another example of how inborn tendencies can be modified.

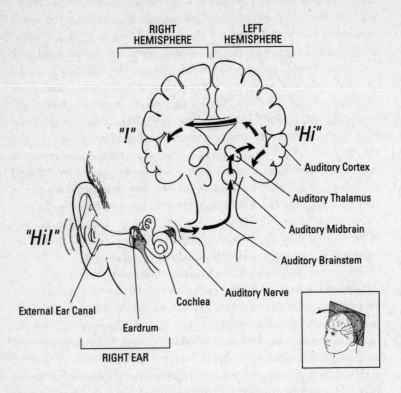

FIGURE 3-1. THE BRAIN'S PATHWAYS FOR HEARING.

A simplified depiction of the auditory pathway. Sounds in the environment are picked up by nerve receptors in the cochlea of the inner ear and transmitted to the brain by way of the auditory nerve (arrow at bottom left). Auditory nerve fibers make synaptic connections in the cochlear nucleus region of the brainstem. Most of the axons then cross to the other side of the brain and ascend to the midbrain where they synapse. (A smaller number of axons—not shown—ascend on the same side.) Midbrain axons then transmit the signal to the auditory relay nucleus of the thalamus. This nucleus relays the message to the auditory cortex. The signal is then distributed to a number of regions in the cortex on the same and opposite sides. In most adults language is interpreted in the left hemisphere; the emotional qualities of language are processed in the right hemisphere.

Doorway to Language

The channels for receiving spoken language are our ears, which send along information to processing centers in the brain. Speaking proceeds in the reverse direction. Every utterance starts as a command to the brain center that controls the musculature of speech, and is transmitted along neural pathways to the muscles of the vocal apparatus. To hear, our ears pick up sound waves, which are vibrations—alternating increases and decreases in air pressure—emanating from a source such as vocal cords, violin strings, a car engine, or a radio speaker. The pitch of a sound is set by the frequency of the cycles of peaks and valleys in the sound wave within a given period of time. The higher the frequency, the higher the pitch. A single frequency creates a pure tone. A mixture of frequencies produces a chord or a noise or a speech sound. The quality of the sound depends on the number, mix, and timing of the constituent frequencies. Loudness depends on the magnitude of the air-pressure wave. The human ear can hear tonal frequencies from about 20 to 20,000 cycles per second. (A bat's ear is sensitive up to 100,000 cycles per second.) The human ear can respond without discomfort to a sound a million times as loud as the softest sound it can hear.[12]

The drum that closes off the inner end of the ear canal vibrates as sound waves strike it, transmitting the air-pressure waves to the chain of tiny bones in the middle ear space. The innermost bone, the stapes, vibrates against the closed but flexible window that leads to the fluid-filled spiral canal of the inner ear, the cochlea. The air wave now becomes a fluid wave. As it ripples through the cochlear canal, which is lined by a specialized tissue called the basilar membrane, the fluid wave activates auditory receptors called hair cells. These cells, which have tiny hairlike projections on them, are arranged along the basilar membrane much like piano keys, in order of the sound frequency to which they respond. High-frequency tones stimulate one end and low-frequency tones the other. Hair cells bend when they are touched by a sound wave. Because the hairs vary in stiffness, length, and manner of attachment to their foundation, they tend to respond only to a narrow range of sound frequencies. Where the cell is placed along the basilar membrane also influences the characteristic sound frequency to which the hair responds.

The hairs touch the roof of the coiled chamber of the cochlea, where auditory nerve fibers, also lined up according to the frequency information they carry, are waiting to relay the hair-cell messages. Here the physical energy of sound is converted into the electrical code used by the nervous system as hair-cell movements release transmitter chemicals that induce electrical impulses in the connecting auditory nerve fibers. In their patterns of electrical firing, nerve fibers code information

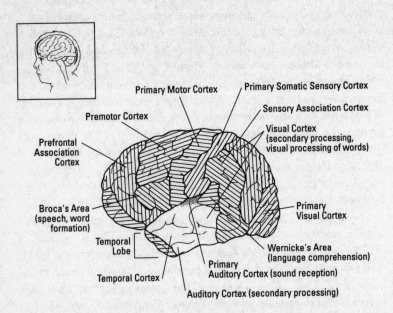

FIGURE 3-2. REGIONS OF THE CEREBRAL CORTEX.

A left lateral view of the surface of the cerebral cortex with some of its regions indicated. Functions such as language, vision, and thought are supported by interconnected brain areas working together rather than by individual regions working in isolation.

The deep indentation that sets off the temporal lobe from the rest of the cortex is called the Sylvian fissure. Most of the primary auditory cortex is on the medial (inner) side of the temporal lobe.

concerning a sound's frequencies, intensity, and time sequencing. The spatial arrangement of the nerve fibers according to sound frequency is preserved as information is passed from neuron to neuron along the path from the auditory nerve to its final destination, the auditory cortex.

The exact tuning of the receptor hair cells and auditory nerve fibers in the human ear is specially adapted to the detection and analysis of the complex sounds constituting speech. Many features of the human auditory system enable us to analyze simultaneously the rapidly changing frequencies of consonant sounds and the relatively constant frequencies of vowel sounds.[13]

Unless a sound comes from a source located exactly at the midpoint between the two ears, there will be slight differences in its timing and intensity as it arrives at the ears; this serves to cue the brain as to the direction from which a sound is coming. Several types of relay neurons in the auditory pathway extract and transmit different features of sounds.[14] Most of the auditory nerve fibers from an ear cross over to the opposite side of the brainstem (right ear nerve fibers to left side, left ear to right side), although some ascend on the side they started from. The brain's analysis of timing and intensity of sounds and its decisions about whether to ascribe a series of sounds to a single source are aided by many interconnections in the auditory pathway.

The auditory projections, transmitting different properties of sound (such as frequency and intensity) along parallel pathways, course the short path from the inner ear through connecting way stations in the brainstem, taking about ten milliseconds to arrive at the thalamus, the busiest neural traffic control center of all. This clump of nerve cells containing anatomically distinct subparts (or nuclei, as neuroanatomists call such aggregations) is located at the root of the cerebral hemispheres, deep in the center of the head. Thalamic nuclei relay incoming messages to cortical brain centers for hearing and all the other senses. Subcortical circuits governing levels of awareness and emotions also send their messages to the thalamic hub; these circuits intersect with incoming sense information. These junctions make it possible to act on emotionally charged information (such as the sound of a gunshot) well before cortical information processing has had time to occur. Recent work suggests that some phonetic analysis also takes place in the thalamus.[15]

Information is fed forward through nerve fibers connecting the thalamus to areas of the primary auditory cortex, which is on both the left and right sides of the brain, in the temporal region behind the ears. A message takes about thirty milliseconds to travel from the midbrain to the cortex, where it is projected—"mapped" is the term used by neurophysiologists—onto several sets of cortical nerve cells more or less ordered in columns. The cortical map is still arranged by frequency, timing, and intensity. These cortical neurons not only have many connections to each other, they also have links back to subcortical brain regions. These connections help to process information about location and loudness, and they probably regulate and fine-tune the system, focusing on sounds of particular interest to the person or animal.[16] Upon receiving the multiple separate inputs of specific features of sound, the secondary auditory cortex begins the task of integration. The stage is now set for the even more strenuous task of analyzing the stream of sounds that constitutes the world of speech.[17]

The sound information, now partially processed, is relayed to cortical association areas that in human beings take up most of the room in our heads and account for its large size. Association areas are located in cortical regions contiguous to the primary and secondary auditory cortices. These regions extract, correlate, and interpret auditory information and related information from the other senses, especially vision. Although the process starts in lower centers, intersensory integration takes place mainly in the association cortex. This has two benefits: information from all sense channels can be processed simultaneously, and ensuing motor responses can be coordinated. At least part of the circuit is functioning at birth; even a newborn will turn his head toward a sound as if to see what he hears.

In nearly all adults, the principal cortical association region for processing speech is in the left posterior temporal cortex slightly above and behind the left ear. Named for a nineteenth-century neuroanatomist, Wernicke's area has long been known to have a special role in speech comprehension, because stroke victims with brain damage in this region lose the ability to understand words. However, recent studies show that linguistic analysis and speech comprehension involve other brain areas as well.[18]

Exactly how the brain binds together all the information from its parallel information-processing pathways is one of the challenging questions of modern neurobiology. Even less is known about how the brain "listens"—that is, how it scans and stores sequential information over the time it takes to process a sentence or a train of thought, while simultaneously it is receiving the next segment of speech for subsequent scanning. Some scientists feel that "this close association of working memory and language may come the closest to defining the special basis for human intelligence."[19]

Association areas in the cerebral cortex receive information from the sensory areas of the cortex—the process we've just described with respect to sounds. The association areas influence perceptions through connections, both cortical and subcortical, to neural systems underpinning emotions, attention, memories, volition, and values. Our consciousness of information flowing in through our senses can vary widely, from exquisitely focused concentration on a single sensory thread to nearly automatic taking into account of the changing environment, as when we drive a car. During sleep the "Do Not Disturb" sign can be posted for sirens, the air conditioner, and the TV, but mothers startle to attention at the baby's first peep. We can be totally inattentive to a stream of talk until we overhear our name mentioned, whereupon we are all ears.

We think about what we are hearing, or we don't. Unlike eyes, ears stay open, but as we have noted, the information is filtered and influenced by processes at many levels from ear to cortex. One of the things our brains do best is select information from a vast menu of possibilities; we do this in many ways, with infinite subtlety and usually without conscious effort. There is much evidence that humans have a special sensitivity to speech compared to other sounds, a sensitivity that seems to be present at birth. Although, as we have noted, a good deal is known from experiment and observation about the interrelationships of developing language, cognition, and attention, our present knowledge of the underlying anatomy and physiology of the neurons carrying out these functions is extremely limited.

Right and Left Brain

A peculiarity of the brain is its specialization for language in only one of the two hemispheres that together constitute the cerebrum. In contrast, the cortical processing centers for most other information, whether visual, tactile, or auditory, are located in both cerebral hemispheres. Each half of the brain receives information from the opposite side of the outside world. Whatever is seen on a person's right is represented in his left visual cortex. When an object, such as a key ring, is grasped by the left hand, the tactile information obtained by the hand's sensors is sent through nerves in the left arm to the spinal cord, where it crosses to the right side and continues onward to the tactile-sensation-processing area in the brain's right hemisphere. Hearing follows this contralateral processing pattern. Sounds, including speech, are initially processed in the auditory cortex of the left hemisphere if they come, say, from an earphone worn on the right ear, and they are processed in the right auditory cortex if they come from the left ear.[20]

Large tracts of neural axon fibers coated with myelin (a substance that assures rapid conductance and gives the fibers their characteristic whitish appearance and designation as "white matter") connect the right and left halves of the cerebral hemispheres. The largest of these fiber tracts is called the corpus callosum. These interhemispheric links weave together strands of information from the left and right sides of the brain, making a seamless fabric. We are totally unaware of the independent operations of the two cerebral hemispheres.

The striking independence of the brain's two halves was demonstrated in a series of experiments on patients with severe and incapacitating epilepsy. As a last resort, they had undergone surgery to sever the connections between right and left hemispheres by cutting through the corpus callosum.[21] This splitting of the right and left brain prevented the spread of epileptic seizures from one side of the brain to the other. (Subcortical and spinal cord left-right connections remained intact.) After surgery the patients got along quite normally; indeed, their lives improved because they suffered many fewer disabling, convulsive seizures. Testing, however, revealed some curious deficits.

If a neuropsychologist presented them with sensory information in such a way that the right cerebral hemisphere but not the left was stimulated, or vice versa, the one hemisphere processed the information independently and did not involve the other. For instance, a split-brain patient *hears* speech presented to his left ear through an earphone, but he understands it poorly because it has been delivered to the right side of his brain—the side not specialized for language—and the major pathway for information transfer to the left brain has been severed. When his eyes are closed and a ring of keys is placed in his left hand, a split-brain patient can show by an action—turning the key in an imaginary lock—that he knows what the keys are used for, but he cannot name the object in his hand, because the connections that would transfer the information to the naming and speech-output centers in his left brain have been cut.

Speech processing is not bilateral. In approximately 98 percent of adults, linguistic analysis is done in left-brain structures. Until the last few decades, virtually all the considerable progress made in understanding the unique role of the left hemisphere in receiving and producing language came about through the study of adults with aphasia who had lost their ability to speak or comprehend language because of a stroke or other brain injury. These patients' difficulties, whether in speaking, in recalling different classes of words such as nouns or prepositions, or in comprehending meaning and context, were assessed on neuropsychological tests. When the patients died, their brains were examined at autopsy and their anatomic lesions were correlated with the signs and symptoms they showed during life. Using these methods, nineteenth-century neurologists and neuroanatomists demonstrated that in most people the parts of the brain critical for linguistic functions are located in the temporal, parietal, and frontal areas on the left side of the brain around the deep infolding of the cortical mantle that is called the Sylvian fissure.[22]

The left brain specializes in language, not sound. People who have left-brain damage may find themselves able to hear spoken words normally but be totally unable to understand them. Deaf people who communicate by sign language, which is produced by hand gestures instead of vocal musculature and interpreted via the visual rather than auditory sense, store their language in the left temporal cortex, just as do hearing persons. If a deaf person has a left cerebral stroke, sign language is disturbed, but not ordinary gestures, which, as in hearing persons, are stored in the right brain. Conversely, a stroke affecting the right side of the brain may leave a deaf user of sign language unable to gesture normally. But she can still sign.[23]

Painstaking anatomic studies explain the ancient observation that people who lose speech from stroke also become paralyzed on their right side. "If I forget thee, O Jerusalem, let my right hand forget her cunning . . . let my tongue cleave to the roof of my mouth," the psalmist sang. Three thousand years later anatomists can tell us how it happens that left-brain injury impairs both voluntary movement of the right hand and the ability to speak: both are functions of the left hemisphere.

The right hemisphere also plays an important role in communication, but in most adults only with respect to nonlinguistic functions such as gestures and patterns of emphasis that express emotion. An adult with left temporal damage in Wernicke's speech area loses the ability to say things that make sense, but the tone quality and expression in his voice are normal. A person with a similarly placed lesion on the right side speaks sensibly, but his voice is flat.

Certain children have been identified who seem to have inborn *nonverbal* communication disabilities. Although they have normal vocabularies and syntax, they have great difficulty in using language appropri-

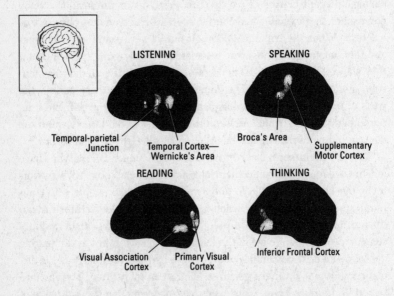

FIGURE 3-3. DIFFERENT BRAIN REGIONS ARE ACTIVE
DURING DIFFERENT MENTAL TASKS.

PET scans taken while subjects are listening to a word, reading it, speaking it, or analyzing its meaning. These are averaged PET images of the brain activity of nine normal subjects. (*Source:* Adapted from Kandel, Schwartz, and Jessell, *Principles of Neural Science,* 3rd ed., p. 13.)

ately in social contexts and in using and interpreting conversational gestures and the emotional tones of speech. Their dysfunctions, thought to involve the communicative centers of the right hemisphere, can be socially disabling.[24]

Left-brain areas devoted to linguistic functions are larger than the corresponding areas on the right side of the brain, and humans are born with these right-left anatomic differences. The differences increase during childhood as functional specialization develops within the rapidly growing brain.[25] It is well established that the left brain of nearly every adult is dominant for linguistic and analytic functions and the right for spatial function, music, and pattern recognition. However, there is no neat dichotomy; both hemispheres contribute, albeit unequally.

Although the general anatomic layout is similar for everyone, the exact contours of various functional areas may be unique to each person. Gender appears to account for some differences in language area maps. In females the right hemisphere typically plays a larger role throughout life than it does in males, and this probably accounts for the fact that women recover better language function than men after strokes on the left side of the brain. Women also have proportionally larger language-associated cortical areas than men.[26] Increasingly, precise neuropsychological testing and functional imaging studies of both normal and abnormal individuals promise better understanding of how language processes are distributed in the brain. These tests can be performed in brain-injured patients, in persons with various language disorders, in normal subjects, and increasingly, thanks to fast and safe techniques we will discuss, in children.

During childhood the right hemisphere seems to play a far larger role in language than it does later in life. Lateralization of language to the left side of the brain is not fixed before adolescence, and children whose left brain has been permanently impaired by a stroke or congenital anomaly have excellent prospects of developing virtually normal language skills. In children, the undamaged hemisphere takes over the functions that ordinarily would have been performed by the damaged side, and does double duty since it also performs the jobs it was originally assigned. The recovery of adults usually entails a reorganization of function within the dominant temporal lobe, rather than a transfer of function to the undamaged side, as in children.[27] The potential to assume functions other than those specified by the genetic blueprint is another example of the extraordinary capacity for organization and reorganization which is the prime characteristic of a child's brain.[28]

Windows on the Brains of Children

Neuroscientists face daunting problems in trying to understand the brain's structures and functions for language in children. Drastic illnesses and injuries to the brain resulting in specific language deficits are rare in this age group. Fortunately, few children die from aphasia-producing brain injury, so autopsy data are also rare. As for children who recover, the change in their behavior is so fast that it is hard to distinguish effects attributable to brain reorganization in response to injury from the effects of normal development. Moreover, small children, especially those who have been ill, are often impatient and fearful in test situations. Rarely do they show great interest in experiments, however elegant or promising, unless they perceive them as play. In most brain research, neuroanatomists and neurophysiologists make use of laboratory animals. But the mysteries of language cannot be unraveled by studying even chimpanzees and baboons, our close nonhuman relatives, since their language capacity is rudimentary at best and may be organized quite differently from that of a child.

Neuroimaging techniques such as CT (computed tomography) and MRI (magnetic resonance imaging) provide detailed pictures of the living brain with a clarity and detail unimaginable a few years ago. They are a boon to the neurologist and neurosurgeon, and they have expanded our understanding of human anatomy, both normal and abnormal. In the past two decades, faster neuroimaging technology has permitted us to study the brain while it processes information. We can, almost literally, see the brain at work. These newer techniques promise to make a significant contribution to the study of language by allowing direct visualization of the brain locations and pathways that are active during the various steps of comprehension and speech. Using PET (positron emission tomography), SPECT (single-photon-emission computed tomography), fMRI (functional magnetic resonance imaging), and advanced electroencephalographic and evoked-response techniques, neuroscientists are beginning to pinpoint functional areas, see their relationships, and watch information processing as it unfolds over time. Since the methods are not risky, do no harm, and are not very unpleasant, they can be adapted with relative ease to the study of children.

PET, which uses radioactive isotopes, has thus far been the most fruitful method for studying normal and abnormal language activity in the brains of adults, but the use of radioactive substances in children is not justifiable unless it will produce information of direct benefit to the child who undergoes the test. Unlike PET (and SPECT, which also requires injection of radioactive materials), MRI is not invasive.[29]

Older MRI machines are slow, however; a session typically lasts about an hour, and patients must lie still the whole time since even slight movements can blur the picture. Functional MRI is an important technological advance because images of the brain can be made nearly as fast as the actual changes in the brain during thinking. With the aid of high-speed computer programs, successive images can be combined to make movies of the brain in action—for example, perceiving a stimulus; choosing among stimuli; thinking up a reply to a question in French or in English; or getting ready to direct a motor response such as pressing a switch with one's finger.

Functional MRI exploits the fact that activated brain cells—for example, those being used to control speech or process a visual image—need more oxygen, the molecule required to produce energy in neurons. When extra oxygenated blood flows through active brain regions, fMRI is able to detect the change because the magnetic signal from the oxygenated blood is slightly different from that given off by deoxygenated blood. The MRI machine scans and images the brain of the person at rest and then repeats the scan while the person is asked to think about something—say, perform a calculation or picture a zebra. Then a computer calculates the difference. In one recent fMRI study, subjects learned to accomplish a task (mentally locating the path through a maze and tracing it with a pencil) while their MRI was being recorded. The images acquired during the test show how activity shifts to different brain regions during successive phases of the learning process.[30] Besides being faster, newer fMRI machines can now be combined with stronger magnets, which enable sharper spatial resolution in the images and thus pinpoint the location of brain activities more accurately.[31]

On a visit to a laboratory at the National Institutes of Health, we watched a monitor showing images of the working brain of an eight-year-old boy as he was invited to think of the names of animals and then to recall all the things stuffed in his desk at school. He was asked to do his thinking first in English and then in French. (His mother, a French neuroradiologist, gave him the instructions.) The images of his brain obtained during rest and under various conditions of brain activity were analyzed, compared, and displayed by the computer.[32]

Studies of this kind reveal locations and pathways for information processing, delineating the bumpy terrain inside our heads much like a road map. However, the road map simile is a bit misleading, especially with respect to a child's brain: the "roads" are constantly under construction, traffic patterns change, and auxiliary pathways keep opening up as a child develops and learns. For example, as new information is acquired, especially if it is complex or difficult, several dispersed areas of brain become active. When the material is mastered, activity related to the task becomes confined to a smaller area.

Imaging studies are revealing just how widespread and dynamic brain language processes are. When the eight-year-old boy we observed thought in English, the active brain areas were not identical to those involved when he thought in French. Recent neuroimaging research confirms that language is organized differently in the brain depending on whether it is acquired in early childhood or in adulthood. Using as subjects fluently bilingual individuals who had acquired their second language either as infants or as young adults, Karl Kim, Joy Hirsch, and their colleagues at Cornell University Medical College recorded fMRIs of the subjects as they silently "described" some event that had happened the day before. They were instructed as to which of their two languages they should use. Later in the session, they (silently) described the same event in their other language. The researchers were especially interested in two of the most important language areas: Wernicke's area (in the left posterior temporal cortex), which has major responsibility for comprehending word meanings, and Broca's area (in the left frontal cortex), which is critical for producing speech (see fig. 3-3, page 72). For subjects who had acquired their two languages as infants, the researchers found that activity in Broca's and Wernicke's areas was exactly the same irrespective of which language was used.

In contrast, bilinguals who had learned their second language as adults showed a different activation pattern. Late learners showed spatially separated and distinct side-by-side areas in their frontal cortical language area (Broca's area) for their two languages. As with the early-bilingual subjects, activation in Wernicke's area was the same for both languages. The researchers took their results to mean that the brain must use different strategies in adulthood for generating the speech sounds (phonemes) of the second language even when, as in this experiment, they do not actually voice the words. As we pointed out earlier, at first infants can discriminate all phonemes; but then, after exposure only to the phonemes of the language (or languages) used around them, they become unable to distinguish phonemes that don't exist in that language. Broca's area becomes dedicated to the production of the language sounds to which an infant is exposed. For a second language learned after the original Broca's area has lost some of its plasticity, an ancillary Broca's area is created.[33]

In another study performed by the Montreal scientists Deborah Klein and Brenda Milner and their colleagues, PET imaging studies were done of native English-speakers who had learned French at about age seven. As adults the subjects were fluent in both languages and used them both every day. In these persons, the same brain areas became active when either language was used, except that when the non-native language was employed, a region of the basal ganglia (the left putamen) lighted up. (The putamen is involved in the production of rote movements.) The researchers thought that perhaps the region was pressed into use when speaking a second language because of the need for additional control of articulation. These and other studies offer evidence that language-related learning and memory are distributed in several brain regions rather than being isolated in specific structures. Moreover, these results confirm that age has a critical influence on the organization of the brain's language structures.[34]

Electrical Signs and Signals

Electrical impulses signal that information is being conducted along nerve fibers from sense receptors in eyes, ears, and skin. These electrical changes start a millisecond or so after a sense organ receives a stimulus and can last for several seconds as information passes through successive synapses in the pathway from the receptors to subcortical and then cortical centers. Electrical impulses are transmitted as well when information passes in the opposite direction—for example, from the brain to a muscle. Recordings can be made of this electrical activity at many sites along the roadway. When, for example, a finger touches something, the electrical record of the touch can be picked up at the finger, arm, neck, or head, or, if the requisite measuring devices are employed, at all these locations simultaneously.

Measurements of electrical activity can be made at each location in the neural pathway. But the detail of the examination and what it tells the examiner depend upon the method used. Surface electrodes on the skin give a general idea of the activity under the electrode. Fine-needle electrodes can also be placed right in or on nerve fibers or cell bodies at various points. This latter method, combined with neuroanatomical examination, is used by animal neurophysiologists, and many advances have been made in the last few years in improving these tools. Obviously, only surface recordings are used in the study of humans except in the rare cases where a more invasive recording will benefit a patient.

As many as twenty or thirty distinct electrical waves are evoked by a single sensory stimulus and can be recorded from the surface of the head; each signifies a different facet of information processing. In deciphering this electrical code, scientists hope to gain understanding of the timing, sequence, and location of information processing without using the invasive neurosurgical procedures that are required for direct recordings from nerve cells. The series of electrical changes that follow sensory stimulation are called evoked potentials, event-related potentials, or (our usage) evoked responses.

As a child gets older, evoked responses change in their wave form, size, timing, and distribution; study of the changes provides insights into how maturation, development, and learning reorganize the brain. In general, with increasing age, evoked responses become faster and more localized. This development is especially rapid during infancy; for example, the large evoked responses to sounds that are found over the occipital (visual) area in young infants are confined, a few months later, to more anterior locations where auditory processing takes place in the mature individual. Evoked responses originating in lower brain centers such as the brainstem mature much more quickly than those from cortical locations, which are still showing maturational changes throughout adolescence.[35]

Evoked responses—unlike MRI and PET data, which reveal tissue densities, energy utilization, and blood flow—are a direct record of the electrical activity of neurons and thus a measure of their most essential function.[36] Neuroscientists in several laboratories are using them to study language processing in children. They have devised experimental situations that make differing demands on linguistic abilities and understanding, and these are reflected in differences in evoked-response waves. For example, hearing the sentence "John spread the warm bread with ———" completed with "socks" rather than "butter" evokes a large wave peaking at about 400 milliseconds after the surprise ending. Researchers term this a semantic deviance response. Brain waves of children as young as five years old show that they get the joke.[37]

In adults, the evoked-response wave that occurs about 200 milliseconds after an auditory stimulus shows differences depending on whether the stimulus is a word, a noise, or a nonsense word. Words usually evoke larger responses than the other stimuli. To find out if this is also true in small children, Helen Neville and her colleagues at the Salk Institute recorded evoked responses to sounds of three types: words the child knew and understood, unfamiliar words, and nonwords (taped words with the tape run backwards). She tested twenty-four normal twenty-month-old children. The children, who wore electrodes placed in standard positions on the left and right sides of their heads, sat on their mothers' laps in front of a puppet show and listened to the sounds, which seemed to be coming from the puppet. The evoked responses, averaged separately for each type of stimulus, showed the expected 200-millisecond response. Words, whether comprehended or not, evoked larger responses than nonwords; comprehended words evoked larger responses than unknown words, especially from the electrodes on the left side of the head.

At around eighteen to twenty months of age, children often show a spurt in their vocabularies, but language facility at a given age varies enormously from child to child. Neville administered various standard language tests to the twenty-month-old children in her study to ascertain the size of their vocabularies. The children were then divided into two groups, one with an average vocabulary of 310 words and the other with an average of 77 words. The children's evoked responses were analyzed to see if language facility (as indexed by vocabulary size) made a difference in the characteristics of the evoked response. Neville found that it did: certain evoked-response waves were larger and appeared more quickly after stimulus presentation in the group with better language facility. There were also other differences between the groups, such as the size of the responses recorded from the various electrode positions. These and other experiments on older and younger subjects seem to indicate that specialized patterns of brain electrical responses develop as children gain language facility.[38]

Evoked responses are also being used to chart abnormal development. In one series of studies, done with my colleague Ann Lodge, I (Ann) found that infants with Down syndrome have unusually large evoked responses to sounds. Unlike normally developing children, those

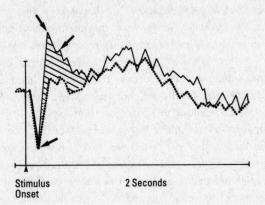

Stimulus
Onset

2 Seconds

FIGURE 3-4. EVOKED RESPONSES REVEAL THAT THE BRAIN
OF A TODDLER PROCESSES COMPREHENDED WORDS
DIFFERENTLY FROM UNCOMPREHENDED WORDS.

The solid line shows an averaged evoked response to words that the child understood. The dotted line shows a smaller response to uncomprehended words. In twenty-month-old children this difference was found in recordings made from the left side of the head. In younger children recordings from both sides of the head showed larger evoked responses to comprehended as compared to uncomprehended words. The difference in evoked responses between older and younger children suggests developing left brain specialization for language.

Brain activity was recorded for a period of two seconds after each stimulus. The evoked responses were recorded and averaged separately for the two conditions (comprehended and uncomprehended words) but they are superimposed here so that a visual comparison can be made. The arrows and cross-hatching indicate parts of the response that consistently differed. (*Source:* Mills, Coffey-Corina, and Neville in Dawson and Fischer, *Human Behavior,* p. 438.)

with Down syndrome do not show decreases in the size of their evoked responses as identical sounds are repeated over and over. These findings, confirmed and expanded by many other investigators, suggest a failure to modulate and control responsiveness to sensory stimuli, a defect that interferes with learning.[39] My group (and many other experimenters as well) found that infants with risk factors such as very low birthweight may have abnormal evoked responses. Abnormal responses in infancy are associated with neurologic abnormalities or learning difficulties that emerge later in childhood.

Evoked responses can also test the theory that the brain circuits for processing the semantic content of language differ from those that process syntactic features. Several researchers have found, for example, that evoked responses to "grammar" words such as auxiliary verbs and conjunctions differ in timing and location from responses evoked by "meaning" words such as nouns, verbs, and adjectives. Although evoked responses may reflect linguistic processing, what they are telling us about these processes is poorly understood at present.

Imaging techniques such as MRI and PET tell us in general where the brain makes language, and evoked responses tell us when. But how language happens is still a mystery. Steven Pinker suggests that language "is probably computed by microcircuitry defined at the cellular, subcellular, and synaptic levels, where manipulation and recording in the human brain is currently impossible." He believes that "there may be discrete language circuits, but current technology would have no way of identifying them, because they might differ in . . . size, shape, and location from person to person, and have . . . shapes that never coincide exactly with brain lesions."

Moreover, the precise routines used by the brain as it processes language information may not be revealed by test methods that rely on behavioral tasks such as naming and repeating words.[40] Research reveals that widely distributed systems and circuits are activated in parallel as language is summoned, but the coherent flow of language emerges from processes that connect and coordinate linguistic elements from moment to moment. How this comes about is not known. It may be that the brain's electrical rhythms—the patterns of electrical activity that characterize the brain during its various states of sleep, wakefulness, rest, and attention—play an important role, but this is mere speculation. However, as data generated by different advanced techniques converge, the window on the elusive language organ keeps opening, little by little.

Chapter Four

HOW MUCH HELP
DOES A BABY NEED?

Children are born with a capacity for language. But how well a child uses words is influenced by many factors—his ability to hear, his general physical and mental health, and especially, by the talk he hears around him. In this chapter we explore the role environment plays in learning language. We include a brief discussion of the harmful effects of adverse physical environments to which millions of children are exposed. The major focus, however, is on how social environments influence the process of language learning, verbal skill and speaking style, and children's readiness to read.

Toxic Environments

By far the largest number of language-handicapped children across the world inherit normal biological potential but are exposed to harmful physical and social environments. There are millions upon millions of children whose development is thus endangered. Some are exposed to a toxic prenatal environment because their mothers are malnourished or drink alcohol or take drugs during pregnancy or have a sexually transmitted disease such as syphilis or AIDS. Many more are born into families lacking access to clean water, a safe place to live, or nutritious food. Millions who are not poor fail to receive the nurture and social stimulation that are as critical to a child's mastery of language as having enough to eat. Many children endure both physical harm and social deprivation, although these risks do not necessarily go together. Children in households where there is plenty of food and good medical care may be parked in front of the television for hours on end and have no one who encourages them in the arts of growing up or celebrates their developmental accomplishments, while a poor child may receive all the encouragement and direction she needs to develop her cognitive, communicative, and social skills.

However, deprivations associated with poverty often lead to impairments of language skills, whatever the culture or the child-rearing practices. For example, low birthweight occurs more frequently among poor families, and a disproportionate number of low-birthweight children end up with a variety of developmental problems, including language handicaps. Complications from ordinary childhood diseases are more common in poor children, who are likely not to have access to proper medical care. Poor children are less likely to be immunized against preventable diseases, and some of these diseases, measles for instance, can have severe aftereffects, including deafness and brain damage. Middle ear infections are common in children, and some children, especially those who don't get good medical care, carry fluid in their middle ears all through their early childhood. Blocked middle ears distort sounds, causing developmental language disabilities, according to some experts. Iron-deficiency anemia, common among poor children, places them at risk for developmental problems. Children who are chronically enervated because of frequent bouts of disease or deficient diet develop slowly. They may be listless, quiet, and easily ignored by busy caretakers. Such children often do not seem motivated; they lack the focused attention needed to develop good language and cognitive skills.[1]

Children who live in old, deteriorating dwellings covered with layers of lead-based paint, who drink water run through lead pipes, or who play in spaces contaminated by lead dust can pay a heavy price as they build up deposits of lead in their bones, blood, and brain. Children with high lead levels are at risk for learning and behavioral problems, and in the worst cases may suffer seizures, coma, and mental retardation. In the United States, lead screening tests, the outlawing of leaded gasoline, and lead abatement programs have reduced children's exposure, but lead is still a potential hazard to the more than 12 million children living in old buildings covered with layers of leaded paint. A standard pediatric textbook estimates that 17 percent of U.S. children between the ages of six months and six years have blood lead levels higher than "acceptable."[2] Other toxic substances, such as plant pesticide residues and heavy metals in foods, also zero in on the growing brains of children. According to some scientists, these exposures are increasing because our environment is becoming increasingly contaminated.[3]

Chronic malnutrition in a mother can be associated with low birthweight in her children; lack of certain nutrients in her diet can damage her fetus. Malnourished children are far more likely to die of infections or to be sicker longer than those who are well nourished. Both malnutrition and susceptibility to infectious diseases are more likely in low birthweight babies than in those born with normal weight.[4] Throughout the world, the most serious threat to children's health and development is not having enough of the right kinds of food. Child malnutrition most often occurs in contexts of extreme poverty and social disorder. Even in sudden catastrophes such as drought and flood, child malnutrition seldom occurs if the social fabric holds and resources are shared.

Healthy adults can withstand months or years of inadequate nutrition or even near starvation without suffering brain impairment. But a baby has little reserve to draw on. The energy requirements for brain and body growth in early childhood are huge, and they must be supplied through steady, just-in-time supplies of the necessary raw materials. A crucial point bears restating: infant development proceeds according to an inborn genetic program that depends on and expects critical environmental inputs. Growth and development are stepwise and cumulative processes. Although there is built-in flexibility in the infant's timetable, which permits protective and adaptive mechanisms to come into play, these fail-safe features can be overwhelmed. If given the chance, deprived children work at catching up, but they still may be left far behind.

Sadly, I (Ann) saw this happening as I observed the rehabilitation of thirty Mexican infants who were hospitalized before they were one year old for treatment of severe malnutrition. All the children came from large, very poor families living in shantytowns in and around Mexico City. Their homes had neither refrigeration nor an indoor water source. They had been breast-fed for only a few weeks, or not at all. Their families had meager social support from public assistance programs or from their extended families.

With proper food and other treatment, all the malnourished children grew, gained weight, and began to act more like children. They smiled, played with toys, and showed interest in their surroundings. But they stayed small for their age, and their development lagged, especially with respect to language. Shortly after the children's admission to the hospital, and periodically for over a year, my Mexican and North American colleagues and I recorded the children's electroencephalograms and electroencephalographic evoked responses to a range of visual and auditory stimuli, including speech sounds. For comparison, we also tested evoked responses of normal children of the same sex and age who attended the day care center for hospital employees' children.

Near the time of their admission to the hospital, the malnourished children's brain-wave evoked responses were small, simple, and slow. Although the evoked responses improved with therapy—that is, they became more like the responses of the children's normally nourished age-mates, the malnourished children continued to have abnormal brain-wave patterns even after nutritional rehabilitation. Apparently malnutrition had left a long-lasting mark on how the children's brains processed visual and auditory information.[5]

Other adversities suffered by these children in their short lives may also have contributed to their abnormal responsiveness. In addition to enduring protein and calorie deprivation, most also had suffered from various illnesses such as diarrhea and respiratory infections, and their long hospitalizations were stressful. The children came to the hospital from environments with many risks and went home to the same environments, except that some supplemental food and follow-up medical care were provided. We wondered whether there was something unusual about these infants; after all, not every child in their families had suffered severe malnutrition.

Research on human malnutrition illustrates the limitations of field studies, where many uncontrolled factors can influence results. Outside the lab, a single risk factor, such as protein deprivation, virtually never operates in isolation. Laboratory studies using genetically inbred animals fed controlled diets and raised in controlled environments are used to tease out the relative impacts of many different risk factors and to define their neuroanatomical and neurophysiological effects with a specificity impossible to achieve in research on humans. These efforts have led to better understanding of the role nutrition plays in brain development and also to more effective nutritional therapies. Such studies are also shedding light on the intimate connections between social factors and biological outcomes.

Studies in both animals and children confirm that severe malnutrition or lack of certain nutrients, especially if suffered prenatally or in infancy, is associated with structural and functional alterations in the brain. But they also indicate that some part of the dull or hyperactive behavior shown by both malnourished animals and children occurs because they are less exploratory and less socially engaged, and thus less likely to encounter situations from which they can learn. They are more likely either to withdraw from novel situations or to become frustrated and irritable in them; this compounds their learning problems. Therapy for malnourished children requires not only adequate nutrition but also special attention to their social and educational needs.[6]

Adverse social and environmental factors can influence development through an accumulation of various kinds of risks. For example, chronically malnourished children, neglected children, and children born with low birthweight (who may also have specific learning disabilities) all tend to stay small in size. Since they may look and act younger than their age, adults tend to baby them. If adults signal low expectations, children may take the cue and perform well below their potential. Or if a child comes to school hungry, or upset by something that happened at home, he may act immature, impulsive, inattentive, or uninterested. He is labeled a behavior problem. His teacher may give up on him. He may give up on himself and fall further and further behind. Poor school performance may then reduce his range of educational and social opportunities, and this will in turn limit possibilities for jobs, friendships, and marriage.[7]

Early experiences establish patterns that tend to recur in one guise or another. Within a given environment, what claims our interest depends partly on what is available, partly on past experiences and the competing experiences of the moment, and partly on our temperament and tastes. The friends we choose and those who choose us, whether we make the chess team, play football, or prefer reading, open a range of different possibilities for later social contacts and experiences.

In certain respects our environment is constantly changing. We move, change schools, experience our parents' divorce or remarriage, and look on as a baby brother or sister joins the family. But for most people critical environmental influences that affect development, learning, and health tend to persist from one stage of life to the next. A child who attends a mediocre elementary school is likely to go on to a middle school and high school that are no better. The advantages of having a father and mother who spend time with us, of eating enough of the right food, and of attending a decent school usually lead to subsequent advantages. Conversely, the heavy weight of deprivation also persists.[8]

Organized efforts to provide food supplements, to immunize children, to clean up the water supply, to get rid of lead-based paint significantly improve children's health. But they often are not available to those who most need them. Worldwide, almost 200 million children younger than five years old are undernourished. Although severe malnutrition is rare in the United States, millions of American children do not have nutritionally adequate diets, and child poverty has increased significantly over the last decades.[9]

Language Partners

The breakthrough that explains the marvelous workings of the language system in the human brain will be an intellectual achievement worthy of a Galileo or a Newton. Our focus here, however, is on a more immediate question: What do we know now about the role parents and other caregivers play in children's language development? Do caregivers play their part naturally, or must they give thought to their interactions with their baby? If being a language partner to a baby is a skill, are parents obligated to see to it that they and the child's other caretakers are performing adequately? If parents do not or cannot facilitate their preschool child's language learning, is there some public responsibility to instruct and support them in this critical aspect of child rearing?

Steven Pinker, a colleague of Chomsky and the author of a widely read book on how language is created, dismisses as "folklore" the idea that parents "teach their children language."[10] In the same vein, a recent cognitive neuroscience textbook states, "Just as is the case with vision, given adequate, early exposure to language, children's language develops rapidly and with few errors, despite little or no instruction."[11] Since reading stories, singing songs, and playing word games with babies will do little either to initiate or to improve language acquisition, according to this view, parents should relax. The chances are that the little one will talk a blue streak when he is ready. By age three the child will, in Pinker's words, be a "grammatical genius."[12]

On the other hand, Catherine Snow, a professor at the Harvard Graduate School of Education, argues that such descriptions of language acquisition make the process sound too easy. We are given a marvelous innate capacity for language, but to realize the uniquely human potential for sophisticated communication takes both effort and help. "Learning language is a long slog, which requires from the child a lot of work . . . it requires a relationship with an adult and a whole set of cognitive abilities."[13]

Clearly, Pinker and other "innatists" recognize the importance of a language partner. (But that partner, as Chomsky reminds us, need not be an adult; siblings and other children will do.)[14] And the innatists agree that both cognitive abilities and proper relationships with adults are required for normal development of language, but for the same reasons that they are required in other areas such as emotions and motor skills. Mastery in all these areas takes "work." Differences among students of children's language acquisition center on questions relating to the uniqueness of brain mechanisms for acquiring language as compared to other knowledge, and on how these mechanisms are brought into play. Theories differ about how brain processes governing syntax and semantics operate and what is needed for them to kick in at the right time and perform at peak efficiency. Do parents hold the key that unlocks the child's door to language? Does the adult open the door, or simply get out of the way so that the child can enter?

The answer depends in large part on what we mean by language. Children come into the world equipped to acquire language. Just as we are born to walk on two legs, so we are born to talk. However, a toddler's locomotor development is pretty much the same whether he is born in Ecuador or Australia. His verbal utterances will depend on whether his mother speaks to him in Spanish or English. Chomsky's great insight was to see the similarities in the grammatical structures underlying all human languages. Children are born with linguistic principles, common to all languages, that are written into their brain substance.

Like walking, the ability to use language is universal among humans. But while an individual may have a characteristic gait, language shows much greater variation from one person to the next; these differences matter more because of the complexities of modern civilization. A significant amount of individual variation is attributable to children's different language-learning experiences. While our ability to convey, receive, and decode complex streams of speech sounds is sturdily built into human brain structure, the richness of our mental lexicon and our agility in deploying it depend on a mix of inborn and experiential factors. Given a bare minimum environment, virtually every toddler learns to walk well enough to get along, although few become marathon runners or ballet dancers. Practically any baby, even one subjected to a barely adequate environment, learns to talk. But many children do not learn to talk well enough to fit them for the daily challenges of contemporary life. Why does this happen?

Two factors are at work here. First, language proficiency is called for in many ordinary transactions of daily life, such as shopping, enrolling one's child in school, answering an ad, and getting and keeping a job. Second, many children do not have the learning environment needed to acquire language proficiency.

In most modern work and social settings, basic requirements for communication skills have become steeper. To do well as a data processor, one need not have won a spelling bee, but no one without the requisite language and literacy skills can succeed at this or many other jobs. In order to keep its assembly line for cellular phones moving at the desired level of quality and productivity, Motorola had to put workers through a six-month remedial reading course at a cost of $5 million because they could not follow the instruction manual.[15] Other employers simply classify applicants with limited language proficiency as unemployable. Although some of the fastest-growing employment opportunities do not call for sophisticated language skills—for example, jobs as fast-food servers, health aides, and data entry clerks—proficiency in speaking, reading, and writing has much to do with someone's chances of getting a job with the prospect of advancement.

At the very time when higher language skills are required for millions of jobs in every part of the economy, more and more children are handicapped because their language-learning environment has not prepared them adequately. Their parents, child-care providers, and schools have not put in enough time, energy, and resources to support their language development.

The contention that the social environment of many young children presents risks to language learning is at first blush puzzling. In today's world, most children are bombarded with talk—on the car radio, at the day care center, on the street, and above all on television. But children develop language and communication skills through social interactions. They need the back-and-forth of face-to-face speech, in the context of joint activity.

Merely being in the presence of adults who are talking to one another does not appear to be of more than minimal help to a child in becoming proficient in a language. For example, children of immigrants who hear their parents and grandparents speak to one another in Spanish, Korean, or Chinese but are themselves addressed only in English develop only a low-level understanding of their parents' native language and little or no active vocabulary.[16] Talk in a social context that includes the children at least some of the time helps them to master language.

How and when adults talk to children differs a good deal from culture to culture. In some cultures, adults direct very little speech to their children until they are old enough to converse. Indeed the interactive style of parent-child discourse common to speakers of English in North America, Britain, and Australia is not much in evidence in many other countries; toddlers learn to talk mostly through their interactions with siblings and other children.

Catherine Snow maintains that "the major function of [adult] speech to the child in the early stages of language acquisition is, not displaying information about syntactic structure, but rather providing a context for the child's utterances. . . . If children reliably hear their own short utterances embedded in discourse, they will discover ways to create longer linguistic contexts for themselves."[17] Snow proposes that a child in the one-word stage of language acquisition participates with her language partner in construction of longer utterances and uses these experiences to move on to create two-word phrases and longer sentences on her own.

The evidence is unpersuasive that infant-directed speech and fine-tuning of adult discourse to the child's level ("parentese") are critical to the child's acquisition of grammar or to her deciphering of the words she hears. But making speech interesting to infants and toddlers serves other purposes. Caregivers use words to signal the infant that she is seen and heard and emotionally connected to a wider world that is influenced by words. The baby soon grasps the notion that vocalizations are signals, and this realization is what Snow calls "the first stage in the ability to communicate."[18]

When the mother shifts her gaze and speaks in response to the infant's visual focus and vocalization—"Yes, you can have a cookie, but first finish these delicious peas"—the child is meeting another requirement for linguistic communication: joint attention. Now she can communicate *about* something, as well as with someone. She looks to her mother for the words that guide her exploration: Is it okay for me to crawl up these stairs? To pet the neighbor's big dog? To punch the buttons on the stereo?[19]

Almost all speech directed to babies is used less to deliver information or model good grammar than to convey social connectedness. Adult speech provides a scaffold, as some psychologists put it, for the infant's efforts to communicate. The words parents speak to babies differ from country to country, but the melodies are much the same. As Pinker notes, the rise-and-fall phrasing to communicate warmth and loving approval, the "sharp, staccato bursts" that signal "Don't touch" or "Stop," the rising pattern that means "Pay attention," and the "low, legato murmurs" that bring comfort are discernible in the speech parents direct to their children in every language.[20]

Mothers and fathers selectively reinforce different aspects of their children's communication, depending on their culture and temperament, what they perceive to be the child's temperament and developmental stage, and what they consider important. Most American parents talk to their boys and girls differently, and a father and mother often differ from each other in how they engage their children.[21] One mother takes pride in letting the toddler take the lead; she mostly responds to or interprets the child's utterances, or acknowledges and describes the objects of his gaze. She is careful to listen for questions, and she answers them simply, often repeating the child's own words in her answer. Another will ask the child to repeat a sentence that is not clear: "Huh? What did you say?" Sometimes she confirms the child's statement by expanding on his theme.

> Child: It's a kitty.
> Mother: With beautiful fluffy fur.

Letting the child set the subject and pace of the conversation and challenging him to be an active participant at least some of the time appear to encourage language learning. However, routinized speech, too, seems to help children master their language. In the repeated ritual of the bath, the bedtime story, or the favorite game, caregivers often use stylized words and phrases to engage infants and provide opportunities to practice communication: "Good night, Moon! Good night, Mommy! Good night, Daddy! Good night, Baby!"

Every two weeks over a twenty-one-month period the psychologist Jerome Bruner observed two little boys, Richard and Jonathan, in their respective homes as each played peekaboo with his mother.[22] At the outset Richard was five months old and Jonathan three months. Bruner describes how the two infants evolved from engaged observers to participants and how the mothers handed over more and more control of the game as the children's comprehension and motor skills matured. The basic game—appearance, disappearance, and reappearance—took different forms. Sometimes the mother hid and reappeared with a "Boo!" and a smile. Sometimes a toy clown was brought on and then hidden. By the time he was twelve months old, one of the little boys could initiate the game by hiding himself. (At about the same age, our grandson Joey discovered the fun of hiding behind a floor-length drape and then suddenly reappearing with an expectant smile.) Although the mothers in each case punctuated the game with verbal exclamations explaining what was happening to the clown—"He's going!" "Here he comes!" "Gone!"—more than language was learned in the process. At six months Jonathan would grab the clown, and his mother would have to coax the toy from his grasp so that the game could continue; at twelve months he had enough understanding and motor control to hand over the clown voluntarily. He was using vocalizations (not yet words) to match his mother's words and had learned much about what Bruner calls "the management of interaction." Both boys took increasing pleasure in the joint activity itself, in the joy of nonthreatening surprises within a safe relationship, and in predictable social rituals. Joey often clapped his hands as he emerged from his hiding place, and his audience would join the applause.

Nursery rhymes and simple games enthrall small children precisely because they become familiar. Perhaps infants and toddlers are mentally anticipating the routines that come next, just as later they will anticipate the words of a familiar bedtime story or the next scene of a video they have seen over and over. Talking to children before they themselves can talk contributes to both cognitive and emotional development in many ways. In routine and predictable situations, like those we have been describing, children appear to use more complex speech and use it more correctly than they do in less structured situations.

Which strategy better promotes language acquisition and the learning needed to develop facility in speech and later in reading? Happily, children learn to talk in either structured or unstructured situations, and most families in the United States offer a mix of both. A key way to foster preschool language skills is what Catherine Snow calls the "embedding" of the child's utterances within discourse and joint activities. Either conversations moved along by adult responses to what a child says or looks at, or predictable bedtime, mealtime, and around-the-house routines will work. The capacity to acquire language is highly buffered and resistant to failure. It works in a variety of learning environments.[23]

Children exhibit a wide range of temperamental differences in their urge to communicate. Within these limits, a caregiving environment in which language is valued and a child's progress in using it is celebrated often makes a difference in how high she sets her language-learning goals and in how much effort, energy, and persistence she will show in reaching them. What caregivers say and do can motivate young children to do the hard work for which nature prepares them.

Parents need to be mindful of the important role they play in their children's language learning. But this does not mean that cramming them with words or ceaseless "enrichment" is a good idea. Children have their own rhythms of engagement and solitude and of speech and silence. They need opportunities to seek out what they want to learn on their own as well as with others.

The linguist Ruth Weir recorded the dreamy monologues of her two-year-old son, Anthony, in his crib as he was falling asleep. One comical feature of this unique set of data, pointed out by the great language scholar Roman Jakobson, is the extraordinary degree to which the toddler's soliloquies "bear a striking resemblance to the grammatical and lexical exercises in textbooks for self-instruction in foreign languages: 'What color—What color blanket—What color mop—What color glass —Not the yellow blanket—The white—It's not black—It's yellow. . . . Yellow blanket—Yellow light . . . There is the light—Where is the light —Here is the light.'"[24]

Perhaps it is only in a linguist's home that a two-year-old engages in language drill as he drifts off to sleep. Yet we see many examples of how the connections between a child and his primary caregivers influence his efforts to master skills of all sorts. The infant who has the assurance of nurture and high expectations is likely to be more confident, more intellectually curious, and more willing to take risks in language as well as in other forms of learning than an infant who is ignored and mostly hears a cacophony of barked commands or telegraphic messages intended for grown-ups. Early experiences with language can make a crucial difference in how well children learn to read and write, and in whether they take pleasure in the art of using language well. A major concern about many day care arrangements in the United States is the high staff turnover rate, which forces the child to begin the dialogue at square one every time a new caregiver appears. Similarly, a day care center with many children and few staff, or a home environment with a depressed mother who is barely available, or an incessant TV with which a baby must compete as he tries to communicate can discourage language learning.[25]

Language and Opportunity

In the summer of 1991 the Carnegie Foundation for the Advancement of Teaching surveyed more than 7,000 kindergarten teachers nationwide to learn what they thought about the readiness of the children who had been in their classes that year to benefit from the more formal education they would encounter in the first grade. The survey asked questions about the children's physical well-being, social confidence, emotional maturity, language richness, general knowledge, and moral awareness. Ernest Boyer, a noted educator and the president of the foundation, found the results of the survey "deeply troubling, ominous, really." Thirty-five percent of the children were not ready for the first grade, according to their kindergarten teachers, and a large number of the teachers thought that the children in their current classrooms were more poorly prepared than those they had taught five years earlier. "When asked to identify the areas in which the children are most deficient," Boyer reports, "teachers overwhelmingly cited 'lack of proficiency in language.'"[26]

The Carnegie survey recorded teachers' impressions rather than pupil test scores and thus may have been biased. But the mere fact that so many classroom teachers across the United States shared a belief in the decline in preschool and kindergarten language skills is significant, because the teachers' discouragement is likely to be reflected in the ways they treat the children.

The British psychiatrist Michael Rutter pointed out in a talk before the World Congress of Neurology that the great majority of children around the world who have poor language skills possess the requisite mental capacity but lack the social opportunities to develop their potential. The cultural contexts in which such opportunities are provided vary widely, but many studies show that they all contain variations on the basic elements we have discussed: encouragement and support for the child's accomplishments; social routines that involve language; engaging the child in conversation; reading to the child; and responding with words to a baby's effort to communicate. To supply these elements the time, attention, and energy of an adult are required, and in many families these resources are in short supply and subject to fiercely competing demands. Lack of parental time is one of the major reasons why children of low-income families are so often unprepared for school, but in an age when it is becoming rarer for families to eat together and rarer still for the TV to be off when they do, opportunities for unstressful, unhurried, and enjoyable conversations between parents and children are lacking in every social class.[27]

In one study researchers received permission to make monthly hour-long visits to the homes of forty children, beginning when they were seven months old and continuing until they were three. The researchers taped the speech of the children and the adults who interacted with them, and recorded the contexts and content of language interchanges, as well as the "pragmatics" of the exchanges (gestures, facial expression, tone of voice). They kept track of the number of different words each child could say and the length of each child's utterances.

All the children developed language skills, and none was classified as language-delayed or language-impaired, but there was great variation in proficiency among them. When they were three, their spoken vocabulary ranged from 266 to 1,692 words, and their mean length of utterance varied from 1.56 morphemes (word units) to 4.51. The three-year-olds with the smallest vocabularies and the shortest sentences were found to have parents who talked to them less, used a smaller variety of words, explained less, asked and answered questions less, and were more likely to prohibit or discourage exploration by the child. These parents were likely to be both poor and poorly educated.[28]

Twenty-nine of the children in the study were tested again at intervals during their elementary school years up to third grade using standard measures of verbal, reading, and academic achievement. None of the children was in remedial or special education. The researchers found that the children's elementary school scores, especially on tests measuring receptive and spoken language and reading skills, were highly correlated with test results that had been obtained when the children were thirty-six months old.[29] Thus children who began school at a disadvantage and received no special help remained at a disadvantage.

Language, Status, and Identity

"Where is Susan?" the teacher asks. "She ain't ride de bus," a Trackton boy answers. "She *doesn't* ride the bus, Lem," the teacher corrects him. "She *do* be ridin' de bus," says Lem, informing the teacher of the true state of affairs. The teacher, who has forgotten or does not know that in Lem's language "ain't" is a synonym for "didn't," frowns and looks away.[30]

Eliza Doolittle, the cockney heroine of *My Fair Lady,* spoke an English-language dialect that was semantically complex, pragmatically expressive, and syntactically correct. But Eliza's dialect restricted her to the life of a street vendor. The musical comedy, and the George Bernard Shaw play on which it was based, remind us that how we talk has much to do with the opportunities life offers us.

Even in supposedly egalitarian societies, language divides even as it unites. Across the world, speaking styles, accent, dialect, and word choices are indicators of social class. A speech style that diverges from what is held to be standard, such as a heavy accent or Black English, is usually a handicap in the mainstream job market, and it tends to limit social and educational horizons. There is a kind of speech and diction that can open the door to a factory job, another that can qualify one as an office assistant, and quite another that must be attained before a managerial career in a major corporation or getting into medical school become more than a dream.

Standard English emerges naturally from homes where standard English is spoken. Children from homes where English is not spoken or where the parents use a dialect usually adapt to school English. This has been true for successive generations of immigrants. Most children learn to use speech appropriate to various social situations, switching with ease from buddy talk in the 'hood to classroom diction, and later, from home speech to job speech.

Learning one's culture and learning one's language are entwined. As we have seen, even the first games and routines like peekaboo and bye-bye as well as more complex speech routines introduce the child to approved social interactions. According to the linguist and ethnographer Bambi Schieffelin, when Kaluli-speaking mothers in New Guinea wish their children to imitate what they say, they end the phrase they want imitated with the directive, "Say it!" However, the mother is not engaging in language drill; rather, she is instructing the infant in proper behavior. For example, in one incident Schieffelin recounts, an older child had just snatched a bit of food from the baby. The mother then repeated over and over to the baby, "That's not yours, it's mine. Say it!" The mother was well aware that the baby wasn't old enough to say it, or even to understand the words. But among the Kaluli food is scarce, and mothers teach their babies how to protect their share. Among the first utterances of Kaluli babies is a quick negative response to an older sibling's aggressive moves.[31]

Teachers (and at a later stage employers) in every society often confuse class- and culture-determined divergences from standard language with linguistic and even cognitive deficits. Cultural anthropologists document the many ways in which class and cultural factors influence language style: the expansiveness of gestures; diction and word choice; when or whether eye contact is to be made; and how to address a person of the opposite sex, someone who is inside or outside one's group, or someone in authority. Children become competent communicators in cultures in which styles of communication differ greatly from the American white middle-class model. However, they may be able to use language effectively within their cultural context but be at a loss outside it.

If language learning did converge at the same developmental endpoint in all cultures and if language style and usage were the same in all cultures, then individual differences in speaking style would be best explained by individual differences in ability. But that is not the case.[32] Different cultures have differing styles of and requirements for language usage. But at school or on the job, judgment of language competence is determined by the dominant cultural standard; linguistic styles that stray too far from the mainstream are deemed inferior and unacceptable.

At the same time, English, like all living languages, is constantly being changed by the people who use it. Schoolteachers sometimes seem to think of themselves as guardians of language purity, but they fight a losing battle. The evolution of language may be especially rapid in the increasingly multicultural and polyglot society the United States is becoming. Changes in English usually occur first in subcultures—among teenagers, computer nerds, scientific subdisciplines, minority groups, immigrants, and border residents. These verbal innovations may stay local or die out, but some flow into the mainstream.

Special language communities now embrace not just Black English in its various forms but Appalachian English, creole dialects, Haitian French, many varieties of Spanish, Korean, Chinese, Vietnamese, Russian, and Ethiopian, and all sorts of other tongues. The hum of languages from all over the world reverberates through subways, streets, and supermarkets across America. We are now a multicultural society in many new ways and to an extent we have never known before. The new immigration of the last thirty years has made many Americans uncomfortable. A movement to require "English only" in schools is once again gaining power. Multicultural education is a contentious issue, and disputes over language are often bitter.

Heavy-handed efforts to disparage or demean the way a person talks or to force people to speak a language not their own often backfire. From playground brawls to bloody wars, conflicts about language are emotionally charged, deeply divisive, and hard to stop. The threatened breakup of Canada, the bloody massacres in the Balkans, the role Great Russian chauvinism played in the erosion of the Soviet Union, and the withering scorn of a teenager for peers whose talk is not "cool" remind us of the extent to which our species uses language as a flag; our ways with words not only tie us to the community we care about, but they are markers of who we are.

Seeds of Literacy

When we talk, we combine a small number of meaningless vocalizations into a large number of meaningful units. Writing was invented when some long-ago ancestor realized that his or her words were made up of special speech sounds, and then discovered that each of these meaningless vocal segments could be represented, however arbitrarily, by distinct optical shapes: the sound "a" by the shape a, the sound "b" by the shape b, the sound "c" by the shape c. Thus was born the alphabet. With this momentous invention, anyone who could speak the language could learn to read and write, provided he or she became conscious of the sound structure of its words—that is, its phonology—and learned its alphabetical code.[33]

A six-year-old learning to read makes a similar discovery, usually with the help of a parent or other teacher. He learns that sounds are visually represented by letters. He learns to read words by "sounding them out." He learns the different ways a letter translates into sounds—for example the, "o" in "do," "don't," and "dog." He learns to listen and to become conscious of the fact that a spoken word is a blend of sounds, not separately uttered, but articulated all together to make a syllable. (The distinctive units of sounds of a language are called phonemes. "Dog" has one syllable and includes three phonemes; "doggy," two syllables and four phonemes.) The letters d-o-g on the page represent the sounds of the word "dog," and that word stands for the dog in the book, his own pet, and "dog" in general. The child also comes to recognize words on a page by their familiar shape.

Preschool children, provided they are exposed to books and other written materials, prepare themselves for reading long before they can understand the words in their book or recognize a single letter. Toddlers love to sit on a parent's lap and have stories read out loud. They point to the cow and pat the bunny. They say "Moo" or may say "Dog"—their temporary generalization for a four-legged creature. They are learning to associate three kinds of representations of real-world objects and actions: words they hear, pictures on a page, and written words. They may "read" the story out loud, sometimes in a mix of words and jargon, often mimicking the reading style of their mother or father.

When we take a walk with two-year-old Joey, he stops at every sign and "reads" it or demands that it be read to him. Our walks are punctuated by "Stop," "For Sale," and "No Parking." Without being able to read, he has already grasped the idea that print makes special patterns, different in kind from the patterns made by autumn leaves or those knitted into his sweater. Print "says something." Children from literate homes have innumerable opportunities to observe how print is used in dozens of ways by the people important in their world—for shopping, reading labels, looking up baseball scores, reading for pleasure and information. Even toddlers come to appreciate the importance of reading in their culture, and they develop the expectation that they, too, will become readers. These attitudes, skills, and knowledge some reading specialists call "emergent literacy." Preschool children learn "to develop and refine their capacities to use symbols, to represent experience, and to construct imaginary worlds, capacities they will draw on when they begin to read and write."[34] The most important role parents can play in the process is to encourage and guide the natural interest children exhibit in reading and storytelling.

Considerable research over the last two decades indicates that a family environment in which infants and toddlers become familiar with books early in their life predicts success at learning to read. But there is no canon of early literacy. There are all sorts of ways children are introduced to books, print, computers, and writing materials. Some anxious parents are so eager for their toddlers to shine in kindergarten that they inundate them with instruction. But commonly, literate parents expect that as a matter of course their children will be literate, and this confidence enables them to be relaxed and playful as they encourage their children's early adventures in the world of words.

Children become prepared for reading as they hear rhymes and simple stories over and over. In the process they become aware of the sound structure of words. They learn to hear, for example, the differences between "bed," "red," and "said"; "bun," "but," and "bud"; and "bell," "ball," and "bull." Research indicates that about a quarter of first-graders in the United States are significantly deficient in phonemic awareness, and these children are at risk for becoming poor readers.[35]

Many studies show that the preschooler who knows the names of letters and recognizes them on the cornflakes box, traffic signs, or television is likely to become a good reader in elementary school. Nothing predicts reading success better, however, than a child's experience of being regularly read to, one-on-one, in the first years of life—especially "when the vocabulary and syntax of the materials are just ever so slightly above the child's own level of linguistic maturity."[36] The reading researcher Marilyn Jager Adams, a developmental psychologist at the University of Illinois Center for the Study of Reading, describes the experience of her own child, which is not unlike that of many American middle-class children. Ever since John was six weeks old "we have spent 30 to 45 minutes reading to him each day." By first grade he had already spent some 1,000 to 1,700 hours one-on-one with a parent or other caretaker with his face in a book; another 1,000 hours or so watching *Sesame Street,* and "at least as many hours fooling around with magnetic letters on the refrigerator, writing, participating in reading/writing/language activities in preschool, playing word and 'spelling' games in the car, on the computer, with us, with his sister, with his friends, and by himself, and so on."[37]

Six-year-olds who lack such experiences are much more likely to get off to a slow start in the first grade. Think of all they must learn if they come to school not knowing what print is for.[38] First-grade teachers in the United States, who must divide their attention among twenty or thirty pupils, typically devote no more than 360 hours to formal reading instruction during the school year.[39] They face an almost impossible task in preparing slow readers to cope with the challenges that will confront them in the higher grades. When slow readers and even nonreaders are promoted through the system, both the students and the school fail.

Culture and Literacy

Fortunately, innate language capabilities are so sturdy that only the most extreme isolation and neglect keep us from talking. Reading is a different matter. Literacy is not written in our genes; well over half the people of the world cannot read at all. Reading depends on being taught to read.

According to many authorities, "the ability of our [U.S.] students to read advanced materials is slowly but steadily declining; . . . among industrial nations, American students' reading achievement is average or even below; . . . compared to its industrial competitors, the United States is raising a disproportionate number of *very* poor readers; . . . already one out of five adult Americans is functionally illiterate and these ranks are swelling by about 2.3 million each year."[40]

The basic myth of American democracy is equality of opportunity, and the vehicle for self-advancement offered to everyone, at least in theory, is free public education. But to take advantage of even the lowest rungs of the educational ladder, a child must be ready to read. As the Commission on Reading of the National Academy of Education predicted almost fifteen years ago, literacy levels only recently considered acceptable will not suffice in the year 2000.[41] In the so-called Information Age the ability to read, understand, and write complex, often technical material is becoming indispensable—not just for the chance to land a better-than-poverty-level job and start along the path to economic advancement, but also for being a good enough citizen and voter, roles that require some understanding of how the rapid technological and political changes propelling America into the twenty-first century are affecting us personally. People who can't read at an adult level are cut off from information they need to make intelligent decisions about their own health, family, education, and job, and they can play only a marginal role in local, state, and national politics.

Earlier in this chapter (page 96) we quoted from a remarkable study of home life in three communities in the North Carolina Piedmont, each with a quite different cultural environment. The author of the study, Shirley Brice Heath, found that the sort of preschool language support and preparation for learning to read we have been describing were prevalent in the "culturally mainstream homes" she observed, even when the parents were poor, had never gone to college, and held nonprofessional jobs.[42] But millions of American children do not grow up in the cultural mainstream. In some families, income levels and social status may be high but books are neither valued nor much in evidence. Time and patience may be in short supply for reading simple stories over and over to a tiny child or for engaging him in talk about the happenings of the day. In some families little effort is made to acquaint preschoolers with what letters look like, what they sound like, and what books are for.

Whether a child is suffering from a biologically based language or reading disorder, a delay in language learning and reading due to lack of social opportunity, or poor adaptation to a school culture and language very different from those of home is often unclear, especially with respect to poor children. Heath gives us a picture of how a mix of these factors can affect reading skills, school performance, and the attitudes of teachers in the three contiguous but socially distinct communities that were the subjects of her nine-year study. She calls the groups Townspeople, Roadville, and Trackton.

Townspeople, both black and white, are "mainstream" and middle class in their outlook and aspirations. They value education and reading. The baby is treated as a participant in family conversations. Mothers talk to their babies face-to-face, responding as if the child's movements and vocalizations are intentional. The parents themselves enjoy reading, and they communicate that pleasure to the children. By and large, the children do well in school.

In Roadville, a white working-class community on the edge of town, parents value reading as a tool for success, but themselves read only an occasional magazine. They begin reading to their children when the children are very young. By two years of age they have been taught to sit passively during story reading, not participating or commenting until the parent quizzes them on what has been read. "'Wendy, stop that,' says one father to a wiggly toddler. "'You be quiet when someone is reading to you. You listen. Now sit still and be quiet.' Often Wendy . . . runs away . . . saying 'No, no.' When this happens, her father goes to get her, pats her bottom, and puts her down hard on the sofa beside him. 'Now you're gonna learn to listen.'"[43]

Heath calls this style of interaction "pre-scripted participation." It prepares Roadville children well for the teaching environment they will encounter in their elementary school. Roadville children are successful in navigating the early grades. But many of them cannot adapt what they learn to new contexts. Their creativity is limited, their imagination unengaged. They soon fall behind. By junior high "most are simply waiting out school's end or their sixteenth birthday, the legal age for leaving school."[44]

The black working-class community of Trackton consists of a few two-family wooden houses at the end of a dirt road. Much of Trackton's social life takes place outdoors, on front porches and in a dirt plaza formed by the cluster of houses. Babies and toddlers are constantly in the eye of older children and adults; they are carried around, played with, cuddled, fed, and admonished by any nearby adult. They are bathed in a never-ending stream of communication, verbal and nonverbal, but the special "baby talk" and "parentese" generally used in nearby middle-class communities, both black and white, is almost never used in Trackton. Everybody talks about the baby as he is admired and passed around, but rarely does anybody talk *to* the baby. In this community it is assumed that no special effort is needed to encourage a child to talk: "When a baby have sump'n to say, he'll say it." Trackton children have little direct experience with the written word before they enter school. Parents do not read to the children or for pleasure. Their literacy level is usually low.

The children of Trackton learn highly adaptive social skills for the isolated community in which they are growing up. When a boy baby becomes a toddler he assumes a special role on Trackton's outdoor stage.

One routine, repeated over and over with variations, consists of teasing challenges by the men of the community. An uncle snatches at the toddler's bottle or cookie, or challenges him verbally, "What you mean, you dunno? You better know sump'n in dat big ol' ugly head. What's yo' name?" If the child whines or cries, the teasing is stepped up. But the toddler who yanks his bottle back or punches at his tormentor, shouting "Stop dat!," is applauded with laughter and approving words: "You gonna be all right, boy, you be just like me."[45]

However, these children have little familiarity with the kinds of language skills that impress teachers at school. Trackton children enter elementary school speaking Black English and depending heavily on context to make themselves understood. They have had little experience to prepare them to read.

The child-rearing culture of Trackton encourages social sensitivities and skills, fosters imagination, and prepares children to look out for themselves. But it has not prepared them for school schedules regulated by the clock, or for acquiring a stockpile of facts by listening to the teacher, or for making themselves understood in standard English. If a Trackton child were dyslexic, one would not expect his classroom teacher to discover it, since her prior experience has led her to expect Trackton children to be nonreaders. She is pleasantly surprised when she gets a reader from Trackton in her class, but does not fret unduly over her nonreaders. Not surprisingly, Trackton children fall quickly into a pattern of failure made all the more painful by the incessant message they hear everywhere around them, both at home and at school: without a high school diploma you can never get ahead.[46]

There are now many more Tracktons than when Heath did her study. At the same time, speaking, reading, and writing standard English has become a survival skill. Except for the few people who can spend their whole lives within their own language community, those who know little English or only an English dialect discover that their prospects are limited to poverty-level jobs, unemployment, and cultural isolation. For some, a criminal career may look like a better bet.

The 7,000 kindergarten teachers who were queried in the Carnegie survey mentioned above were asked "What would most improve the school readiness of children?" The majority replied, "Parent education."[47] Interested parents can learn in a relatively short time to read stories to their children in ways that excite the imagination. They can help their children become aware of the sounds of language, for example, by playing rhyming games and repeating nursery rhymes. One study of middle-class two- and three-year-olds found remarkable gains in children's verbal expression and vocabulary after their parents had received just one hour of training in interactive story reading. The control group (children whose parents had not received the training) lagged some six to eight months behind on standard tests.[48]

At the Family Place, a community center for families that I (Ann) helped start in 1981, we designed a six-session course for poorly literate Spanish-speaking parents. We videotaped small groups of parents as they interacted with their infants and toddlers and then parents and instructors together commented on the videotape and tried out ways to evoke and enhance the children's efforts at communication.[49] Several years later, in preschool and kindergarten, these children were found to have better facility in both Spanish and English than children of parents who had not received special training. Such "family literacy" programs equip parents with language and literacy skills and open their eyes to how they can help their children acquire these skills.

Awareness of the stages of child development, knowing how to use conversation with a child in everyday life, interacting effectively with children at various stages of development, engaging a child with appropriate play materials and books, and knowing how to encourage a child's efforts at communication are not skills automatically conferred by parenthood. But in many cases they can be learned.

Special education and remedial teaching efforts take time, commitment, and resources, but when they are done well, they end up saving society money. Under our present self-defeating practice, many nonreaders are promoted through the system until they receive a diploma they cannot decipher and soon find that all they can look forward to is a succession of poverty-level jobs or worse. As the sheriff of Alexandria, Virginia, puts it, "My jail is full of the failures of Alexandria's schools."[50]

Chapter Five

LANGUAGE OF THE HEART

Discussions about the meaning of childhood, the special requirements of children, and the role of parents generate heated disagree-
ments about the most basic questions: What do children need in order
to develop into normal, happy, and caring adults? When do they need
it? Who should provide it? The answers have changed over the course
of history in response to differing cultural and economic forces, and,
more recently, also as a result of the research of child psychologists and
other scientists. How much influence inborn temperamental tendencies
exert compared with experiences with caregivers is a matter of dispute.
We will discuss recent research bearing on these issues.

Bringing Up Baby

The child-rearing attitudes and practices of humans are much more varied than those of other species. In eighteenth-century France, for example, about half the infants born to well-to-do urban families were sent
away for a year or more to wet nurses in the countryside on the theory
that they would benefit from the healthy air. Among the Efe!, a semi-

nomadic people in Congo, a newborn is given to another lactating woman to hold and nurse, and many different caregivers share responsibility for the child. Infant feeding practices, for example, how long or whether to breastfeed and the correct moment to introduce solid food, are equally varied and subject to the swings of cultural fashions.[1]

Across the world small babies are laid to sleep alone or with others, in cradles, hammocks, and cribs, on papoose boards, in the parents' bed, or in clothing that secures the infant to mother's back or front. They are swaddled, wrapped, loosely covered, uncovered, laid face up or prone. In traditional cultures mothers normally learn their caregiving routines from their own mother or some other older woman and believe that they are caring for their baby in the best or the only way. Modern women, however, may instantly change their ways under the influence of outside authorities and in the light of new knowledge or circumstance. When pediatric studies confirmed an association between sudden infant death syndrome (crib death) and the custom of placing infants on their stomachs for sleep, surveys showed a flip from one year to the next in babies' sleeping position, and a decrease in the incidence of sudden infant death.[2]

Millions of parents who have never heard of, much less read, Sigmund Freud, John B. Watson, B. F. Skinner, John Bowlby, or Arnold Gesell have interacted with their babies under the influence of these experts. Over the years, pediatricians, therapists, social workers, and family court judges have often reflected various theories of child development in their advice and decisions, and versions of the theories have filtered into the daily life of parents through popular books on parenting, TV, newspaper and magazine articles, novels, and movies.

Consider the authoritative advice of the behaviorist John B. Watson, whose famous book *Psychological Care of Infant and Child* was published in 1928. For Watson, infants were potter's clay: they would become whatever their environment—meaning mother, mostly—molded them to be. Mother's power to shape her children's behavior was total and her responsibility awesome. Some of Watson's wisdom was disturbingly counterintuitive: "Never hug and kiss them, never let them sit on your lap. If you must, kiss them once on the forehead when they say goodnight."[3] The child thus trained, he promised, will learn not to cry or whine for attention.

As difficult as listening to the wails of an unconsoled baby must have been for sleepless Depression-era mothers, the very different advice later offered by the British child psychiatrist John Bowlby also could generate maternal guilt. "Intimate attachments to other human beings," he wrote, "are the hub around which a person's life revolves not only when s/he is an infant or a toddler, but throughout adolescence and the years of maturity as well and on into old age."[4] Bowlby considered it critically important that a mother communicate her affection for her infant in the early months of life so sensitively that the child becomes "securely attached" to the person he comes to know and trust above all others. On this foundation "the rest of his emotional life is built—without [it] there is risk for his future happiness and health."[5]

Bowlby presented his theory of attachment in a series of books and papers beginning in the 1950s. He had been struck by Konrad Lorenz's studies showing that newly hatched birds bonded to the first moving object they saw, whether their mother or the human experimenter, and by the work of other ethologists, notably Harry Harlow, who described the importance of the mother-infant relationship in monkeys.[6] Bowlby argued that in humans the relationship between mothers and infants is organized by the infant's innate, unlearned behavioral signals—sucking, clinging, following, smiling, and crying—which bind each to the other. If the mother is physically or emotionally unavailable, or the child fears that he will be abandoned, he becomes chronically anxious. If the primary caregiver is remote, depressed, uncaring, or inconsistent and unreliable, or if the people who fill that role come and go with great frequency, the resulting distortions of the primary relationship, Bowlby theorized, can lead to difficulties in forming deep relationships with others in adult life.

On the basis of early attachment experience, Bowlby believed, every infant develops an internal working model of himself and others. A securely attached infant is one who is confident that his mother, father, or some other primary caregiver will respond to his needs. His confidence that the adults who care for him are trustworthy gives him a sense that the world is an essentially safe place. Out of this sense of security comes the confidence that he can meet new challenges. His security is the underpinning of his developing autonomy. Insecurely attached infants and toddlers have a different working model of human relationships; they tend to be more wary of others, more uncertain about whether their environment is threatening or benign. As babies they are more hesitant to explore the world around them; as they grow, they are more apt to be overly self-protective, anxious, or angry.

By focusing on early interactions between infants and caregivers and postulating that these have profound impact on later life, attachment theory has become an influential concept in psychology.[7] Over the last forty years the theory has influenced how parents, child development specialists, pediatricians, day care providers, and therapists think about emotional development. Later in this chapter we will discuss some of the ample evidence from observation of both humans and nonhumans that lends credibility to Bowlby's thesis—and suggests some reservations as well.

Bowlby challenged Freudian orthodoxy by ignoring Freud's theories concerning an instinctual tension-reduction drive, repression, infant sexuality, and the Oedipus complex. He agreed with classical Freudian theory in ascribing great importance to the early relationship between parents and their child. But the Freudian theories predominant in the first half of the twentieth century dealt with children's fantasies and dreams about their parents rather than with the real-world details of the relationship. As one prominent psychoanalyst explained it in the 1920s, psychoanalysis was concerned "simply and solely with the imaginings of the childish mind, the phantasied pleasures, and the dreaded retributions." Indeed, classical analysis was interested in children only because universal myths of childhood, in particular incest fantasies, figured importantly in the treatment of adult psychiatric problems.[8] Bowlby, on the other hand, believed that "real-life events—the way parents treat a child—is of key importance in determining development."[9]

Bowlby's theories raised issues of responsibility. If infants' emotional destiny is fixed by early experience—Bowlby did not believe this to be the case, but sometimes his work was so interpreted—then some adult, usually the mother, is faulted for the child's failures in later years. During much of this century, mothers have been blamed for ruining their children—and many have blamed themselves—because they have overwhelmed them with their own emotions, been aggressively overprotective, smothered them with demanding love, showed too little love and too much anger, toilet-trained them too late or too early, weaned them too early or too late. Indeed, not so long ago mothers were blamed for making their children autistic by treating them insensitively.

In the late 1920s, Arnold Gesell, an eminent pediatrician at Yale, began to popularize a more comfortable idea: that development proceeds according to a built-in schedule and, within broad limits, is hard to derail. All normal children learn to talk and walk, and develop other skills, within more or less the same time span. Gesell stressed the benign implications of nature's timetable: "The inborn tendency toward optimum development is so inveterate that [the child] benefits liberally from what is good in our practice, and suffers less than he logically should from our unenlightenment."[10]

Far from settling the controversies over parents' role in their child's emotional development, recent revival of interest in the durable effects of a baby's innate propensities has fueled the debate. Over the last two decades the hypothesis that physical and behavioral development are controlled by the child's genetic endowment has become so fashionable, and belief that early childhood experience makes the critical difference so unfashionable in some scientific circles, that, by 1991, Sandra Scarr, the president of the U.S. Society for Research in Child Development, was arguing that children "make their own environment . . . based on their own heritable characteristics." According to this view, a child unconsciously picks and chooses from among the many elements in the environment only those that fit his or her inherited proclivities. For example, a naturally outgoing three-year-old will plunge happily into a playground group and take part, while a shy child will hang back on the fringe of the group. No matter how hard the teacher tries to influence the two children, their social experiences will be different. Likewise, boys and girls will often choose different items—toys, activities, playmates—from the same environmental menu. Observation over time shows that the sum of each child's social experiences adds up quite differently, depending on their differing biological predispositions.

By and large, the advocates of this position hold, children become what they are biologically programmed to be. As long as parents are "good enough" at caring for their offspring, Scarr maintained, it does not matter much what they do. They should relax and avoid "needless sacrifices and emotional turmoil." Another prominent psychologist concludes that parents' behavior has relatively little influence on their children's cognition and personality compared to that imposed by inborn constraints.[11]

But what is "good enough," and what does it mean that "parents have little influence"? In the American marketplace of ideas two basically contradictory notions about children are contending with one another. Many people hold both simultaneously. One is the old-fashioned notion that families—again, read "mothers"—are responsible for nurturing their babies so that they become industrious, competent workers and engaged, morally sound members of the community. Children who don't turn out well have been raised wrong. The other view, much influenced by some interpretations of behavioral genetics research, is that inborn genetic traits are so strong that, unless disaster strikes, environment plays only a minor role in determining the sort of adult any child will become.

The most compelling evidence for the latter hypothesis comes from studies of sets of twins who were separated from each other and from their biological mothers shortly after birth. It turns out that identical twins, although reared by different adoptive families, are often astonishingly alike as adults, not only in physical characteristics but also in behavior. If one twin was affectionate, drank diet soda, and liked sports cars, the other tended to have the same qualities and preferences, even down to liking the same brand. If one twin was a salesman or liked hunting and science fiction, the other was likely to have the same kind of occupation and interests. These twins, with their virtually identical genes, were much more like each other than like their adoptive brothers or sisters, even though they had shared a home and had a similar upbringing.[12]

The twins and their adoptive siblings all presumably received "good enough" parenting. Behavioral geneticists interpret these results to mean that in an environment that is not severely deviant or damaging, personal development moves along a track whose course is strongly affected by biological endowment. According to this view, given the same parents, the same home, the same school, children are influenced only by the factors in these environments that fit their innate predispositions; thus, what seems superficially to be the same environment is in fact different for each person. And it is these "unshared" factors that matter.

But even identical twins, whether raised together in the same home or raised apart, are not exactly alike. Parents and friends can tell them apart with no trouble. Dissimilarities between identical twins are nearly always attributable to environmental influences, some of which begin well before birth.[13] For example, identical twins rarely have the same birthweight. This suggests that prenatal nutrition or other factors influencing growth differ for each member of the pair. Birthweight may also affect postnatal environment in critically important ways. A healthy five-pound baby goes home in a few days, while his or her "identical" four-pound twin may remain in the hospital for many weeks. This may cause parents to treat the twins differently.

A recent study makes a good case that firstborn and later-born siblings exhibit striking differences in personality and character and in the lives they lead because parents, without necessarily meaning to do so, treat first- and later-born siblings differently, and the siblings themselves interact with one another and with their parents differently depending on birth order.[14] Thus, the happenstance of a child's birth order, a factor that is fixed but not genetically determined, influences her environment in ways that strongly affect her behavior. Current estimates made by behavioral geneticists for the relative influence of heritable factors and environment are about 50-50, although the ratio shifts considerably depending on the trait studied.[15]

The Nature of Mother Love

For most mammals, just being exposed to newborn offspring induces physiological changes that promote caregiving. For many human parents, the most profound experience of love they will ever have comes with the birth of a child. A mother and father gaze at their baby, and their joy echoes Adam's on seeing Eve for the first time: "Now this at last, bone from my bone, flesh from my flesh."[16]

Processes in the body, brain, and culture that foster these bonds begin well before birth—in expectant parents' hormones and imagination, in friends' and families' smiling approval, in advertisements for pink and blue baby gear. Consider this study of one aspect of the program that prepares a parent for the task of child rearing: Linda Mayes, a pediatrician at Yale Medical School, questioned expectant parents, mostly middle-class New Haven couples, about their thoughts and feelings before and after the birth of their child. All of them thought a great deal about the baby, and often their ruminations had a special quality: they were unbidden, preoccupying, compelling, even intrusive. The amount of time the parents spent preoccupied with thoughts and daydreams about the baby kept increasing from the moment they learned that they had conceived until about two weeks after the baby's birth, stayed very high for three months, and then very slowly began to fall off. When their preoccupation was at its height, mothers reported that they were thinking about the baby every three minutes! (Fathers said that they thought about the baby every forty-five minutes.)

In the weeks before the baby's birth, the parents undertook all sorts of projects. Women who had never sewn a seam began to hem curtains. Expectant parents busied themselves cleaning, painting, wallpapering, and rearranging furniture to get things just right. As new parents, the couples found themselves possessed by happy, excited, and expectant thoughts, but also by worries. They checked on the baby when they had just checked moments before. They worried about germs. Fathers, especially, were afraid of dropping the baby; they had irrational fears of harming the infant.[17]

Although a nudge from a gene does not determine human feelings or behavior, species survival in all mammals is promoted by wired-in programs that promote nurture of the young.[18] Humans have come up with innumerable elaborations on these programs, and individuals differ greatly in the extent to which they respond. When Mayes's description of parents' "nesting behaviors" was presented at a meeting of about three hundred physicians and other scientists, there were smiles and murmurs of recognition from the audience. But not, one can be certain, from every parent in attendance.[19]

Researchers have pointed out the many similarities that can exist between parental love, especially in its initiation and early stages, and obsessive-compulsive disorder. This seems to be true with respect to not only the thoughts and behaviors we have mentioned, but also, remarkably, the brain pathways involved. The normal involuntary preoccupations of new parents, which serve to keep babies safe, and the abnormally intrusive thoughts and compulsive rituals, such as repetitive handwashing, suffered by persons with obsessive-compulsive disorder may share some underlying brain circuitry, neurohormonal influences, and genes.

The hormone oxytocin seems to play a role both in rituals of nurture and in obsessive-compulsive rituals.[20] Oxytocin has been found to be a vital stimulus to nurturing behaviors. Found only in mammals, it is a component of the extremely complex system that regulates reproductive behavior, influencing uterine contractions and milk release in females, and sexual function in both sexes. Oxytocin is secreted in the hypothalamus, the master center for regulation of vital survival functions such as temperature control and food and water intake. Oxytocin-secreting neurons influence many brain systems, including brainstem centers governing sleep and wakefulness, limbic centers governing emotions, and hippocampal centers governing memory. Neural receptors for oxytocin undergo changes during an individual's development. Their numbers wax and wane with sexual activities and social behaviors, but their most characteristic shifts occur with maternal (and, in some species, paternal) behaviors.[21]

Neuroscientists looking for genetic links in the bonds between mothers and offspring have discovered a gene called fosB, which may be a linchpin of maternal caregiving. The fosB gene normally is active in an area of the hypothalamus known to be important for nurturing behaviors. Researchers have managed to inactivate this gene in mice and have found that the animals with the gene deletion (which seem otherwise normal) are profoundly indifferent to their young, ignoring them until they die.[22]

Deviations can occur in the physiological systems that promote the nurture of human infants.[23] Severe postpartum depression is one example. Another comes from recent research suggesting that the reason some cocaine-addicted mothers show utter disregard for their babies (their behavior is often more extreme than that of alcohol- or heroin-addicted mothers) may be that receptors in the maternal behavior system we have just described are co-opted to the craving for cocaine.[24]

Love Is a Basic Need

What happens when caregiving fails is tragically clear. Infants deprived of the caring touch of a parental figure do not thrive even if their other basic needs—for food, drink, warmth, and physical protection—are met. They lose interest in food, in their surroundings, and in life; if the emotional deprivation is severe enough, they die. As early as 1760, a Spanish bishop noted in his diary: "In the foundling home the child becomes sad and many of them die from sadness."[25]

In ten U.S. orphan asylums studied in 1915, mortality rates for children under two ranged from 32 percent to 75 percent. Over the next three decades the sadness, loneliness, and retarded development of young children in hospitals and orphanages aroused the concern of psychiatrists and pediatricians in a number of countries. They found institutionalized children to be emotionally flat, listless, uninterested, and unconnected. Five-year-olds who had been moved from one foster home to another every six months—it was thought to be bad for the child to become attached to any adult before he or she was adopted—appeared to lack the capacity to control their feelings. They were hyperactive, given to temper tantrums, and unable to engage in group play. Toddlers clung to strangers. A child would rush up to a male visitor never seen before, crying "Daddy!" or plaintively ask a female stranger, "Will you be my mommy?" They seemed confused about the cast of characters in their life, especially themselves.

But until the mid–twentieth century, most institutions caring for children were preoccupied with preventing the spread of disease. Infants were fed lying in their cribs, with their nursing bottles propped on a folded diaper. Children were touched as little as possible. The idea that babies had emotional needs was hardly recognized. In a 1941 paper entitled "Loneliness in Infants," the pediatrician Harry Bakwin described the lengths to which hospitals had gone to isolate babies, notably the antiseptic box into which each infant was placed so that "she can be taken care of almost untouched by human hands."[26] In a 1960 study of children in an Iranian orphanage where similar conditions prevailed, 60 percent of two-year-olds could not sit up unassisted, and 85 percent of the four-year-olds could not walk on their own.[27]

In 1945 the psychoanalyst René Spitz published a study of two sets of infants, one group raised in a foundling home for abandoned children and the other in a nursery attached to a women's prison. In the foundling home, each nurse was assigned seven infants. Each crib was covered with a sheet, with the result that the babies could not look out. In the prison nursery the babies were cared for by their mothers, who lavished affection on them in the time allotted for mother and child to be together.

By a number of developmental measures, the foundling-home infants were the more advanced in the first four months of life (suggesting that they were not born more handicapped). But by the end of their first year they had fallen far behind the prison babies. Only two of the twenty-six children in the foundling home could walk and talk by the time they were three, while the children reared by their prisoner mothers were developing normally.[28]

Spitz's basic findings have been corroborated by many other studies that have demonstrated a wide gap in IQ between institutionalized children and those raised in more homelike settings. In one research effort conducted in the 1930s, thirteen institutionalized toddlers were removed to a residence for older "feeble-minded" girls, and each was "adopted" by one of them. Under the care of these retarded but affectionate young women, the average IQ of the emotionally starved toddlers jumped from 64 to 92, evidence that compassionate care promotes cognitive development as well as emotional well-being.[29]

During the Second World War, children from cities all over Europe were sent away from their families to live in rural areas. This practice, meant to protect the children from air raids, led in many instances to the emotional deprivation we have described. John Bowlby collected the findings on the mental health of the separated children in *Maternal Care and Mental Health,* a report published in 1951 under the auspices of the World Health Organization. Other efforts that documented the effects of maternal deprivation, including a touching 1953 film showing the desperate protest, grief, and despair of a child in a hospital that held to the then nearly universal policy of severely restricting parental visiting hours, were influential in revising caregiving practices in hospitals and other child care institutions.[30] Parental visiting hours were increased. Caregivers were instructed to hold babies and respond to them; bottle propping for feeding was prohibited in many institutions.

But knowledge that challenges entrenched institutional practices is often ignored. In the 1990s, Western observers who visited Romanian institutions for abandoned and orphaned children found conditions to be "harsh" and "deplorable." There was "no personalized caregiving." In some institutions, the children were washed by being hosed down with cold water. Predictably, the babies were severely retarded, in both physical and mental development. Happily, when such institutionalized children are removed to good foster or adoptive homes, their behavior and their performance on intelligence tests often greatly improve. But the longer infants are exposed to deprivation, the more likely it is that their deficits will be permanent.[31]

There are good mothers and bad, and most are somewhere in the middle. Fathers are often nurturing, too, and so are others who are biologically unrelated to the baby. Infants are accommodating, but the evidence is persuasive that a baby *must* have someone he or she can count on who does what parents do—consistently, dependably, lovingly, and over the long haul.

The Power of Attachment

Harry Harlow's experiments in the 1950s in which he separated monkey infants from their mothers offered striking support for a number of Bowlby's theories. The monkey infants' need for what Harlow called "contact comfort"—prolonged and extensive tactile communication with another monkey—was so great that they would desperately cling to a cloth-covered object he provided them, even though this inanimate "surrogate mother" offered no nourishment.[32]

Harlow and his colleagues found that isolated monkey infants were impaired psychologically, physically, and socially. When an infant that had been isolated for six months—a very long time in the life of a primate—was returned to the monkey colony, it stayed by itself, neither playing with others nor defending itself when attacked. Some of the animals crouched and rocked in the corner; much like some autistic children, they clasped themselves and chewed on their fingers and toes. The younger the baby and the longer and more total the isolation, the worse the symptoms; but there were also large individual differences. Some animals were relatively unscathed by their experience of isolation; others were devastated.

Many years later monkeys deprived of contact comfort in infancy still showed radical differences from mother-reared animals both in behavior and in physiology, even though they spent the rest of their lives in more normal living conditions. Their lives were shorter. Their cognitive abilities were impaired; in tests, they failed to process information as effectively as normal monkeys. Some animals had depressed immune function; tests done at autopsy revealed abnormal brain immunochemistry. Some evidence suggested that animals showing persistently abnormal movements, such as endless rocking back and forth, had altered brain chemistries indicating involvement of motor regulation systems. Some of the monkeys were overly aggressive, a behavior pattern consistent with their abnormal serotonin levels; others were unduly submissive. Some would not mate, and some that did ignored or abused their progeny, especially their firstborn. It was discovered that attachment patterns can cross generations; the characteristic ways a female monkey infant related to her mother were likely to show up again in her own offspring.[33]

Isolation experiments with infant monkeys and great apes began at a time when the "best" medical practice was unwittingly subjecting institutionalized human babies to the emotional pain and developmental risks of social isolation. When the cruel effects of abnormal social environments on both human and nonhuman primates were finally noticed and understood, practices began to change.[34] In recent decades—thanks in part to rising concern, sparked by the animal rights movement, about mistreatment of research animals—monkeys have not been subjected to long periods of social isolation. But shameful violations of accepted guidelines for treatment of helpless children and helpless animals still occur. Advocates for humane treatment have plenty of work to do.

Researchers now study lesser degrees of social separation in nonhuman primates. In one such program, headed by Stephen Suomi, a student of Harlow's and now the director of the Laboratory of Comparative Ethology at the National Institute of Child Health and Human Development, infant rhesus monkeys were reared apart from their mothers but in the company of other juvenile monkeys. When these "peer-reared" animals were in familiar, socially stimulating, and stable surroundings, they usually seemed normal as they passed through adolescence into adulthood. When, however, they encountered new or stressful situations, such as annual isolation from their social group for a four-day series of tests, the monkeys who had been deprived of maternal rearing reacted very differently from their peers who had been mother-reared during the critical first months of life. Although none of the animals enjoyed the tests, peer-reared animals were far more distressed and fearful, and physiological measurements also indicated stress. The scientists concluded that patterns of response which had disappeared under benign conditions were still latent and could reappear years later when triggered by a stressful experience.[35] An infant's reaction to separation predicted its response to other social challenges during its adolescence and even adulthood, although its behavior and physiological responses changed with age. For example, protest cries and a look of utter desolation were more common in babyhood; aggressiveness was more common in older animals.

Primate research suggests that individual differences in responses to separation are based in part on inherited traits; some baby monkeys are more easily and more profoundly stressed by separation than others. Researchers found this to be true even of separations that occur naturally, as when a mother rejects her baby during weaning and the breeding season. Most infant monkeys take such separations more or less in stride, while about 20 percent become frantically distressed and seem overwhelmed by despair. Typically, they cry for long periods and stop playing. Levels of stress hormones such as adrenocorticotrophic hormone (ACTH) and plasma cortisol sharply increase, and the infants' heart rate goes up, indicating heightened activity in the sympathetic nervous system. Serotonin and dopamine systems also give evidence of stress responses.[36]

Suomi and his colleagues had observed certain mother-infant pairs who were similar in temperament. Both members of a pair were either highly reactive or very unflappable. The reactive animals became extremely excited and upset by novel or mildly stressful stimuli, while the others remained calm. The researchers conducted a series of experiments designed to learn whether the infants' temperamental tendency to calm or excitable behavior (which was presumed to be inherited) could be modified by the quality of maternal rearing they received. The researchers placed newborn infants from presumed high-reactive and easygoing lineages in the care of foster-mother monkeys chosen because they had exhibited either unusually nurturant maternal behavior or "typical" behavior for their species. Both high-reactive and easygoing infants developed normally in the care of their foster mothers. The experimenters noticed that the high-reactive infants with unusually nurturant foster mothers were actually accelerated in their development. Whether high-reactive or easygoing, these monkeys explored more boldly and displayed less distress during weaning than the babies being fostered by "typical" mothers.[37]

At six months of age the infants were separated from their foster mothers for a four-day test period, during which each was housed by itself. High-reactive infants, whether they'd had nurturant or typical foster mothers, became much more upset than their easygoing counterparts. But when they returned to their foster mothers, all the infants did well and the high-reactive babies once again appeared precocious compared to the others.

A few months later, all the infants were moved into larger groups with other juvenile rhesus monkeys. Each group also included an old male-female pair with a history of exerting a good influence on the social life of young monkeys. The foster grandfather broke up fights and controlled the more rambunctious members, while the foster grandmother was available for the youngsters desiring close physical contact.

Suomi describes the results of these social maneuvers:

> In this larger group setting, high-reactive monkeys who had been reared by a nurturant foster mother immediately established close social relationships with these old adults, particularly the old female. With the old adults providing a basis of social support, these high-reactive youngsters became the most dominant member of the peer group. In contrast, high-reactive monkeys who had been reared by "typical" foster mothers avoided the older monkeys and wound up at the bottom of the dominance hierarchy. (Easy-going monkeys, whether reared by nurturant or typical foster mothers, were somewhere in the middle of the dominance hierarchy.)[38]

These studies showed that individual monkeys with similar predispositions to high reactivity fared very differently in the social hierarchy depending on the social support they received both as infants and later on in life. Although the reasons for this outcome are far from clear, Suomi's results suggest the interplay of several factors: inherited predispositions to respond in a certain way to novel and challenging situations; quality of early nurture; elements in the current social situation, including the availability of social support; and the responses of others to the animal's behavior. Sufficient nurture, both past and current, seemed to buffer the animals from unfavorable consequences of their natural tendency to overreact.

Do similar effects occur in human groups? Humans, of course, have ranges of responses not available to nonhuman primates. But as Suomi concludes: "It seems likely that most, if not all, of the more general principles that can be gleaned from the monkey data can, in fact, apply to the human case. A wealth of data suggests that early attachment relationships do have long-term consequences in humans, especially under conditions of stress and challenge. Moreover, the pattern of individual differences in the behavioral and physiological responses to challenge observed in rhesus monkeys seems strikingly similar to the pattern of individual differences reported for human infants and young children."

Babies in Strange Situations

Mary Ainsworth, an American psychologist who worked in London in the early 1950s as an assistant to John Bowlby, went on to devise a laboratory test to assess the quality of human infants' attachment to their mothers. Her Strange Situation test, published in 1978, is still widely used.[39]

After an initial study in Uganda, in which she observed the interactions of mothers and infants in their homes, Ainsworth moved to Baltimore and undertook a larger observational study, achieving similar results despite the great cultural differences between the two populations.

During the first year of the Baltimore infant subjects' lives, Ainsworth and her assistants conducted eighteen four-hour home visits, closely monitoring the interactions of each of twenty-six mother-infant pairs in the study. A striking assortment of behavior patterns was observed. A few mothers ignored almost all their infant's cries; others reacted promptly to nearly every whimper. Some mothers were quick to pick up cues, such as coos, gurgles, and body movements, responding in ways that were pleasurable and soothing for both the infant and themselves. A few months later these women were playing with their child, eliciting smiles, vocalizations, and joyful bouncing. Meanwhile, the encounters of less sensitive mothers with their babies were muted or brief; they approached the infant in silence or with no trace of a smile and they struggled as their babies wriggled in their arms or spat up while being fed. Mothers who showed more sensitivity in the first quarter of the year's observations maintained a more harmonious relationship with their child through the first year.[40] Maternal behaviors that Ainsworth characterized as "sensitive" or "insensitive" were highly correlated with the quality of the infants' relationship with their mothers—that is, their attachment.

These different patterns of mother-child interaction and relationship in the home prompted Ainsworth to develop a laboratory test to classify patterns of attachment. The "Strange Situation" was designed for babies a little over one year old, an age when they could freely explore their surroundings but before they were fluent in language. Mother and baby start out together in an unfamiliar room filled with inviting toys. At one point a friendly stranger enters the room. Then a series of brief separations and reunions are staged as the mother leaves and then reenters the playroom. The procedure is designed to be mildly and then moderately stressful. In the strange room, the baby first has to decide whether it is safe to leave the mother in order to explore the new toys. Then come the stress of her departures and the relief of her reappearances. Most infants cry and stop playing when their mother leaves; but when she returns, they are easily comforted, and they return to their play.

The success of a baby in using her mother as "a secure base from which to explore" and in deriving comfort from her when she is distressed are measures of attachment security. In experiments using the Strange Situation, it was found that babies' behavior on reunion with their mothers provides the most reliable and consistent measure of attachment security, so the classification of a baby's attachment is based mainly on reunion behaviors.

Ainsworth found that roughly 55 to 65 percent of infants behaved in ways that caused them to be classified as "securely attached."[41] A baby so classified explored the playroom while her mother was in the room. She might or might not show distress when she left, but greeted her warmly on her return, either by going directly to her to be picked up, or by showing through a smile or a little utterance that she was happy to see her. After a period of being held or staying in close proximity, she resumed her play.

The remainder of the infants Ainsworth studied exhibited behaviors thought to indicate insecure and anxious attachment. They fell roughly into two categories, one termed "resistant/ambivalent" and the other "avoidant." Resistant/ambivalent children, about 10 or 15 percent of those tested, did not venture far from their mother while she was in the room and they were distressed when she left. When she returned, however, a resistant/ambivalent baby was hard to comfort and took a long time to settle down. When his mother picked him up or patted him, he cried and stiffened or even took a swipe at her. He squirmed to be put down and then cried to be picked up again. He sought contact but also resisted it. Resistant/ambivalent infants did not seem to be able to use their mother's help in modulating their high degree of arousal and distress.

A child in the second category of insecure attachment, the "avoidant," showed minimal distress when his mother left; when she returned, he ignored or even avoided her attempts to interact with him. About a quarter of the infants tested by Ainsworth fell into this category.

Classifying this latter pattern of behavior as a manifestation of insecure attachment is controversial; critics maintain that "avoidant" infants may just be especially independent. In answer, attachment researchers point to longitudinal studies that find "avoidant" infants to have a different developmental course from "securely attached" infants. The former actually have *more* difficulty being independent in their childhood and adolescent years. The explanation given for this seeming paradox is that securely attached infants have their dependency needs well met, and from this secure base they are able to move on with confidence.[42]

By now, children all over the world have participated in this twenty-minute laboratory drama. About 90 percent of large samples of children can be readily assigned to one or another of the categories defined by Ainsworth. Longitudinal studies of normal children and children in a number of special populations—those born with low birthweight or with handicapping conditions, abused children, children raised by foster or adoptive parents, and those experiencing differing types and amounts of day care—have extended Ainsworth's findings, given rise to several subclassifications, and tested their predictive significance.

One more recently described category is the "disorganized/disoriented." On reunion with the parent, such an infant may start to approach her, then freeze. He may come toward her but with head averted. Or he may scream during her absence but move away from her when she returns. These incoherent reactions are common among children of abusing and psychotic parents, but are also seen in infants whose parents are highly inconsistent in how they treat the child. Their contradictory and unpredictable parenting makes it hard for their children to develop effective ways to cope in stressful situations. Disorganized attachment also seems to be more frequent among children whose parents have themselves suffered highly traumatic experiences in childhood, leaving them with unresolved feelings of fear and helplessness.[43]

Studies in a number of countries, including the United States, Canada, Britain, Japan, Germany, and Israel, have found similar patterns of infant attachment across many cultures, although the percentages of children found in each category vary a good deal. In general, Ainsworth's finding that the mother's (or primary caregiver's) sensitivity to the infant predicts the baby's attachment classification has been validated.[44] Infant attachment classification has been shown to be useful in predicting important facets of the child's future development. For example, preschool and young school-aged children who had been classified as insecurely attached in infancy were more likely to have behavior problems than those who had been classified as securely attached.[45]

Culturally influenced child-rearing practices seem to play a role in attachment patterns. In studies of infants in Bielefeld, a city in northern Germany, half were found to be "avoidant," a much higher proportion than found in studies of American babies. In Regensburg, a city in the southern part of Germany, the figures were much like those in the United States. The observers found that mothers in Bielefeld demonstrated less overt affection and tenderness in caring for infants than did middle-class American mothers and those in the south of Germany. Bielefeld mothers tended to discourage physical closeness and actively encouraged their infants to be exploratory and independent.[46]

As they raise their children, parents communicate the values of their culture, usually unconsciously. Most American parents tend to encourage self-reliance and individualism by the emotional cues they give, the routines they set, the games they encourage, and the toys they buy. On the other hand, many Japanese mothers encourage emotional dependency and loyalty. In both cases the caregivers are passing along social signals about character and emotional relationships they have internalized over their lifetime. In a similar manner the differing cultural values and expectations for girls and boys are transmitted early in children's lives.[47]

One tendency in child rearing is to repeat the practices of our own parents. In every nursery there are ghosts, says Selma Fraiberg. This practitioner, with vast experience in observing infants and their families, offers an evocative description of the psychological processes that cause parents to echo their own upbringing.[48] In the cases she analyzes, the parents were neglectful or had committed acts of abuse, but the insight also applies across a wide range of normal attitudes and practices. Parenthood, especially the first time around, opens up the Pandora's box of the past. We will see in the next chapter why this phenomenon is not only a poetic metaphor but a neurophysiological fact—or so current research on emotional memories suggests.

Temperament and Experience

The Harvard child psychologist Jerome Kagan has not only challenged the validity of the Strange Situation test but questions attachment theory itself. Kagan argues against the idea that psychological life is formed in any lasting way by early relationships or that "the events of infancy seriously influence the future mood and behavior of the adolescent." Dismissing popular ideas of the overriding importance of the mother-infant bond for the child's future happiness and adjustment as "intuitively pleasing" but wrong, Kagan maintains that the child's own temperamental predispositions are the major determining factors in the kind of person he becomes in later life.[49] Kagan also questions the underlying values of attachment theorists, who in his view are overly concerned with security: "In the forties and fifties, the children now called attached were called overprotected and that was a bad thing."[50]

According to Kagan, whether children are independent, sociable, and easygoing, or timid, shy, and easily distressed, depends primarily upon their inborn traits. True, babies' temperamental predispositions are modified by how they are treated and by their assimilation of parental expectations and values, and this can be very important in many cases. "If your parent values autonomy, you'll be autonomous; if your parent values dependency, you'll be dependent."[51] But the most enduring influence on the course of development, Kagan maintains, is exerted by inborn predispositions grounded in biological endowment.

The second-century Greek physician Galen believed that the "humors," four bodily fluids, determined whether a given individual would have a sanguine, melancholy, phlegmatic, or choleric temperament. In line with this ancient idea, modern temperament theorists believe that the differences among people—some shy and timid, others fearless and adventurous; some outgoing and effervescent, others hesitant and thoughtful, and still others passive, even sad—flow from the genetic cards a person is dealt. Temperament also defines a person's characteristic emotional range and the settings of his emotional thermostat, causing individuals to differ in their sensitivities to various stimuli, thresholds for triggering reactions, and response characteristics.

In Kagan's Laboratory for Child Development, he and his colleagues noted the differences in the way twenty-one-month-old toddlers played with one another. While most of them readily and joyfully engaged with others, a smaller group, about 15 to 20 percent, hung back, clung to their mothers, and looked on. These "behaviorally inhibited" children had exhibited higher than average heart rate at birth, and when they were toddlers their heartbeat accelerated rapidly if they were exposed to a novel situation in the laboratory. Almost four years later the same children were back in the lab. About two-thirds of the timid toddlers were now anxious five-year-olds, still afraid to meet new people and reluctant to taste unfamiliar food or try doing something they had never done before. None of the bold, outgoing toddlers had become timid.

Kagan's longitudinal studies indicated that timid, inhibited children tended to develop into shy, anxious adolescents and adults, especially if their shyness persisted throughout childhood. One study, which surveyed 754 boys and girls in the sixth and seventh grades, found that 44 of them had already suffered at least one panic attack. At thirteen or fourteen these same shy children smiled and talked less, avoided unfamiliar situations, and were more anxious in social activities than their peers. They also were prone to feelings of guilt and self-reproach.[52]

Kagan points out that his findings with respect to humans are consistent with animal research on the anatomical and neurophysiological underpinnings of emotional behavior. He postulates that fear-prone infants are born with nervous systems that are easily triggered by fear-inducing stimuli. They react strongly to events other children shrug off, and their fear responses last longer and are more intense. Kagan notes that timid children compared to others show more arousal of the autonomic nervous system. Even mildly stressful stimuli such as a bad smell or being picked up by an unfamiliar person trigger such autonomic responses as increased heart and respiration rates and dilated pupils. There is an increase in levels of urinary markers of norepinephrine, a stress hormone associated with autonomic nervous system activity. Animal research has demonstrated that a pivotal structure in the brain's emotional alarm system is the amygdala, an almond-shaped cluster of several groups of neurons buried deep in each temporal lobe of the brain. (We will talk further about the amygdala in the following chapter.) Kagan speculates that children who are unusually shy and fearful are born with an easily excitable amygdalar fear system.

A child's temperament, according to Kagan's view, affects the parent-child relationship; for example, parents tend to react differently to an inhibited or clinging child than to one who is more outgoing and fearless. Moreover, parents' styles of child rearing, their values, and their expectations interact with their children's behavioral tendencies. Some parents shelter their timid, sensitive children, guarding them from unfamiliar experiences. Another parent might push his fearful child into new experiences, hoping they will "toughen" his tender sensibilities.

Kagan makes the sensible suggestion that parents can "engineer emboldening experiences" by showing their own interest in unfamiliar objects and new experiences, encouraging the child to explore them, allowing the child to resolve mild challenges and uncertainties by himself, and setting clear limits on acceptable behavior. Timid toddlers need opportunities to master the fears to which they are prone so that they learn to cope with life's normal ups and downs. Kagan has found that about one-third of the inhibited children he has studied grow out of their timidity by kindergarten. He believes that gentle pressure from parents helped them to be more self-confident and outgoing.[53]

The uninhibited, easygoing, exploratory child is more likely to exhibit secure attachment than the timid child, but, according to Kagan, this is due much more to his fearless temperament than to his experience with his caregivers. Temperamentally inhibited babies, on the other hand, become more upset and fearful than uninhibited babies in the Strange Situation test and thus are harder to comfort; it is this, rather than an impaired mother-child relationship, that causes them to be classified as "insecurely attached."

Attachment researchers note, however, that attachment characterizes a relationship rather than an individual; they point to the finding that infants' attachment to their fathers may differ from that to their mothers. They also maintain that infants' temperament does not directly influence the quality of attachment because, as University of Pennsylvania psychologist Jay Belsky puts it, "even a difficult infant, given the 'right' care, can become secure." Whatever the child's temperamental tendencies may be, the way she behaves in the Strange Situation will be shaped by her relationships with her attachment figures.[54]

A study in the Netherlands lends support to this view. Dymphna van den Boom identified a group of one hundred newborn infants who were highly irritable and hard to soothe.[55] Van den Boom provided counseling to fifty of the one hundred mothers when their babies were between six and nine months old, helping them to monitor the infants' signals accurately and to learn effective strategies for calming their fussy babies. At one year of age, 62 percent of the babies whose mothers had received counseling were found to be securely attached on the Strange Situation test. In contrast, only 28 percent of the babies in the control group, whose mother had not received counseling, were classified as secure. Thus, the babies' experience with their mothers seemed to have a greater influence on the quality of their attachment than did their temperamental tendencies.

Influences flow both ways: an infant's own qualities can have a strong impact on the parent and affect the quality of care he or she receives. Parents who are not conscious of the role their infant's temperament plays in their relationship can, as the child psychiatrist Stella Chess noted many years ago, "develop enormous guilt feelings due to the assumption that they must necessarily be solely responsible for their children's emotional difficulties. With this guilt comes anxiety, defensiveness, increased pressures on the children, and even hostility toward them for 'exposing' the mother's inadequacy by their disturbed behavior."[56] On the other hand, in order to help a difficult baby, caregivers need to provide the quality of nurture that decreases the baby's distress. Chess makes this important point: A child's temperament does not signify parental failure (or success), but neither does it indicate that sensitive care is unimportant; it does indicate that what constitutes sensitive care is different for different babies.

Megan Gunnar and her colleagues at the University of Minnesota have performed a series of experiments in which they have assessed babies' temperamental predisposition to fearfulness, their attachment to caregivers, and the ways in which they cope with stressful situations. Gunnar measures levels of the stress hormone cortisol under various conditions. Whether and how much cortisol levels rise under stress seems to be influenced by whether the baby is securely attached. The researchers found that when a securely attached fifteen-month-old is given his measles shot, he screams loudly and clings to his mother, father, or whatever adult has brought him to the doctor's office. But his cortisol level does not rise. In contrast, the fifteen-month-old who is insecurely attached as measured by the Strange Situation test screams just as loudly when he feels the prick of the needle, but he is not as likely to reach for his caregiver for comfort. His cortisol level shoots up. Secure attachment appears to offer support in coping with stressful situations.[57]

Children have different coping styles and resources. Coping behaviors depend on a child's developmental stage as well as on his temperament.[58] In stressful or threatening situations, a child copes by sucking his thumb or nuzzling his security blanket, by distracting himself in play, by hitting, by shutting his eyes and closing out the threat, or by resorting to various other learned maneuvers. When our then three-year-old son, Michael, went out to play in the yard of the house to which we had just moved, he was accompanied by Brave Willie Sheriff, a friend only he could see.

But a small child's main coping resources are the adults he depends on, his attachment figures. This was brought home to us when our two-year-old daughter, Beth, fell down and gashed her forehead. She shrieked loudly, of course, but quieted down, thumb in mouth, as we drove to Children's Hospital to get her stitched up. In the emergency room, the resident physician and the nurse prepared for their work by wrapping their little patient's body, arms, and legs in a "mummy pack," a swaddling device used to keep children from moving during medical procedures. By this time Beth was screaming in terror. The doctor gave the customary instruction to her parents to leave the room. "I'm staying," Ann said. "And she needs to suck her thumb." He hesitated, and Ann said, with all the authority she could muster, "Give her her thumb!" Beth was then allowed to keep her coping resources: her thumb and her mother. Her screams subsided, and she was asleep before the procedure was over.

Emotional growth depends upon continuous interaction between an individual's unique emotional makeup and a parade of life experiences. But there is something special about the first relationships. Allan Schore, a psychiatrist and the author of a treatise on the neurobiology of emotional development, offers an arresting summation in neurobiological terms: "The experiences that fine-tune brain circuitries in critical periods of infancy are embedded in socioemotional interchanges between an adult brain and a developing brain." Primary caregivers, he contends, not only play a key role in modulating the infant's emotional state, but also "indelibly and permanently shape the emerging self's capacity for self-organization."[59] In the next chapter we will examine this idea in the light of recent neurophysiological discoveries concerning the neural underpinnings of emotional development.

Chapter Six

I AND THOU:
EMOTIONAL RELATIONSHIP
AND THE DISCOVERY OF SELF

In this chapter we will explore the beginnings of emotional development, the child's emerging consciousness of self, and how social interactions influence the processes of emotional regulation. We will describe recent research on the neural underpinnings of emotions, especially fear. Studies of experimental animals and of individuals suffering brain lesions illuminate the workings of the brain's emotion systems, showing how emotion and reason are intertwined. Children's intellectual development is inextricably bound up with their emotional development.

Emotions: What They Are
and What They Do

Infants arrive equipped with built-in capacities on which emotional development depends. They are biologically prepared to direct their attention; from their first breath, they show that they are responding to their surroundings. They turn to the breast and suck. They are born with vision acute enough to show their preference for faces over other visual stimuli. They can discriminate between the syllables "pa" and "ba," can hear the difference between C and C sharp, and can show that they prefer their mother's voice above all others. They have an inborn need for tactile contact, nestling and seeming blissfully at peace when they are cuddled and stroked. Babies who are rarely touched fail to thrive, and tiny premature infants who are gently handled on a regular basis gain weight faster than babies who are touched and held less often.[1]

Although newborns exhibit only a limited emotional repertoire, normally it is enough to get them what they need. An infant can send distress signals through flailing arms and legs, contorted face, and crying. She can show her contentment by relaxing peacefully in her mother's arms, and her interest in something new by her alert regard. These are messages for the infant's caregivers: "Get over here! I need you"; "Everything is fine now"; "Thanks for waving that beautiful bright rattle at me." Adult caregivers don't depend much on cognition to interpret an infant's communications; they clutch at the heart. The basic signaling and response patterns of infants and mothers, developed and perfected over evolutionary time, keep helpless offspring alive, nourished, warm, near, and learning.

All infant mammals cry when they are separated from their mother. In mammals other than humans, and probably in humans too, maternal calls to separated offspring are also instinctive. Separation cries, whether of infant mice or humans, cause mothers to gather up their offspring, feed them, and care for them.[2] The neurophysiologist Paul MacLean points out that the region of the brain's cortex involved in producing separation cries also receives neural messages from centers in the thalamus involved in the perception of pain. MacLean studied the brain circuits for the "affiliation cry" squirrel monkeys give when they seek one another and found that lesions in a part of the cingulate cortex eliminated the cry.[3] The cingulate cortex, lying deep within the brain, is part of the brain's limbic system, the evolutionarily ancient system for emotion. The instinctive dread of abandonment is so basic that even a grown man socialized over many years to be stoical may cry for his mother under conditions of extreme stress, as when he lies wounded on a battlefield.

Crying, like laughter, is a physiological response which serves many emotions, but it is not an emotion itself. We cry for joy as well as for sorrow. We cry in frustrated anger. Emotions evoke expressions and actions to satisfy the body's needs. Infant birds, mammals, and humans, born utterly helpless and dependent, must communicate their needs to their caregivers, and this they do through patterns of behavior that depend on neither experience nor memory nor thought. The addition of ever more sophisticated levels of control, regulation, and nuance over our innate emotional response patterns is a driving force of human development.

In his book *The Expression of Emotions in Man and Animals,* published in 1872, Charles Darwin noted the correlations between emotional states—such as fear, sadness, and anger—and characteristic facial expressions, bodily movements, and postures, and these have been much studied by psychologists ever since.[4] One function of emotions is to signal to others what we feel. Similarly, we infer from the overt manifestation of the emotions of others—the smile of a friend, or the snarl of a dog—what their next move is likely to be. In Darwin's words: "The movements of expression in the face and body, whatever their origin may have been, are themselves of much importance in our welfare. They serve as the first means of communication between the mother and her infant; she smiles approval, and thus encourages her child on the right path, or frowns disapproval. We readily perceive sympathy in others by their expression; our sufferings are thus mitigated and our pleasures increased; and mutual good feeling is thus strengthened."[5] Millennia before language developed in our species, emotive facial and vocal expressions and body language served the purposes of communication, and they serve similar functions in a baby. Emotional communication becomes wedded to language as the capacity for verbal expression emerges.

In the last three decades, psychologists and anthropologists all over the world have gathered impressive data supporting Darwin's observations.[6] Certain emotions are associated with characteristic facial expressions that do not appear to vary significantly from culture to culture. People look happy, sad, afraid, angry, or surprised in much the same way across time zones, climates, and cultures. An Eskimo and a Hungarian can, in emotionally charged situations, read each other's faces.[7] Facial expressions of strong emotion are largely involuntary, although early on, by about three years of age, we learn to control or disguise them according to the "display rules," as anthropologists call them, of our culture. Even a newborn baby shows facial expressions recognizably appropriate to an external stimulus that is pleasant or unpleasant, although her reactions may be slower and less differentiated than they will be in a few months. Pricked with the pediatrician's needle, the baby will most likely increase her movements and then cry. When she is touched on the lips with a citric acid–soaked piece of cotton, she will purse her lips and wrinkle her nose.[8]

We can all recognize emotions in others and in ourselves. Yet people, including scientists, find it difficult to agree on what an emotion is.[9] One reason emotions are so hard to characterize is that they well up from depths below the realm of language. Emotions roil our guts or lift our hearts. Dread is an indescribable heaviness in chest and limbs. Joy is ineffable, although it can be evoked in poetry.

How a scientist describes an emotion depends not only on her personal and cultural context but on the methodology she employs. Anthropologists are becoming increasingly aware of the ambiguities of emotional experience and expression as well as the difficulties of using the terms of their own language to describe analogous (but subtly different) affective states in other cultures.[10] Developmental psychologists have studied the effects of age and experience on the processes that characterize an emotion, but these effects are still incompletely understood. Upon seeing a stranger enter the nursery, an infant's sober face does not mirror that of the three-year-old upon being left with a new baby-sitter, and it is surely different from the apprehension a high school senior feels as he opens the thin letter from the college of his choice. Whether a child's anger is measured by a tantrum or a change in heart rate influences the questions a researcher asks and the results she gets. As the physicist Freeman Dyson notes, "It is hopeless to look for a description independent of the mode of observation."[11]

All emotions are, to a greater or lesser degree, forceful, arousing, motivating, and hard to put under voluntary control. They always have a quality of pleasurableness (joy, love, pride) or the opposite (disgust, fury, dejection). Each emotion tends to be triggered by a characteristic set of stimuli—praise usually evokes happiness or pride, and loss evokes sadness—but the same stimulus will evoke a different emotional reaction depending upon an individual's temperament and circumstances. Praise can cause some people to feel ashamed or sad.

Emotions serve to label incoming information as significant or not, compelling attention to what is salient, preparing the body's reactions, and activating a rapid, coherent response to dangers, challenges, and opportunities. Emotions vary in intensity because of differences in how incoming information is appraised, but they always serve to direct attention, set priorities, mobilize energy, and heighten responses. Chronic negative emotions such as anger and fear exact a physical and mental toll. But even intense joy can eventually tire us out. Something in us needs a measure of emotional equilibrium, a middle ground between excitement and repose; where that place is differs from individual to individual. Humans, and other animals as well, also exhibit great differences in emotional range. Some individuals tend to be excitable, some phlegmatic; some are fearful, others unflappable. This background emotional tone we call mood, or, if it is a characteristic and enduring habit of mind, temperament.

In thinking about emotion it is often helpful to make certain distinctions between overt emotional expressions and actions, internal emotional processes, and subjective emotional experience or feelings. You see a bear in your path. Danger! You feel terrified. You run. Perception, appraisal, actions, and the bodily responses that underlie them are at least theoretically measurable by scientists. But your feeling of fright, although intensely real, is indefinable. Subjective feelings are essentially private, although we spend a great deal of time and effort trying to communicate them to one another.

Emotions are accompanied by feelings, but not all feelings are evoked by an emotional experience. For example, fear comes with a feeling of tightness in the chest, but so does a heart attack. Happiness suffuses your cheeks with a warm rosy glow, but so does a run on a hot day. Part of the physiology of these reactions is shared, but the stimuli evoking them are different, as are their neural controls. A triggering event (an intruder, a cry of pain from a child in the night, the approach of someone you loved long ago) sets in motion a whole series of appraisal processes and patterns of action which, initially, are involuntary and outside of consciousness. You startle, then freeze. You are out of bed and on your feet before you know it. You run toward your long-lost lover, beaming. Awareness of your beating heart, sweaty palms, or flushed face comes later, as do your judgments concerning the stimulus event. "It's just the dog thumping around" or "How worried should I be?" or "Where were you?"

Developing Emotions

All animals, including humans, have emotional reactions that appear to be programmed and instinctual and involve little or no cognitive processing. For example, young chicks flee from the shadow of a hawk although they have never seen one before. A laboratory rat shows signs of fear when it encounters a cat for the first time. The automatic clutch and cling of a newborn whose head falls back may be a response to an innate fear of falling; likewise, the baby's startle at loud noises is probably an inborn fear response.

Psychologists have differing theories about how emotional states emerge. Some believe that infants are born with genetic programs that allow certain discrete emotions to appear at the appropriate stage of maturation.[12] Others hold that infants are born with just two basic emotional states, "a negative or distress state and a positive or satiated state."[13] The baby moves not only between these poles but also along the continuums of withdrawal and engagement, attention and inattention.

Babies have an innate drive to learn and a biological preparedness for emotionally laden social interactions. Anyone who observes normal babies knows that they are often as eager to engage in social play as they are to eat. In a baby, playing is learning. Moreover, from the first the baby "knows" he is a social being. Experimental evidence suggests that an infant is "primed"—that is, he naturally shows the ability to act appropriately in social interactions without trial-and-error learning. The impetus for learning and social interaction comes from subcortical centers, some psychologists speculate, and this motivating energy, which we see in the curiosity and playfulness of a baby, makes an essential contribution to developing cortical functions such as language and imagination. Children's cognitive development goes hand in hand with playful social interactions. In an adult, intellectual functioning can be separated (to a degree) from emotional state, but in a young child learning is inextricably bound up with the emotions.[14]

Like infants' perceptual and cognitive abilities, emotional sensitivities may also develop earlier than was once thought. By the time he's about four months old, a baby will look sad, his face sober, his body held stiff, when his mother abruptly puts him down and leaves the room to answer the phone. Around the same age his face will light up and his whole body show his delight when a familiar figure enters the nursery, or a favorite routine, such as the bath, is repeated. By the time a baby is four to six months old, vigorous expressions of anger are beginning to emerge.

From the time of Darwin's nineteenth-century writings on emotion, anger has been usually defined as the characteristic response when achievement of a goal is frustrated by an obstacle. If an infant is capable of anger, it implies that she is also capable of having a goal, and a sense that her efforts to achieve it are being frustrated. Parents can see this development and it has been amply confirmed in psychologists' laboratories. A one-month-old whose arms are restrained might look distressed and try to increase her movements, but her negative response is undirected. By four months she might look at the experimenter's restraining hands as she tries to free herself, and her face will express anger. By seven months she is more likely to look at the experimenter's face as she struggles or at her mother standing by, as if to ask for help.[15]

The psychologist Michael Lewis and his colleagues found that infants become distressed when their expectations are violated. The infants had learned to pull a string to turn on an amusing picture projected on a screen and accompanied by a tape-recorded song. When the experimenter adjusted the string so that a pull no longer produced the picture and song, some babies acted sad and others acted angry. The string mechanism was later readjusted so that a pull would again be rewarded by the display. Those infants who had previously reacted with anger rather than sadness showed higher levels of interest and joy as they relearned the task. Thus, early on infants show temperamental differences in their response to a frustrating situation.[16]

At seven or eight months infants begin to exhibit fear when they are exposed to certain novel experiences. The almost universal wariness of strangers that infants show in the fourth quarter of their first year of life requires not only memory of familiar faces but the ability to compare what they remember with what they see. A slightly younger baby may exhibit surprise in unprecedented situations. According to one study, upon seeing a midget walk toward them infants were both surprised and fascinated.[17] The happy and contagious excitement expressed by laughter develops in the middle of the first year of life, often in response to parents' tickling and "I'm gonna getcha" games.

As a child matures in cognitive skills and motor control, and assimilates the wealth of daily experience, she comes to exhibit a more complex tapestry of emotions, and her versatility in expressing them increases. She becomes an expert in smiles. She giggles, laughs, and whoops with joy. Or her brow furrows, her lower lip shoots out, she whimpers miserably or shrieks in fury. She is beginning to learn a word or two along with intentional gestures to express her feelings and desires. A six-month-old can cry to be picked up; at twelve months she raises her arms, looks be-seechingly at her father, and says a syllable that to her signifies "up."

By the end of her first year she is crawling. Soon she is up on her feet and on the go. Her ability to enter into a larger, more stimulating world is accompanied by expressions of elation and joy, reinforced by de-lighted caregivers. The newly mobile infant is beginning to exhibit emo-tional reactions different from those of a few weeks earlier. She feels new power, new possibilities, new challenges, and new pleasures. The pioneer developmental psychiatrist Louis Sander describes the infant self at this stage as "the intentional self." The child now can explore a wider field, set herself tasks, and carry them out with a gratifying sense of growing competence, and with these achievements she typically ex-hibits a radiant happiness not seen before.

The psychoanalyst Margaret Mahler calls the toddler stage (normally between ten and eighteen months) "the practicing period." As the child masters new skills, he is "exhilarated by his own capacities, continually delighted with the discoveries he is making in his expanding world, . . . enamored with the world and with his own omnipotence."[18] Out of this general feeling of being pleased with himself emerges pride, the emo-tion associated with the successful mastery of some task or the achieve-ment of a goal.

Up to this point most of the signals affectionate caregivers send the baby have been positive and approving. But now in many American homes, parental annoyance and expressions of disapproval rise sharply as the newly mobile child crawls toward the stairs, sweeps a vase from the coffee table with a flick of the forearm, or totters headlong toward the oven. Up to the time her child is ten months old, one researcher es-timates, 90 percent of maternal behavior consists of "affection, play, and care-giving," but when a toddler reaches the thirteen- to seventeen-month stage, his mother is saying "No!" to him in one form or another every nine minutes."[19]

Each emotion plays multiple and changing roles throughout our lives. Some scholars think there may be "universal" elicitors such as the menace in the approach of a large animal. But most associations that trigger fear and other emotions are learned through personal experi-ence and cultural conditioning. Disgust, for example: almost without ex-ception, normal adults are repelled by touching feces, but many a baby will experimentally taste her excrement and enjoy decorating the walls with it. Toilet training likely helps a child acquire the culturally required aversion as she comes to understand the feelings and expectations of her caregivers. Disgust, the experience of revulsion characterized by a wrinkling nose, pursed lips, and churning stomach, continues to protect us from swallowing at least some contaminated objects, even as the adult emotion, its bodily responses, and its neural circuitry are put to more abstract use, as when we feel nauseated at witnessing or even hearing about some brutal or loathsome act.[20]

Dissecting Fear

Each emotion produces a cluster of physiological changes and action patterns; in fact, some psychologists once believed that emotions are fully defined by bodily changes and the sensations they produce. "What kind of emotion of fear would be left if the feeling, neither of quickened heart-beat nor of shallow breathing, neither of trembling lips nor weakened limbs, neither of goose flesh nor of visceral stirring, were present, it is quite impossible for me to think," wrote William James in 1890.[21]

Neuroscientists now propose that there are unique, specialized brain circuits for each of the basic emotions. Using the laboratory rat as an experimental model, Joseph LeDoux of New York University has delineated the brain areas and neural connections that underlie fear, and he suggests that eventually neural maps can be constructed for a wide range of emotions. LeDoux studies a specific indicator of fear in the laboratory rat, its propensity to "freeze" when suddenly endangered. A rat is placed in a box with a wire-mesh floor, through which an electric current is passed; this gives the animal a mild but unpleasant shock to its feet. The experimenter turns on a brief sound and then, shortly afterward, the shock. After a few such pairings the animal shows that it fears the sound. When the sound comes on, the rat stops dead in its tracks and crouches motionless. Its fur stands on end. Its blood pressure and heart rate rise. Stress hormones are released into the bloodstream. The rat has learned to associate a formerly neutral signal with an unpleasant consequence, and now the tone alone inspires fear. The rat's conditioned response is exactly the same as its instinctive response when it encounters a cat.

Building on the research of other neurobiologists, LeDoux and his colleagues undertook a systematic series of experiments to discover which brain regions in rats control and influence this fear response. In order to test their hypotheses as to which anatomic locations were involved, the experimenters electrically stimulated various brain locations and injected tracer substances at the site of stimulation, or they made lesions in various parts of the brain pathway they thought might play a role. They took advantage of the well-established finding that certain tracer chemicals injected into a neuron cell body would be disseminated to its projecting axons and dendrites, and even across synapses, thus delineating the particular pathway and connections of that neuron. Similarly, when a neuron was killed by an injection, its axons and dendrites would degenerate and change in appearance; in this way the projections of a cell could be ascertained through microscopic examinations. Lesion, labeling, and tracer techniques could be used as well to find the neuron cell body belonging to a fiber or to follow the pathway of an axon to its synaptic connection with the next cell in the chain. After interfering with a specified part of the presumptive pathway, the researchers then watched the animal's behavior in the sound-shock situation described above to see if or in what way its behavior was affected. Then they killed the animal and examined its brain to document the location of the lesion or tracer substance.

These experiments established the critical role of several nuclei (small clusters of neurons) nested together in almond-shaped collections at the base of the cerebral hemispheres, one on each side of the midline deep within the temporal lobes. Nineteenth-century anatomists named these nuclei "amygdalae," from the Latin word for almonds. LeDoux and his colleagues found that when a subregion of the amygdala, the central nucleus, was stimulated, changes in heart rate and blood pressure typical of fear occurred and the animal also froze. Lesions made in this region abolished the conditioned fear response; after the operation, the animal heard the sound but was indifferent to it.

When a lesion was made in only one bundle of nerve fibers projecting from the central nucleus, it interfered with the heart rate response but not with blood pressure, stress hormone release, or the behavioral freeze. A lesion in another projection left heart rate unchanged but interfered with another component of the fear response—for example, the normal outpouring of stress hormones during fear. In this way researchers established the importance of the central nucleus of the amygdala in controlling the basic ways fear is expressed by the body.[22]

Similar techniques are being used to investigate the role of other subregions of the amygdala. For example, it has been found that the lateral nucleus of the amygdala is also part of the pathway for fear. Other regions of the amygdala are important in aggressive displays such as the menacing growl of a dog and the rising fur on the back of its neck.

The amydgala, in LeDoux's phrase, is "a hub in the wheel of fear."[23] One of the most fascinating aspects of research on the amygdala is the neuroanatomical explanation of the sudden turn the wheel takes when danger strikes. As we have discussed in an earlier chapter, the thalamus is the principal center for incoming traffic in the two-way highway connecting the senses to the cortex and the cortex to joints and muscles. The cortical round trip takes roughly 200 milliseconds. But there is another, speedier road.

Charles Darwin describes an incident during which this faster road was taken: "I put my face close to the thick glass-plate in front of a puff-adder in the Zoological Gardens, with the firm determination of not starting back if the snake struck at me; but as soon as the blow was struck, my resolution went for nothing, and I jumped a yard or two backward with astonishing rapidity. My will and reason were powerless."[24] A moment later, Darwin remembers that he is in a zoo, that the animal poses no threat, and that his involuntary response confirms his theories about the preservation of adaptive behaviors during evolution. When Darwin jumped back from the puff adder's strike, it was because a direct message from his thalamus to his amygdala had delivered the image "Snake!" and his amygdala barked out the order "Jump back!" The thalamus-amygdala round trip takes less time than the cortical trip. The quick response system of the amygdala can mean the difference between life and death. Afterward, more measured cortical responses can modify emergency perceptions and responses.

But the impulsive and involuntary emotional feelings and behaviors controlled by the amygdala's rapid response system can sometimes cause trouble. "Emotional hijack" is Daniel Goleman's compelling metaphor for the explosive and uncontrollable rage, fear, or excitement that overwhelms rational appraisal and judgment in most people at some time and in some people too much of the time.[25] Powerful phobias such as fear of heights or germs or crowds also may be at least partly based in the amygdala's fear response system.[26]

We have described research that shows how the brain of a laboratory rat deals with a stimulus causing fear. Do the same or similar processes occur in humans? The answer is a qualified yes. The expansion of the cortex in humans, with its capacity for weighing options and restraining impulse, makes possible many modifications of basic emotional responses. But the circuitry at the level of the amygdala is similar in all mammals, and the behavior patterns it initiates are much the same. In humans, if an electrical discharge stimulates the amygdala—as can happen in temporal lobe epilepsy—dread is evoked. Damage to the amygdala in humans can abolish or alter fear.

In humans, lesions confined to the amygdala are rare, but a few cases have been reported. One involves a woman identified as D.R., who had undergone surgery for uncontrollable epilepsy. Lesions made during the surgery damaged the amygdala. Afterward, although D.R. easily recognized the faces of people she knew, she could no longer interpret their facial expressions, especially when the face showed fear. Presented with pictures of faces depicting emotions readily identified by normal people, D.R. could not recognize fear or anger. Even though her hearing and comprehension of spoken words and sentences were normal, she had poor understanding of vocal expressions of emotions. For example, she could not identify angry and fearful intonations in sentences or words read out loud to her. She also could not label a growl as an angry sound, nor did she immediately realize that a sound such as a scream signifies fear. Her deficits were quite specific to certain emotions; she could still identify laughter as happy, and sobbing as sad. Moreover, she was as aware of her loss as an amputee is of an absent limb.[27]

The limited evidence we now have about humans confirms the importance of the amygdala for appraising potential threats. (An angry face or growl may signify danger; another person's fearful expression may signal a threat to both of you.) Without the capacity to evaluate threatening situations rapidly, protective strategies such as running away or self-defense would be delayed. It is unlikely, however, that D.R. would be left totally defenseless. Mammals have a number of routes to self-preservation, including the social claims they make on others. D.R.

might not have a clutch of fear as the car bears down on her in the crosswalk, but she would know enough to step back, and if she didn't move fast enough, someone near her might well grab her. In humans, the neocortex, especially parts of the frontal cortex with their wealth of connections to evolutionarily older cortical and subcortical centers, permits learning and judgment to modify the automatic adaptive responses we have inherited from our ancestors. But not always. Even the eminently rational Charles Darwin could be hijacked.

Emotional Connections

Emotions influence the whole body, from the top of the head to the tips of the toes. A cat's hair stands on end when she is enraged; she cannot help stretching out her toes as she yawns luxuriously after a satisfying meal. The immensely complex systems that mediate, influence, and respond to emotional promptings are located throughout the body. Emotions feed into and are fed by closely related and overlapping brain systems whose anatomic locations range from brainstem to prefrontal cortex. Subcortical systems exert control over hunger, thirst, attention, and sleep; govern hormone production and immune function; regulate mating, reproduction, and maternal caregiving; influence memory formation, storage, and retrieval; and they are intertwined with cortical processes such as language, judgment, and moral reasoning. A circlet of interconnected structures at the base of the forebrain, the limbic system, is sometimes referred to as the emotional brain because of its pivotal role in emotional processes.[28]

An emotion may be initiated in any one of many body systems, triggered by an external event or some internal trigger such as a pain or a memory. Within the brain, numerous components of emotion systems overlap, interlock, and control responses that sometimes appear similar. This makes the exact neural basis for a behavior extremely difficult to pinpoint. Indeed, as Gordon Shepherd points out, "a given behavior may be mediated by many potential mechanisms."[29] Brain systems governing emotions receive direct and indirect messages from within the body and, through the senses, from the environment. Emotions can commandeer the pathway governing voluntary movement that courses through the spinal cord. In this way emotion can control action.

Emotions influence and are influenced by bodily states. This occurs through the neurohormonal and immune systems and through a subsidiary nervous system, the autonomic nervous system, itself divided into two subsystems, the sympathetic and parasympathetic branches. (These subsystems have actions that generally oppose each other in a coordinated fashion, thereby promoting the equilibrium of the body.) The autonomic nervous system, which regulates smooth-muscle tone and contraction, controls the size of the pupil of the eye, heartbeat, respiration rate, blood vessel caliber, blood pressure, digestive functions, gland secretion, and much more. It has ancillary centers of control throughout the body—in the heart, in the gut, in the reproductive organs, and elsewhere. Their existence reminds us that the central brain, which supervises and coordinates the body as a whole, is relatively new; prior to its evolution, local command and control sufficed. The central brain's "basement" level, the brainstem, which regulates breathing, metabolism, the rhythms of waking and sleeping, and preprogrammed postures and movements, is in intimate touch with the autonomic nervous system. It supervises the inside world of the body and its metabolic states.

The autonomic nervous system performs its functions more or less automatically, but it is linked to higher brain centers for emotions which both influence the system and are influenced by it. Fear—triggered, as we have seen, in the amygdala—can constrict muscles in the walls of blood vessels in the digestive tract, thereby decreasing blood flow. At the same time the blood vessels in arms and legs become *less* constricted, thereby permitting an increase in blood flow. These involuntary changes in the body serve as cues: "The bear is coming closer! Don't just sit there eating lunch! Take off!" The amygdala sends control messages via the branches of the autonomic nervous system. These have the effect of balancing metabolic requirements in various parts of the body as circumstances change. "One test for the presence of emotion," writes Shepherd, "is whether a given perception or motor act is accompanied by changes in the autonomic nervous system, such as faster heart rate or increased perspiration." Invertebrates do not have an autonomic nervous system. During sexual arousal and copulation, the heart rate of the octopus does not change.[30]

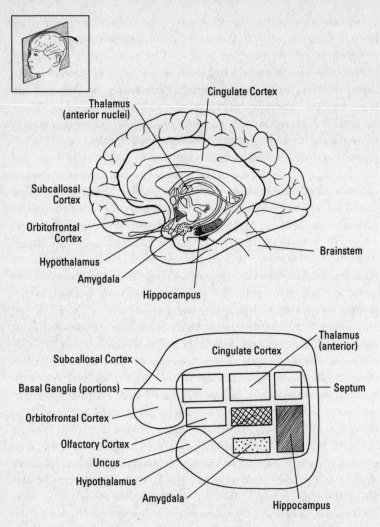

FIGURE 6-1. THE ANATOMY OF EMOTIONS.

At top, the medial (inner) surface of the cerebrum showing the limbic system (outlined). The brainstem and part of the thalamus have been removed to expose limbic structures. At bottom, limbic structures are also depicted. Their many interconnections are not shown. (*Source:* Adapted from Guyton and Hall, *Medical Physiology,* 9th ed., p. 753.)

Hormones and other neuroactive molecules have a tremendous influence on emotion circuitry and, through this circuitry, on all kinds of body processes, including cognition. Orchestration of neurohormonal function takes place in the hypothalamus and the pituitary gland. The hypothalamus is a peanut-sized collection of neurons in the base of the cerebrum. It has direct contacts with the pituitary gland. The pituitary is the control center for hormone production and is often referred to as the master gland because it produces hormones that in turn direct the production of other hormones elsewhere in the body. Thyroid, adrenal, stress, reproductive, and other hormones come under neural control in the hypothalamus, and the hypothalamic-pituitary axis in turn receives feedback from hormones circulating in the bloodstream. The hypothalamic-pituitary system also has copious control and feedback loops connecting many brain regions, including the amygdala and other limbic regions and the cortex. It is in close two-way communication with regions in the brainstem and midbrain. Acting in concert, these regions coordinate wakefulness and attention with motivational urges such as hunger, thirst, sex drive, and perhaps curiosity.[31]

Stress is the normal response of the body to fearsome or painful stimuli that disturb its equilibrium. It is managed largely by interactions among the hormones of the adrenal and pituitary glands and the hypothalamus, the "stress axis." Normal levels of stress hormones such as cortisol and epinephrine are necessary and beneficial. In the first moments after a stressful stimulus is encountered, the stress hormones epinephrine and norepinephrine are released. Emotional arousal is increased and memory formation is enhanced. But sustained stress can produce numerous pathological effects throughout the body and the brain. Stress increases the production of cortisol, a hormone secreted by the adrenal gland. Chronic excess of cortisol has been shown to accelerate the loss of certain types of neurons, including those of the hippocampus, a center vital for the formation of memories.[32] Chronic stress adversely affects memory and learning, and this may have particularly pernicious effects on children's development.

As the physiologist Jaak Panksepp points out, there is harmony between the effects a hormone or neuropeptide produces in the brain and in the rest of the body. (Neuropeptides are chemical substances, produced by neurons, that have hormonelike effects.) For instance, in the body, insulin promotes the storage of energy; in the brain, it appears to regulate food intake. Oxytocin facilitates childbirth and nursing by its effects on the uterus and breasts; in the brain, it regulates maternal caregiving behavior.[33] In the last decade the feedback loops linking the immune system and the nervous system have come under increasing scrutiny and have been found to have important interactions. For example, depressed individuals and individuals suffering from stress have decreased immune responses.[34]

Paul MacLean has imagined the mammalian forebrain as evolving from three main "neural assemblies," which can be identified in present-day brains from reptile to human.[35] As brains evolved, newer structures, especially neocortical structures, came to control and transform the functions of the evolutionarily older assemblies. The most primitive and deepest part of the forebrain choreographs the "daily master routine," the complex but more or less automatic species-typical behaviors engaged in every day: eating, sleeping, eliminating, and foraging. The same part of the brain also controls subroutines such as courtship and defense, which are evoked by special stimuli. The neuroanatomical control of master routines resides in the basal ganglia, a group of neuronal clusters at the base of the forebrain.[36] ("Ganglia" is an alternative term for nuclei.)

The limbic system evolved, according to MacLean's theory, in the brains of ancient mammals. This system consists of a number of interconnected neuronal clusters and several folds of cerebral cortex located in the deepest layers of the cerebral hemispheres.[37] It provides part of the neural underpinning for the behaviors of attachment between mothers and infants, including nursing, vocalizations to maintain contact, and play. Lesions in these circuits have been shown to interfere with maternal caregiving. Animals without a neocortex, such as reptiles, show no maternal affection; as they emerge from the egg, newborns instinctively hide from their mothers to avoid being eaten.[38]

The emotional brain superimposes a level of control and coordination on the body's responses that is vital to all higher cortical processes. In its capacity as mediator between the reasoning brain and the body, the emotional brain informs and motivates the thinking brain. It imbues thinking with feeling in such a way that they are not separable. MacLean believes that the limbic system also plays a role in maintaining "the continuing sense of personal being" and "the conviction that we attach to our beliefs."[39] Limbic structures also may be critical in enabling an animal to recognize a member of its own species and in social affiliation. Long before the highest level of the brain, the neocortex, fully evolved, the emotional brain was already in place. As communication links between old and newer cortical centers evolved, the neocortex came to facilitate, modulate, interpret, and regulate emotional life.

Over the course of mammalian evolution, the emotional brain performed two distinct functions, which still serve to define what an emotion is. The first involves evaluation. Is this incoming information significant? How much attention should it command? Is it pleasant or unpleasant? What emotion is appropriate to the set of stimuli being processed? Second, emotions prepare the body for action. As the Latin root indicates, "emotion" connotes movement. When we are "moved," bodily changes take place. Tears flow. Eyes widen in joyful surprise. Legs fly off the ground.

In other animals, emotions are nearly always elicited by direct physical stimulation or need, but in humans emotions are often evoked and transformed by words. "Sticks and stones can break my bones but words will never hurt me." The old playground rejoinder to a taunt is patently a whistle in the wind. A word or two spoken under the right circumstances can trigger overwhelming emotion. Words can lead to a homicide, a love affair, or panic on Wall Street.[40]

The Beginnings of Self-discovery

In the twentieth century, psychologists have come up with a variety of theories to explain what the self is and what it does, where it resides, how it becomes conscious of itself, and how it comes to think well or ill of itself. In recent years consciousness and self-consciousness have begun to intrigue neuroscientists as well. How does a brain become a conscious mind? How and when does a child develop a sense of self?

For Freud, the self, the ego, was "the ghost in the machine" that organizes perception, memory, and thinking. The ego mediates conflicting demands of conscience (the superego) and instinctual animal drives (the id). Only the ego is self-aware. William James, on the other hand, gave a lordly definition that pictures the self as an inventory: "A man's me," he wrote, "is the sum total of all he can call his, not only his body and his psychic powers, but his clothes and his house, his wife and children, his ancestors and friends, his reputation and works, his lands and horses, and yacht and bank account." He feels "triumphant" if they prosper and "cast down" if they "dwindle and die away."[41] James contrasted this experimental objective self, the "me," with the subjective self, the "I," which interprets and evaluates.

Erik Erikson expounded the idea that a coherent identity "provides an individual with a stable sense of self and a frame of reference for making sense of experience." He believed that "identity confusion" and threats to identity are the source of many emotional problems of childhood and adolescence. Similar in some respects is the idea of Carl Rogers and others that people strive to develop and maintain a coherent and stable conceptual system. The self is an organization of conscious, relatively stable beliefs and values about one's person.[42]

The psychiatrist Daniel Stern describes a process in the infant and young child of ever more complex organization and reorganization of the emerging self. "There is a sense of self that is a single, distinct, integrated body; there is the agent of actions, the experiencer of feelings, the maker of intentions, the architect of plans, the transposer of experience into language, the communicator and sharer of personal knowledge."[43] Other scholars would include as essential to a self the sense of the body's boundaries and its continuity over time, and an awareness of the capacity to communicate feelings and meanings to other selves.

Parents unconsciously recognize the emergence of self in their children and facilitate the process. There are periods in the life of a baby when rapid changes are especially evident—at two to three months, at nine to twelve months, at fifteen to eighteen months. The smile and coo of a three-month-old have become much more social than before, and his actions and activity patterns are more regular and coordinated. A ten-month-old baby has learned that he can share an experience with another person. He looks at his mother and then at his ball as his mother follows his shifting gaze. He and his father play peekaboo, each partner happily observing the correct sequence of play. An eighteen-month-old is discovering the power conferred by locomotion and language. He can distance himself from his mother by choice, and he can return to her. By what he says he can reach out to her and influence her behavior. At each age, developmental achievement and parental response contribute to the child's growing sense of self.

Drawing on the wide range of research indicating that babies come into the world biologically prepared for social behaviors, Robert Emde has attempted to integrate these findings with psychiatric theory. A baby's "affective core" functions as an "internal executive," organizing the infant's growing sense of coherence and stability in her environment, her increasing control over her body, and her developing power to manage her relationship with her caregivers and to regulate her emotions.[44] Development is not simply the addition of new capacities but a continuing process of reorganization. The self is not just a collection of traits and dispositions. It is a processor of awareness, intentionality, recognition, continuity, and change, which is shaped and reshaped by experience.[45]

A basic indicator of self-consciousness is self-recognition. A one-year-old infant gazes at his reflection in the mirror with interest. He may even try to look behind the glass to see who is there. Six or seven months later, he will still be captivated by the image in the mirror. If his mother has secretly put a red dot of lipstick on his forehead during his nap, he will look long and hard at the red dot on the forehead of the baby in the mirror. After all, he has been fascinated by unusual features of an image for some months. But now he rubs his own forehead instead of the reflection in the mirror. Not only does he recognize himself, but he perceives the red dot as foreign to his mental image of himself.[46]

But what causes all this to happen? At present, neuroscience offers at best a few clues; testable hypotheses have not been framed. In his book *Affect Regulation and the Origin of the Self,* Allan Schore reviews neurobiological research bearing on "the origin of the self" and presents interesting data in support of a theory of the American philosopher and psychologist George Herbert Mead: "The process out of which the self arises," Mead wrote, "is a social process which implies interaction of individuals. . . . Selves can only exist in definite relationship to other selves."[47] The self is not only a social being; it is a social creation.

In the first months of life the caregiver is the choreographer of the emotional communication system from which self-awareness arises. At this stage a parent's principal regulatory function is to modulate the infant's state of arousal, gently stimulating him when he shows interest and soothing him when he appears overstimulated or distressed. Little by little the relationship becomes more reciprocal as the baby develops goals and intentions of his own. The process picks up at the beginning of the second year, when the infant is becoming a toddler. Normally, parents have become more attuned to their child's emotional spectrum, sensing impending emotional storms, knowing by now when the baby's exuberant joy is about to give way to frantic wailing. They are more adept at anticipating frustration and interceding before the child loses control. This joint experience in emotional regulation, as Alan Sroufe puts it, "paves the way for later self-regulation."[48] But emotional regulation remains a joint effort for a good many years.

At first, touch and perhaps smell are the senses most used in the communication between an infant and her caregiver, although voice and vision are also important. After about three months, visual information assumes ever greater importance in the developing emotional relationship between parent and child. The infant now has greater capacity for prolonged visual attention. She fixes her gaze on her father's face and picks up emotional clues in his expression as he gazes back. By this time she also knows how to break off the gaze. Her parents adjust their responses according to the baby's facial expressions, body movements, and vocalizations. "The more the mother tunes her activity level to the infant during periods of social engagement, and the more she allows him/her to recover quietly in periods of disengagement," Allan Schore notes, "the more synchronized their interaction." Facial and vocal mirroring and exquisitely subtle but unconscious mutual adjustments in movements and touch are "fundamental to the ongoing affective development of the infant."[49]

Edward Tronick, a child development specialist at Children's Hospital in Boston, calls the behavioral interaction between parent and infant on which the processes of emotional regulation depend an "affective communication system." A six-month-old baby grabs at a teddy bear, but it is just out of reach. He looks angry and distressed, but then he puts his thumb in his mouth and becomes calmer, an example of what Tronick characterizes as "self-directed regulatory behavior." He tries for the teddy again and fails, becomes distressed again, but this time the caregiver talks to him in a soothing voice. The infant calms down, then reaches again, and fails once more. Now the caregiver, noticing what the baby wants, moves the desired object within reach. He grasps it and explores it with hands and mouth. The caregiver has picked up on the baby's signals and by helping him deal with both failure and success, she has aided his own early efforts to both achieve a goal and regulate his emotions.

Even the most attentive and sensitive parent misses some emotional cues, and this fact, true of any relationship including the first ones, gives the infant useful experiences in mild frustration and in self-regulation. It also motivates him to develop his skills in communication. But persistent and chronic failure to connect with another sets the stage for much later unhappiness. Tronick theorizes about how this happens: Failing to communicate with his primary caregiver, the infant withdraws and comforts himself by thumb-sucking or some other device to dampen his feelings of frustration and sadness. With repeated failures of social communication, he begins to deploy these self-regulatory behaviors in an automatic, inflexible, and indiscriminate manner. He gives up trying to assess each new situation on its merits, adopting instead a coherent but isolating stance that, in some cases, leads to depression or another psychopathological outcome. Certain children who are continually frustrated by their inability to communicate may also exhibit outbursts of rage.[50]

Clearly mothers, fathers, and other caregivers differ widely in their capacity to read the emotional cues of babies and to regulate their own behavior in response. Some exhibit nearly flawless intuition while others tend to miss or ignore nearly every cue. Or they respond in heavy-handed, mechanical, or wildly inconsistent ways. The skill of communicating with an infant is no more automatic than the skill of being a friend or lover. A caregiver's acuteness and sensitivity depend on many factors, including temperament, childhood experiences, patience, and emotional stability. Parents who are able to focus attention on the infant in the time they spend with the child and resist other demands are more likely to be sensitive to the baby's cues. Some parents find that even brief periods of meditation can help prepare them to be fully present to a small child.[51] A number of successful educational efforts in communities in the United States and in other countries indicate that parents can be taught to be more aware of a child's emotional needs and how to respond to them.[52]

During the child's first three years of life, emotional regulation is changing from a largely external process, in which the child responds to parental signals and physical control, to an internal process in which "the self-monitoring self," to use Louis Sander's term, plays an increasingly important role. Gradually the processes of cognitive and emotional development are completely enmeshed in the emerging self; the separate self blossoms. At the same time the child is decreasing his dependence on his primary caregiver as he moves along the path toward greater autonomy and self-regulation.[53]

The importance of social relationships to the development of self-awareness and independence is of course not a new idea. In the last century the Danish philosopher Søren Kierkegaard beautifully described the role emotional interaction plays in one of the great developmental milestones of childhood:

> The loving mother teaches her child to walk alone. She is far enough from him so that she cannot actually support him, but she holds out her arms to him. She imitates his movements, and if he totters, she swiftly bends as if to seize him, so that the child might believe that he is not walking alone. . . . And yet she does more. Her face beckons like a reward, an encouragement. Thus the child walks alone with his eyes fixed on his mother's face, not on the difficulties in his way. He supports himself by the arms that do not hold him and constantly strives towards the refuge in his mother's embrace, little suspecting that in the very same moment that he is emphasizing his need of her, he is proving that he can do without her, because he is walking alone.[54]

Emotions Right and Left

As with language, the right and left halves of the cerebrum seem to play differing roles in emotion. Thus, certain lesions within the right frontal region leave a patient apathetic and emotionally shallow, while lesions in the corresponding region on the left side are associated with sadness, depression, or forebodings of catastrophe. Electroencephalographic evidence suggests that the left frontal region becomes active when individuals experience the range of emotions that accompany an approach to the outside world (joy, interest, and anger); emotions associated with drawing back from the external environment (distress, sadness, disgust) activate the right frontal cortex. Richard Davidson and Nathan Fox found evidence of this brain asymmetry in newborn infants. Given a bad-tasting substance, the neonates wrinkled their face in disgust as an EEG recorded heightened electrical activity in their right frontal cortex. Infants and children who consistently show a relatively higher activation of the right frontal cortex tend to become more upset in stressful situations.[55]

Mapping of the brain areas and processes that underlie various emotions is still in its infancy. Differing methods of study give results that are not easy to compare or reconcile. But progress is being made. For example, Mark George, Robert Post, and their colleagues at the National Institutes of Health have used PET scans to study the brain activity of normal adult volunteers during sadness and happiness. (PET—positron emission tomography—the reader may recall, measures blood flow and metabolic activity; increases in a certain region reflect greater neuronal activity in that region.) The experimenters induced emotional states by asking the volunteers to recall sad and happy personal events and to try to feel the emotion they felt then. When the women volunteers were sad, *increased* activity was found in subcortical and cortical limbic structures on both left and right sides. On the other hand, during happiness, *reductions* in brain activity were observed, especially in the right prefrontal area and both temporal areas. Men showed a somewhat different activation pattern.[56]

As research results proliferate and are better understood, and as interpretations converge, there is reason to hope that more targeted and rational therapies can be devised for patients who are not just normally happy or sad but incapacitated by mania or depression. Similarly, better understanding of the roots of chronic anxiety or anger may also illuminate more effective ways to help.[57]

Neuropsychologists believe that an infant's growing capacity for emotional self-regulation depends upon the inhibitory role played by the frontal cortex. With increasing neocortical development the baby shows signs of being able to plan his behavior and inhibit or delay his response to an emotional stimulus that even weeks earlier would have elicited an immediate reaction. By the time he's twenty months old, a toddler can sometimes control his impulsive behavior. Frustrated that his mother is not giving him the attention he wants, he may be able to pause and take stock of the situation instead of exploding in a temper tantrum.

Ample behavioral research supports the hypothesis that the interaction of parents and infants influences emotional regulation, but how this is reflected in developing patterns of neuronal connectivity is unknown. Throughout this book we discuss a growing body of evidence that parents' characteristic responses to their infants' behaviors shape the course of development. According to current thinking, this interaction will influence which synapses and neuronal assemblies are reinforced and strengthened, and which are pruned and lost. It will be recalled that the brain has a hyperabundance of neurons and synapses in the first three years of life. Many will be eliminated, much as a sculptor chips away at a marble block so that a face can emerge. A caregiver can reinforce the baby's joyful emotion by a supportive look or touch, or he can ignore what is happening and walk out of the room; how he reacts can heighten the child's anger or cool it.

In their daily interactions with their infants, caregivers help design the child's cortical map by the emotional messages they send or fail to send. EEG studies of infants of depressed mothers appear to support this hypothesis. Geraldine Dawson found that 40 percent of babies of a group of depressed mothers exhibited reduced left frontal brain activity; in many cases, when the mother's depression lifted, their infant's brain activity "returned to normal." It is surmised that brain regions chronically activated during persistently negative emotional states may be excessively stimulated, while regions for processing positive emotions are underexercised.[58]

As cognitive abilities develop, the child is better able to call up and interpret memories of earlier emotional interactions. As his locomotor skills improve, enabling him to come and go at will, he develops a clearer sense that he is an independent agent. Before venturing into the unknown, he still looks back at his mother—at least sometimes—for a clue that will help him decide whether to take the exploratory step he has in mind. As a richer store of differentiated emotions and experiences becomes available to the toddler, he is better able to evaluate events and internalize the behavioral standards modeled and counseled by his caregivers. He is practicing the art of self-regulation and thereby preparing to become a competent participant in the widening circles of school and neighborhood he will enter.

He is also becoming increasingly aware that his own goals do not always coincide with those of his parents. His accelerating reach for autonomy inevitably involves conflict with the very persons he loves the most.[59] This is an especially challenging time for parents, who are called upon to deal with their concerns about keeping their child's behavior within acceptable bounds without squelching his adventurous spirit. As the toddler seeks to establish his independence, he tests his relationship with his caregivers. It is now his turn to say "No." Especially after a hard day at work, parents sometimes find it easier to control a child with their anger than with sweet reason, or to hedge him about with all sorts of rules, or to physically confine him in a playpen or bouncing seat, or to switch on the television to distract him. Providing assured protection, making children mind, containing excessive exuberance, while simultaneously encouraging play and exploration, is a balancing act.

How information is conveyed to a baby—pleasurably or unpleasantly—influences how the infant acquires and retains knowledge and experience. A baby's participation in playful and affectionate interactions with her various caregivers provides opportunities to practice regulating arousal, focusing attention, and juggling the many aspects—social, emotional, and cognitive—of communicative interchange.[60]

Words with Feeling

The emerging ability to represent feelings with words exerts a profound influence on a child's emotional life. Just as caregivers use words to send emotional messages to infants not yet able to grasp their semantic significance, so infants and toddlers use preverbal utterances to make emotion-laden connections with the important people in their life. When language facility increases in the second year of life, the child begins to be more explicit about what she is feeling. Her equivalents of "It hurts" and "Comfort me" now pepper her interchanges with her mother.

Even before a child is two he will point to a nearly invisible scratch on his arm or say that he is very tired, in the hope of being excused from picking up his toys or finishing his supper. Around this time he will tell a lie to avoid punishment or throw the blame on a brother or sister. Studies indicate that in their third year children are able to talk about causes of events and feelings, but they are most likely to talk in this mode so as to draw the caregiver's attention to a need, to express feelings of distress, or to enlist support for getting or doing something they want.[61]

The child development researcher Judy Dunn gives an example: A two-year-old girl sees chocolate cake on the table. "Bibby on," she demands. Her mother replies, "You don't want your bibby on. You're not eating." Child: "Chocolate cake, chocolate cake." Mother: "No more chocolate cake." The child starts to whine: "Why? Tired." The mother, seeing that the child is lively and not fatigued, says knowingly: "You tired? Ooh!" The child tries again: "Chocolate cake." Mother: "No chance."[62]

However, children have no less need to express happiness, pleasure, and love. Around two some children will spontaneously offer verbal expressions of affection, and many more show their enjoyment of affectionate social routines: "Kiss Grandma." "Daddy home soon." They enjoy and expect approbation and are happy to learn the good manners of love. And they need such support of positive emotional states as much as they need comfort in their distress. Although the reinforcement of positive emotions is as important an aspect of emotional regulation as the damping down of anger, fear, and other disturbing emotions, it may seem less urgent to the caregiver. Supporting young children's positive emotional experiences requires caregivers to make time to listen to their stories, to recognize and offer praise for successes, to encourage exploration, and to acknowledge and share pleasurable feelings.

As their language skills develop, young children find other ways to use words to enrich their lives or to solve problems. By the time they are around two years old, children will use words to console a brother or sister who is distressed: "Stop crying, mate. Stop it crying." (In this example from Dunn's research, a thirty-month-old boy is trying to comfort his older brother, who has just been scolded by their mother.) While toddlers exhibit empathy in their behavior even before they can talk, language opens up many new opportunities and strategies for comforting another person (or making him feel worse). Thus, the younger brother now turns to his mother and tries to induce her to comfort the older boy: "Len crying Mummy! Len crying. Look. Me show you. Len crying." As the episode wears on with Len still crying, baby brother chimes in, "Stop crying Len. Smack your bottom."[63]

Language skills enliven play. Three-year-olds can tell jokes and enjoy funny stories about family happenings. Julian always laughs when he tells the story of how he and his grandmother thought they were locked out of the house one afternoon when really the door was just stuck. Sharing a joke creates intimacy and helps a child place himself in the family narrative. Children's pleasure in making their parents and siblings laugh is evident. But a child soon learns that his mother may not find scatological references as funny as his brother does. He is becoming alert to the fact that words and behavior have different meanings in different contexts.

Teasing can be jocular and a little risky as in this exchange: Mother asks, "Do you like your Mummy Ned? Child: No yes! (Smiles) Mother: No yes? No yes? Child: No yes!" A child's developing language skills permits him a richer internal narrative about emotions. In play, children work out their understanding of how people relate to one another. "You be the baby and I be the mommy," says a thirty-six-month-old boy to another child of the same age. "Say wah, wah, wah, and I read you my book. Say wah, wah, wah some more and I give you juice." "Baby dinosaur," replies the second child as he charges around the room shouting "Wah, wah, wah!" and making dinosaur sounds. Dunn reports that not until their third year, when children are almost fluent in their speech, do they show great interest in pretend play about emotional states.[64]

A Tapestry of Reason, Emotion, and Memory

There is a strong tradition in the philosophies and religions of the West that proclaims life to be a never-ending struggle between reason and passion. Children are below the age of reason. They are creatures of passion. The mature, upright man or woman has been taught to subject emotions to the authority of reason. When the eighteenth-century philosopher David Hume declared in his *Treatise of Human Nature* that "reason is, and ought to be, the slave of passions," the statement was considered outrageously contrarian. But faith in reason has been periodically challenged by waves of religious sentiment and by celebrations of feeling as the only authentic guide for human behavior; indeed, these currents are still running strong in our own time.

However, as more is being learned about the neurobiology of emotional development and emotional regulation, it is becoming clearer that the lines separating reason from passion are much fuzzier than philosophers and psychologists have contended. Brain circuits for cognition and for emotion are distinct, but they work in tandem. As Antonio Damasio, a professor of neurology at the University of Iowa College of Medicine, puts it, the brain systems on which both emotion and reason depend are "enmeshed" and "interwoven." Specific brain systems are involved in reasoning, and some of these also process feelings. "It is as if we are possessed by a passion for reason, a drive that originates in the brain core, permeates other levels of the nervous system, and emerges as either feelings or non-conscious biases to guide decision-making."[65]

Damasio has advanced the theory that the brain notes and remembers the bodily changes that accompany emotion-laden experiences. "Somatic markers"—body-based signals that focus attention—persist as part of association and memory at both subcortical and cortical levels. When an experience is recalled consciously, or its memory is triggered unconsciously, or the individual has a similar experience, it is accompanied by a positive or negative "gut response."

Much or perhaps all of the learning and socialization that takes place in early childhood is marked by pleasant or unpleasant somatic markers. They bias learning, decision-making, and actions. For example, a thought or image associated with pleasant markers such as a smile, a decrease in stress hormones, and muscle relaxation creates a positive bias that influences one's actions, beliefs, or decisions, not only this time but the next. Positive somatic markers act as incentives, negative markers as disincentives. A few of these dispositional preferences are innate, but most of them are built up as a child encounters people, contexts, events, social conventions, and rules.

Damasio's theory implies that "emotion is part and parcel of what we call cognition. If there is severe impairment of the emotions, we cannot have rationality."[66] He speculates that certain sociopaths—individuals who can commit murder in cold blood—have a pathological diminution or absence of feeling. (Tests reveal that sociopaths often have an abnormally high threshold for emotional arousal.) Their conduct is also irrational, since they run the risk of lengthy imprisonment or execution. The developmental impairment of sociopaths, Damasio theorizes, could "come from abnormal circuitry and abnormal chemical signaling and begin early in development." Social and cultural factors, he suggests, are likely to interact with biological factors to aggravate sociopathy.[67]

The amygdala, which we've already discussed as a key center for emotions, has also been found to be a critical structure for producing and storing emotional memories. This special type of memory is evoked when an emotionally charged episode or experience is recalled. The emotional brain is activated by the memory; in the case of a fearful memory it opens "the floodgates of emotional arousal, turning on all the bodily responses associated with fear and defense."[68] Other events can evoke feelings tinged with pleasurable emotions from the past. Physiologically, the person is to an extent reliving the experience. An example of an emotional memory is the fear that surges up sharp and fresh each time you travel on the mountain road where you were once involved in an accident fatal to a friend. The present moment evokes feelings and bodily responses that are associated with the past event.

Research indicates that memories for past events and contexts are made and stored separately from emotional memories. While the amygdala is the repository for emotional memories, the hippocampus, twin structures deep within each temporal lobe with rich connections to both the amygdala and neocortex, is the storehouse for memories of events and contexts.

Someday, you hope, you will be able to remember your friend and his death without the intensely painful emotional reaction. When that happens, you will be drawing upon event memory stored in the hippocampus. You will remember the episode that took place at that turn in the road perfectly well, but it will no longer evoke a conditioned fear/grief response. Usually memory systems work together, but their separate neural basis can be teased apart in animal experiments and observed in patients who have suffered damage to one or another memory system.[69]

In the infant's brain, the hippocampus matures more slowly than does the amygdala. Perhaps this difference explains why infants do not remember specific episodes, including traumatic events, but even years later may be aroused by a stimulus that triggers an emotional memory. These memories may be laid down in the amygdala without the child's retaining a corresponding memory for the actual event, which requires a maturely functioning hippocampus. Emotional memories may be experienced as a phobia, a panic attack, post-traumatic stress syndrome, or "free-floating anxiety."[70]

Some psychologists speculate that the separation in a young child's mind between emotional and event memories could contribute to false memories. For example, an adult might retain an emotional memory from early childhood of a trauma such as sexual abuse without being able accurately to remember the identity of the perpetrator or the exact circumstances of the violation. Trying to make sense of his strong feelings, he might unconsciously construct an account at variance with the actual but irretrievable facts, which have not been stored in memory. Although this explanation of false memories is plausible in light of what we now know about memory, it has by no means been fully accepted.

LeDoux suggests that one reason why childhood emotional trauma is so potent in adult life, as psychologists believe, and so hard to deal with, as therapists confirm, is that these emotional memories may antedate language. The infant lacked the capacity to make sense of emotion-laden experiences because at the time he had no words to explain them. And so years later, unprocessed, chaotic feelings come tumbling out to trigger poorly understood emotions and irrational behavior.[71]

Brain connections that have slowly evolved over the course of millions of years in response to dangers and opportunities no longer a part of daily life can be a source of trouble. Voracious sexual appetite and immediate aggressive response to perceived threats, adaptive qualities in thinly populated hunter societies, have become social problems now that the six billionth inhabitant of our planet is about to be born, responsibility for defense has been handed over to bureaucrats, and meat is purchased rather than speared. Although innate patterns of behavior have been conserved because they were selected over millions of years, learned modulations, controls, and diversions—for example, punching a punching bag instead of your co-worker—have come to be just as essential for survival in the complex world modern humans have constructed.

A powerful emotion such as anger over a frustrated goal mobilizes energy and attention that will, if not too intense and overwhelming, lead to efforts at mastering the challenge, a discovery of one's own powers captured in the triumphant outcry of the three-year-old: "I can do it all by myself." But anger at obstacles or at the agent who is placing the obstacles in one's path can also turn aggressive. If over and over again, a child is frustrated in his goals, especially if he perceives that he is being teased, humiliated, or abandoned, healthy anger turns into learned helplessness, despair, and hatred. This terrible sequence, we will argue in a subsequent chapter, is the experience of more and more children in our time.

Chapter Seven

EMPATHY, CONSCIENCE, AND MORAL DEVELOPMENT

When a thirteen-year-old boy apprehended after mugging an old blind woman was asked by one of his interrogators how he felt about the pain he had caused her, his answer was chilling: "What do I care? I'm not her."[1] It is not just the lack of remorse in his response but his inability to connect with the feelings of another person that terrifies us; his emotional isolation makes him seem inhuman. The capacity to share the feelings of others is necessary for developing family relationships and wider social arrangements. In this chapter we will look at research on how empathy develops in children and the role it plays in moral judgment and moral behavior. We will also discuss recent research on how children internalize moral principles.

Early Signs of Empathy

David Hume believed that empathic feelings—the predisposition of human beings to share the concerns of others, to wish them well, and to be dismayed when they suffer or are hurt—are "the chief source of moral distinctions."[2] Recent developmental research is yielding evidence that supports Hume's insight. Very young children recognize the joy or distress of their parents and react to emotional signals, whether smiles or sad looks. There is also evidence that babies are born prepared to make emotional connections with others besides their primary caregivers. Newborns cry when they hear other infants cry; experiments show that their distress at hearing the wailing of another small child is greater than when they are exposed to a synthesized rising and falling sound that mimics crying, or to some other loud noise.

Martin Hoffman, a professor of psychology at New York University, calls this reflexive crying "empathic arousal," and he sees it as a precursor of empathy.[3] Analogous behaviors are also seen in adults—for example, contagious yawning and the emotional arousal triggered by the mass excitement of a cheering crowd. Neuroscientists believe that subcortical brain areas enable empathic arousal; in the words of a research team at the National Institute of Mental Health, the behavior is "an innate, hardwired response connecting us to the emotional plight of others."[4]

However, some doubt that it is correct to dignify early mimicry with the word "empathy." Catching the mood of another, they say, is not the quality Hume wrote about but merely a behavior shared with other animals that has proved adaptive. An antelope will pick up on the fear of another antelope, and this "mood contagion" can cause an entire herd to flee. Wolves howl in unison, and a dog may whimper at seeing his master in distress. But while mood contagion and motor mimicry are not the same as empathy, as we understand the word, they have been put to the service of the more differentiated and complex emotion that does deserve the name. In biology it is a common phenomenon that a reflexive behavior pattern is reconfigured as a more complex behavior at a later stage of development. In humans there are analogous examples of other subcortical precursors of higher brain function—for example, the stepping reflex. When a newborn is held upright with both feet planted on a flat surface, she will make walking motions even though the circuits for cortical control of motor behavior needed for walking will not be fully in place for a whole year.

To develop the capacity to experience empathy in Hume's sense— that is, to feel the feelings of others—a child must have some notion that the plaintive infant cries that distress him are coming from another baby and not himself. To share the feelings of another also requires some capacity to react to an event, whether joyful or distressing, from that other's perspective. These capacities underlying empathic behavior appear to be part of our inherited endowment; they emerge during maturation in response to normal social experiences. Comparisons of twin pairs show that identical twins are more similar in their empathic feelings and behaviors than fraternal twins.[5] Scientists are piecing together neurobiological evidence and behavioral observations that may one day explain why Jane can enter into what Mary is feeling while Mary has barely a clue as to Jane's emotional state.

The word "empathy," a translation of the Greek *empatheia,* literally "feeling into," was coined by a psychologist in the first decade of the twentieth century. As we understand the word, empathy involves picturing another person's situation and having a response that causes us, at least to some degree, to experience that person's emotion. Sympathy, on the other hand, is the sorrow or concern for another's welfare which can follow from empathy. Neither empathy nor sympathy necessarily results in "prosocial behavior," the infelicitous term psychologists use to describe acts intended to benefit others. Indeed, police interrogators and practitioners of brainwashing who are good at their jobs use their capacity for empathy to form an emotional bond with their subject in order to elicit cooperation. Empathy can also cause distress to the empathizer since he shares the pain of the other person. This personal distress can in some cases lead him to turn away, or to give assistance solely to reduce his own distress. Altruistic behavior, as it is usually defined, is motivated purely by unselfish considerations. But often the mix of motives cannot be untangled.[6]

There are many documented instances of children responding empathically to the pain or discomfort of another child. Here is one from a teacher's observation of toddlers in a nursery school in 1937: "Heinrich [two years old] was on the Kiddie car. Wallis [a younger toddler] was on the bicycle nearby. Wallis fell off the bicycle, pulled it over on himself. He wriggled and struggled to get out. Heinrich left the Kiddie car, pulled the bike so that Wallis could get out. He rode off as soon as Wallis jumped up."[7] As early as fourteen months of age a child may try to comfort his mother when he sees her crying or sad, although more typically he demands to be comforted himself. He may also feel so agitated at seeing his mother cry that he hits her to make her stop. This irrationally self-centered behavior is understandable in a two-year-old. But we see a similar phenomenon in abusive parents who justify hitting their infant with the excuse "I couldn't take it anymore. She just wouldn't stop crying."

Stages of Empathy

Reciprocal behavior is necessary for conversation, for play involving another person, for performing string quartets, or indeed for almost any other social activity that comes to mind. Waiting, watching, listening, mimicking, and responding synchronously—the rhythmic activities involved in taking turns—can be observed in children in the early months of life. Even infants take turns.[8]

There are many indications of young children's biological preparedness for friendly social interactions, such as smiling and hugging, sharing food or toys, communicating fascination with an object by pointing it out to mother, feeding and caring for dolls or a dog, and helping around the house. One mother reports that her nine-month-old baby regularly crawled over to the bedside to "help" her make the bed in the morning; by eighteen months he was helping push the mop and dusting the furniture. Although the child is mimicking behavior of his caregivers or siblings, this sort of play also suggests that he has learned what will elicit pleasure and approval.

In the early weeks and months of life, rudimentary mental representations are formed as sensory information flows into the child's brain, emotional coloring is added, memories are compiled and consulted, information is analyzed and integrated, the preverbal language of empathic communication is practiced, and action plans are elaborated. Connections inside a baby's brain are being made, reinforced, and broken at a rapid pace. According to current speculation, all this activity creates a set of unique circuits that over time will cause the child to be increasingly conscious of his own emotions, able to interpret the emotions of others, and aware that his emotions affect and are affected by the emotions of others. These growing cognitive and affective abilities are neither consciously learned nor consciously remembered, but they become skills as the baby practices them in a variety of social situations. As in other types of learning, the neural connections underlying social behavior patterns are strengthened and elaborated through repeated use.

According to Martin Hoffman, who has for many years studied the development of empathy, a child passes through four developmental stages.[9] In the first stage, roughly the first year of life, the baby becomes distressed upon hearing another infant cry as "distress cues from the dimly perceived other are confounded with unpleasant feelings empathetically aroused in self." An eleven-month-old girl sees another child fall and start to cry. She herself feels an urge to cry, "but she puts her thumb in her mouth, and buries her head in her mother's lap, as she does when she herself is hurt." Her distress, though triggered by what has happened to another child, is focused on herself. Another baby will put her own fingers in her mouth upon seeing a child hurt his hand.

Between ages one and two children begin to understand that the distress of others, though it causes them distress, is not their own, although the boundaries between the self and others are still not distinct. Hoffman has described this second stage as "egocentric empathy." A toddler sometimes imitates the distress of another child, for example, falling down and whining upon observing another child who has fallen down and has burst into tears. The child who is imitating the other's distress may be creating internal cues that help him vicariously experience the other child's emotion. Children of fourteen months or older have been known to take a crying playmate to their own mother instead of their friend's mother, even though she is also present.

The encounter of Angela and José is typical of empathic behavior at stage three: Angela, twenty-nine months old, was excited when José, a younger child, came to visit, but she did not like it when he began shrieking and pounding his fists on the floor. Angela's mother put the small boy in a high chair and tried to soothe him with cookies, all of which he threw on the floor. Angela, who customarily ate other people's cookies whenever she could and was not known to share her own, picked up the cookies, put them back on the high chair tray, climbed up on the kitchen table beside José, and began to stroke his hair. Angela is clearly distressed at José's temper tantrum, but she has no doubt that his unhappiness belongs to him, and she makes several appropriate attempts to comfort him. By this age she has developed smoother-functioning capabilities for organizing, integrating, and regulating her own emotions, and she has also developed more competence in using her empathic arousal in the service of effective help.[10]

Studies indicate that children who tend to become very agitated in the presence of another child's distress are less likely to help the child, as if they are too overwhelmed by their own feelings to act on behalf of the other person.[11] As two- and three-year-olds develop increasing capacity to organize their perceptions and their relationships to others, they come to exhibit a wider range of emotions on perceiving another's distress—not just concern, but fear, surprise, sadness, withdrawal, anger, indifference, or even enjoyment.[12] (An example that will come to any parent's mind is the all too apparent pleasure a sibling may exhibit when a brother or sister is admonished.)

Between the ages of three and five, children are developing strategies for adjusting the way they feel and act in a given situation. Dale F. Hay, a child development specialist at Cambridge University, calls this "the management of empathy."[13] Preschool children begin learning how to balance self-interest with the interests of another or even of a group. They can twist the truth either to be tactful or to avoid blame. They learn the social conventions surrounding emotional display, gradually discovering the conditions under which helping or showing concern is deemed "appropriate." In these years they begin to deal with their feelings of guilt, shame, pride, and boastfulness.

"It's like taking candy from a baby." Before the age of fifteen months or so children willingly share food, toys, or whatever they have in their hand. A little later they become less willing to share. Some students of development also have found that as a toddler enters his preschool years he is less likely to help others. Hay, who has conducted observational studies in preschool classrooms, notes that children in this age group help others relatively little, compared with younger children. He proposes several reasons for this trend, speculating that by age three children have picked up cues that "prosocial actions are not always socially appropriate." A parent walking with a young child shakes his head no at a beggar holding out a cup and hurries the child along. The message is clear: you share with family and friends, not strangers.

Children's predispositions to be compassionate are subjected to all sorts of developmental, cultural, and temperamental influences. By about three years of age children have developed not only a sense of self but a sense of guilt, evidenced by their greater willingness to comfort and help another if they have caused the pain. But children this age may not readily distinguish between distress they observe and distress they have caused; they may feel responsible in both instances. On the other hand, some normal children who are responsible for inflicting pain may show less concern, more aggressive behavior toward their victim, and even obvious enjoyment of the distress they have caused.[14]

Older children are less likely to be emotionally aroused by another's distress. They are more able to make decisions on the basis of cognitive appraisal about whether to respond. For example, the appraisal might include an assessment of responsibility ("It's the teacher's job, not mine"), reciprocity ("Did she help me when I was in trouble?"), or self-interest ("Do I risk getting hurt if I help?"). By this age children have also developed a repertoire of social skills that enable them to get what they want without having to act conciliatory. They are becoming more adept both at negotiation and at manipulation. They have refined the techniques used in rivalry with brothers and sisters that stop short of (or are combined with) physical combat. Three-year-olds are more or less expert in teasing, blaming, playing one person off against another, and wheedling support from a parent. As Hay notes, they are learning how not to be good.[15]

The fourth stage in empathic development, according to Hoffman, occurs later in childhood, at about eight years, when a child is more able to make rational assessments of various situations and to make judgments based on the moral framework he is developing. The child has a greater ability to imagine the pleasure or pain of another person because of his own wider experience and greater command of language, which enables sharper mental representations and better understanding of abstract concepts. At this point a child has greater awareness of another person's general life situation, and so his empathic response is influenced by what he knows about the individual's health, successes, or disappointments. For example, a ten-year-old who sees her brother fall will feel especially concerned if she knows that he suffered an epileptic seizure a month ago. At this stage a child can also feel empathy for a group or a class, such as homeless people. Her empathic response can also be influenced by what her friend ought to be feeling, given what she knows about what is happening in her friend's life. Deborah has

learned that the mother of her friend Martha has just been seriously injured in a car accident. She sees Martha at play, laughing and singing,
happily unaware of the accident. At four years of age Deborah would
have been unable to combine what she sees with what she knows. But at
eight years Deborah does not share Martha's happiness because she is
anticipating the distress Martha will soon feel.[16]

Early Caregiving and Empathic Development

Parents' child-rearing practices influence empathic development. Psychological tests measuring empathy were given to a group of thirty-one-
year-old men and women whose families had participated twenty-six
years earlier in a study of child rearing.[17] Mothers had been interviewed
when their child was five years old about their own and their spouse's
parenting practices. The mothers were rated on such measures as
warmth, strictness, and tolerance of their child's "dependent behaviors,"
which were thought to reflect the mother's nurturance, her responsiveness, and the amount of time she spent interacting with the child; fathers were rated on their degree of involvement with their child. In
addition, their kindergarten teachers rated the children on such behaviors as activity level, ability to get along, and quarrelsomeness.

The children, now adults, were given several standard personality tests
that included measures of empathy; the adults' empathy scores were examined in the light of their parents' child-rearing practices and their
teachers' assessments.[18] The latter had no bearing on how the children
eventually turned out; playground ruffians were as likely to end up compassionate as boys and girls who were well-behaved. However, the researchers found strong relationships between certain parenting patterns
and their children's empathy as adults: Empathic adults were more likely
to have had mothers who discouraged aggression in their child, and to
have had both mothers and fathers who were highly involved with the
child and enjoyed the parental role. These researchers conclude, but-
tressing their view with findings from other studies, that empathy is fostered by a parenting style in which children are expected to be responsive

to parental requirements, and parents accept a reciprocal responsibility to be responsive to the reasonable demands of their child. The analyses indicated that the active involvement of fathers with their children was a startlingly strong factor associated with adult empathy—a sobering finding, given that in so many families today the father is absent.

What parents communicate through their own behavior and teaching influences children's empathic responses and readiness to help. A number of studies indicate that parents who were affectionate and sympathetic, those who explained clearly and emphatically the importance of kindness and regard for the rights of others, and those who tried to inhibit their children's aggressive behavior were more likely to raise children who were concerned and helpful. As one would expect, abusive parents produced children who had troubled peer relationships. Abused children were less likely to aid a distressed child, and were more likely to become aggressive or to withdraw.[19]

Cultural Influence and Empathic Development

"There is no such thing as a baby." This provocative proclamation by the influential British psychiatrist D. W. Winnicott was meant to make the point that no human being, young or old, can be understood in isolation from his or her social environment. From birth every person is enmeshed in and formed by a web of emotional connections that is continually reshaped and reorganized. How empathy develops in a child is influenced not only by his interaction with caregivers but also by the culture in which his family is embedded. The interactions of parent and child, as the child development specialist Arnold J. Sameroff puts it, "are a blend of social and biological codes." For intuitive parental behaviors, such as baby talk and picking up a baby when he cries, the biological dimension is dominant, while practices and beliefs about toilet training, feeding, and desirable behavior in social situations are more culturally conditioned. As the child gets older, social and cultural influences widen to include neighborhood, school, church, and playmates.[20]

The way parents and others treat children depends greatly on the prevailing cultural attitudes about who children are. Consider all that flows from two radically different metaphorical renderings of child rearing. Plato compares the process of instilling virtue in a child to bending a piece of warped wood. Winnicott conceives of a baby as nothing but the sum of a complex of human interactions. Each of these exercises in pedagogical hyperbole is based on a very different unspoken premise. The Platonic prescription assumes that parents and teachers know how to bend children without breaking them; Winnicott's insight fails to do justice to the stubborn stuff within every child who comes into the world. Both metaphors capture cultural attitudes that are still influential. As a child grows up, he incorporates prescriptions about personal behavior derived from his people's history, customs, and religion. For example, in some societies hospitality to a stranger is a sacred obligation, and this belief influences even young children's interaction with guests.[21]

The views of human nature that parents pick up from their culture help to shape their child's empathic development. It makes a difference whether parents believe that human beings are basically self-centered or are naturally disposed to share the feelings of others and to help people in trouble or in pain. Long philosophical traditions across many cultures support both beliefs. In the fourth century B.C., the Chinese philosopher Mencius pronounced it to be "a feeling common to all mankind that they cannot bear to see others suffer." Similarly, in 1909 the American sociologist Charles Horton Cooley, rejecting the prevailing presumption in philosophy and in the social sciences that human nature is inherently selfish, declared that the "improvement of society does not call for any essential change in human nature, but, chiefly, for a larger and higher application of its familiar impulses."[22]

However, from ancient times other philosophers and theologians have argued that egotism and selfishness play such a dominant role in the development of human character that they usually overwhelm whatever altruistic impulses we may have been born with or are socialized to develop. Over the centuries something closer to Jeremiah's view that "the heart is deceitful above all things, and desperately wicked" has been the more influential assessment of human nature in the Judeo-Christian West.[23] In the twentieth century both Darwinian theorists and free-market economists have emphasized the positive consequences of innate selfishness; in the ceaseless struggle that defines existence, only the selfish are fit and only the fittest survive. When this view is taken to its extreme, even an apparently altruistic act is seen as driven by a desire for prestige, approbation, power, or a return favor.

But Darwin himself, in *The Descent of Man,* took the view that our species is endowed with an "instinct of sympathy," a developed form of the "social instincts" that constitute adaptive behavior in many animal species. The biological basis for empathy may have emerged in human beings as an adaptive counterweight to aggressive impulses.[24] Had there not been selection for empathy, it is unlikely that the complex living arrangements human beings have devised and depend on would have survived the catastrophes, wars, and social disorganization that have accompanied the human journey.

There is a plausible scenario of natural selection for empathy in humans. Child mortality over evolutionary time has been extremely high. During most of human history, demographers believe, women gave birth to many babies but more than half the children died before reaching reproductive age. Given limited physical resources and a shortage of time and energy for child care, it is likely that mothers would have invested more in babies who were physically robust and temperamentally predisposed to establish close emotional connections with their caregivers. These appealing babies—"cute babies," we call them—would have elicited preferential treatment, which would have made their survival more likely. By the same token, the mothers who were in touch with the emotional signals of their children would also have reached out most effectively. These more sensitive mothers would have been more likely to bring their children through the rigors of childhood. The surviving children would likely inherit and in turn pass on the predisposition for empathy.

It is not surprising that in what is probably the most violent century in recorded history, the twentieth, altruism has not been widely seen as an influential factor in human behavior. Capitalist ideology, now embraced around the world, is based on the assumption that the self-promoting behavior of millions of people, each pursuing his or her own interests, fuels the engines of economic and social progress and preserves individual freedom. Popular contemporary elaborations of evolutionary theory celebrate the "selfish gene" aggressively promoting its own survival.[25]

Yet without selfless behavior the human race likely would not have survived. The utter dependence of children on someone else to take care of them during their long period of development—often including many caretakers who do not share the infant's genes—demands extraordinary sacrifices of other people's time, energy, interests, and pleasures. Jumping into an icy river to save a stranger who is drowning offers no obvious genetic advantage, although selfless acts such as these are often explained away by invoking the notion of reciprocal altruism (I help you this time; you help me next time). But every day people act courageously to rescue others or show kindness to strangers, and they consider this to be normal human behavior.

In 1985 an earthquake wreaked havoc in Mexico City, killing and injuring many thousands and leaving parts of the damaged city without essential services for many weeks. At the time, our daughter Julie was living in a part of the city that was hit hard. Together with sheer gratitude at being alive, her most profound impression was of the extraordinary behavior of a gang of teenagers who had long been causing trouble in her working-class neighborhood because of their drunkenness, brawling, and thievery. But when the disaster struck, they became local heroes, pulling victims from the wreckage and helping to build shelters. At great personal risk they unearthed deeply buried water mains and organized a bucket brigade to bring water up out of the ground. These young social outcasts were able in this extreme situation to engage in selfless high-risk activities and were applauded for it by the community.

A few thousand people hid Jews from the Gestapo in Nazi-occupied Europe at great personal risk for no apparent reason other then their compassion and humanity. In a study of Gentiles who risked their lives to save Jews during World War II, the rescuers were found to have come from families and communities in which unselfish behavior was taught, modeled, and expected. At the same time, like the Mexican adolescents, the rescuers tended to be risk takers and nonconformists.[26]

Every society is faced with conflicts between individual self-interest and community interests. As individuals are socialized, they learn by example, by intuition, or by intimidation that there are advantages in treating other people well—at least certain other people. Their primary concern may remain their own survival and welfare, but even as children they come to see the various ways in which these are entwined with the welfare of the family and the surrounding community. In his

Theory of Moral Sentiments, Adam Smith, perhaps the most influential celebrator of selfish behavior as the driving force behind wealth and progress, wrote that the capacity to experience the pleasure and pain of others is part of human nature. Human beings are incapable of being totally selfish because we cannot help sharing the feelings of others. Moreover, despite the pain, guilt, and ambivalence it may cause, people welcome emotional connection that draws them into the lives of others because the alternative—a life of personal isolation, loneliness, and fear of one's neighbor—is far worse.

Our innate capacity for empathy gives rise to the assumption that other people think and feel much as we do. This unconscious theory of mind which, seemingly, most people share, makes it possible to believe that others can make a fair assessment of our behavior. In discussing the basis of moral standards, the Harvard sociologist Christopher Jencks builds on this point: "We therefore develop standards of what others 'ought' to think about our conduct. To do this, we try to see our behavior objectively, that is, as others would see it. This means trying to evaluate our behavior from a perspective in which our selfish interests count no more than the interests of others. These moral standards are, in principle, independent of any particular individual's judgment."[27]

The same capacity that allows us to revel in another's happiness also enables us to imagine the pain of another human being, offering a choice whether to try to alleviate it—or, indeed, to cause it. The choice to help someone else is characteristic of our species, and it happens every day. But so does the intentional infliction of pain.

The Neural Basis of Empathy

Under experimental conditions a rhesus monkey is taught that a sound will be followed by an electric shock. Then it discovers that it can abort the shock by pushing a lever right after the warning signal. The monkey is then shown another monkey in a distant room on a closed-circuit TV (without audio). This monkey has also learned to associate the warning sound with a shock, but has not been given the means of avoiding it. The first monkey pushes the lever to abort the shock the distant monkey is about to receive. The first monkey has not heard the signal and has no reason to believe that it is in any danger itself. How does it know a shock to the other animal is imminent? It picks up the distressed look on the face of the other monkey.[28]

Leslie Brothers is a psychiatrist who is interested in how the brain decodes complex social signals. She has studied the neurophysiology of responses to various facial expressions in animals. In her experiments, small recording devices were inserted at several locations in monkeys' brains, including the temporal lobes and the amygdala, the control center for emotions we discussed in the preceding chapter. The animals were then shown a variety of videotapes or pictures of monkeys engaging in various natural social activities. The pictured behaviors, and the facial expressions that were part of the behaviors, caused specific nerve cells in different parts of the observer monkeys' brains to fire. The resulting electrical responses were picked up by the recording electrodes. (The experimenters could tell what the observer monkeys were looking at by monitoring the direction of their gaze and their eye movements.)

Specialized neurons in the observer monkeys' visual cortex fired only in response to their seeing specific facial expressions or gestures; the experiments showed that the observer monkeys' neurons had distinct preferences in faces, responding strongly to some and weakly to others. Some brain cells responded more to eyes, others to the mouth or hair. Still other cells responded to facial expressions rather than features or were sensitive to facial positions, registering whether the face was looking in the observer monkey's direction or looking away. Certain cells responded vigorously to pictures of threatening expressions, others to a view of an animal in a crouching posture. These socially sensitive neurons were mostly located in the superior temporal area and amygdala.[29]

Brothers and John Allman, a neurobiologist at the California Institute of Technology, comment in the journal *Nature* on two human patients, D.R. and S.M., who have lesions in the amygdala and, as a consequence, cannot correctly read other people's facial expressions. (D.R., the reader may recall, is mentioned in another context in chapter 6.) According to Brothers and Allman, there is "growing evidence that the amygdala has a central role in social communication." But they note that patients with brain abnormalities in other locations or with other imperfectly understood brain abnormalities, such as autism, also have deficiencies in "social cognition." Autistic people are unable to make normal emotional contact with others even though no damage to the amygdala is evident. They are also inattentive to facial expression, and they fail to interpret correctly where another person is directing his gaze. Patients in a paranoid delusional state wildly misinterpret social signals, but they also have no clear-cut amygdalar damage.[30]

Some investigators postulate a neural system that includes the amygdala, the temporal poles, and the orbitofrontal cortex as the underpinnings of social ties (see fig. 6-1, p. 146). It has long been known that damage in any of several temporal, frontal, and limbic regions can cause abnormalities in the ability to make social connections. The impairment may be quite delimited. Damage in the right temporoparietal lobe can leave patients unable to verbalize their own feelings. Or, they may be incapable of judging—from the sound of someone's voice or the look on someone's face—what he or she is feeling. A different right-hemisphere impairment renders patients unable to express their emotions either in appropriate body language or with voice intonation, even though they are capable of feeling the emotions. Although it is known that the regions of the cortex affected by these disorders are closely connected to the limbic system, particularly the amygdala, neither the anatomy nor the physiology underlying these problems is fully understood. Brothers believes that the evidence points to the existence of specific nerve cell assemblies and circuits for the social cognitions on which empathic responses depend. But as yet no neural system or neurotransmitter for empathy has been identified.[31]

Biological Preparedness, Shared Feelings, and Moral Codes

Empathy does not necessarily lead to altruism. Nor is an empathic person necessarily a moral person. People seem predisposed to show empathy toward people who look more or less the same as they do, come from the same backgrounds and economic and social circumstances, and act in similar ways. An individual's personal code for treating family members, coreligionists, and fellow citizens does not necessarily apply to infidels or foreigners. As Martin Hoffman puts it, "The bloody ethnic conflicts of our time demonstrate that people who have strong empathic feelings towards members of their own group may show intense hostility to some other group."[32]

Despite the rapid pace of globalization and the dramatic rise in international travel and communication, the capacity to empathize with others of different races, cultures, and beliefs remains limited. This is a problem given our present reality, which is forcing new relationships across the world. In our dynamic, unsettled historical moment new forms of collaboration and conflict across cultural, racial, and geographical boundaries are emerging that require a redefinition of the meaning of self-interest. One can only hope that the capacities of the human brain will permit successful adaptation to the new conditions under which humans must live.

Though its presence does not insure moral behavior, emotional sensitivity is a foundation stone on which moral codes are built. Children begin to learn notions of right and wrong from their parents very early in life. By age three, according to Robert Emde, "the child's self is a moral self," thanks primarily to the relationship with her parents. Before the infant develops the capacity for reflective self-awareness or moral judgment—indeed, even before she has any idea of what a "rule" is—she is beginning to internalize rules of behavior that are "acquired piecemeal through day-to-day interactions with caregivers." She is unaware that this interchange of social signals is already shaping her moral behavior. But Emde argues that the capacity of very young infants for reciprocal behaviors is a forerunner of morality, since all moral systems have at their center some version of the Golden Rule: Do unto others as you would have them do unto you.[33]

Until the eighteenth century most philosophers and theologians in the Judeo-Christian tradition insisted that to act morally one must listen to reason and keep a firm rein on passion. Knowledge of the difference between good and evil was easily accessible to anyone who believed the Bible and the universal moral principles derived from natural law. But by the eighteenth century David Hume, reflecting the growing desire for individual self-expression and personal freedom in his time, argued for a subjective definition of morality. Whatever made one feel good *was* good, and whatever produced unpleasant feelings was by definition bad.[34]

There are problems with both natural-law definitions of moral behavior and a moral code based on an individual's emotions. In a world of great cultural diversity, that which is held to be good in one society or among one group or class may be held to be bad in another. Even in recent times murder, torture, and slavery have been held to be moral under some codes. Deciding who is to be included in the moral universe is, as already suggested, a first-order problem. To equate morality with the prevailing norms taught by parents and educators is a tempting simplification, but it does not tell us how to act morally in an immoral society. One need only recall Hitler's educational program to indoctrinate German youth in racial hatred and blind loyalty to a genocidal leader. Clearly, socially prescribed rules and morality are not necessarily the same.

It is equally true that one's own feelings at the moment of decision are not necessarily reliable signals on which to base moral behavior. In totalitarian societies, well-indoctrinated children who informed on their parents were socialized to feel proud and patriotic. In our own society, acting on the impulse to harm, to exploit, or to steal from another can, depending on one's character and emotional maturity, make a person feel better than to resist the impulse.

Empathy is only part of the scaffolding on which moral behavior develops. Moral decisions involve evaluation and judgment. Indeed, for most of this century the cognitive dimensions of morality have elicited more interest from theorists than have the emotional underpinnings. In *The Moral Judgment of the Child,* the Swiss psychologist Jean Piaget, who spent many hours playing marbles and other games with boys and girls, developed an influential theory of moral judgment that details the stages by which children learn fairness, as evidenced by what he called the jurisprudence of marbles. He concluded that only by age seven or eight did children begin to understand rules.[35] Like Freud, he believed that infants and toddlers were too self-absorbed and dependent to be capable of either empathy or moral judgment. But numerous observational studies over the last two decades confirm that moral development begins well before a child enters elementary school. Children as young as three show by their behavior that they are using both conventional standards (reliance on the authority of parents and customs they have learned) and principled standards for distinguishing right from wrong.

Lawrence Kohlberg, building on Piaget's work, developed a theory of how moral reasoning evolves in stages. At first, morality is based on what feels right, next on what conforms to parental expectations and the teachings of other authority figures; finally, moral growth culminates in the comprehension and acceptance of "objective principles" of morality. The child comes to apprehend that "what is correct and virtuous is defined in terms of universalizable standards" such as justice, natural rights, and respect for all persons.[36]

These cognitive theories are controversial. There is disagreement about how and when children learn moral principles and whether, in a multicultural world, there are such things as universalizable standards. There is disagreement about when and how, and indeed whether, children make distinctions between conventions—customary practices in their culture such as eating or not eating pork or beef, or proper ways to address their parents and teachers—and universal standards: harmful actions such as pulling another child's hair or hitting a baby are wrong; sharing resources such as food and toys is right; destroying someone else's property is wrong.

Some psychologists start with the assumption that humans are born with "a biologically-based preparedness" to understand and to adopt standards.[37] Like linguistic competence, which is naturally attained as a child matures in a normal environment, moral competence—that is, sensitivity to right and wrong—develops as the relevant cognitive abilities mature. By the second year of life a toddler has developed enough to have an internal image of a prototype. He feels disquieted, even upset, if a familiar object is not where it should be or if something about it looks wrong. This ability to evaluate objects and behavior against a standard is evidence that he can reflect on the meaning of what he experiences.[38]

Between ages two and three, the child is internalizing everyday rules about what to do, when to do it, and how to please. He takes pleasure in "getting it right." He scans the room, looking to adults for signals that he is doing the right thing, being a good boy. Depending on what messages he picks up, he feels pride or shame. Sometimes, children are tougher judges of their performance than their parents are. When she was four years old, our daughter Julie, effusively praised for a painting she had done, looked at it coolly and said, "Well, yes, it's very good for four." As self-evaluation develops, the child describes acts as good or bad, and by the third year a child may call himself "bad." Aggressive boys, especially, often judge themselves severely, indicating their low self-evaluation either by stating outright how little they like themselves or by demanding repeated declarations of parental love.

Cross-cultural studies indicate that children everywhere, even in their second year of life, show signs of awareness when something does not appear right. Young children in the United States, India, Mexico, and in other cultures where this research has been carried out exhibit the same sort of uncertainty or discomfort upon encountering an object, a doll for example, that is broken or dirty, and they manifest the same chagrin over failing a self-imposed task such as building a tower out of blocks. Since parents around the world do not train their children on the same schedule or in the same ways, these strikingly similar reactions suggest that all children do indeed have some predisposition for evaluation. Small children in all cultures, including those belonging to isolated tribes only recently encountered by Western explorers, exhibit the same spontaneous facial expression—a look of disgust or apprehension—on being presented with an object that is missing a part or is dirty or defaced.

Why do children around thirty months old begin to notice cracked toys, headless or defaced dolls, and torn clothing, while nineteen-month-old infants brought into the same laboratory playroom will take no notice? One hypothesis is that by the later stage of development the child better understands her parents' emotional signals indicating that something is wrong. The parent looks displeased, or says she is displeased, or may even have swatted the child or her siblings for breaking toys or dirtying her clothing. Gradually, a standard emerges that is based largely on avoiding unpleasant parental reactions.

But there is evidence that young children can form a mental representation of what is correct, harmonious, and fitting, and that this awareness is independent of parental admonition or correction. In one experiment, two-year-olds in the United States and in a Mayan village in Yucatán exhibited the same heightened interest in a distorted human face, scrutinizing it longer than they did a normal face. Some became anxious, indicating by word or gesture that they feared that the squashed nose had been hit. When our twenty-month-old grandson, Julian, climbed on hands and knees up the wooden staircase in our old house in Vermont, he always paused at one stair that had a quarter-sized knothole in it. Sometimes he would put his eye to the dark hole. Something bothered him. Stairs are not supposed to have holes in them.

In the third year of life, Kagan notes, a child will show concern by pointing to an object or saying "Fix," but only if the deviation from the normal appears to have been caused by some event the child evaluates as bad. Two-year-olds can understand and use evaluative language. Coloring the sofa with a crayon and kicking the dog are bad. Catching the ball and picking up toys are good. This sense of the fitting may help explain why a boy barely two is careful to speak Estonian at home and English at the day care center without being taught either language or being corrected for speaking the wrong language in either place.[39] But a two- or three-year-old's evaluations may be severely limited by cognitive immaturity, lack of experience, and egocentricity. A child this age can blame himself for today's flooded basement because last week he was chided for turning the faucet on. Almost all children blame themselves if their parents divorce.

Moral Judgment

Two-year-olds show signs of having internalized parental rules. As they learn the moral code of their culture, "Do it because I say so" becomes "Do it because it is the right thing to do." However, parents' signals are often ambiguous or inconsistent. The parent waits to see what happens, and may even show some pleasure at the motor skills and adventurous spirit the child is exhibiting. But before long the parent is expressing mild disapproval, and then suddenly uttering a firm, loud "No" just as the little hand is about to knock over the vase. The child is developing and testing what Robert Emde calls "strategies of negotiation" through emotional communication. In the course of this early playful learning, both parent and child adjust their expectations, and the child expands his understanding both of the rules and of the different ways they can be interpreted. What mother, father, or older brother permits in a given situation is not necessarily the same; the child tests the waters, learning just how far he can go with each of them. On the other hand, chronically unpredictable parental reactions to a child's transgressions can lead to moral confusion and behavior problems.

By the age of thirty-six months, children show that they have a conscious awareness of dos and don'ts. They can talk about moral dilemmas, wrestle for solutions, and think about alternative outcomes. Three-year-olds can grasp the idea that moral principles may bump up against one another. Jane knows that the bathroom shelf is off limits, but a playmate has skinned her knee. A Band-Aid will make it feel better. Should she get it? At this stage, while she grapples with the answer, Jane feels the presence of her mother even though she is nowhere to be seen.[40]

There is considerable experimental evidence that after thirty-six months of age children begin to grasp the distinction between conventional and moral standards. In many households, lapses in table manners or faulty dress are one thing, lying or hitting quite another. A child of this age growing up in the United States is likely to label only the latter as "bad" and to feel a stronger and more unpleasant emotional reaction—shame, guilt, or both. For children older than three, modeling adult behavior still plays an important role, but relationships with other children become increasingly important in developing feelings of "moral reciprocity, kindness, cooperation, and justice."[41]

Honesty in word and deed appears near the top of most short lists of "universal" virtues: "The truth will make you free." "To thine own self be true." "Honesty is the best policy." As a general rule children are taught by parents that lying is "bad." But what exactly constitutes a lie is culturally conditioned. Parents often give an absolutist verbal message about the importance of telling the truth, and then dilute it by what they say and do. Instruction in courtesy, kindness, and social graces further shapes a child's understanding that not all lies are forbidden. In Japan, Kagan reports, children are taught that it all depends on whom you lie to and why. It is considered ethical to camouflage the truth or skirt it entirely "to maintain social harmony," provided one is not lying to "a member of one's inner group."[42]

Throughout history, understandings of moral rectitude and enforcement of moral codes have shifted with changes in social situations. The obligations of one individual to another were prescribed in feudal society, and even fifty years ago in extended families and in small-town America they were clearer than they are today. Fewer children now are taught that God is watching them, and fewer experience the informal oversight of neighborhood adults. Family values are still widely celebrated, but there is increasing confusion and controversy about what a family is, what role it is supposed to play in our lives, and what obligations it involves.

Moral behavior depends upon a capacity for making moral judgments, and these require both an ability to weigh the relative values inherent in alternative choices and some appreciation of standards of conduct. Neuroscientists are beginning to identify specific brain areas which, if damaged, impair moral judgment. In his book *Descartes' Error,* the neurologist Antonio Damasio describes his patient Elliot, who had had a large tumor removed that was pushing up against the frontal lobes.[43] The excision of the tumor necessitated removing some frontal lobe tissue that had been injured by the growth. A relatively small amount of brain tissue was lost, but it happened to include critical neural structures for social decision-making.

Prior to his illness Elliot had been an intelligent, well-informed man, a good husband and father, and a fine employee with a good job. After the operation Elliot could still converse intelligently and perform creditably on IQ tests. His memory was excellent, and his answers to test questions such as "If you needed cash, would you steal it if there were absolutely no chance of ever being discovered?" showed that he understood ethical principles and dilemmas. But in real life he had lots of trouble. He could not keep a job, because he was unable to set personal priorities, make decisions, choose among options, or stick to a task in order to arrive at some rational goal he had set himself (even one as simple as getting out of bed in the morning at a set time). His personality was radically altered. He was emotionally neutral and detached, never getting excited or upset about anything. He could not comprehend, much less meet, the standards of conduct that had previously guided his life.

Damasio thinks that the absence of emotion in Elliot's reasoning prevents him from weighing the moral significance of various options. Brain imaging studies done on Elliot revealed damage to the right frontal cortex and, to a much lesser extent, the left frontal cortex, as well as destruction of the white matter underlying the right frontal cortex. (The white matter is made up of myelinated nerve fibers that normally connect separate brain areas.) Because of the lost connections, a large part of Elliot's frontal brain no longer functioned.

Damasio has compared two groups of patients with prefrontal brain damage. One group acts like Elliot; their brain lesions are quite similar to his. Like Elliot, they have impaired capacity to make rational choices in personal matters and moral judgments in social situations, although they operate quite well in the impersonal world of abstract thought, language,

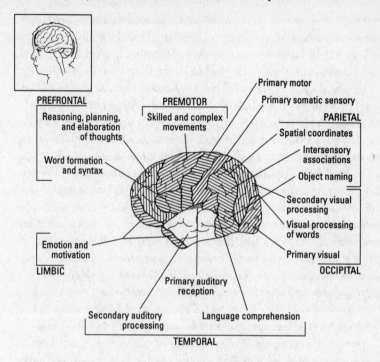

FIGURE 7-1. ASSOCIATION AREAS OF THE CORTEX HAVE DIFFERING BUT COORDINATED FUNCTIONS.

Prefrontal cortex: Reasoning, planning, elaboration of thoughts, syntax, and speech

Temporal cortex: Secondary auditory processing, auditory association, language comprehension

Limbic cortex: Emotion, motivation

Occipital cortex: Secondary visual processing, visual association, visual processing of words

Parietal cortex: Processing of the body's spatial coordinates, intersensory association, visual recognition and naming

Premotor cortex: Plans for skilled, complex, and coordinated movements

Those cortical locations which initially receive sensory information from subcortical pathways are labeled primary auditory, visual, and somatic sensory areas. The primary motor cortex, which initiates voluntary motor control, is also indicated.

Identification of functions specific to each area should not be taken too literally. Mental tasks are carried out through numerous interconnected systems working in concert. Demarcations of the various regions differ somewhat from person to person.

and logic. The second group of patients, with lesions that do not involve these brain locations, continue to be as morally and socially responsible as before their brain damage. But they show other impairments in intellect, language, or memory, depending on the location of their lesions.[44]

In recent decades, research has established that the prefrontal area (the region immediately behind the forehead) plays a critical role in the organization of the complex cognitive processes needed for moral judgment. Anatomical mapping studies done in brains of nonhuman primates, studies of brain-injured patients, and functional imaging studies using PET and fMRI have revealed functional connections of the prefrontal cortex with many other cortical regions important in higher-level information processing. These studies also reveal links between the prefrontal cortex and other brain regions important for emotions and memory, such as the amygdala, hippocampus, and hypothalamus. But no connections have been found between the prefrontal cortex and brain areas in which sensory information is initially received, such as the primary auditory and visual cortex. Instead, information arrives in the prefrontal cortex only *after* being highly processed and integrated—that is, combined with other information that gives meaning to sensory data.

The prefrontal cortex is an organizer of experience, a regulator of various processing systems that control memory, attention, and other higher brain functions. It is also the only place in the neocortex where information processed in limbic circuits is integrated. Some neuroscientists maintain that, indeed, it is the unique site in the brain for the interplay between intellect and feelings.

How Conscience Develops

The inner voice we call conscience reminds us of the difference between right and wrong and encourages or inhibits morally relevant behavior. No one has located it in the brain or described how it functions by monitoring physiological responses. Yet everyone hears the whisperings of conscience—even, we think, at some point in his young life, the thirteen-year-old mugger we described at the beginning of the chapter. Where do these promptings come from? What makes us listen?

By the time a child is ready for school, her interactions with her caregivers have provided her with a life-shaping moral education of one sort or another. Humans are born with intimations of life's spiritual dimension and a deep yearning for meaning. Some scholars conclude that no human society without religious beliefs has ever existed. Parents, whether they are devout or secular, are the earliest transmitters of spiritual values; their moral code and conduct are the most important influences on the child's development of moral understanding and behavior. But moral education is also a lifelong process. Our inner authority figures speak to us at various moments through poetry, philosophy, or religious teachings. We hear echoes of the advice of friends and mentors and live with the memories of the examples they set. But traditional religious belief—"Train up a child in the way he should go: and when he is old, he will not depart from it"—and twentieth-century psychiatric theory both assume that early interaction with primary caregivers is the most powerful force in shaping a child's moral consciousness.

Conscience is used to describe the process by which external standards become part of a child's own character. When this happens, a child will regulate his own behavior even when parents are not present, refraining from acts likely to evoke parental disapproval. In one experiment, for example, young children were tempted by a talking puppet to play with toys their parents had said should not be touched. Even though no adult was in the room, a number of the children told the puppet in almost the same words: "Didn't you hear my mommy? We better not play with those toys."[45]

At around two and a half, children begin to take intentions into account, but imperfectly. While a younger child will assume that breaking a dozen of Mom's best china cups is more serious than breaking one of them, an older child will also judge the seriousness of a transgression by whether it was committed "by accident" or "on purpose."[46]

Parental messages that convey displeasure are needed for the development of conscience. On the other hand, children who are especially quick to pick up the angry or aggressive content in adult words, body language, and behavior are also prone to be angry and aggressive themselves, and these children have difficulty internalizing moral codes. A child's own anger or lack of inhibition can stunt the growth of conscience. In one study, children with significant conduct disorders and little evidence of conscience were found to be exceptionally free of fear and anxiety. When confronted with a fear-arousing situation, these children did not respond with increased heart rate, higher skin conductance, and other normal indicators of autonomic arousal.[47]

Psychologists are guided in understanding how a child internalizes moral standards and precepts by following the behavioral development of young children and their interactions with their parents. Grazyna Kochanska and her collaborators at the University of Iowa studied the disciplinary styles of a group of mothers. They found that five-year-old children of "authoritative" mothers had fewer behavior problems and were more likely to obey rules than the children of "authoritarian" mothers. Authoritative mothers influence a child's behavior by giving clear instructions in how to behave, how to share with others, and how to help with chores. They communicate their high expectations and emphasize positive instructions rather than prohibitions. Authoritarian mothers, on the other hand, are more controlling, reactive, and negative in interacting with their children. It appears that a child's ability to regulate his own behavior develops more smoothly provided the parents' child-rearing style emphasizes moral appeals or reasoning rather than expressions of power. In the longitudinal study on the family origins of empathic concern we discussed earlier in this chapter, the distinction between authoritarian and authoritative parenting styles was also seen as predictive. Empathic adults were more likely to have experienced the more positive "authoritative" parenting.[48]

In the last twenty years, with rising interest in genetic explanations for behavior, researchers have been trying to understand how inborn traits affect the development of conscience. Temperamental differences among children—degrees of anxiety and shyness; high or low thresholds of arousal of angry or empathic feelings—influence how a child deals with moral messages. If the parental injunction arouses too little emotional response, the child may simply ignore it. If the message arouses too much of a response, the memory may call to mind not the behavior that prompted the message so much as the menacing parental figure who spoiled his day. Kochanska found that the more a child focuses on the negative feelings he experiences because of parental anger and parental power, the fear or shame at being caught, the punishment and threats of future punishment, the less likely he is to internalize the message, even though he may comply. When the parent asserts moral standards in ways that elicit a moderate level of arousal, the content will become dissociated in memory from its context—that is, it will be internalized as the child's own moral guide.

Fearful children experience high internal discomfort and are sensitive even to slight cues of parental displeasure. In one of her experiments Kochanska studied the strength of conscience in seven- to nine-year-old children who had been observed as toddlers. She found that fearfulness in a toddler did not by itself predict strength of conscience. But fearful toddlers whose parents deemphasized the use of power in their rearing of the child were found to have strong consciences when they reached school age.[49]

Parents employ many different strategies to gain compliance, from physical control and punishment to more subtle anxiety-producing threats, such as withdrawal, a hurt or disgusted look, or some other indication that the child's behavior may be taxing the relationship. Cautionary tales, fables, and religious instruction are often used to deliver moral messages. Their effects may depend on how well-attuned the parent is to the child's individual temperament and how much insight the caregiver has into his or her own feelings and motives. Needless to say, every child has to deal with the disparities between what her role models preach and what they practice.

Shaming is a widely used means of inculcating social values and teaching civilizing skills. It plays an important role in the development of conscience. But shame is an especially painful emotion. It is experienced as an attack on the self and is often accompanied by a wish to shrink, hide, disappear, or even die.[50] Charles Darwin noted that a child does not exhibit shame (and such related emotions as shyness, embarrassment, and guilt) until he develops a certain level of self-consciousness. These emotions come with a telltale clue: blushing. According to Darwin, our faces redden because we have done (or left undone) something that makes us anxious about our reputation. We blush, he wrote, when we are "thinking about others, thinking of us."[51]

The degree to which shame is used to socialize children varies widely across the world. Many societies, in Asia particularly, use shaming as the primary strategy for inculcating moral values. In Puritan New England, offenders were put in the stocks, objects of derision for all who passed by. In the early decades of this century schoolchildren who misbehaved were put in the corner wearing a dunce cap. Late-twentieth-century America scarcely qualifies as a shame culture, but as everywhere, American parents and teachers shame and humiliate children at times. Some child psychiatrists, believing that the risk of repeated shaming is that the child will learn to inhibit not just proscribed behavior but his own feelings of happiness and self-confidence, think that shaming should never be deliberately employed. Parents shame their children quite enough without intending to do so.[52]

For a child who is developing standards by which to live, internalizing the judgments of those he loves can be a painful process. Consider the following exchange: A little girl is exultant, having just captured a toad in the grass. Eager to share her pleasure, she brings it to her mother, but instead her mother shrieks in disgust. The child suddenly realizes that her own judgment is off the mark. Her pride is deflated by the unexpected contrast between her mother's sense of the moment and her own, and the dissonance will remain in her memory. It is quite likely that her brother at the same age would have been treated differently, since boys are usually given more latitude to be exploratory and adventurous and to get their hands dirty. Cumulative differences in experiences of this sort are instrumental in shaping gender differences, not only in behavior but in standards for judging behavior.

Chapter Eight

CHILDREN'S ANGER AND ADULT VIOLENCE

We will discuss research on the emergence of anger in children and how parents help children regulate their angry feelings and aggressive impulses. We also focus on children who are unable to take this crucial developmental step, and who start on the road to delinquency and crime. Because the high level of violence in the United States is such a major problem, the causes of criminal behavior are the subject of much study. A substantial body of research indicates that a combination of adverse social and economic factors such as extreme poverty, abusive or neglectful parents, and living in a violent environment, along with personal vulnerabilities such as impulsivity and attention deficit disorder, puts a child at risk for delinquency. We will look at some of the research on the causes of aggressive behavior and on the efficacy of crime prevention programs.

Angry Babies

Unmistakable signs of anger usually appear in an infant between four and six months of age.[1] Before this time, when a baby undergoes an unpleasant experience—an inoculation, for example—her facial expression may be, first, one of surprise, then one of distress. She squirms and begins to cry. Her heart rate and level of cortisol, a stress hormone, usually rise.[2] By the time she's around a year old, her anger has become more than a way of energizing behavior in the face of pain or frustration. It is now directed at the person the baby holds responsible: the physician, or even her mother who is standing by. At home, she now looks indignantly at her brother when he forcibly pulls the teething biscuit from her mouth.

When her mother leaves the room, a year-old baby might look sad, but she might also mount what John Bowlby calls a "bitter separation protest."[3] In chapter 5 we talked about the response of young children to lengthy separations from a parent in strange surroundings such as those of a hospital or orphanage. Under these conditions, and depending on individual susceptibilities, children become withdrawn and depressed after a time of angry protest. Observers can begin to see links between pain, fear, anger, sadness, and depression even in infants.

A frustrated two-year-old can fly into a rage; neither his own immature capacity for emotional self-regulation nor his caregiver's interventions keep him from spinning out of control. Fortunately, babies usually do not sustain a highly excited state for long. A two-year-old's tantrum is said to last on average less than 4.7 minutes, and when it's over, it's over. He does not as yet bear a grudge. There are, however, perfectly normal two-year-olds who can kick and scream for an hour, and of course these are the episodes parents remember.[4]

As brain systems mature and the infant's store of experience grows, primitive emotions undergo a staged process of reorganization. The frontal areas of the cortex, where capacities for judgment and choice reside, come to exert inhibitory control over the limbic system, and increasingly nuanced anger develops out of the more undifferentiated emotional state observable earlier. Over time, as his capacity for representational thought and imagination develop, a child begins to attach meanings and memories to experience, and his anger is kindled and shaped by his interpretations of what is happening to him. His increasing power over words affects the ways he experiences anger and how he expresses it; earlier experiences with frustration, anger, and sadness influence the appraisal and expression of subsequent experiences. Cumulative experiences interacting with temperamental factors cause him to develop a characteristic style of response.[5]

In 1931, Florence Goodenough reported on her observations of small children's anger.[6] At home, 40 percent of angry outbursts occurred as objections to such routines as being dressed, having face and hands washed, and being coaxed to eat or confined in the high chair at mealtimes. Another 40 percent occurred because of frustrations during play. Siblings provide ample occasion for anger, and for practice in the regulation of anger. Joey at two, frantic at seeing his mother nursing his new baby sister, tries to insert himself between them, and when he fails, he strikes out wildly. Although his mother tries to soothe him, Joey soon gets carted off by his father. Parents see unmodulated anger in a child as unpleasant or even dangerous, and their efforts to suppress or socialize its display begin early. Joey is getting the message that he must find a way to express his frustration in a socially acceptable way. A few weeks later he is willing to curl up close to his mother and suck on a bottle as his mother reads him a story while his sister nurses. He is not quite resigned. Sometimes he looks sad or angry, and occasionally he pulls his mother's hair or pinches her, even though he knows such behavior will not be tolerated.

Parents are likely to deal with their toddler's anger by employing such strategies as coaxing, diversion, affectionate tolerance, ignoring, or gentle physical restraint to help them deal with their feelings. But as children grow older, mothers and fathers become less permissive. Differences in responses to girls' and boys' anger emerge, at least in middle-class homes in the United States. Parents are more likely to ignore a girl's anger or tell her to stop; boys are more likely to receive attention. They are cajoled, threatened, isolated, or spanked.[7]

There are sizable differences in how anger is regarded and dealt with from family to family, and, within the same family, from child to child. In some homes where anger is pervasive, family members yell and hit. In other homes overt expressions of anger are not tolerated, and a mother might respond to a child's provocation with a stony glare, or she might act sad, disappointed, or disgusted. These expressions induce shame, which is an effective brake on the child's activity, but shaming, if overdone, can lead to chronic humiliation and lay the basis for later personality disturbances.[8] Other research suggests that mothers who habitually respond to toddlers with anger will raise children who are more likely to persist in angry, noncompliant behavior. These children also are less likely to respond empathically to someone in distress. In the preschool setting, children who regulate their anger poorly are likely to be disruptive or aggressive if they are temperamentally outgoing; if they are shy and inhibited, such children tend to be anxious and wary.[9]

Even when the children themselves are not the target, witnessing an eruption of anger or an act of aggression affects them. Children as young as a year appear to be upset when their mother and father verbally attack each other. Infants whimper or freeze. When they are a little older, they may cover their ears or leave the room. Upon witnessing angry conflict among adults, some children become aggressive toward their peers. After observing a laboratory simulation of conflict between two adults, those children who had previously been classified as aggression-prone engaged in more intense and more prolonged conflict with peers than those who had been classified as low or moderate in aggressive tendencies.[10]

In a day care center, three- and four-year-old children were observed fighting over toys even when there were duplicates, or over a particular space on the floor even when the nearby space seemed to be no different; the motive seemed simply to be "I want what you have."[11] As they mature, children learn ways other than physical struggle to achieve their ends. Five-year-old Julian, who wants the truck three-year-old Joey is playing with, offers him another truck, saying "This one is better." Or he negotiates: "It *was* your turn. Now it's mine." Or he tries to distract Joey's attention from the coveted object by making exciting "brm . . . brm . . ." noises with the truck he wants Joey to want.

If his maneuvers fail, an older child may (if no one is looking) take the truck forcibly, or he may decide that he doesn't really want that old, bad, broken truck anyway. Under the watchful gaze of an adult, he may turn magnanimous: "Let him have it. He's just a baby." Or he may simply shift his attention to some other activity, abandoning his goal of gaining possession of the truck if he judges the price of attaining it is too high, or if something else claims his interest. By the time he is five years old his displays of anger are usually tuned appropriately to social situations. No longer so much at the mercy of his sudden and immediate impulses, he is beginning to be able to reframe situations, using his growing cognitive maturity to see them in a more positive light. He has developed childhood versions of strategies he will employ all his life.[12]

When a child enters preschool, and later in school, other children assume great importance in socializing expressions of anger. Provocative behavior on the playground often leads to a fight, although some children characteristically withdraw rather than engage in conflict. Giving in to an attacker tends to terminate the dispute, but it also increases the chances that the attacker will repeat her behavior. But even if her angry or aggressive behavior results in short-term gain, the end result may be rejection by her peer group. Sadly, children who are rejected because of their aggressive behavior tend to perpetuate both their behavior and their status. They are likely to perceive hostile intent in the actions of peers, and the perceived threat makes them more likely to respond aggressively. Then nobody wants to play with them.[13]

At about four years of age, children have some rudimentary notion of fairness. Now a child is not merely frustrated because he cannot have the toy he desperately wants; he also believes that he has been wronged. Why shouldn't his mother give it to him? "You promised," he scolds, his eyes brimming with tears. Or he yells at the boy with whom he is competing in a board game, "You cheated!" At this point the children have several options, from overturning the board and hitting each other to working out some way of continuing their play. Children who get along reasonably well with others both within the family and in outside social groups learn to defend their interests without rupturing relationships. Children who are popular with their peers and are rated as socially competent by their teachers are less likely to become involved in angry conflicts. When they do, however, they tend to deal with provocations in a direct but unaggressive manner that preserves the relationship.[14] If a young child is chronically unsupported by his parents and teachers in his efforts to regulate his anger, is physically or verbally abused and humiliated, or is regularly exposed to aggressive behavior, he runs the risk of becoming a behavior problem in his preschool years and of engaging in delinquent behavior in adolescence.

What factors make some children more violence-prone than others? There is ample documentation that aggressive tendencies first manifested in early childhood persist into adulthood; this is especially true of males. Although the defiant, truant, incorrigible playground bully often becomes better adjusted as an adult, as many as a third of these children go on to become violent in their personal relationships, are unable to keep a job because of hostile behavior, or end up as criminals.[15]

On the basis of their review of a broad range of studies, Rolf Loeber and his colleagues came to the conclusion that children who go on to engage in persistent antisocial behavior are likely to have felt the effects of such parental behavior as harsh, inconsistent discipline; inadequate supervision; lack of involvement; or rejection.[16] Studies of the early experiences of violent criminals have detected recurring patterns of parental behavior: the parents are abusive or violent to each other; they explode in rage at the child but ignore him much of the time; they fail to supervise him or even notice what is happening to him; they neither explain to the child why his behavior is unacceptable nor reason with him about what he is doing; they neither discuss nor model nonviolent ways to resolve conflicts; they rarely touch the child or talk to him except when they are hitting him. The message they communicate is that anger is a weapon, might makes right, violence is power, and the willingness to harm confers status and compels respect. Could there be a more antisocial model of human relations to present to a child?[17]

Many developmental theorists now postulate that reciprocal influences—from parent to child and from child to parent—are continuously at work. For example, faced with a demanding or defiant child, an uncertain parent who does not know how to be firm will vacillate between forcing obedience and yielding. Failure to obtain compliance increases the difficulty of obtaining compliance in subsequent encounters. Out of desperation or weariness, the parent gives the child a hard slap.

In the same situation, a more self-assured parent might be more consistent. By the same token, an easygoing and good-humored child would be more likely to emerge unscathed from confrontations with a tense, depressed, or angry parent. Risk of emotional and behavioral problems also decreases if a child has other resources—an understanding grandparent, some special talent for music or sports, or a good school. Parents, too, are more likely to defuse conflicts with a child if they have friends and outside interests, and if they are willing to seek help.

Children, especially difficult children, need opportunities and motivation to engage in satisfying, helpful, and praiseworthy activities. They also need adults who notice and celebrate signs of their progress as they develop the social skills they need. "You are *such* a good boy to share your grapes with Kenny!" "This room looks great. Every toy picked up." "Yes, you were very mad a minute ago, and I was too, but we made up (and we'll always make up) because we love each other."[18]

Research suggests that infant attachment status predicts later conduct disorder. For example, in a follow-up study of seven-year-old boys, those who had earlier been classified as insecurely attached as toddlers were found to be more noncompliant and hostile than those who had been classified as securely attached.[19] One of John Bowlby's first papers told the stories of forty-four young thieves. In their short lives he found some common experiences, notably early separation from or loss of their primary attachment figure. The loss—perceived as abandonment, Bowlby theorized—triggered feelings of worthlessness, self-loathing, and humiliated fury. ("She left because I'm no good. She's bad.") One defense against such feelings, according to Bowlby, is for the child to withhold love and affection. Such children are impervious to appeal and unmoved by punishment. On the surface, some seemed adaptable and eager to please. But behind their hardboiled masks of amiability and indifference, Bowlby wrote, is "bottomless misery, and behind the apparent callousness despair." The hunger for love and rage at its absence manifested themselves in these children in antisocial and delinquent acts.[20]

Another study showed that children were more likely to be aggressive if their mothers had been placed in a foster home or institution in childhood and also were in a bad marital relationship.[21] Perhaps the mother was unable to give sensitive care to her children because her own emotional needs had not been met in childhood and were not currently being met. Not surprisingly, many studies confirm that the children of young, poor, unmarried, socially isolated parents growing up away from their extended families and in high-crime neighborhoods are at higher risk for developing insecure attachment and later emotional disturbances than children living in less troubled circumstances.

Another persuasive hypothesis, not inconsistent with Bowlby's but suggesting an alternative path to delinquency, is that persistently disruptive and demanding behavior in preschoolers has its roots in chronic miscommunication between child and caregiver. For example, an inexperienced or inattentive parent who overlooks an infant's subtle bids for attention, responding only when the baby escalates his demands, may be unwittingly reinforcing irritable crying or temper tantrums. Certain children who feel angry, frustrated, and insecure at not getting the adult help they need to manage their emotions worsen their situation as they act out their feelings, thereby incurring adult wrath or disengagement.

A cycle of coercive behaviors by both child and adult comes to define their relationship.[22]

Happily, most children have mothers and fathers who guide them on the path toward emotional self-regulation. The incidence of tantrums usually falls sharply by the middle of the third year. By this time a toddler has become more attached to her father, and the paternal presence can lend support to a child as she seeks greater autonomy and sorts out her ambivalent feelings about her mother.[23] (In most families in the United States, the mother is the child's primary attachment figure during the first months of life, and the mother is also likely, during the toddler period, to be the primary rule setter and enforcer of acceptable behavior.) This age can be a difficult transitional time for parents, because children often vigorously oppose their caregivers as they try to develop and carry out their own agendas. Children's anger, if it is not too intense, can support the process of emotional development. It effectively mobilizes and focuses energy for self-assertion and self-protection, and for overcoming obstacles. But prolonged, unmoderated anger is a warning signal.

Anger, Impulsivity, and Aggression

Much of what we know about the causes and later developmental consequences of a child's inability to control anger is derived from epidemiological and clinical studies of children who exhibit alarming antisocial behavior, such as frequent unprovoked fighting, cruelty to animals, setting fires, or wantonly destroying property. Antisocial behavior serious enough to constitute delinquency usually does not show up until adolescence. But for about 3 to 5 percent of delinquents, aggressive antisocial behavior began earlier in childhood.

It may start in the preschool years, with argumentative, irritable, defiant, disruptive, and reckless behavior that increases in frequency and intensity until it becomes serious enough to warrant the psychiatric diagnosis of conduct disorder. Conduct disorder, which comprises a constellation of worrisome behaviors, such as lying, stealing, truancy, and fighting, that persist over a period of months, is the most common problem seen in child mental health clinics in North America. However, among psychiatrists, social workers, and criminologists the criteria for making the diagnosis vary considerably. Many researchers and practitioners make a distinction between children who are runaways, truants, and rule breakers at an early age, and those who are aggressive and violent. Those in the latter group have a worse prognosis for violent behavior in later life. Understandably, aggressive, bullying, or hostile children are avoided by most schoolmates. Rejection by their peers confirms them in their view that the world is a hostile place, and they become loners or seek out companions who share their dark outlook and antisocial impulses. By the time they reach puberty, these children may already be part of a gang and have committed assault, burglary, or worse.[24]

Juvenile delinquents whose aggressive antisocial behavior began before adolescence make up a very small segment of the population, but they are believed to be responsible for half the crimes committed by children and adolescents. Because they are markedly more aggressive than those who begin to exhibit antisocial behavior in adolescence, they are responsible for an even greater proportion of violent offenses. Some of these children experiment with delinquent behavior and are able to quit, but the earlier they start, and the more persistent and aggressive their behavior, the less likely it is that they will stop voluntarily. Children with conduct disorder are at high risk for drug and alcohol abuse, and many more of them have access to guns than in earlier generations.

If an irritable, impulsive, stubborn child is hyperactive as well, or has a learning disability or attention deficit disorder, his risk for delinquent behavior is heightened. As many as 40 percent of children with attention deficit disorder have behavior problems. Whether children with attention deficit and hyperactivity also develop serious conduct disorder seems to depend on how strong their families are. "Families who provide a supportive, consistent environment with clearly defined limits presumably allow [children with attention deficit disorder] to develop enough social skills that they can function reasonably well in school and with their peers."[25]

Children who are chronically unable to control their urgent impulses to get what they want are often angry. How well a preschool child can tolerate frustration has been shown to provide important clues as to his personality and behavior in adolescence. Walter Mischel and his colleagues at Stanford University devised an experiment in which four-year-olds were tested for their ability to delay gratification, and then evaluated years later as high school students. The four-year-olds were told they could have two marshmallows if they waited until the experimenter returned from an errand. One marshmallow was placed on a dish in front of each child. The experimenter told the child that if he couldn't wait, it was all right to eat it before the experimenter got back, but then he wouldn't get the second marshmallow.

The children who had enough self-control to wait long enough for the bigger reward (about two-thirds of the group) devised all sorts of strategies and behaviors to help them resist temptation. They sang to themselves, made up games, or even covered their eyes. The others usually grabbed the marshmallow as soon as the experimenter left the room. In a follow-up fourteen years later, it was found that the adolescents who had been impulse-resistant as four-year-olds were better able to cope with frustration. They were less impulsive and more confident, assertive, and successful in human relationships. The marshmallow grabbers, on the other hand, tended to be more "stubborn, indecisive, mistrustful, envious, argumentative and pugnacious."[26]

Inability to delay gratification in order to achieve a future goal is a serious handicap. Good impulse control is rewarded in our society. Poor impulse control in childhood is a predictor of delinquency. (Again, it must be emphasized that most impulsive children do *not* become delinquent.)[27] Success in school depends upon a student being able to tear himself away from television to learn irregular verbs or quadratic equations. And in fact, when the children who had resisted their marshmallow-grabbing impulses were compared to those who couldn't wait, it was found that the impulse controllers had dramatically higher scores on their SAT tests fourteen years later.

But billions of dollars are spent each year on advertising messages designed to undermine impulse control, and many of these buy-it-now messages are aimed at children. American children hardly can be expected to ignore these drumbeats—certainly their parents don't—but they can be helped to control their desires: to "wait a second," to "squash it," to "cool it," to "count to ten," and to choose to act in a manner that will increase their chances for happiness. They can acquire this crucial component of "emotional literacy," as Daniel Goleman calls it, if parents and teachers are patient and consistent in supporting the child's own efforts at self-control in the face of the ordinary frustrations of life. How successful children are in moderating their impulses depends on the thousands of little social interactions of daily life, the most important of which are with parents.[28]

Paths to Violence

The developmental prospects of boys who exhibit early antisocial behavior have been studied a good deal, those of girls much less. It is not that girls do not engage in unacceptable or disruptive behavior; indeed, some studies suggest that by adolescence there is not much gender difference in the prevalence of conduct disorder. But compared to boys, the behavior of adolescent girls is markedly less aggressive, and girls are much less likely to come to the attention of the police. This is partly because of the nature of their offenses: girls are more likely to shoplift than to hold someone up with a gun.[29]

John Richters, an investigator at the National Institute of Mental Health, reminds us that a child may end up at the same place by taking one of several routes.[30] One person may start life temperamentally impulsive or irritable because of a genetic vulnerability. Another child may have suffered brain injury or exposure to a neurotoxic agent such as alcohol or lead.[31] A child's self-esteem may be low because he is repeatedly ignored or rebuffed at home and at school. He finds his companions in similarly rejected children, and they reinforce one another's anger and alienation. Another child might acquire deviant values from a violent family. Still another might learn that aggression is necessary for survival in a hostile, dangerous inner-city neighborhood. He might be pressed into joining a gang because otherwise he would be defenseless. A child without respect, loving care, and guidance at home might find the family he needs in the gang. To gain status among his adolescent peers, reckless or violent acts may be required of him.[32] Numerous studies confirm that risk for delinquency is worsened by poverty and by the lack of beneficent influences such as a loving father, good neighbors, a religious community, and teachers willing to reach out to a troubled child.[33]

It has been repeatedly shown that many aggressive children and adolescents have significantly lower than normal levels of serotonin, a neurotransmitter involved in many neurobiological processes that affect emotional states. Some of these individuals also give evidence of low reactivity in their autonomic nervous system; this is taken to mean that they have a lower than normal level of anxiety and inhibition. In several studies, levels of the stress hormone cortisol have been found to be lower in aggressive boys than in unaggressive boys. Testosterone is the hormone most often linked with aggression in humans, but the reported effects are extremely complex and levels can go up or down depending on a host of interrelated and incompletely understood factors. None of these differences in physiology imply causality or invariably predict a certain behavior pattern. The autonomic and neuroregulatory functions of persons whose reaction patterns are learned and reinforced by experience may be indistinguishable from those that have been largely determined by a toxic agent or some inborn predisposition. Some progress is beginning to be made in understanding how various hormones, acting at critical times, affect brain development and the function of the brain systems that underlie aggressive behavior.[34]

Although genetic predispositions or a history of experiences such as abuse, neglect, or injury play a role in some instances of delinquency, these factors are not in themselves sufficient to explain a person's present behavior. For example, the threshold of excitability in a neural circuit may be regulated by a gene, but the gene is switched on or off by epigenetic—that is, environmental—influences. An adolescent boy may have an inborn tendency toward impulsivity, but he will not commit a felony in the absence of a chain of special circumstances—a car with the keys left in it, a friend who dares him to take it, and an incident at school that has left him seething. The variety of experiences, memories, relationships, physiological changes, and temperamental predispositions that play a role in antisocial behavior makes for uncertainty as to what combination of influences and circumstances determined any particular person's fateful act. However, research in individuals and high-risk groups can both increase our understanding of how violence is triggered and suggest points where interventions may be beneficial.

Life experiences shown to be associated with criminal behavior in a given population do not reliably predict how any individual in the group will behave over time. Studies of abused children show about 10 to 25 percent going on to commit violent crimes, which means that 75 to 90 percent do not. A study of boys from high-crime neighborhoods in Eugene, Oregon, confirmed the intuitive assumption that the earlier a child commits a crime, the higher the risk that he will embark upon a criminal career. The researchers found that boys who had been arrested by age fourteen were eighteen times likelier to become chronic offenders than those who were first arrested later in life or were never arrested. But to conclude that early arrest amounted to anything like a prediction of individual destiny would result in a major error. If one were to predict that a boy arrested by age fourteen would go on to a criminal career, one would be wrong 65 percent of the time.[35]

Abused children may grow up to be abusers themselves. It is likely in most cases that this comes about because of emotional scars. But some individuals who exhibit violent behavior may have suffered extensive brain damage. Brain injury at any age can impair the processes of emotional control, but it can be especially devastating in children. Early frontal-lobe impairment may cause a learning disability that affects insight, foresight, social judgment, empathy, and abstract reasoning ability. Bruce Price, M. Marcel Mesulam, and their colleagues describe two adult patients who had long arrest records and troubled histories of unpredictable, erratic, impulsive, and assaultive behavior. In conversation and in more formal testing, the patients were found to be extremely immature in moral and social judgment, although their IQs were low-normal and neurological examinations revealed no striking abnormalities. But both had had frontal-brain trauma as young children. And MRIs performed when they were adults showed sizable areas of frontal brain damage.[36]

There is considerable evidence that the frontal brain is important for regulating social behavior and inhibiting aggression. In a group of 279 Vietnam War veterans with severe brain injuries, those with frontal-lobe damage were found to be two to six times as violent and aggressive as veterans who had not suffered frontal-lobe injury. Studies of fifteen death row inmates convicted of one or more murders revealed that they had collectively suffered at least forty-eight serious head injuries, a number of which resulted from severe beatings by a parent. It has been reported that brain scans of children who have been badly neglected reveal underdeveloped frontal cortical and subcortical limbic areas, about 20 to 30 percent smaller than normal.[37]

In 1995 over 3 million children in the United States were reported to have been abused or neglected; just under a million cases were investigated and confirmed. New research supports the belief of many health professionals and police across the country that the official figures, which rose 61 percent between 1985 and 1995, are, nevertheless, greatly understated.[38] Some of these victims of abuse will treat their own marriage partners and their own children the way they were treated. According to one study, parents who were subjected to beatings as children are five times more likely to use harsh corporal punishment on their own children than those who were not so badly treated. Adults, especially males, who were abused as children are also more likely than adults without a history of abuse to engage in violent criminal acts outside the family.[39]

The criminologist Cathy Widom and her colleagues found that arrest rates for violent crimes were almost as high for adults who had been neglected in childhood as for those who had been physically abused. In her study, 16 percent of a group of adults who had been abused as children had arrest records for violent crimes; in adults with a history of neglect but not abuse, 13 percent had such records.[40] Widom cites other studies suggesting that "neglect may be potentially more damaging to the development of the child than abuse . . . particularly in the areas of language development, psychosocial development, and empathic responsiveness."[41]

Middle-class and upper-class children are by no means immune from neglect and abuse. One reason is that so many parents in the United States suffer from depression, which spares neither the affluent, the powerful, nor the accomplished. Studies indicate that 12 percent of mothers of young children are clinically depressed and 52 percent report depressive symptoms. Depressed mothers often have difficulty engaging with their small children, picking up on their cues, and providing a warm, reassuring presence. They may lack the patience to resolve conflicts with their children in a calm and consistent way, and so they either retreat and give up, or become harsh, even abusive, in trying to control them.[42]

For fifteen years David Olds and his colleagues in Elmira, New York, have been following a group of 400 children born into high-risk situations. Their mothers were mostly adolescents, unmarried, and indigent.

About half (216) of the mothers were regularly visited at home by nurses during their pregnancy; slightly over half of these (116 mothers) were also visited during the two years after the baby's birth. The nurses sought to influence the quality of parental caregiving by providing instruction in parenting, modeling appropriate interactions with the children, offering emotional support, and helping the mothers deal with issues such as family planning, education, and employment. Among the visited families, reported child abuse and neglect were 46 percent lower than for the control group, which was not visited. The visited mothers also had fewer subsequent births, spent less time on welfare, and had 69 percent fewer arrests than the control group. Similar promising results seem to be emerging from a more recent home-visiting program involving the children of 1,139 high-risk women in Memphis. Like the New York mothers, the Tennessee mothers who received home visits showed a reduction in the incidence of child abuse.[43]

Born to Kill?

American who are afraid to be on the streets after dark and law enforcement officials and politicians looking for an answer for anxious constituents are understandably attracted to the idea of an early warning sign of criminality hidden in the criminal himself, in his DNA. If budding criminals can be identified in childhood by genetic markers, then they can be educated, medicated, segregated, incarcerated, or whatever it takes to prevent them from acting out their genetic destiny.

The genetic approach to crime prevention has had a certain allure. Although most teenagers—87 percent, according to one national survey—engage in one or another form of antisocial behavior, such as petty theft, vandalism, or drunk driving, before they turn twenty-one, only a small percentage end up as criminals. Indeed, a consistent finding in criminological research is that a very small percentage of the population is responsible for a large percentage of violent crimes. One such study tracked 13,150 males born in Philadelphia in 1958 and found that 7.5 percent of the group were responsible for 61 percent of all the homicides and 75 percent of all the rapes committed by members of the group.[44] So, identify that 7.5 percent before they start their criminal careers and the promise of eliminating almost two-thirds of violent crime opens before our eyes!

But nature is not so obliging.

Although there is now wide acceptance of the idea that genes influence behavior, there is less understanding of the continuous interaction between genetic and experiential information. These strands are the warp and woof of behavior. As the neurobiologist Torsten Wiesel puts it, "Genes controlling embryonic development shape the structure of the infant brain; the infant's experience in the world then fine-tunes the pattern of neural connections underlying the brain's function. Such fine-tuning of the fabric of connections making up the brain must surely continue through adulthood."[45] Genes are expressed if they are switched on by some specific information for which they are biologically prepared; it is highly doubtful whether it will ever be possible to identify genes that reliably predict future behavior patterns.

But there is a danger that genetic markers will be treated as firm predictions, a scarlet letter stamped from birth on medical, police, and insurance records. Children branded as potentially violent could well be treated in ways that increase their risk. Being stigmatized or ostracized does not usually make people sweet-tempered. Genetic prophecies based on weak data and weaker theory could be self-fulfilling. Yet some investigators who are searching for genetic predictors of violence are undaunted. As one of their number puts it, this research may one day make it possible to examine a young boy and "predict with 80 percent accuracy that your son is going to become seriously violent." The psychiatrist Stuart Yudofsky promises, "With the expected advances, we're going to be able to diagnose many people who are biologically brain-prone to violence."[46]

"People want simple explanations for hard-core problems," observes Anne Fausto-Sterling, a geneticist at Brown University. "If there was an antitestosterone drug that we could inject to make young boys nice, that would be a lot easier and cheaper than transforming schools or society or whatever is at the heart of the problem." The Harvard neurobiologist Evan S. Balaban is equally skeptical. "I would say, don't hold your breath if you think looking for genes is going to help you understand violence. I would put my money on clever environmental manipulations, because in the end you're going to go there anyway."[47]

Still, crime does run in families. Researchers supported by the U.S. Department of Justice have amassed data on the population of state and local penal institutions across the country and have found that more than half of all juvenile delinquents imprisoned in state institutions, and more than a third of adult criminals in local jails and state prisons, have immediate family members who have also been incarcerated. But speaking Latvian, sending your child to parochial school, and taking piano lessons also tend to run in families. Do young delinquents inherit a "criminal gene," or do they learn antisocial behavior from family members? Were they abused, neglected, and rejected by their parents? Did they have bad role models? The explanation, suggests Marvin Wolfgang, a professor of criminology and law at the University of Pennsylvania, may be a shared environment in which crime is likely: "low socioeconomic backgrounds and disadvantaged neighborhoods, where a high proportion of people will be sent to jail whether they are related or not."[48]

Studies of twins indicate that heritability does indeed play a role in criminality, but the story is complex:

> A Swedish adoption study in 1982 found that the rate of criminality in adopted children was 2.9 percent when neither their biological nor their adoptive parents had committed a crime; the figure rose to 6.7 percent if their adoptive parents were criminals and to 12.1 percent if their biological parents were criminals. That might seem to be a clear demonstration of the relative weight of environment and genetics in determining antisocial behavior. If *both* sets of parents were criminals, however, the chance of the child's being criminal as well was 40 percent. Together, genes and environment appear to be several times as powerful as either force acting alone.[49]

In reviewing numerous twin studies, Michael and Marjorie Rutter agree that results indicate a "modest genetic component." The Rutters, however, also point to major environmental influences in delinquency: "family discord, poor supervision of the children, weak parent-child relationships, social disadvantage, and large family size."[50]

Studies that purport to show a causal link between race and criminality have sparked considerable controversy. African Americans are disproportionally represented in the prison population. According to a 1995 survey, 32 percent of black men between twenty and twenty-nine years old were in jail or prison or were under probation or parole supervision, compared to 6.7 percent of white men in the same age group.[51] Although clearly there is an association between being an African-American male and being involved with the criminal justice system, this does not prove genetic influence. Nor, even assuming such influence exists, does it reveal which genes trigger criminal behavior and how they do it. Moreover, to say that hereditary influence is present does not mean that environmental influences are excluded or unimportant, although that is the meaning often intended in everyday usage.

Skin color is genetically determined to a large degree, but how having dark or light skin affects behavior depends upon a chain of interactions of hereditary factors and environmental circumstances. In the United States, dark skin alters one's environment in myriad and often unfavorable ways. Being black triggers a variety of social interactions— in school, on the street, in the workplace, on the highway, with the landlord, with creditors—that increase the risks of ending up in the hands of the criminal justice system. There is an infinite supply of hypotheses to explain this reality without overtly or (as is more often the case these days) covertly assuming genetically based racial inferiority as the root cause. A black man is more likely to be suspected, more likely to be framed, more likely to have given up on the system, more likely to lack opportunities for honest work, more likely to have had disruptive early experiences, more likely to have seen family members unfairly treated, more likely to have grown up fatherless in a bad neighborhood and gone to a poor school. Even in kindergarten he will have been made to feel that he was not expected to do as well as white children.

Genes and Aggression

Attack is one possible response to threat. Another is flight. Immobility, the freeze response of the rat waiting for a shock it cannot avoid is yet another. Extreme differences in behavioral response to stress coexist in the same individual and in a normal population, whether nonhuman or human. The tendency to respond one way or another depends not only on the triggering situation but on characteristics of the individual. That laboratory animals with one or another characteristic response can be selectively bred confirms that observable neurophysiological and behavioral patterns have a genetic base.

When I (Ann) was a student at the Jackson Laboratory in Bar Harbor, Maine, a research facility noted for its hundreds of genetically pure lines of inbred mice—generation after generation of mice with identical genes—I assisted in an experiment in which two hungry male mice were given one food pellet. Mice from one of the inbred genetic lines always shared the pellet, each nibbling at one side of it until it was eaten. Mice from the other line always battled over the pellet, and the winner jealously guarded his trophy as he consumed it. If mice from the two different genetic lines were paired, the fighter mouse would grab the food pellet and attack the other as it tried to nibble. After several provocations, however, the nonaggressor mouse would fight, and, since it was a larger breed, would almost always prevail. In fact, it sometimes killed the aggressor if they were not separated in time.[52]

Much more recent studies have taken laboratory mice similarly bred for specific types of behavioral responses to threat and used them to study the differences in neurotransmitters, hormonal responses, neurophysiological patterns, and even genetic mechanisms underlying the behavioral differences. In one series of experiments, inbred aggressive mice exhibited high activity in their sympathetic nervous system and low levels of corticosteroid stress hormones if they were victors in a fight. Other animals, who were bred to be more passive under threatening conditions, had high parasympathetic activity, and if they were defeated, high levels of stress hormones. Testosterone was generally lower in the more passive animals. The researchers found that aggressive and nonaggressive animals differed in the number and distribution of serotonin receptors in the limbic system.[53]

New methods now make it possible to map an animal's genes—that is, find where they are located on a particular chromosome—then clone one or many of them, alter them, put them back or insert them into another animal, substitute one gene for another, or eliminate one or another gene. Mutated animals then can be bred to create lines of genetically identical animals. Such inbred genetic lines provide an effective means for studying how a gene contributes to development and behavior. New methods are now being developed that will make it possible to knock out genes (or a gene protein) in adult animals and in specific locations.

Several research groups are studying aggression in mice, using various forms of gene "knockouts." They eliminate a single targeted gene and then see what happens to the mutant offspring of the genetically altered animals. In one series of experiments, the gene for one of the synaptic receptors for serotonin was knocked out. A line of mice lacking this receptor was then bred. The mouse mutants, both males and females, were found to be much more aggressive than nonmutant animals.[54] Although males and females behaved similarly once they started to fight, they became aggressive under different experimental conditions. Males, both mutant and nonmutant, reacted aggressively when an intruder mouse was introduced into their cage, but the mutants were more aggressive than nonmutants.

Female mice were not troubled by an intruder except when they had just given birth, in which case they responded with an aggressive attack. Mutant mothers were much more aggressive than nonmutant mothers. Moreover, their aggressive attacks waned in intensity and frequency as the usual time for weaning approached. The researchers drew the conclusion that aggression in males and females, although elicited by different triggering situations, is governed by a similar neural pathway in both sexes. They also concluded that the serotonin receptor altered by the gene knockout is a critical regulator in the pathway on which aggressive behavior depends.[55]

In another promising line of research, scientists are seeking to knock out a serotonin receptor gene in adult animals (rather than creating the knockout animals by transferring the mutant gene to the mouse germline and breeding for the mutation). If these attempts are successful, researchers will be able to compare the effects of acute genetic alteration in the adult animal with the effects in animals that have always lived with the altered gene and perhaps have compensated for it in some way during their development.[56]

Such experiments are beginning to be used to identify genes that contribute to behavior, and also to understand critical physiological and environmental factors that switch genes on and off. The extraordinary complexity of this task is only barely suggested by the fact that, to date, fourteen types of mammalian serotonin receptors have been cloned, which act in various pathways in the central nervous system and have a variety of effects. A well-known example is the effect of serotonin on mood. (Several studies have already shown that pharmacologic agents, such as fluoxetine [Prozac], that elevate serotonin levels inhibit aggressive behavior under some conditions.)

Serotonin is just one of many neurotransmitters that affect aggressive behavior. To sort out the complex and interrelated physiological systems underlying aggression will require considerably more research. Testosterone, dopamine, norepinephrine, adrenocorticotropin, vasopressin, prolactin, and nitrous oxide all play some role. Alcohol and drugs such as cocaine shift the equilibrium in neurotransmitter systems, as do many other pharmacologic agents, and their study in laboratory animals will shed light on the neurophysiology and neuropharmacology of both aggression and substance abuse.

Well-groomed Rodents

Mouse breeding experiments provide strong evidence that aggressive behavior has a genetic component. Yet as the researchers whose work we have described above note, "another line of research has provided increasing evidence for a decisive role of early experience in programming of circuits underlying stress-response patterns in adult life."[57] Research with mice and rat pups and other infant mammals including monkeys has shown that maternal behavior affects the development of infants' physiological and behavioral responses to stress. Licking, grooming, nursing, maintaining physical contact—all normal maternal behaviors—seem to regulate the developing specialization of the infant's limbic and cortical neurons, and these in turn govern autonomic reactivity and stress hormones in both mother and offspring. The psychologist Myron Hoffer calls these interactive processes "hidden regulators."[58]

Researchers have found that the care given infant animals affects the expression of the genes involved in brain pathways governing stress. For example, when infant laboratory rats are gently stimulated by their mother's licking and grooming, the expression of the glucocorticoid (cortisol) receptor gene in the infants' hippocampus, limbic system, and frontal cortex is increased. If the rat pups are separated from their mother, the gene becomes less active.

Nurturing diminishes hypothalamic-pituitary-adrenal stress responses through complex feedback mechanisms: high activity of receptor genes in these forebrain locations inhibits production of stress hormones.[59] Separation from the mother, or physical trauma, does almost exactly the reverse: infants' levels of stress hormones and reactivity to stress are increased, because the genetic mechanism for inhibiting stress hormone release is less active. These results provide evidence that differing amounts of maternal nurture at a sensitive period in development cause individual differences in neural programs governing stress.[60]

Even more important is the finding that the effects persist on many levels throughout the animals' lives. As adults, animals that had received more maternal licking and grooming showed more exploratory behaviors (an indication of lower anxiety), and their brains were found to contain more receptors for anxiety-reducing pharmacological agents (an indication of less susceptibility to anxiety). When the "well-groomed" infants were exposed to stress as adults, they had a lower outpouring of stress hormones, and genes in their hippocampus and hypothalamus showed lowered stress-related activity. These experiments confirm that animals behave differently in stressful situations for the rest of their lives depending on their early experiences. They also uncover intervening physiological steps in this process, even down to the level of gene activity that is regulated by their early experiences with their mother.[61]

A behavioral response pattern is influenced by many factors. The laboratory mice that I (Ann) observed at Bar Harbor had a gene or genes "for" aggression, but the animals did not fight when they had enough food and when they did not encounter provocative intruders in their cage. Moreover, as we have seen, early experiences can permanently alter tendencies toward one or another type of behavior. But even animals with a particular genetic predisposition and a particular set of early experiences can often be induced to change their ways at any age, at least to a degree. Recall the beneficial effects nurturant foster mothers had on the stress-hormone levels and behavior of the excitable, motherless young rhesus monkeys discussed in chapter 5. Converging evidence suggests that not only do hormones affect behavior, but behavior affects hormones. Likewise, not only do genes affect behavior, but behavior affects the expression of genes.

Uncontrolled Anger:
An American Crisis

Anger is an emotion that can save your life or cut it short in a flash. How we deal with our angry feelings affects every social relationship—not just those in the family and at work or school but also the interaction with a stranger whose car suddenly swerves in front of you. According to a 1997 survey by the federal Centers for Disease Control and Prevention, this country has the highest rates of childhood homicide, suicide, and death by gunfire of any of the world's twenty-six richest nations. The United States is the most violent of developed nations, and American children are not well shielded from the consequences of that violence. Almost three-quarters of all the reported murders of children in the industrialized world take place here.[62]

At Children's Hospital in Washington, the major cause of fatal head injury in infants is not car accidents, as one might assume, but a violent shaking or a blow inflicted by an adult who is supposed to be taking care of the child. "More than 95% of serious intracranial injuries during the first year of life are the results of abuse," states a standard pediatric textbook.[63] For children between one and four years of age, the leading cause of death was accidental injuries; and the fourth leading cause was homicide.[64] The lethal mix of guns, drugs, lack of effective supervision, and uncontrolled adolescent anger has transformed schools and cast a grim shadow over inner-city neighborhoods across America. Indeed, it is hard to think of any nation not at war with another nation or ravaged by civil strife where children are subject to so much violence.

Of the 20,000 homicides that occurred annually in the United States during the 1980s, about half the victims were young males. According to Deborah Prothrow-Stith, a former commissioner of public health in Massachusetts and a researcher of adolescent violence at the Harvard School of Public Health, "In 47 percent of the cases an argument can be established as the cause, whereas violence during the commission of another crime, such as robbery, accounts for only 15 percent." "He dissed me" is a commonplace explanation for a shooting or knifing occasioned by nothing more provocative than a dirty look or an insult. Indeed, the most usual setting for an adolescent homicide is one in which two people who know each other are drinking and arguing, and one or both have a handgun.[65]

The anger and recklessness of young men accounts for much of violent inner-city crime. For African-American males between the ages fifteen and twenty-four, homicide is the leading cause of death; they are seven times more likely to be murdered before they reach adulthood than young men in Canada. Killings in which preadolescent children are either victims or perpetrators have also increased dramatically since the early 1980s. According to a 1993 study, about 44 percent of eighth-graders in Chicago-area schools reported being in physical fights every day.[66]

Anger is not the only emotion that triggers violent behavior. A clutch of fear can mobilize the body to launch a preemptive strike. "He was going to hit me so I hit back first," a young woman says, explaining why she attacked her boyfriend. An adolescent who has just committed a robbery panics at the thought that his victim will identify him in a police lineup and puts a bullet through her head. (In contrast, a hardened criminal may plan and carry out an act of violence without anger.) Other acts of violence are committed to punctuate a life of boredom. In the world of psychopathology, violence is also used to exert control over others, heighten a sexual experience, build self-esteem, give meaning to one's life—in short, to satisfy all sorts of unmet emotional needs.

Anger serves many positive purposes. It may spur a child on to master a difficult task. In later life, the same emotion may impel him to fight corruption and injustice. Anger can help clarify and support relationships among friends by clearing the air. An angry glare from a parent can stop an incipient fight between two children.[67] Indeed, under certain circumstances, for example when witnessing cruelty, *not* to be angry is a moral failing. But, increasingly, anger is becoming what the psychologist Paul Ekman terms "the most dangerous" and "the least adaptive" of human emotions because it impels too many among us to strike out with weapons that kill faster than we can think.[68]

Witness to Violence

How aggressive a child becomes and how violently he expresses his aggressive urges are influenced not only by his picture of himself, but also by the view of his surroundings he has constructed from what he feels, observes, and learns—what the psychologist James Garbarino calls his "social map."[69] From an early age he is learning what is socially accept-able not only from what his caregivers say and do but also from cultural messages beamed from outside the family. Movies, television, and rap music celebrate violence, and an insistent message in political discourse is that violence works: The threat of force protects national security. The death penalty prevents crime. A gun in the bureau drawer protects the family.

As is clear from best-selling novels and high-grossing movies, Ameri-cans are fascinated and entertained by violent crime. (We are not unique in this; blood-dripping movies and TV programs are a major American export.) The most insistent transmitter of cultural signals is television. In many households in the United States the TV is almost al-ways on during waking hours. Psychologists have conducted literally thousands of studies on the impact of television violence on children. The number of simulated acts of violence children see by the time they leave elementary school is staggering: about 100,000 for the average American child. An American Psychological Association report review-ing 3,000 studies of the effects of television watching on children con-cluded that there is "absolutely no doubt that higher levels of viewing violence on television are correlated with increased acceptance of ag-gressive attitudes and increased aggressive behavior." Saturday morning programs aimed specifically at small children featured twenty to twenty-five acts of violence an hour. Several studies concluded that when tele-vision was introduced into a community, there was a rise in aggressive behavior by children. A longitudinal study of boys found a significant re-lation between exposure to television violence at eight years of age and antisocial acts—including "serious, violent criminal offenses and spouse abuse—twenty-two years later."[70]

Television viewing does not take place in a vacuum. The well-documented increase in television violence from the 1970s to the mid-1990s has coincided with an increase in parental neglect, a decrease in the numbers of fathers at home, a decrease in supervision, and a falloff in the time parents spend playing with their children, helping with homework, and simply being there. For many children in the United States there is no one around to monitor what is on the screen or to in-terpret what the child is seeing and hearing.

A group of probation officers who work with juvenile offenders in Brooklyn, New York, are convinced that in the adolescents they encounter, "real-life arrests that appear regularly on the local [TV] news, images typically of young black and Hispanic men," help perpetuate violence more than televised murder fiction does. The emerging worldview of troubled adolescents is confirmed. "If [arrests of people like themselves] is what they see over a period of time, of course they think, 'That's all I can be.'"[71]

It is only in the last few years that studies have been undertaken to determine how much real-life violence children in the United States actually witness. In 1993, John Richters and Pedro Martinez of the National Institute of Mental Health published a study of 165 children, ranging in age from six to ten years, who were living in what is described as "a low-income, moderately violent neighborhood" in Southeast Washington, D.C. Over a third of the fifth- and sixth-graders said that they had witnessed shootings, muggings, arrests, someone being attacked or chased by a gang, or someone carrying, exhibiting, or using a weapon. Almost 30 percent had seen someone being wounded, 22 percent had seen someone being physically threatened, and 23 percent had seen dead bodies on the street. Nine percent said that they had actually witnessed a murder.[72] A similar investigation in a housing development in a violent neighborhood in New Orleans produced even more appalling data. Over 90 percent of the children in the development had witnessed acts of violence, over half had been victims of violence in some form, and 26 percent had witnessed a shooting. In the New Orleans study, mothers reported that they taught their children to keep their heads below the windowsill when watching television, to avoid stray bullets.[73]

What are the emotional consequences for young children of living in neighborhoods in which acts of violence are everyday events? Some become timid and withdrawn and develop phobias. Nightmares are common. "Bang, bang. You're dead" play, a favorite of many small boys, becomes more realistic, and because of the abundance of real guns in their environment, sometimes much more dangerous. Children are forced to deal with the loss of a friend or a relative at a very young age, and often they must work out their complicated feelings on their own. Some seek out the "protection" of gang membership.

While there is very little research on what effects living with everyday violence has on very young children, there are disturbing inferences to be drawn from developmental theory. The psychiatrist Robert Emde worries that in a chronically violent environment the ordinary daily routines of a baby and his caregiver are distorted. In normal situations, a small child comes to expect certain reactions of the caregiver that reassure and instruct. Taking his cues from his parents, the toddler is encouraged to explore his environment. He is also developing a sense of standards, which lays the foundations of moral behavior.

In a violent environment, however, a mother's wariness, alertness to danger, or depression may restrict opportunities for positive interactions that support development. The child's sense of security is undermined, and the normal processes undergirding early moral development interrupted. As Emde puts it, the "opportunities for experiencing empathy . . . and other kinds of positive shared meaning" are restricted. The sense of trust on which a hopeful view of life is based is not likely to develop when the insistent message is "Keep your head down!"[74]

For children who have difficulty regulating their anger, exposure to real-life violence and hostility tends to confirm them in the view that the world is dangerous and unfriendly. An experiment involving two groups of boys, one with a history of aggressive behavior and the other made up of unaggressive boys, illustrates how easily emotionally vulnerable children can be affected by what they see and hear. The boys in both groups were asked to watch videotaped vignettes of interactions among children their own age, some of which depicted provocative or aggressive behavior. Each boy was asked to imagine that he was part of the scene, and then interpret whether the intentions of the boys in the video were hostile or benign. Under relaxed circumstances the aggressive boys made accurate judgments almost as often as the boys who were not aggressive.

Then a disturbing event is staged in the laboratory: The experimenter calls a recess so that he can bring in a new boy from the next room, but the unseen boy is heard through the wall loudly and aggressively predicting that he will get into a fight with the others once he joins them. All the subjects become upset to a degree, but the behavior of the aggressive boys changes markedly. They now see much more hostility and they attribute many more sinister motives to the children in the videotaped vignettes. An acute emotional upheaval has altered the way they process information and impaired their judgment.[75] In violent neighborhoods across the nation emotionally fragile children do not need to be tricked into perceiving hostility all around them.

Breaking the Cycle

Parents begin teaching their child very early how to resolve conflict by how they act. Take, for example, this familiar occasion for a clash of wills between a toddler and her parents: the child cries after being put to bed. Mother or father looks in to make sure nothing is wrong. Baby stops momentarily, but then starts up. Father picks the child up, whereupon she stops crying. After checking her diaper or giving her a drink, he resettles her in her crib. And then the baby starts to cry again. Children who are temperamentally irritable can keep up this behavior for hour after weary hour; so can any overly fatigued baby.

Although parents are the responsible partners in this transaction, it is not always easy for them to behave responsibly. A child's cry is extraordinarily compelling. As in so many dramas of everyday life, there is no one "right" resolution. In the bedtime routine, toilet training, and in many other daily interactions parents may find themselves at odds with their baby. How they resolve these conflicts becomes a learning experience for the child.

Parents teach young children how to resolve conflicts in a number of other ways, too. If one parent abuses or insults the other, their words and actions send a disturbing message. On the other hand, when children watch their parents resolve conflicts peacefully despite their differences, they are more likely to learn to succeed in acknowledging and regulating their own feelings. Children as young as five can sense that their parents have settled an argument amicably even when they were not present when peace was restored.[76]

Parents often negotiate with their child to gain their compliance. A study of ninety-five mothers interacting with their two-year-old children in a laboratory playroom when it was time to go home revealed a variety of strategies. Some mothers used play to encourage the child to help put toys away: "Let's drive the car to the garage." Others made a point of explaining the reason for their directive: "We need to clean up for the next little boy or girl." Combining a clear request with some explanation, persuasion, or enticement was more effective in securing the child's compliance than simply asserting control or relying totally on persuasion. In the process the mother is introducing the child to strategies of conflict resolution that rely on negotiation rather than intransigence, verbal rather than physical challenge, and mutual respect rather than coercion and brute power.[77]

Since harsh parenting has been found to be a risk factor in adolescent delinquency, a number of early-intervention programs have been started across the country to introduce parents to noncoercive strategies for exerting authority. A review of forty such programs found that those that combine educational efforts to improve the children's verbal and cognitive skills with parent education and other family support services "had moderate to large effects on antisocial behavior and delinquency."[78]

One of these, the High/Scope Perry Preschool Project in Ypsilanti, Michigan, followed a group of 123 African-American children born into poverty up to age twenty-seven. Sixty-eight of the children had been given the opportunity to participate in high-quality preschool programs. Their parents had frequent meetings with their children's teachers, and project staff members regularly visited the families at home. At age twenty-seven the preschool intervention group had half as many criminal arrests as the group that had no intervention. They also had higher earnings and higher educational attainment, and were likelier to own a home and be committed to marriage. Investment in the program, according to one analysis, resulted in an estimated return to the public of $7.16 for every dollar invested, owing primarily to savings in the justice system and savings for the victims of crime.[79] Helping children overcome adversity, a moral obligation in a compassionate society, also proves to be a good financial investment.

According to a 1997 study of juvenile crime prevention and rehabilitation commissioned by Congress and carried out by University of Maryland criminologists, most crime prevention programs, including boot camps and drug classes in schools, start too late and fall far short of their goals. More effective, according to this review, are long-term interventions that change the thinking and behavior of troubled young people or ameliorate the conditions under which they live. The researchers point to favorable results from programs that include regular visits by nurses and counselors to the homes of infants and young children in troubled families, an early start to head off problems before they become a way of life.[80]

A recent report from an ongoing study of 343 neighborhoods in Chicago supports the hypothesis that the social cohesion of a neighborhood—that is, the collective determination of the residents "to live in safe and orderly environments that are free of predatory crime"—is a highly significant predictor of lower rates of violent crime. The researchers characterized the 343 neighborhoods according to numerous demographic and social factors; they found that factors such as home ownership, residential stability, and less concentrated social disadvantage (poverty, youth, unemployment, female-headed families) were associated with fewer reports of personal victimization, violent crimes, and homicides. Their analyses indicate that collective, informal neighborly activities—such as acting together to organize informal play groups for children, to prevent truancy, and to confront drug traffickers—create an environment that builds hope and confidence, what the researchers call "collective efficacy." Where the neighbors trust one another and share similar values, they are more likely to work together for the common good. They are more likely to command better public services such as police patrols, fire stations, garbage collection, public playgrounds and basketball courts, and housing code enforcement than are residents of more demoralized neighborhoods where trust levels are low and people do not exercise informal social control. Strong social connections at the local level are vestiges or reinventions of community, and they appear to be important in discouraging violent crime.[81]

The research presented in this chapter suggests that if violent crime in America is to abate, early interventions in the lives of at-risk children are required. These interventions can and must address the children, their families, and their neighborhoods. All this can help, but without substantial progress in improving education, living conditions, the effectiveness of police presence, services, and employment possibilities in the demoralized city blocks of our country, violence and its malignant consequences will continue to be a major problem.

Chapter Nine

BEATING THE ODDS

All new parents hope life will be good to their newborn baby. They silently vow to cherish and protect their child. But many experience a clutch of fear as well, for they know that they cannot guard him from all chance, accident, and misfortune. In this chapter we will look at how experiences that increase a child's risks and experiences that make it possible to overcome these risks intersect and interact in the course of development. We will also discuss programs designed to decrease risks, minimize their effects, or surmount them.

Risk and Resilience

In 1955, Emmy Werner embarked on a study of all 837 children born that year on Kauai, one of the islands that make up Hawaii. Her goal was to trace how risks impacted on the lives of a particular group of people in a particular time and place. The participants in this remarkable study were mostly children and grandchildren of poorly educated plantation laborers, either native Hawaiians or immigrants from Japan and the Philippines.

The children grew up enjoying some advantages over their fellow citizens on the U.S. mainland. The quality and availability of medical, public health, educational, and social services compared favorably with that of most communities of similar size on the mainland. The school system made unusually determined efforts to reach dropouts, and only 3 percent of the group failed to complete high school. (The national dropout rate at the time was over 11 percent.) In their preschool years, the children enjoyed surroundings of natural beauty and a relatively tranquil social environment. No war or natural disaster disrupted their lives. However, beginning in the 1960s, an influx of tourists, drugs, cults, and other unsettling cultural changes brought new stresses and challenges into the lives of Kauai's children just as they were approaching adolescence.

Werner and her colleagues have followed the progress of most of these children over half a life span. The Kauai Longitudinal Study presents a kaleidoscope of the multiple interactions of risk and protective factors that influence development from infancy to adulthood. Over the years Werner has periodically reported on how the children's lives have unfolded.[1] She monitored and analyzed the effects of biological and social risks, stressful experiences, and protective factors on participants' lives, and how these affected their ability to cope with adverse circumstances.

About two-thirds of the group led relatively uneventful lives as children and went on to successful young adulthood. Their births were uncomplicated, their home environments supportive, and their circumstances not unusually stressful. They coped adequately with school, work, and personal relationships. Nevertheless, a few of these low-risk individuals, about 10 percent, became troubled adults. Werner defines "trouble" as at least two of the following conditions: a broken marriage, a criminal record, or a chronic mental health disorder.

About a third of the whole group experienced serious difficulties in early life. By two years of age these children had already faced such risks as prenatal and perinatal medical complications, persistent poverty, poorly educated parents, a parent's mental illness or alcoholism, divorce, desertion, or chaotic family environment. Twelve children (1.4 percent of the whole group) died before their second birthday, almost all because of congenital anomalies or complications of low birthweight. (Another seventeen had died by age thirty-two, most during adolescence.)

One-third of these high-risk youngsters did not experience great difficulties in growing up. The other two-thirds evidenced "serious learning and/or behavior problems by age 10 or had a record of delinquencies, mental health problems, or pregnancies by age 18." But about a third of these adolescents in serious trouble were able to turn their lives around, and by the time they had reached young adulthood, they had grown into "competent, confident, and caring" men and women.[2] Even among those who had had multiple problems as children, teenagers, and young adults, about half had developed stable lives by age thirty-two. By the same age, the high-risk children who were unable to change course, about 18 percent of the entire group, had chronic mental health problems, criminal records, or other serious impediments to a happy and successful life.

What protected the children who escaped major long-term effects of adversity? What enabled some of the at-risk children but not others to "grow out" of their propensity to get into difficulties? The researchers sought to identify the factors that made it possible for seventy-two individuals who faced high risks in childhood to be successful in friendships, marriage, and in their job, given that other children who were exposed to similarly adverse circumstances at birth or in childhood took quite different paths that led to far more troubled lives.

The fortunate children Werner describes as "resilient." The word suggests a child's capacity to cope with stressful events or adapt to adverse circumstances. Some years ago, such children were called "invulnerable," but fortunately this hyperbolic term has been dropped. Even the toughest child is likely to be wounded by a pile-up of negative experiences, even though investigators may not readily detect the scars. Resilience—being able to bounce back and move on—is not, as we shall see, an attribute or a state of being, but a *process* that depends upon the kinds of challenges a child faces as well as his or her stage of development and temperamental qualities. Many observers have found, for example, that low birthweight babies with mild neurological abnormalities during their first year of life were doing well by the time they entered school and had no difficulties, *if* the children came from stimulating and supportive homes. If, on the other hand, the children came from disrupted or deprived environments, they did badly.[3]

The high-risk but resilient children in the Kauai study had personal qualities that caused family members to delight in them and treat them well. They were "easy to deal with," "affectionate," "cuddly." By age two they were alert, exploratory, and independent and "more advanced in communication, locomotion, and self-help skills than children who later experienced serious learning and behavior problems."[4] In elementary school they made friends easily, could read better, and were more adept at reasoning than the high-risk children who did poorly in school. They had a variety of hobbies and outside interests and shared household responsibilities. By the time they completed high school they had a healthy respect for who they were and what they had accomplished. On psychological tests they were found to be "more nurturant, responsible, and achievement-oriented" than their high-risk age-mates who had already experienced problems. The resilient girls were more "assertive and independent" than their peers.

The experiences that protected the high-risk children in the Kauai study almost always included emotional support of one sort or another provided by an adult "who accepted them unconditionally, regardless of temperamental idiosyncrasies, physical attractiveness, or intelligence." For the most part, the resilient children were not separated from their primary caregivers for months at a time during the first year of life; parents stayed together and fathers did not walk out on the family. All the resilient children had established a close bond with one or more caregivers when they were infants. Firstborn boys who did not have to vie for attention with younger siblings were well represented among this favored group. (The birth of a sibling before the firstborn reached age two was found to be particularly stressful.)

As the resilient children grew up, grandparents, teachers, and neighbors often served as role models and confidants. In cases where their parents stayed together during their adolescent years, children who exhibited delinquent behavior did not become adult offenders. In contrast, as Werner and her colleagues report, "five out of six among the delinquents who went on to commit adult crimes came from families where one parent was absent for prolonged periods of time during their teens." The Kauai researchers found that boys tended to be more vulnerable to adverse experiences in the first decade of life than girls, but in the second decade girls had more trouble coping with stress. Other studies in Europe report similar findings.

By age thirty-two all but two of the high-risk but resilient children had achieved a level of education and vocational success equal to that of the low-risk children. Seventy-six percent of the women and 60 percent of the men had good marriages. Most had children and were judged to be "caring parents who respected the individuality and encouraged the autonomy of their offspring." Many ascribed their ability to cope with the cumulative challenges of early adulthood to their religious faith, which gave them a hopeful outlook on life.[5]

The authors of the Kauai study conclude that three types of protective factors were especially significant for improving the outcomes of children at risk: (1) the individual's personal competence, as evidenced by at least average intelligence, language and communication skills, sociability, and self-control; (2) emotional support within the family in times of stress; and (3) "external support systems whether in school, at work, or church, that reward the individual's competencies and determination, and provide a belief system by which to live." The resilient individuals in the study exhibited "confidence that the odds can be surmounted." This self-confidence was of crucial help in coping with adversity. Werner has reviewed other studies of high-risk children raised at different times and in different cultures—Berkeley, Oakland, Baltimore, Boston, Sweden, England, and Denmark—and she concludes that similar protective factors were at work.[6]

Just as the consequences of bad choices constrict future choices—dropping out of school makes it harder to get a job—so positive feedback can promote a favorable chain of circumstances. Signs of improvement at school, success at a job, making good friends, or being helped by a mentor can increase self-confidence, encourage more thinking and planning about the future, and open up possibilities never seriously considered before.

Resilience is usually measured by observable achievement, such as performing well in school, eliciting positive reports from parents and teachers, and exhibiting acceptable behavior at home and in the classroom in the face of adverse circumstances or multiple biological and social risks. However, as some studies show, the survivors who beat the odds may feel more vulnerable than they appear. Werner noted that some of the high-risk children of Kauai who as adults were successful in meeting their responsibilities did not have satisfying lives. Males, especially, found it difficult to establish committed intimate relationships. Some studies indicate that apparently resilient children who by and large fulfill social expectations and succeed in school may be suffering emotional distress. The problems show up in the psychiatrist's office or in interviews, or in ratings on such traits as assertiveness, sociability, and sense of well-being.[7] A study of abused children in Israel found that those who did well—they were neither aggressive, despairing, nor abusive—often had difficulty expressing emotion, appeared isolated, and had trouble forming satisfying relationships.[8]

We have had our own experience helping to raise a child who faced a number of serious risks. Dennis came to live in our house in the mid-1960s and stayed for six years.[9] We celebrated his eleventh birthday soon after he came, the first birthday party he had ever had. Dennis had been living in Junior Village, a Dickensian orphanage in Washington, D.C., that was later closed because of public outcry. A friend of ours who had taken an interest in him asked if he could go to the school we were just starting. The authorities were willing to release Dennis from the institution if we would take him into our home.

When Dennis joined us, we knew several things about him. His mother was an alcoholic who lived on a small government disability check, and his father had died before he was born. He had lived in a rough neighborhood until the authorities removed him from his mother's care because he spent his days on the street, his nights sleeping in unlocked cars, and as little time in school as he could get away with. We met his mother on several occasions, and she expressed her love for Dennis but felt she could not care for him. By this time she was chronically ill.

Dennis was charming, a beautiful child with an angelic smile. Having lived by his wits for much of his young life, he knew how to manipulate adults, but he was genuinely kind and exhibited tender feelings for others in the family. He was childish for his age: he was afraid of the dark, he wet his bed, and he loved being read to from books for young children. He himself could not read at all. After he had been with us for a while and we realized how severe his learning problems were, it dawned on us that he was probably suffering the effects of prenatal exposure to alcohol.

Dennis became a loved member of our family. But as he entered adolescence, his behavior problems became more serious. He was caught taking part in a couple of petty thefts. He would disappear for days at a time to his old haunts. Although quick to anger, especially if he felt some injustice was being done to him or to another person, we never had any indication that he injured anyone. However, he was expelled from a special school for learning-disabled teenagers in which we had enrolled him, because in a fit of anger he kicked through a wall. "I'm a born loser and I'll die one," he said bitterly.

By the time he was twelve years old he was experimenting with marijuana and alcohol and he became a regular user of both. After many fruitless efforts to help him, including counseling and drug programs, we finally told him that he could not stay unless he was ready to try to conquer his addictions. He was seventeen years old. Dennis thought it over for two days, and then came to us looking downcast and said that he could not promise to try. Heartbroken but determined, we watched him leave.

Over the years we kept in touch, and he came to the house on birthdays and holidays. But in young adulthood it was evident that he was an alcoholic and a multiple substance abuser. We repeatedly offered to help him, and he entered more than one rehabilitation program. But he always walked out, and soon he was so high or drunk whenever he phoned or visited as to be incomprehensible. Over the next years our contacts were sporadic. We learned that he had fathered several children and took care of none of them.

Then, a few years ago, Dennis called. Now thirty-five years old, he was cold sober and had a steady job. You could hear the pride in his voice. He had experienced a religious conversion, and the African-American fundamentalist church his sister attended had become an anchor in his life. He had developed some ability to read. He had had no further brushes with the law. He lived with his sister, who was deeply religious and insisted on the highest standards of behavior and sobriety. Dennis's problems are by no means over. He subsequently lost his job because he got angry at the boss. But he keeps finding work and is able to support himself. Most important, he has been sober for several years. Given the prospects he faced just a short time ago, he is doing well. We still see him and include him in family gatherings.

We often speculate about what has made it possible for Dennis, thus far at least, to turn his life around. Perhaps the years spent with us helped. We like to think so. His good looks and open manner helped him in his childhood because people were drawn to him and wanted to help. He has always had strong religious feelings. Our guess is that the key factor was his own family: his sister, certainly; his older brother, who was married and had a steady job; and ironically, his mother most of all. She damaged him by her own prenatal indulgence, and she damaged herself to such an extent that she could not care for him. Yet to the end of her life she communicated a love for him that eventually strengthened his determination to lead a life he could respect.

Stories of high-risk children who beat the odds inspire admiration and hope; yet it seems that few such children emerge unscathed. The emotional costs are often high. We know a marvelously effective counselor who attributes her sensitivity and understanding to what she has learned in the process of recovering from childhood sexual abuse, and a father who, having been deserted by his own father, spends hours playing catch or just hanging out with his own sons. Adults who overcome adversity often impart a special wisdom to the next generation, not just by what they say, but because of who they have become.

What Is It About Poverty?

There are risks in assessing risk factors. For example, a few years ago a comparative study was conducted in Atlanta of homicides within the family where the killer and the victim belonged to the same race, and it came to a disturbing conclusion: The relative risk of homicide within black families was almost six times greater than that within white families. These findings were confirmed in a later study of 349 intraracial domestic homicides in New Orleans. But when the same data were re-analyzed according to a single measure of socioeconomic status—degree of household crowding—the disparity in risk between blacks and whites essentially disappeared. Looked at in this way, the significant variable was not race but poverty.[10]

But poverty in itself is no more a cause of low achievement or antisocial behavior than race is. Most poor people and most black people do not flunk out of school or commit crimes. The majority of children who drop out of school have never been poor.[11] But growing up poor is the context within which a chain reaction of hardships and failures often occurs. At every stage of the development process, a person brings to each new experience "attitudes, expectations, and feelings derived from a history of interactions that, in turn, influence the manner in which environmental cues and stimuli are interpreted and organized."[12]

Being poor in the United States carries with it special emotional burdens and is hurtful in special ways. Mother Teresa detected a more profound hopelessness and anger among inner-city poor people in this country than she saw among the desperately poor in Calcutta with whom she worked for many years. In strictly economic terms, the poor of the United States are clearly better off than poor people in most of the world. Most have running water and inside toilets, refrigerators, and television sets. Even the smallest welfare check or a week's wages from McDonald's would be a princely sum for someone living on the street in Calcutta or Cairo. But in the United States the processes of family breakdown and erosion of community are more advanced than in many other countries. Many poor Americans lack the support of family, friends, or neighbors who in previous generations would have been there to help.

Another special feature of being poor in America is the insistent message, broadcast twenty-four hours a day, that buying things is what life is mostly about. Money defines worth. Americans celebrate the opportunities a competitive society offers individuals to make money, and tens of millions of people have come to these shores penniless and have prospered. But this prosperity of a majority of Americans brands the chronically poor as "losers" caught in a web of personal failure for which they are often despised and feared. If poor people lose hope, their despair can lead to anger, resentment, humiliation, and self-blame.

The accumulation of risk factors associated with poverty begins even before birth. If a woman has limited access to prenatal care, the likelihood of a stressful or premature delivery increases; perinatal complications increase the child's risk of developmental problems. A mother who is poor is more likely to smoke, drink, use drugs, or be infected with the AIDS virus, and the results can be devastating for the fetus. Infants of poor parents are more likely to be born underweight and have cerebral palsy; they are more likely to receive poor medical care. They are less likely to be properly immunized. They are more vulnerable to chronic diseases, such as asthma and ear infections. They are more likely to be poorly nourished. At age five they are less likely to be ready for kindergarten; they are more likely to fall behind in elementary school and drop out of high school. Girls are more likely to become single teenage mothers, and boys are more likely to get involved in the drug trade or gang violence; both are far less likely to have a legitimate job that pays a decent wage. The odds that somewhere along this perilous route they will either commit a crime or become the victim of one are far greater than for the average American.[13]

Risk factors that adversely affect a child's learning, judgment, and capacity for emotional control tend to pile up. Michael Rutter and his colleagues conducted longitudinal studies of British families in two very different environments, one on the rural Isle of Wight and the other in an impoverished borough of London. The researchers found that the sheer number of risk factors is a powerful predictor of mental health disorders and behavioral problems in children. Severe marital discord, overcrowding and large family size, low socioeconomic status, and poorly educated parents are all risk factors. When other serious sources of family stress are added, such as a mother's psychiatric problems, a father's criminal behavior, or the child's placement in a foster home, the likelihood that a boy or girl will be emotionally and cognitively damaged goes up significantly.[14] Some children must run the gauntlet of all these risks.

Low socioeconomic status often means that parents' money worries are chronic, jobs are insecure, and time is scarce. Housing that poor families can afford is usually in bad neighborhoods with inadequate schools, few recreational facilities, and low-quality municipal services. The most visibly prosperous segment of the neighborhood economy may be the drug market; flashy drug dealers in big cars may easily excite the imaginations of bored, unsupervised children. A depressed mother has neither the money, the time, nor the energy to seek treatment. If a parent is chronically depressed or abuses alcohol or drugs, children's risks increase significantly.[15] The criminal father may be in jail or out pursuing his career on the street. The hardworking father may lose his job, and with it the respect of his wife and his children as well. Jobless fathers often become absent fathers.

A temperamentally difficult child in a poor family is less likely to receive the emotional support he needs. A middle-class family might well seek therapy or enter the child in a special school or camp. Especially if they lack the support of a spouse or other family members, "lower-income parents . . . are more likely to attribute children's behavior to willfulness and stubbornness."[16] This can lead to increasing conflict between parent and child, and to greater defiance. Many single mothers do not have either financial or emotional support in raising their family, and they may be under such pressure to earn money that they do not pay attention to their children's emotional needs. Children lack the all-important support of their father to encourage them in their quest for greater autonomy, keep them out of bad company, set clear limits to unacceptable behavior, and support their own efforts to control their aggression.

Having dark skin compounds the problems of poverty in many ways. Black and Hispanic families in the inner city often pay higher rent than white families of similar means because, despite antidiscrimination laws on the books, the supply of available housing is much more limited for them than it is for whites. In many neighborhoods across the country landlords will go to considerable lengths not to rent to African Americans. Surveys conducted in Harlem and other low-income black and Hispanic neighborhoods have found that residents pay more for the same basket of groceries than affluent families in the suburbs. So the purchasing power of inner-city families is often less than that of whites with the same income.

Genetic Risk and Developmental History

Many studies confirm that psychopathology runs in families. Such conditions as attention deficit disorder, conduct disorder, anxiety disorders, and depression regularly appear across generations. Family history can be a powerful predictor of psychological and behavioral problems. Yet in none of the family studies of the disorders just mentioned does a regular pattern of inheritance emerge. How the interplay of genetic and environmental factors allows a given individual to escape the disorder is not known.

A few brain disorders attributable to a single gene have been identified; Huntington's and Tay-Sachs diseases are two examples. Any individual with the gene for these diseases whose life is not otherwise cut short will succumb to it and die. But geneticists believe that multiple genes are involved in all or virtually all complex disorders that affect behavior. One family member may have the combination of genes and experiences that cause attention deficit hyperactivity disorder. A second family member with the predisposition may not manifest the clinical disorder because of protective factors—inborn, environmental, or both. Their sibling may escape the disorder because he does not possess the predisposing genes. Adding the genetic dimension complicates the problem of understanding resilience and the role of protective experience in enabling some children to overcome unfavorable odds. Any given family member not exhibiting symptoms in a family with psychiatric problems—for example, a child of schizophrenic parents who is free of the disease (as about 85 to 90 percent of offspring of schizophrenics are)—may have escaped because of protective factors in his environment (for example, a sensitive caregiver), or because he was never at risk: he was never dealt the genes that would make him vulnerable; or, if he was, the environmental conditions that allow the genes to be expressed were not present.

Richard Rende, a Columbia University psychiatrist, and the geneticist Robert Plomin speculate that, with the great advances that are being made in genetics, at some point "specific indexes of genetic markers of *small, probabilistic effect* will be found that represent genetic risk for behavioral maladaptation." This will make individual risk profiles possible; where risk is established, the individual's unique balance of risk and protective factors can be investigated. This could lead, someday, to therapies and social interventions tailored to the individual's needs. Rende and Plomin point out, however, that the contribution of genes to mental disorders is "significant but moderate," influencing clinical outcomes but not determining them.[17]

Genetic influences can also reduce specific risks. For example, individuals with sickle cell anemia are unlikely to get malaria. Sickle cell anemia arises from a genetic flaw that causes red blood cells to be abnormally shaped. The sickle-shaped red blood cells resist infestation by the malaria parasite. Michael Rutter speculates that somewhat analogous effects may be present in autism. He suggests that the genetic factors responsible for the inability of autistic individuals to make social connections may also be responsible for their often remarkable capacity to focus their attention and master a task by themselves, a helpful trait for some with this disorder. In the same vein, a number of studies indicate that genes influence intellectual capacity; high intelligence usually confers a degree of protection on individuals who are at risk because of some unfavorable genetic or environmental influence. Finally, genes influence temperament, predisposing some children to take in stride negative experiences that defeat other children who are more susceptible to fear, rage, or despair.[18]

Genetic research suggests that our shared genes cause us to resemble other family members, while environmental factors are responsible for the differences. However, even identical twins can share the same physical environment, live in the same room, play with the same toys, eat the same breakfast food, wear identical clothes, and yet differ from each other in important respects. They make different choices in the ways they relate to people and circumstances. How and why this happens is still uncertain.

One current explanation, mentioned earlier, is that each twin experiences life differently because of his or her unique relationships and life-shaping experiences. A person's developmental history, especially his or her record of adaptation to challenges and stresses in the past, influences responses to later risks. "From a developmental point of view," Alan Sroufe writes, "behavior is not simply the interaction of genes and environment but genes, environment, and the history of adaptation to that point."[19] Children, and adults as well, develop inner resources through their experiences in successfully coping with stressful situations. Similarly, maladaptation predisposes to future problems and disorders.

Marital stress, divorce, alcoholism, and the chronic depression of a parent, all risk factors for children, are common occurrences; yet these pivotal events in the life of a family usually do not affect each child in the same way. Identical twins have the same genes, but in the case where one of them happens to have schizophrenia, the other usually does not. However, the children of both twins are equally at risk for the illness. This finding suggests that the schizophrenia-inducing genes are present in both twins even though the mental illness shows up in only one. The speculation is that chains of life experiences unique to the individual influence the expression of the genes involved and determine whether a person will be ill.[20]

A Meaningful Difference:
Intervening in the Lives of Children

Adults intervene in the lives of children in all sorts of ways. Usually, they do not act in behalf of a government program or research institute or any other institution. Parents, of course, are the primary intervenors. But a teacher, impressed with a child's gifts, sometimes offers special instruction and encouragement. A grandmother, a neighbor, or a family friend reaches out to a troubled child and becomes a mentor. William Julius Wilson has documented the special importance of such role models for those who have surmounted the multiple risks of growing up in the inner-city ghetto.[21] If we want to help vulnerable children, Michael Rutter reminds us, we need to focus our efforts on the protective processes that change life trajectories. These processes will reduce the impact of risks and the likelihood of negative chain reactions. They will increase a child's self-confidence and the sense of being in control of his or her life.[22]

Since the 1960s, various public and private agencies have undertaken a range of interventions designed to improve American children's prospects of healthy development, school success, and satisfying and productive lives. These include such public health measures as improving prenatal and perinatal care; research to lower the incidence of low birthweight and cerebral palsy; ridding homes and schoolrooms of lead-based paint; head-injury prevention by means of car seats, bike helmets, and the like; preventive health care; developmental screening; provision of food supplements to nursing mothers and preschool children; and the offering of nourishing school lunches.

Among the strategies to decrease children's risk are programs that offer educational enrichment and support. Project Head Start, the largest and oldest such program in the United States, has been in business since 1965 and has served more than 14 million children. Federal grants

matched by states are used to fund centers across the nation to improve
the learning, social skills, and health of poor children in their preschool
years. Most centers are sponsored by community action agencies and
other nonprofit organizations. In well-run Head Start programs, parents
are much involved. In fact, the organized efforts of enthusiastic parents
and Head Start graduates have protected Head Start's funding from being cut and kept it growing. In 1994, 740,500 children were served. This
is about 53 percent of all income-eligible four-year-olds and 21 percent
of eligible three-year-olds, but fewer than one percent of eligible children under the age of three.[23] Head Start programs differ from one lo-
cality to another, but usually they run for only part of the day and part
of the week. In such a large national program with so many local variations, quality is bound to be uneven, and in fact studies indicate a considerable range in quality.[24]

Head Start was billed from the outset as the heavy artillery in Lyndon
Johnson's War on Poverty. It was hoped that attendance would boost IQ
scores; indeed, IQ scores of Head Start children did go up, in some cases
dramatically. But most IQ gains faded by the time the children reached
the third grade. On the basis of an initial evaluation in the 1970s, a number of politicians and scientists pronounced Head Start a failure. However, subsequent studies that followed Head Start participants to
adulthood have reported significant success in many important areas.
Children who attended Head Start, compared to nonparticipants whose
backgrounds were similar, had a lower incidence of school failure (as
measured by having to repeat a grade), lower high school dropout rates,
lower teen pregnancy rates, fewer health problems, lower rates of aggressive behavior, and fewer brushes with the criminal justice system.[25]

Even though Head Start has made a dramatic difference in the number of poor children attending preschool, many remain unserved. In
1993 fewer than half of three- to five-year-old children from families
with incomes below $10,000 attended preschool. (In contrast, 81 per-
cent of children from families with an income of $75,000 a year or
above have preschool education, an indication of how much Americans
value early enrichment programs.)[26] The weight of the evidence indicates that children benefit from Head Start; however, the question
arises whether their gains would be greater and more enduring if the intervention began earlier, was more intensive, and went on longer.

It has been found, for example, that African-American children are more likely than white children to lose the gains they have made in Head Start by third grade. This may be because they are relatively disadvantaged to begin with and are likely to end up in worse elementary schools.[27] Other questions concern the effects of various types of interventions on different populations of children. For example, is a school-like curriculum better, or should children's self-initiated activities guide the program? What about home visits and programs aimed at parents? What about programs targeted at special groups that will reduce the impact of such risks as premature birth or prenatal drug exposure? As the psychologist Michael Lamb concludes from his recent review of the relevant studies, "Unfortunately, little effort has been made to specify the influential aspects of intervention programs so that attempts can be made to fine-tune their effectiveness."[28]

There have been some studies, however, designed to answer these questions. Craig Ramey and Sharon Landesman Ramey tested the hypothesis that the more disadvantages and risks a child faces, the earlier support programs should begin, the more intensive and comprehensive they should be, and the longer they should last. They undertook a project involving poor African-American children, in which the interventions for the experimental group could last from infancy to the child's eighth birthday. The subjects of the "Abecedarian Project" were 111 healthy full-term boys and girls born to very poor families in Chapel Hill, North Carolina. Three-quarters lived in mother-headed households. Most of these women had not finished high school.

The children were randomly assigned either to receive five years of preschool intervention or to act as controls. Control children were cared for at home or enrolled in regular day care programs. The experimental group attended a full-day fifty-week-a-year program in which one trained caregiver worked with three infants, responding to them in individualized ways to develop their cognitive and language capacities and their social and motor skills. Older preschoolers in the experimental group participated in rich and varied programs. The caregivers provided liberal amounts of what Craig Ramey describes as "holding, tactile contact, love and social responsiveness." Besides the educational program for the children, families received other help—health care and social services, transportation, and parent education.

At age five the whole group, experimental and control, was again randomly divided, with half attending regular kindergarten and the other half a special enrichment program in which one teacher worked with six children. The enriched program included not only a regular kindergarten and elementary school curriculum but also special instruction in language, literacy, practical skills for helping around the house, and artistic appreciation and expression. The experimental school program lasted through second grade. All children in the experiment were tested at least yearly during the eight-year study period, and then received follow-up testing when they were twelve and fifteen years old.

The researchers found that the children in the enriched preschool program did better than the control group on many measures of cognitive and academic development. The effects were still evident in their most recent test, at age fifteen. The differences between the experimental and control groups as a whole, although statistically significant, were small. The greatest differences were in the children deemed most vulnerable because of their mothers' poor scores on intelligence tests. All the children in the experimental group whose mothers were mentally retarded had IQ scores at least 20 points higher than those of control children with mentally retarded mothers; they averaged 32 points higher than their own mothers. School-age children who had been in the preschool experimental program did better than the control group in follow-up tests of reading, math, and IQ at ages eight, twelve, and fifteen.

It is especially noteworthy, but not at all surprising, that the children who received continuous intervention from birth through their eighth year performed the best of any group on the follow-up tests. Next best was the preschool enrichment group whose special program ended at kindergarten. However, the children whose enrichment *began* in kindergarten showed no significant improvements on their test scores compared to the group that never received any enrichment.

The Rameys' findings are further confirmation of the critical importance for learning of the preschool years. "Intellectual development is to a significant degree alterable by the quality of the environment the child experiences," Craig Ramey concludes. "This is particularly true for vulnerable children. . . . But beginning education at age five is too late."[29]

Since resources are limited, the question arises as to which children to target for early intervention. The economically deprived children of the Abecedarian group clearly benefited from intervention, and the subgroup of those children whose mothers were mentally retarded benefited even more. Confirming this in another study, Craig Ramey found that children of mothers who had less than a high school education derived the most from intensive early intervention, perhaps because the homes of these children are relatively more deprived and less intellectually stimulating.[30]

Another high-risk group comprises low-birthweight, prematurely born infants. They are at higher risk for cognitive and behavioral impairments than full-term babies. Researchers addressed the question of improving the prospects of these children in "The Infant Health and Development Program," a research effort involving 985 low-birthweight, premature infants in eight locations across the country. The 377 children in the "intervention" group were offered home visits beginning shortly after birth to instruct and support parents in interacting with their child. When the babies were one year of age, they entered a center-based program modeled on the one developed in the Abecedarian Project. The intervention program lasted until the children were three. The control group, the other 608 children, were merely examined periodically. All the children received periodic medical and developmental tests, were referred for services as needed, and were helped to find places in community preschools when they were three.

The researchers have reported results of tests up to the age of eight.[31] In tests done at three years, the performance of children in the intervention group was clearly superior to that of the controls. They had significantly higher IQs and vocabulary test scores, and their behavior was rated better. The heavier low-birthweight infants—those who had weighed between 2,000 and 2,500 grams (4.4 to 5.5 pounds)—benefited about twice as much from the intervention program as the babies who were more underweight at birth. For example, the IQs of children who were heavier at birth and had also participated in the program averaged 14 points higher than those of children with similar birthweight who had not participated; the IQs of children who had been lighter at birth were only 7 points higher. But by five years of age, and again in the eight-year tests, only the heavier low-birthweight infants were still showing beneficial effects of the intervention program, and these effects were quite modest.

Why didn't the smaller premature babies enjoy more lasting benefits from the early intervention? The researchers speculate that these infants, who are at greater biological risk, may have sustained neurological damage for which the intervention did not compensate. They suggest that future efforts to raise the cognitive skills of small premature infants may need to last longer and also better take into account the individual needs of each child. Why did the gains fade by five and eight years of age even in the premature children who still showed other benefits of the birth-to-age-three intervention? Perhaps, as the Rameys suggest, interventions in the lives of high-risk children work best when they not only start early but also are sustained over a long period.[32]

Even where the IQ gains of children in early-intervention programs fade in elementary school, several studies show that some advantages in reading and cognitive skills are preserved. Social skills are also helped by the preschool experience, especially for children from impoverished families. Gains in emotional intelligence—increased empathy, self-control, and attentiveness; decreased aggressiveness; and other indications of social development—often occur. In 1994, reflecting the growing view that earlier is better, Congress established an "Early Head Start" pilot program for infants and toddlers below age three.

Skepticism about childhood intervention programs is fueled by widespread concern about their efficacy. The studies do not present a clear picture, in large part because investigators have focused on differing measures of success and because the quality and character of programs differ greatly from site to site. Critics properly note that the studies with the most impressive results were carried out in model programs in which the intervention was more intensive, the staff was better paid and better trained, and the cost was almost double the national average. The costs of programs to improve learning skills of low-birthweight and other high-risk children are high. Because there are many competing demands on public funds and philanthropic money, careful systematic evaluations of interventions are needed. Such an evaluation is currently being done for Early Head Start.[33]

However, critics who conclude that early intervention programs do not work go far beyond the evidence. What studies show is that early intervention benefits children when the goals are clear, expectations are realistic, and sufficient funds, skill, energy, and commitment to do the job are mobilized. Gains are rarely dramatic, but the preponderance of evidence shows that they make a difference that matters. W. Steven Barnett, a professor at the Graduate School of Education at Rutgers University, analyzed thirty-six assessments of model demonstration projects and large-scale public programs to ascertain their long-term effects on children from poor families. He concludes:

> The weight of the evidence establishes that [early child care and education] can produce large effects on IQ during the early childhood years and sizable persistent effects on achievement, grade retention [not having to repeat a grade], special education, high school graduation, and socialization. In particular, the evidence on grade retention and special education is overwhelming. Evidence is weaker for persistent achievement effects. . . . Evidence for effects on high school graduation and delinquency is strong but based on a smaller number of studies.
>
> These effects are large enough and persistent enough to make a meaningful difference in the lives of children from low-income families: for many children, preschool programs can mean the difference between failing and passing, regular or special education, staying out of trouble or becoming involved in crime and delinquency, dropping out or graduating from high school.[34]

Years ago Albert Solnit, a physician and a specialist in child development at Yale and a veteran of the War on Poverty, reminded citizens and policymakers to pay attention to what has been learned over the past decades: "It should not be necessary," he said, "to learn anew that services [to children] must be sustained . . . yet policy-makers are always hoping to find some intervention that will serve as an inexpensive, one-shot 'immunizing' agent. Most services cannot and do not work like polio vaccine . . . we persist in behaving as though a good meal now and then . . . will suffice. Sustained, adequate, daily nurture is needed throughout childhood."[35]

The Family Place

As I (Ann) examined my infant patients at Children's Hospital and talked with their parents, I became increasingly aware of the many families with medical, psychological, and material needs that could not be addressed in a traditionally structured medical facility. In 1981, with a few members of my church, I started a community center for expectant parents and families with young children. The Family Place, as it is called, was designed to provide a broad range of support services and resources for low-income families. We contacted groups around the country and became aware that others were experimenting with some of the same ideas. We were all concerned about adolescent mothers and their babies, for it was clear that these young people had great needs that were not being met.

The Family Place, located on a busy street in a low-income neighborhood, offers prenatal and parent education programs and social services in a welcoming atmosphere. People can participate in a variety of activities, such as parent classes, health programs, meals, support groups, job-skills workshops, and holiday celebrations. The staff helps refer participants to medical and social service agencies. About five hundred families now attend Family Place's two centers each year. Many tell us that what they value most is the feeling that they are welcome and respected. In our effort to make the centers warm and friendly places, the Family Place invites use of a washing machine and dryer, offers activities that encourage the participants to help one another, and provides child care while parents are in classes. Several paid staff and volunteers are former program participants. For the children there are sunny playrooms with books and toys, cribs for naps, and smiles and hugs.

It is not unusual for a participant mother to make Family Place her first stop after she leaves the hospital with her newborn. Many participants have no family nearby to admire their new baby, or answer a first-time mother's thousand questions, or provide hand-me-down baby clothes or a stroller. About a quarter of visitors on any given day are homeless. Others live with abusing men. Some are very young, and almost everyone lives in crowded, substandard housing.

Does Family Place work? It depends what you mean. Its scale is very small. It reaches only a tiny minority of families in the city and does not address pressing issues such as the shortage of child care and decent housing. But for some participants Family Place has quite literally been lifesaving—preventing suicide, effecting a connection with medical services that would not otherwise have been made, preventing child abuse. For others it has provided a desperately needed relationship of trust and counsel during a crisis. It has supplied information and afforded a congenial setting for focusing on children's needs during times when children tend to get shoved aside because of all the other urgent pressures in parents' lives.

Some program participants have returned to school, found better housing, or otherwise improved their family life. Of course, there are other parents who do not benefit from the opportunities the program offers. But over the last seventeen years Family Place has given several thousand families a sense of belonging and a chance for a better life. Centers like it are springing up all over the country in response to local needs. They are only part of an effective effort. A far larger mobilization of local and national public and private resources is needed to insure that American children have the chance to realize their potential. We are hopeful that the growing awareness of how important the early years of life are for normal child development will foster a sense of urgency and a determination to build a social network to insure that all children's needs are met.[36]

Chapter Ten

CARING FOR CHILDREN

Most people would agree that parents are the most influential figures in children's lives. Throughout the book we've offered many examples, drawn from various studies, supporting the view that parents establish a unique relationship with their child through the care they give. Today, however, many children do not live with both parents, and most preschool children in the United States are not cared for during the working day by a parent but by unrelated persons in places other than the child's home. In this chapter we discuss the effects of nonparental care on children's development.

The Revolution in Child Care

In 1970, Richard Nixon's second year in the White House, over 90 percent of preschool children in the United States lived with both their parents. Divorce was becoming more common, but social stigma, legal obstacles, and expense still served to limit the formal breakup of marriages.

In the next two decades, the divorce rate took off. In the 1990s about half of all recent marriages ended in divorce; half of these divorces took place within seven years. This means that many divorced couples have children still too young to go to school. For many couples "staying together for the sake of the children" is no longer a persuasive reason to keep a fraying marriage together. Although most American children still live in two-parent families, an increasing number of these families involve stepparents and stepchildren. Another striking trend of recent decades is the increase in numbers of children born to unmarried mothers, up from five percent of all births in 1960 to twenty-eight percent in 1990. In 1989, 67 percent of teenage mothers were unmarried when they gave birth. In the 1990s the birthrate among adolescents slowly but steadily declined, although marriage rates remained low.[1]

By the mid-1960s more and more American women were having second thoughts about spending their adult lives as homemakers. Stimulated by a new wave of feminist thinking, many women were expanding their horizons, developing their capabilities, and taking on challenges outside the family. The awareness that nearly half of marriages do not last also encouraged many women to prepare themselves for a career or to take a job.

Mothers of young children entered the labor market in droves in the 1970s and 1980s; between 1980 and 1990, the number of women who had very young children and were joining the labor force jumped by 25 percent. By the mid-1990s, 60 percent of children under three had mothers in the workforce.[2] In most of these families both parents were working. But in cases in which mothers were divorced or never married, they were usually of necessity the sole supporters of their household: nearly half of divorced and never-married fathers contributed little or nothing to the support of their offspring. (In 1994 only 18 percent of court judgments against fathers for child support were actually collected.)[3] According to the U.S. Census Bureau, while the median income of all families with children under six was $32,215 in the mid-1990s, for female-headed households it was $17,443.[4]

By 1995 more than half of all mothers of children under one year old were working outside the home.

So who is taking care of the children?

In 1995 there were about 21 million children under five years of age who were not yet in kindergarten. Parents took care of 40 percent. But well over half of preschool children—13 million of them—were in the care of someone other than a parent during the working day. Other relatives looked after 21 percent. Thirty-one percent were in day care centers. Fourteen percent were in so-called family child care—purchased care in a private home other than their own—and 4 percent were in the care of sitters or nannies in the child's home. (These numbers add up to more than 100 percent because about 9 percent of parents use multiple child care arrangements.)[5]

The largest shift in care occurred for the youngest children. In 1970 less than 20 percent of infants were in nonparental care during working hours; by 1995 that figure had shot up to over 45 percent.[6] The National Institute of Child Health and Human Development (NICHD) examined the child care arrangements made by the parents of 1,281 healthy infants born in 1991 in ten areas of the United States. The families in the study were selected from diverse economic, social, racial, ethnic, and educational backgrounds. The researchers found that only 18 percent of the infants in the study spent the entire first year of their lives at home in the care of their mothers. When mothers went to work, fathers cared for the children in 12 percent of the families—that is, working couples shared child care. But nearly three-quarters had begun to use some form of nonparental care by the time their child was four months old. Nearly 60 percent of the infants spent more than thirty hours a week in nonparental care.

The NICHD study found that the initial arrangements for nonmaternal childcare were about evenly split among fathers, relatives, and family child care homes, with about 25 percent of children in each setting; the remainder of the infants were cared for in child care centers or by a nonrelative in the baby's home. During the baby's first year, however, more and more infants were switched to center or family child care as fathers and grandparents became less available. Over 40 percent of the infants were moved from one nonparental child care setting to another during the year; one third were in three or more settings before their first birthday. Child care arrangements were particularly unstable when the mother worked a variable schedule and family income was low.[7]

A majority of young children are now spending the day with a variety of caregivers, away from their own homes; many of them are very young infants. Of course, there is nothing new about entrusting children to the care of someone other than their mother. In many cultures siblings, kin, and neighbors play a large role in child rearing; similar arrangements were common in the United States in earlier times and still exist. For centuries children in well-off families have been brought up by servant girls and nannies, and this is still a favored choice of working parents who can afford it.

Indeed, as Michael Lamb notes, anthropological studies indicate that the organization of human society in earlier times required shared child care so that mothers could carry out their various roles in food production and household management. There are, he says, no societies today in which exclusively maternal care is the typical practice. But the peculiarly American myth that throughout history mothers have been the sole caregivers of small children has often been used to brand alternative forms of child care unnatural or deviant.[8]

Nor are child care centers a modern invention. There have been day nurseries in the United States for more than 150 years. The first one opened in 1838 in Boston, to take care of the children of sailors' working wives and widows. In the United States, as in other industrial countries, child care arrangements were instituted in response to national needs to bring women into the workforce. During the Civil War the federal government funded nurseries to serve mothers who were working in hospitals. In the dark days of the Great Depression of the 1930s, the Roosevelt administration established publicly funded child care programs as part of its job-creation strategy. As the United States mobilized for World War II, and women were needed to work in war-related industries, over a million and a half children were placed in child care centers. Once the war ended, however, federal funds for day care were abruptly halted. Demobilization brought men back to the factories, and most mothers became full-time housewives once again.[9]

What is new in present-day child care arrangements is that so many children are in the care of strangers, unrelated persons previously unknown to the family, and so many of these children are very young.

Ideally, every child care setting should offer children not only safe custodial care that is convenient and affordable for parents, but also an environment that will enhance their development. The combination has been relatively rare. Programs focused on enrichment were and are usually part-day, and they are expensive. In earlier years, the consequence was that the children of low-income working mothers were placed mainly in custodial baby-sitting arrangements, while the children of middle-class families attended nursery schools that offered preschool education. But as more middle-class women have entered the workforce over the last three decades, and the need for full-time child care has grown, better-off families have also had to settle for custodial care, often of poor quality.

Is Day Care Harmful?

The debate over whether long hours in day care are harmful for children, especially for infants, has persisted for more than half a century. Because it evokes strong feelings about women's work and women's rights, maternal and paternal obligations, and nostalgic images of a mythic golden age when Mother did it all, controversy over child care has been exceptionally heated. As more women enter the workforce, often within weeks of their baby's birth, many feel guilty, anxious, and torn. Many would rather stay home longer. Political and religious conservatives who oppose out-of-home child care have fueled maternal guilt. But many influential child development specialists have also been worried. Benjamin Spock and Penelope Leach, both authors of best-selling baby books, cautioned against too early and too much day care. John Bowlby thought that putting infants in day care was a terrible idea. Women "go out to work and make some fiddly bit of gadgetry which has no particular social value, and children are looked after in indifferent day nurseries. . . . I think that the role of parents has been grossly undervalued, crassly undervalued."[10]

Especially in the 1970s and 1980s, some feminists attacked critics of nonmaternal care as sexist supporters of patriarchy and heaped scorn on mothers who elected to stay home. Defenders of nonmaternal child care also weighed in. The psychologist Sandra Scarr dismissed the idea that mothers are irreplaceable and wrote a book telling women to stop feeling guilty: "Why the guilt trip? Working mothers spend as much time as nonemployed mothers in direct interaction with their babies." She supplemented this assertion with the more defensible observation that lonely, depressed, or angry mothers who would much rather be out working than changing diapers are not likely to be good caregivers.[11]

As the child care controversy was heating up, and ever more mothers were going to work, researchers were prompted to collect quantities of data on children in various caregiving situations. Was day care really bad for children? During the 1970s and 1980s, many studies were conducted on nonparental child care and its impact on the cognitive and emotional development of toddlers and older preschool children. Few studies were done of infant care, probably because it was so rare. In fact, before the 1980s it was taken for granted by policymakers that nearly all children younger than three would be cared for by their mothers at home and that the very few with employed mothers would be cared for by relatives or by domestic servants.[12]

The welter of data fueled the debate. Some studies indicated that among children "who attend relatively high quality day-care centers, nursery schools, or early childhood programs in the pre-school years [cognitive and language development] is advanced over the development of children from comparable family backgrounds who do not."[13] Still another set of studies indicated that children in day care programs are more confident and assertive and less fearful than children who have been raised entirely by their parents at home. They get along better with children their own age and exhibit stronger social skills. Some skeptics pointed out that many studies with more optimistic conclusions either were carried out in university communities where parents were well educated and the quality of day care providers was well above the national average, or were expensive research programs on the effects of enrichment on children's development. Yet another set of studies shows that children in day care tend to be more irritable, more boisterous, and more likely to use bad language and have temper tantrums. A longitudinal study of 123 children in Göteborg, Sweden, published in 1997 found that the more months children spent in day care centers before they were three and a half, the better they performed on cognitive tests at age eight. However, none of the children had started out-of-home care in their first year, and the quality of care in Swedish centers is consistently high.[14] A number of studies found that a high-quality day care center can promote mental growth and social skills, especially for children who come from unstimulating or stressful home environments.[15]

Observers have also commented that in addition to supporting individual children's developmental processes, child care centers can provide a benign and supportive environment in which to learn how to interact with other children. Centers in urban areas are likely to have children of many races and ethnic backgrounds. Children are enriched by their contacts with other cultures.

The most contentious questions arose over whether out-of-home care is advisable for babies during the first and second years of life, when the need for a stable relationship with an attentive caregiver is especially important. Jay Belsky, a University of Pennsylvania psychologist whose concerns about possible harmful effects of day care on infants provoked considerable controversy in the 1980s, concluded that, on average, "extensive nonparental care initiated in the first year is a risk factor for developments such as insecure attachment to the mother, noncompliance, aggressiveness, and possibly withdrawn behavior."[16]

In 1991 the National Institute of Child Health and Human Development began the large study of the effects of nonmaternal care on children's development mentioned earlier in this chapter. By far the most ambitious U.S. study on the subject ever conceived, the NICHD project has collected massive amounts of data at its ten study sites—data on the family and home environment, the child care environment, and on individual differences among the more than 1,000 children participating in the study. The NICHD sample, selected from urban and suburban neighborhoods and rural areas, includes families that differ widely in socioeconomic status, race, and ethnic background. The child care arrangements chosen by the families also turned out to be diverse, from care by the mother only to many types and combinations of nonmaternal care.

To gain a comprehensive picture of how multiple, interacting factors affect child development, researchers closely observed the infants, their parents, and the nonparental caregivers chosen by the parents. Periodically they interviewed the adults, tested the children, and observed and graded the children's homes and child care settings. Data were collected for the children's first three years of life—at one, six, fifteen, twenty-four, and thirty-six months—and yearly thereafter through age seven. Conclusions already published concern the effects of day care on children's attachment to their mother at fifteen months of age, on their cognitive and language development up to three years of age, and on the quality of the mother-child relationship. (Studies of the children's relationship with their fathers have not yet been published.)

At fifteen months each child was given the Strange Situation test to assess attachment. The researchers found that the proportion of children who were securely and insecurely attached was not affected by caregiving arrangements in themselves. About two-thirds of the children cared for exclusively at home were securely attached, as was a similar proportion of those who had received out-of-home care. Neither the age at which an infant entered day care nor the number of hours a week spent away from home made a difference. Nor did the quality of day care in itself matter significantly. The researchers concluded that infant day care in itself does not lead to insecure attachment.

What *did* matter was a combination of insensitive mothering and poor-quality day care. The risk of insecure attachment increased in cases where the mother's caregiving was judged to be relatively insensitive and unresponsive and the quality of child care was relatively poor. Children who were placed in several different child care situations in the first fifteen months of life also showed increased risk of insecure attachment. There was a correlation between relatively insensitive interaction between mothers and children and lower-quality day care. It was also found that mothers were less engaged in interacting with their children when they spent long hours in day care. These effects were small but statistically significant. Thus risks at home appeared to interact with and reinforce the risks in day care.[17]

The NICHD study also found that "more positive care-giving and, especially, language stimulation in the child-care setting were [positively] related to children's better performance on cognitive and language tests when they were 15, 24, and 36 months of age." Children in day care were not at a disadvantage compared to those in maternal care. The conclusion drawn from the research thus far is that the family environment and the child's characteristics are the most powerful predictors of both the mother-child relationship and cognitive and language outcomes; compared to the effects of the home environment, the effects of day care were small. But day care variables, especially warm and skillful caregiving and language stimulation, did make "an additional significant, though usually smaller, contribution to explaining individual differences in these outcomes."[18]

After decades of research it is becoming clearer that the effects on children of out-of-home care are more complex than previously believed or assumed. The answer to the question "Is day care good or bad for a child?" is "It depends." The role parents play in their child's development turns out to be crucial even when the child spends eight hours a day or longer at a day care center. On the whole, sensitive parents served to buffer the potential negative effects of a poor-quality center and to reinforce the effects of a high-quality center. Sensitive parents were more likely to find good day care. They were likely to visit, to notice the details of their baby's day, to ask the right questions and know the right answers to the questions they ask. The researchers observed that children in better-quality child care had mothers who were more sensitive and involved with them than the mothers of children in inferior child care arrangements.

The quality of child care does matter. Children's language and cognitive development were more advanced in higher-quality settings where caregivers were affectionate with the children, paid attention to their efforts to communicate, and responded to them verbally. In settings where learning and stimulation are minimal, young children lose precious opportunities to advance on their developmental journey.

What Is Quality Child Care?

Much of the care that parents arrange for their children is far from ideal. High-quality day care is unaffordable for millions of families with small children unless they (or the centers their children attend) receive some form of subsidy from a corporate, church, philanthropic, or government program. Under the welfare reform legislation of 1996, mothers who used to be able to stay home must now go out to work. Their children are competing with other low-income children for subsidized child care for which there are already long waiting lists in many parts of the country. (A 1995 survey reported by the U.S. General Accounting Office indicated that 40,000 children in Texas, 19,000 in Florida, and 7,000 in Minnesota were on waiting lists for subsidized child care.)[19] Additional funds for child care have been appropriated by the federal government and by the states, but whether these will be sufficient to meet the need is by no means clear.

Recent data indicate that the need for nonparental care is similar among married and single mothers, black and white families, and across the income spectrum.[20] Many children are receiving mediocre care or worse despite what their parents pay. In 1970 the White House Conference on Children called the lack of affordable, good-quality child care "the most serious problem facing children and families in the United States."[21] The 1995 Cost, Quality, and Outcomes in Child Care Centers Study, conducted by researchers at Yale and the state universities of North Carolina, California, and Colorado, indicates that the situation is considerably worse than when that statement was made, if only because so many more families are affected.

The study examined the relationships among "the costs of care, the nature of children's child care experiences, and their effects," using interviews and observations from 401 centers in four states. Eight hundred twenty-six young children—225 infants and toddlers and the rest of preschool age—received individual assessments. The study team concluded that "child care at most centers in the study is poor to mediocre." Results were about the same in for-profit and nonprofit centers. Almost half of the infants and toddlers were subjected to a physical environment of "less than minimal quality." Only 14 percent of the children of all ages were in care judged to be developmentally appropriate, and less than one percent were in care rated as excellent. The researchers defined as "inadequate" centers in which minimum standards of health and safety are not met, "no warmth or support from adults [is] observed; no learning encouraged." Most children in day care centers, the researchers further concluded, are receiving care that is "sufficiently poor to interfere with [their] emotional and intellectual development."[22]

Infants and toddlers, who are at a developmental stage when sensitive caregiving is especially important, are subjected to the worst care. In the 1995 study just mentioned, only 8 percent of children under three were in care rated good or excellent and 40 percent were in care rated as poor. "When I say poor," one of the researchers explained in an interview, "I mean poor—broken glass on the playground, unchanged diapers."[23] (Only 10 percent of older children were in care rated this low.)

Many parents seeking child care prefer to place their children, especially their babies, with a motherly person who cares for a few children in her own home. Such family day care homes are often in the neighborhood. Many accept infants, and they offer more flexible hours than is customary for day care centers, including weekend and evening care in some cases. They also tend to be cheaper. A General Accounting Office survey published in 1994 found that 55 percent of poor mothers use "informal" child care: a relative, friend, or neighbor who is not working looks after the children, sometimes in some sort of barter arrangement.

It sounds rather nice, and sometimes it is. But on closer examination the overall situation is dismaying. In 1991–92 the Families and Work Institute undertook a project called the Study of Children in Family Child Care and Relative Care. It examined care provided by 226 family child care providers in California, North Carolina, and Texas. Two hundred and twenty-five children were studied, more than half under thirty months of age. The authors concluded that, typically, family child care homes ranged between "just below adequate" and "not quite good"; assessments were based on physical surroundings, caregiving practices, and opportunities to learn. "Adequate care" was defined as "custodial, neither developmentally enhancing nor harmful to children." Only 9 percent of the providers gave high-quality care. The average provider was rated as nonresponsive or inappropriate in interactions with the children close to half the time.[24] The National Association for the Education of Young Children has estimated that 82 to 90 percent of all family child care is unregulated.[25]

There is a good deal of agreement among specialists in child development about what constitutes high-quality care, although there are differing approaches to measuring it. There clearly are certain necessities, such as meeting the children's nutritional needs and providing a safe, cheerful physical environment. Children should not be subjected to fire hazards, lead-based paint, cigarette smoke, bad sanitation, or conditions likely to cause an accident or needlessly increase the risk of disease. Child care providers should have training in first aid so they know what to do in case of accident or illness. A grim, bare, crowded basement offering little to stimulate or interest an infant or toddler other than a television set simply will not do. Many child care situations fail at this most basic level.

It is the caregivers, however, who ultimately determine whether child care is poor, mediocre, or excellent. It makes a difference whether caregivers know how to encourage language learning and motor skills. The ability to talk to an infant, to listen to his vocal responses, and to decode the meaning of gestures and facial expressions is an essential skill. A sensitive caregiver also needs to develop an intuitive grasp of what will challenge a child and what will discourage him. She (occasionally he) must be attentive, involved, and alert to what the infant is trying to communicate; she must respond in appropriate ways. Caregivers should be sensitive to temperamental differences among the infants or toddlers in their charge. Since the developmental patterns and schedules of children vary, one-size-fits-all child care can be harmful. This is particularly true if a child has special problems, such as the developmental difficulties associated with premature birth. Such children may need more time to be quiet and to be held and more individual attention and encouragement from the caregiver. As parents know, caring for small children is demanding work.

Many workers in child care centers and in family care situations are wonderfully intuitive and engaged. "You're loved all day long by these little people," a San Diego day care worker told a journalist to explain why she was there. "I take twelve home in my heart at night. The money is just not the object."[26] But many more see their work as just a job, and not a good one at that. Turnover rates are high. Studies find that on average 37 to 41 percent of the staff is gone by the end of a given year. (Schoolteachers' annual turnover is about 12 percent.)

It is not surprising that so many caregivers leave. Caring for infants and toddlers imposes great responsibilities, but the pay is pitifully small and the work offers little status or prestige. In 1993 the mean wage for teachers in child care centers was $7.22 an hour ($15,000 a year) and $5.70 ($11,860) for assistants. Family day care providers earn even less. A 1996 study concludes that real wages for child care staff have not changed significantly since 1988. Other research concludes that there has been a large decline. Fewer than a fifth of all child care centers provide health insurance for their employees, and women who provide family day care typically receive no benefits. Kennels pay their attendants better, and stories abound of day care workers quitting to become supermarket grocery baggers. The low pay child care workers receive and the low prestige of the occupation reflect "the low priority given to children's care and women's work in American society."[27]

What factors indicate good-quality day care? According to Sarah L. Friedman, a psychologist at the National Institute of Child Health and Human Development who has reviewed many studies of day care settings, the ratio of adults to children was the best predictor of quality.

Where the ratio was high, the children's play, verbal skills, and social interaction were more advanced. There were fewer behavior problems and less anxiety, aggressiveness, and hyperactivity. A second significant factor was group size. Large groups were noisier and more distracting, and caregivers were less likely to respond to children's individual needs. A third factor was the educational level of child care providers. Better-educated caregivers were likely to be more encouraging to the children in their care, better able to provide guidance, and less quick to dampen their exploratory impulses. The children were more likely to develop verbal competence, higher cognitive development, and better social skills. Training in child development and early education was a fourth factor that had some positive impact on the quality of care, but the caregiver's overall educational level was a better predictor, especially for care providers to older children. For infants, the caregiver's formal education seems to matter less than warmth and sensitivity.[28]

Even though almost all child care workers are poorly paid, child care is expensive. In the late 1990s, according to the Children's Defense Fund, the average cost of child care was $3,400 per year per child. But costs vary greatly. A year of high-quality care for an infant in centers in some cities can cost well over $10,000. Child care expenses often take a big bite, about 18 to 21 percent, from the income of poor and near-poor families.[29]

"*I Wish I Were There to Tuck You In*"

Major changes in the economy are making it harder for many parents to give their children the time and loving attention they need. Some researchers contend that over the last quarter-century the total time parents spend with their children has fallen 40 percent. Between 1960 and 1986, according to the Stanford economist Victor Fuchs, parents in white households reduced the time spent with their children by an average of ten hours a week. In African-American households the time reduction was twelve hours a week.[30] Some researchers question whether parental time with children has declined this steeply. One analysis comparing the time employed and unemployed mothers spend in child care distinguishes between "primary time" with the child (feeding, bathing, play) and "secondary time" in which the child is near but is not the focus (household chores, shopping). The authors conclude that employed mothers reduce secondary rather than primary time with their children.[31] To be sure, over the centuries most young children have probably spent most of their time with caregivers in situations where they were not the primary focus. But whatever the studies show, millions of working parents are convinced that there are not enough hours in the day.

Time pressures are directly related to the increasing need for both parents not only to work but to work longer hours. Commuting time has also increased. The average workweek expanded from forty-one to forty-seven hours between 1973 and 1989. A *Wall Street Journal* survey in the late 1980s found that almost 90 percent of senior executives worked ten hours a day or more; small entrepreneurs put in an even longer average workday.[32] In the 1990s many corporations cut their U.S. workforce. The fear of losing one's job as a result of the downsizings and mergers of the last two decades keeps people at their desks long after five o'clock.

Unlike the more than one hundred countries which offer new parents some form of paid leave, U.S. law does not require either the employer or the government to provide financial support for parents' care of infants. The Family and Medical Leave Act of 1993 merely prohibits dismissal of an employee for taking time off after the birth or adoption of a child, up to twelve weeks.[33] Many low- and middle-income working parents, even in two-earner families, cannot afford to take unpaid leave even for a few months. Few places of employment permit a parent to take sick leave to care for a child with chickenpox or the sniffles. Many workers would not dare give a meeting with their child's teacher as the reason for seeking time off. Moreover, the Family and Medical Leave Act does not apply to the majority of working women in the United States, because they are employed in small businesses with fewer than fifty employees. Such small businesses are exempt from the law.

Nights and weekends are for "quality time" with the kids, but this is often defined as brief togetherness in front of the TV, a trip to the supermarket and cleaners, reading a few pages of *Goodnight Moon*, and the presentation of a toy or some other guilt offering. By the time they are four or five, many children spend less time directly interacting with their parents than with the TV. Hallmark has done a brisk business in greeting cards to accommodate the marital partnerships of trial lawyers, surgeons, and workaholic executives with no time when duty calls even to lay eyes on the kids. Dad can slip a thoughtful "Have a super day at school" card under his son's cereal bowl on his way out to make the 6:25 A.M. train, and if Mom knows she has to work late, she can put a tender "I wish I were there to tuck you in" message from Hallmark on his pillow as she leaves for the office.

Stress on the job interacts with stress at home, especially when fathers take little responsibility for either housework or child care. Although more fathers are doing more at home than in the 1950s, most of the burden still falls on mothers, including mothers who work full-time. How to share the "second shift," the full day's work that still needs to be done after Mom and Dad get home from their paid jobs, is a source of tension in most marriages these days, and figures importantly in divorces. One researcher estimates that about one-third of fathers are "involved" enough to participate fully in rearing their children; others give lower figures.[34] The sociologist Arlie Hochschild, reviewing studies of the way working parents spend their time, found that married women in the labor force add nearly four hours in housework and child care to their paid workday. Fathers spend thirty minutes on these tasks.[35]

As a rule, working parents make great efforts to reserve time just to be with the children even though the pressures of a high-speed economy make it hard. Mothers and fathers are constantly making choices about where their children fit into their lives. Some choose a reduced income, postponed ambitions, and a more modest standard of living to purchase time to be with their children. Others keep examining the corners of their lives to see where precious time can be retrieved. Still others make cooperative arrangements with other parents of young children so that they can help each other raise their families. Parents know that they have the greatest influence on the character of their children, and most do not want to forgo the joys of watching and encouraging their development. But to carry out their child-rearing responsibilities, parents need a supportive social environment. Surrogate caregivers need help, too: better education, training, supervision, and pay.

SUMMING UP:
SHAPING THE MIND

A theme running through this book is that human relationships shape the minds of children. Advances in genetics and neurobiology are bringing us nearer to comprehending some of the specific processes through which the interweaving of genes and experience takes place. They have shown us with new clarity how social relationships play an important role in brain processes at many different levels, and have demonstrated that the converse—that biological processes affect social relationships— is just as true. A life is woven with strands of one's individual genetic material and unique experiences. This emerging tapestry is enmeshed in the social fabric.

A growing body of research findings on the experiences babies need for healthy development can serve to guide parents and other caregivers. Although discontinuities occur, early development often exerts a powerful influence over later development. In many cases brain research confirms ancient wisdom and common sense. Babies need closeness, nurture, communication, play, and engagement; they need quiet, stability, and predictability. They need challenge, the stimulation of new experiences, and the opportunity to explore their surroundings in safety. All children need to feel that they are treasured, that their developmental accomplishments are celebrated, and that their parents' devotion is rock solid. Research also tells us that children enter the world biologically primed to get what they need by signaling to their caregivers and responding in such a way as to cause caregivers to pay attention to their needs.

Exactly how critical "critical periods" for learning actually are, and how long windows of opportunity in specific areas of development stay open, are disputed. The human brain is malleable. Neuropsychologists regularly observe its capacity for reorganization in the face of brain damage. Brain organization and reorganization continue throughout life, and these processes can be enhanced by interventions like those we have described. But there is wide agreement that in the first two or three years of life the brain is taking shape with a speed that will never again be equaled.

More is becoming known about the biological systems at work in parents which prepare them for their roles. But there are circumstances under which these systems can be overwhelmed: a chaotic or dangerous environment, mental illness, marital conflict, drug addiction, abuse, the demands of a job, or other stress. Poverty often serves as an incubator of stress, but affluent families are not exempt. In every social class there are parents who are unresponsive to their children's needs, and children who are unable to make their needs understood. For one reason or another some parents lack the energy, skills, or inclination to spend focused and unhurried time with a young child, encouraging communication and making emotional connections. Outright abuse and neglect are serious public health problems in the United States, affecting millions of children.

Neither neuroscience, developmental psychology, nor cultural anthropology tells us that there is only one right way to raise a child. Far from it. Being a good parent can take many forms. What constitutes sensitive care for one child may well not work for another, because parents and children interact in a variety of ways that are influenced by their respective temperaments, the history of their relationship, the parents' childhood experiences, the family, culture, and many other factors. If one can generalize from results of the Strange Situation test, then roughly two out of three small children in the United States are securely attached to their primary caregiver. They feel secure enough to take the first steps toward independence. Most parents are also secure enough in their relationship with their child not to keep crossing the invisible lines between sensitive care and overprotection, between emotional availability and emotional neglect.

We have given illustrations of sensitive care and its power—in descriptions of the mutual gaze of a mother and her newborn child; of the total relaxation of a baby settling into the arms of a familiar caregiver, of the excited back-and-forth of a peekaboo game, of the respectful attention accorded a three-year-old as he works to explain something to his father. Child development researchers have recorded on videotape the exquisite attunement that some mothers and babies can establish in responding to one another. But such pictures can make other parents uncomfortable, because they fear they are unable to duplicate this choreography in their own home. Some parents become anxious when they are reminded of how important they are. So while research data can guide parents, it can also make them feel guilty and inadequate, especially when findings are oversimplified and exaggerated implications are drawn in media accounts. The achievements of neuroscience are truly extraordinary. No grand theory, however, integrates this rapid accumulation of knowledge. Much more is unknown than known about the workings of the brain.

If children are to thrive, those responsible for them must make the necessary emotional and material investment. It is also important, however, to appreciate the abundant evidence that children are sturdy. Within broad limits, the processes of development are hard to derail. If children are exposed to reasonably varied and stimulating experiences, they will take from that environment what they need for their development. Moreover, while early experiences leave their mark, they are not destiny. People exhibit resilience throughout the life span. Resilience is not an inborn trait but a developmental process that depends on cumulative experience and relationships. There is no scientific argument for giving up on any individual because of a traumatic childhood.

Early experiences influence how an individual perceives later experiences, but the reverse is also true. In adulthood or even earlier, we can revise our perceptions and understandings of painful or damaging events when something or someone prompts us to make the effort. How resilient a child turns out to be is certainly influenced by temperament and early emotional experiences; but, as longitudinal studies indi-

262   THE YOUNGEST MINDS

cate, later experiences—a relationship with a mentor, the discovery of music, a good marriage, and an infinite variety of other possibilities— can be healing and restorative.

On the other hand, research also tells us that the sheer number of risks a young child faces predicts with some accuracy whether he or she will be able to do well as an adult. It is the job of adults to remove as many stumbling blocks as possible from children's paths. Studies have shown that reducing children's risks enhances their prospects. Head Start does just that, and children who have experienced Head Start or some other enriching preschool program do better than those who have not. The Kauai study and other similar long-term observations of children's development show how the loving interest and support of adults help protect children from risks they face.

For a number of reasons, raising a child in the United States is difficult as we enter the new century. Divorce rates are high, and fewer children have the experience of living with both parents throughout their childhood. Many parents cannot find jobs that pay a living wage. Long hours at work keep them from being home as much as they should be. The television intrudes too much. High-quality child care is often unavailable or unaffordable. Many families move often and so do not put down roots in a community. In the cities and suburbs where most Americans now live, the support of extended families and neighbors is hard to find. Raising one's children without support from other adults outside the nuclear family can be an overwhelming task. Over human history it has not been the normal practice.

Studies we have discussed in this book indicate the importance of outside help for parents and children. Sometimes this help is available in the form of friends and family. Interventions such as parent education programs can help. Parents can be taught, either by a professional worker or by an experienced parent who acts as a mentor, to be aware of their child's capacities at various points in his development, to be more responsive to his needs and more creative in avoiding or solving conflicts. They can be helped to listen more to what a child is trying to communicate. Depressed parents or abusing parents can benefit from nurses or social workers who visit them at home and help them develop better strategies for interacting with their children, despite their pain. A society concerned about children's welfare finds ways to assist and encourage parents in carrying out the critically important task they have undertaken.

A number of the model programs we have discussed are designed to prevent learning and emotional problems. Average gains are often small, as indicated by tests, but they have been shown to make a significant difference in many lives. High-quality enrichment programs that begin in infancy and last long enough to sustain children's language, cognitive, and emotional gains are especially effective. They are expensive. But if such programs prepare children for learning in school and help them not to fall behind or drop out, they are a bargain. A major reduction of school failure and its emotional and economic consequences would have many obvious advantages for our whole society.

Developmental psychology confirms the unsurprising proposition that parents, or primary caregivers who assume this role, are the most important influence in the lives of small children. The best evidence available from current research indicates that nonparental child care does not adversely affect infants' attachment to their parents. Even when babies spend the whole day in the care of others from the time they are a few weeks old, they become attached to their mother and, usually somewhat later, to their father. It has also been shown that high-quality day care can enhance children's development, especially if their home environment is not stimulating.

However, studies of child care settings in the United States indicate that many are of distressingly poor quality. This has been shown to be especially risky for infants and toddlers whose parents are relatively insensitive to their developmental needs. Over half of children under two years of age now attend some form of day care, and it is the arrangements for these youngest children that have been found to be the worst. Many day care centers and family care homes offer little more than custodial care. Failure to give preschool children rich exposure to language, books, and loving nurture sets them up for school failure. Child care arrangements that meet the urgent developmental needs of America's children cannot be achieved without substantially greater investment of public funds for subsidizing paid parental leave and high quality out-of-home care.

Throughout this book we have included many examples of the interplay of hereditary endowment and experience. Infants' perceptions are formed by the language they hear and the sensory environment they experience. Every member of our species is born with built-in expectations for hearing language, seeing faces, and feeling the nurturing touch of caregivers. Compelling evidence from many sources—molecular biologists, cognitive psychologists, parents, teachers, and other observers—shows that "education" begins very early. Infants and toddlers soak up knowledge and experience with amazing speed and accuracy. Everyone concerned about children's welfare—parents, the school system, the public, and policymakers—has a responsibility to see to it that this prime time for education is not neglected.

We are led, moreover, to the conclusion that the development of children's intellect is inseparable from their emotional and moral development. A child's emotions are the filters through which knowledge is acquired and integrated. We know the terrible consequences of severe deprivation—becoming unable to speak, or to see, or to make normal social connections—but the effects of lesser deprivation of the experiences, guidance, and emotional support that infants expect and need are more difficult to assess. While brain research has shown that abuse and neglect leave traces on the brain, neuroscience cannot yet tell us what imprint ordinary daily encounters between a parent and a child make in any particular case. Nevertheless, both observational and experimental studies have yielded important clues about what it takes to be a good parent. It is becoming clearer that parents, or those who act as parents, are partners in the development of their child's mind.

ACKNOWLEDGMENTS

We are grateful to the colleagues and friends who read part or all of the manuscript and for their many helpful suggestions: Sharon Alperovitz, Beth Barnet, Julie Barnet, Michael Barnet, Robin Broad, Noam Chomsky, Mauricio Cortina, Sarah Friedman, Janet Kotler, Stephan Ladisch, Barbara Lenkerd, Ethelbert Miller, David Mrazek, David Nathan, Phillip Nelson, Julian Nichols, Roger Packer, Marianne Schuelein, Eleanor Szanton, L. Gilbert Vezina, and Paul Wellstone.

Andrea Baird, Pamela Beecroft, Melissa Chiang, Lisa Goldstein, Amy Jacobs, Melissa Labriola, Emily Lundahl, and Victoria Martin were excellent research assistants over the years we have been working on the book. Gail MacColl, Sharon Murray, Tommie Robinson, David Rush, Lisa Weisman, and Ira Weiss provided helpful information and comments.

We wish to thank the librarians at Children's National Medical Center—Deborah Gilbert, Shirley Knobloch, Donald Snyder, Catherine Warren, and Carolyn Willard—for facilitating our research. We also thank Joyce Hurwitz for the illustrations.

We greatly appreciate the editorial guidance and judgment of Alice Mayhew, the careful reading and helpful suggestions of Roger Labrie, and the skillful copyediting of Jolanta Benal. We are grateful for the encouragement and advice of our agent, Lynn Nesbit.

Finally, we acknowledge our gratitude for the generous support of our research by the Jennifer Altman Foundation, the Baker Foundation, the Nathan Cummings Foundation, the Harlken Foundation, and the Michael Gellert Foundation.

Of course, any errors are our responsibility alone.

NOTES

1. HOW THE BRAIN TAKES SHAPE

1. Whether these capacities are *uniquely* human is a matter of some controversy. Throughout the book we will draw on relevant animal research, but the extent to which animals share the capacities most critical for the social arrangements on which the survival of the human species depends is not a focus of this book.

2. William James's characterization is discussed in Edelman, Gerald M., *Bright Air, Brilliant Fire: On the Matter of the Mind* (New York: Basic Books, 1992), p. 6.

3. Rakic, P., "Specification of Cerebral Cortical Areas," *Science* 241: 170–76, 1988.

4. Walsh, C., and Cepko, C., "Widespread Dispersion of Neuronal Clones Across Functional Regions of the Cerebral Cortex," *Science* 255: 434–40, 1992.

5. Elbert, T., Pantev, C., Wienbruch, C., Rockstroh, B., and Taub, E., "Increased Cortical Representation of the Fingers of the Left Hand in String Players," *Science* 270: 305–307, 1995.

6. "fire together, wire together": Shatz, C., "The Developing Brain," *Scientific American*, Sept. 1992, pp. 61–67. Also see Wolpaw, J., Schmidt, J., and Vaughan, T., *Activity-Driven CNS Changes During Learning and Development* (New York: Annals of the New York Academy of Sciences 627, 1991).

7. Shepherd, Gordon M., *Neurobiology*, 3rd ed. (New York: Oxford University Press, 1994), p. 9.

8. The cortex size comparison is taken from ibid., p. 652.

   Neural chatter: Nelson, P., "Palimpsest or Tabula Rasa: Developmental Biology of the Brain," *Journal of the American Academy of Psychoanalysis* 21: 525–37, 1993.

9. "Trillion nerve cells": This is the estimate offered by Carla Shatz (University of California–Berkeley) at the White House Conference on Early Childhood Development and Learning, April 17, 1997. Estimates vary from 100 billion to a trillion.

10. Stellar, H., "Mechanisms and Genes of Cellular Suicide," *Science* 267: 1445–49, 1995.

    The process of programmed cell death is called apoptosis.

11. Nelson, P., Fields, D., and Liu, Y., "Neural Activity, Neuron-Glia Relationships, and Synapse Development," *Perspectives on Development Neurobiology* 2: 399–407, 1995.

12. Rakic, P., Bourgeois, J.-P., Eckenhoff, M., Zecevic, N., and Goldman-Rakic, P., "Concurrent Overproduction of Synapses in Diverse Regions of the Primate Cerebral Cortex," *Science* 232: 232–35, 1986. Rakic studied twenty-two monkeys.

    Indeed, as Rakic asserts, research findings "reveal how children can use their cortical synapses for far more complex logical deductions than hitherto recognized." This quotation (on p. 124), introduces the section "Neural and Psychological Development" in Gazzaniga, M., ed., *The Cognitive Neurosciences* (Cambridge, Mass.: MIT Press, 1995), pp. 123–231. The section contains many examples of young children's "complex logical deductions" from recent research, and we give others throughout this book.

    Limited anatomical data from humans suggest that the frontal association cortex may follow a slower time course for synapse formation and elimination than the more posterior cortical areas. See Huttenlocher, P., "Synaptogenesis in Human Cerebral Cortex." In Dawson, G., and Fischer, K., eds., *Human Behavior and the Developing Brain* (New York: Guilford Press, 1994), pp. 137–52.

13. On metabolic rate, see Chugani, Harry, "Neuroimaging of Developmental Non-linearity and Developmental Pathologies." In Thatcher, R. W., Lyon, G. R., Rumsey, J., and Krasnegor, N., eds., *Developmental Neuroimaging: Mapping the Development of Brain and Behavior* (San Diego: Academic Press, 1997), pp. 187–95.

14. On visual deprivation, see Hubel, D., and Wiesel, T., "Receptive Fields, Binocular Interaction and Functional Architecture in the Cat's Visual Cortex," *Journal of Physiology* (London) 160: 106–54, 1962.

    On enriched environment, Greenough, W. T., "Possible Structural Substrates of Plastic Neural Phenomena." In Lynch, G., McGaugh, J., and Weinberger, N., eds., *Neurobiology of Learning and Memory* (New York: Guilford Press, 1984), pp. 470–78.

    On mouse brain growth, see Kemperman, G., Kuhn, H., and Gage, F., "More Hippocampal Neurons in Adult Mice Living in an Enriched Environment," *Nature* 386: 493–95, 1997. The increase in formation of new neurons was in part of the hippocampus, the dentate gyrus, a brain site where, as previous research has shown, adult mice can form new neurons.

15. Greenough, W. T., Black, J., and Wallace, C., "Experience and Brain Development," *Child Development* 58: 539–59, 1987.

16. The comparison between numbers of stars and numbers of neurons was made in the National Academy of Sciences' Seventh Annual Symposium on Frontiers of Science, Irvine, Calif., Nov. 2–4, 1995. Quoted in *Science* 270: 1294, 1995.

17. The quotation is from a discussion of critical and sensitive periods in Shore, Rima, *Rethinking the Brain: New Insights into Early Development* (New York: Families and Work Institute, 1997), pp. 36–41, 63. For further discussion see Bornstein, M., "Sensitive Periods in Development: Structural Characteristics and Causal Interpretations," *Psychological Bulletin* 105(2): 179–97, 1989.

18. On gene expression: Although every cell in the body (with such notable exceptions as eggs, sperm, and mature red blood cells) contains all the genes in the genome, only a subset of genes is active in each organ and tissue. Activation depends on exquisitely precise regulatory sequences in the gene and in its molecular environment. Whether transcription (the crucial initial step in a gene's production of its functional products) is able to take place or not is determined by proteins that bind temporarily to special DNA sequences immediately preceding the gene. These gene regulators either repress or activate gene transcription.

    Regulators also switch sets of genes on and off in a coordinated manner during development and as different physiological processes occur. The activities of cells are regulated and coordinated in many ways: hormones and neurotransmitters play vital regulatory roles in the brain, as well as in other organs. Hormone and neurotransmitter molecules carry messages from cell to cell. As we said earlier, a particular message can be received by a cell only if it has a specific appropriate receptor at entry points on the surface wall (membrane) of the cell. These points are like keyholes. They allow entry only if the right key is put in the lock and turned.

2. THE HOUSE OF MEANING

1. The biologist E. O. Wilson discusses human impacts on natural phenomena in an interview in *Modern Maturity,* May–June 1995, p. 63.

2. The "housing us in meaning" quotation is from Thomas, Lewis, *The Lives of a Cell* (New York: Viking Press, 1974), p. 90.

3. Susan Goldin-Meadow in Wanner, E., and Gleitman, L. R., eds., *Language Acquisition: The State of the Art* (New York: Cambridge University Press, 1982), pp. 51–77.

4. Emde, R. N., and Robinson, J., "The First Two Months: Recent Research in Developmental Psychobiology and the Changing View of the Newborn." In Call, J., Noshpitz, J., Cohen, R., and Berlin, I., eds., *Basic Handbook of Child Psychiatry,* vol. 1 (New York: Basic Books, 1979), pp. 72–105.

5. Bakwin, H., "Loneliness in Infants," *American Journal of Diseases of Children* 63: 30–40, 1942; Bowlby, J., *Maternal Care and Mental Health* (Geneva: World Health Organization Monograph Series [2], 1951); Spitz, R., "Hospitalism: An Inquiry into the Genesis of Psychiatric Conditions in Early Childhood," *The Psychoanalytic Study of the Child* 1: 53–74, 1945.

6. See, for example, Hubel, D., and Wiesel, T., "The Period of Susceptibility to the Physiological Effects of Unilateral Eye Closure in Kittens," *Journal of Physiology* (London) 206: 419–36, 1970.

7. Curtiss, S., "The Independence and Task-Specificity of Language." In Bornstein, M., and Bruner, J., eds., *Interaction in Human Development* (Hillsdale, N.J.: Erlbaum, 1989), pp. 105–37.

8. Noam Chomsky discusses language acquisition in many books and papers including *Rules and Representations* (New York: Columbia University Press, 1980). Those who challenge his theories usually accept the fact that both genetic and environmental factors are involved in language acquisition, but they have different hypotheses about how the environment influences the manner in which the genetic code controls an individual's development with respect to language acquisition and cog-

nition. For a recent discussion of one such view see Plunkett, K., Karmilov-Smith, A., Bates, E., Elman, J. L., and Johnson, M. H., "Connectionism and Developmental Psychology," *Journal of Child Psychology and Psychiatry* 38(1): 53–80, 1997.

9. "language is embedded": Luria, S., *Life: The Unfinished Experiment* (New York: Scribners, 1973). Luria is quoted in Fromkin, V. A., "The State of Brain/Language Research." In F. Plum, ed., *Language, Communication, and the Brain* (New York: Raven Press, 1988), p. 3.

   "children reinvent language": Pinker. S., *The Language Instinct: How the Mind Creates Language* (New York: Morrow, 1994), p. 32.

10. Chomsky, Noam, *On the Generative Enterprise: A Discussion with Riny Hybregts and Henk van Riemsdijk* (Dordrecht, The Netherlands: Foris, 1982).

11. Berko, J., "The Child's Learning of English Morphology," *Word* 14: 150–77, 1958.

12. Our discussion of Chomsky's ideas follows Pinker, Steven, *The Language Instinct: How the Mind Creates Language* (New York: Morrow, 1994), pp. 40–42. Experiments with preschool children supporting the hypothesis that, in Pinker's words, "the mind contains blueprints for grammatical rules" have been performed by researchers including Crain, S., and Nakayama, M., "Structure Dependence in Children's Language," *Language* 62: 522–43, 1986.

13. Bates, Elizabeth, and Marchman, Virginia A., "What Is and Is Not Universal in Language Acquisition." In Plum, F., ed., *Language, Communication, and the Brain* (New York: Raven Press, 1988), pp. 19–38.

14. Example from de Cuevas, John, "No, She Held Them Loosely," *Harvard Magazine,* Sept.–Oct. 1990, pp. 61–67.

    However, children do not make these charming mistakes very often, apparently because they treat an encounter with an irregular verb as they do any new word: they enter it into their mental lexicon quickly and accurately. Fei Xu and Steven Pinker calculated the rates for overregularized-past-tense errors using a large data set from nine children aged thirteen months to eight years and found that such errors occurred less than one percent of the times the children used past-tense verb forms. See Xu, F., and Pinker, S., "Weird Past Tense Forms," *Journal of Child Language* 22: 531–56, 1995. Pinker believes that regular verb inflections are generated by rules, while those for irregular verbs depend on associative memory.

A recent report on three adult aphasic patients suggests that "regular and irregular past tenses are supported by different neural systems which can become disassociated by damage to the brain." The patients could analyze regular past-tense forms of verbs but not irregular ones, or vice versa, suggesting that "mental dictionary and mental grammar may be kept in different parts of the brain." Marslen-Wilson, W., and Tyler, L., "Dissociating Types of Mental Computation," *Nature* 387: 592–94, 1997. Also see commentary by Pinker, S., *Nature* 387: 547–48, 1997.

15. Fromkin, V. A., "The State of Brain/Language Research." In Plum, F., ed., *Language, Communication, and the Brain* (New York: Raven Press, 1988), pp. 1–18.

16. The figures for developmental progression to thirty months of age are medians from Fenson, L., Dale, P. S., Reznick, J. S., Bates, E., Thal, D. J., Pethick, S. J., "Variability in Early Communicative Development," *Monographs of the Society for Research in Child Development* 59, 1994. For older children, estimates are from Pinker, S., *The Language Instinct: How the Mind Creates Language* (New York: Morrow, 1994). Children's rates of language acquisition vary considerably.

17. The question "How many words does this child know?" is deceptively simple. How shall we count them? Just root words ("jump" but not "jumping"; "die" and "dead," but not both "kill" and "killer"; "happy," but not "happiness" or "unhappy"; "Mom" or "Mommy," but not both)? Compound words ("birth," "day," and "birthday")? Or every utterance that denotes a differing concept ("dog," "dogs," "dog's")? And what are you willing to count as "knowing" a word—any meaning in the dictionary? Use in context? And from what source do you draw your word lists? (An unabridged dictionary? Lists that include slang and regional word usages?) Different researchers use different approaches to these questions and therefore arrive at differing estimates of vocabulary size and its growth. Although these are rather technical questions, they have practical implications as a child comes into a school system and is tested and, sometimes, pigeonholed.

18. "I feel sure, from what I have seen with my own infants, that the period of development of the several faculties will be found to differ considerably in different infants." Darwin, C., "A Biographical Sketch of an Infant." Originally published in *Mind,* July 1877, pp. 285–94. Reprinted as Supplement No. 24 to *Developmental Medicine and Child Neurology* 13(5): 3, 1971.

19. Fenson, Larry; Dale, Philip S.; Resnick, J. Steven; Bates, Elizabeth; Thal, Donna J.; and Pethick, Stephen J., "Variability in Early Communicative Development," *Monographs of the Society for Research in Child Development* 59: 163–89, 1994.

The test forms and norms are published as *The MacArthur Communicative Development Inventory* (San Diego: Singular Publishing Group, 1993). The *Inventory,* originally developed for children learning English as their first language, has now been "normed" for languages other than English.

20. Bates, E., and Marchman, V. A., "What Is and Is Not Universal in Language Acquisition." In Plum, F., ed., *Language, Communication, and the Brain* (New York: Raven Press, 1988), p. 21.

21. Darwin, C., "A Biographical Sketch of an Infant." Originally published in *Mind,* July 1877, pp. 285–94. Reprinted as Supplement No. 24 to *Developmental Medicine and Child Neurology* 13(5): 3, 1971.

22. Shinn, M. W., *The Biography of a Baby* (1900; reprint, New York: Arno Press, 1975, in the series *Classics in Child Development*), pp. 225ff.

23. The creation of large computerized child-language databases, such as CHILDES (Child Language Data Exchange System), which became operational in 1984 (see MacWhinney, B., *The CHILDES Project: Computational Tools for Analyzing Talk* [Hillsdale, N.J.: Erlbaum, 1991]) has enabled child language researchers to list the words used by a single child or a group of children, compute word frequency, and study word combinations and length of utterances.

24. Brown, R., *A First Language: The Early Stages* (Cambridge, Mass.: Harvard University Press, 1973).

25. Papousek, H., "Conditioned Head Rotation Reflexes in Infants in the First Months of Life," *Acta Pediatrica* 50: 565–76, 1961; Grimwade, J., Walker, D., Bartlett, M., Gordon, S., and Wood, C., "Human Fetal Heart Rate Change and Movement in Response to Sound and Vibration," *American Journal of Obstetrics and Gynecology* 109: 86–90, 1971.

26. DeCasper, A. J., Lecanuet, J., Busnel, M., Granier-Deferre, C., and Maugeais, R., "Fetal Reactions to Recurrent Maternal Speech," *Infant Behavior and Development* 17: 159–64, 1994. DeCasper, A. J., and Spence, M. J., "Prenatal Maternal Speech Influences Newborns' Perception of Speech Sounds," *Infant Behavior and Development* 9: 133–50, 1986.

27. Golinkoff, R., Hirsh-Pasek, K., Cauley, K., and Gordon, L., "The Eyes

Have It: Lexical and Syntactic Comprehension in a New Paradigm," *Journal of Child Language* 14: 23–45, 1987.

28. Bowlby, J., *Attachment* (New York: Basic Books, 1969), p. 272.

29. Zesking, P. S., and Lester, B. M., "Acoustic Features and Auditory Perceptions of the Cries of Newborns with Prenatal and Perinatal Complications," *Child Development* 49(3): 580–89, 1978. Malatesta, C. Z., "Developmental Course of Emotion Expression in the Human Infant." In Zivin, G., ed., *The Development of Expressive Behavior: Biology-Environment Interactions* (New York: Academic Press, 1985), pp. 118–219.

30. Meltzoff, A., and Moore, M. K., "Imitation of Facial and Manual Gestures by Human Neonates," *Science* 198: 75–78, 1977. Mehler, J., Bertoncini, J., Barriere, M., and Jassik-Gerschenfeld, D., "Infant Recognition of Mother's Voice," *Perception* 7: 491–97, 1978. Bower, T. G. R., *Perceptual World of the Child* (Cambridge, Mass.: Harvard University Press, 1973). Bruner, J. S., *Child's Talk* (New York: Norton, 1983), pp. 28ff. Fernald, A., "Approval and Disapproval: Infant Responsiveness to Vocal Affect in Familiar and Unfamiliar Languages," *Child Development* 64: 657–74, 1993. Tronick, E., Als, H., Adamson, L., Wise, S., and Brazelton, T. B., "The Infant's Response to Entrapment Between Contradictory Messages in Face-to-Face Interaction," *Journal of Child Psychiatry* 17: 1–13, 1978. Cohn, J. F., and Tronick, E. Z., "Three-Month-Old Infants' Reaction to Simulated Maternal Depression," *Child Development* 54: 185–93, 1983.

31. Frankenberg, W. K., and Dodds, J. B., *Denver II Infant Development Test* 1988. Available from Denver Developmental Materials, Inc., P.O. Box 6919, Denver, CO 80206-0919.

32. Bates, E., Camaioni, L., and Volterra, V., "The Acquisition of Performatives Prior to Speech," *Merrill-Palmer Quarterly* 21: 205–26, 1975. The quotation is on p. 216.

33. Reeder, K., "How Young Children Learn to Do Things with Words." In Dale, Philip S., and Ingam, David, eds., *Child Language: An International Perspective* (Baltimore: University Park Press, 1981), p. 135.

34. Columbo, J., and Bundy, R. S., "Infant Response to Auditory Familiarity and Novelty," *Infant Behavioral Development* 6: 305–11, 1983. Eimas, P. D., and Miller, J. L., "Organization in the Perception of Speech by Young Infants," *Psychological Science* 3: 340–45, 1992. On newborns' understanding of phonemes, see Aslin, R. N., Pisoni,

D. B., and Jusczyk, P. W., "Auditory Development and Speech Perception in Infancy." In Haith, M. M., and Campos, J. J., eds. (Mussen, P. H., series ed.), *Handbook of Child Psychology*, vol 2: *Infancy and Developmental Psychobiology* (New York: Wiley, 1983); Werker, J. F., and Tees, R. C., "Cross-Language Speech Perception: Evidence for Perceptual Reorganization During the First Year of Life," *Infant Behavior and Development* 7: 49–63, 1984; Best, C. T., McRoberts, G. W., and Sithole, N. M., "Examination of Perceptual Reorganization for Non-native Speech Contrasts: Zulu Click Discrimination by English-Speaking Adults and Infants," *Journal of Experimental Psychology. [Human Perceptual Performance.]* 14: 345–60, 1988.

On Japanese "ra" and "la," see Goto, H., "Auditory Perception by Normal Japanese Adults of the Sounds 'L' and 'R,'" *Neuropsychologia* 9: 317–23, 1971; Miyawaki, K., Strange, W., Verbrugge, R., Liberman, A., Jenkins, J., and Fujimura, O., "An Effect of Linguistic Experience: The Discrimination of (r) and (l) by Native Speakers of Japanese and English," *Perception and Psychophysics* 18(5): 331–40, 1975; and Strange, W., and Dittman, S., "Effects of Discrimination Training on the Perception of /r-l/ by Japanese Adults Learning English," *Perception and Psychophysics* 36(2): 131–45, 1984.

35. Bahrick, L. E., and Pickens, J. N., "Classification of Bimodal English and Spanish Language Passages by Infants," *Infant Behavioral Development* 11: 277–96, 1988.

36. Kuhl, P., Andruski, J., Chistovich, I., Chistovich, L., Kozhevnikova, E., Ryskina, V., Stolyarova, E., Sundberg, U., and Lacerda, F., "Cross-Language Analysis of Phonetic Units in Language Addressed to Infants," *Science* 277: 684–86, 1997. In this experiment, infant-directed speech of English-, Swedish-, and Russian-speaking mothers was analyzed. The vowel sounds of these languages differ, and this was reflected in the infants' vocalizations.

37. On infant sensitivity to word boundaries, clauses, and segments, see Christophe, A., Dupoux, E., and Mehler, J., "Do Infants Perceive Word Boundaries? An Empirical Study of the Bootstrapping of Lexical Acquisition," *Journal of the Acoustical Society of America* 95: 1570–80, 1994; Fischer, C., and Tokura, H., "Acoustic Cues to Grammatical Structure in Infant-Directed Speech: Cross-Linguistic Evidence," *Child Development* 67(6): 3192–3218, 1996.

On pattern of prosody, see Jusczyk, P. W., Cutler, A., and Redanz,

N. J., "Infants' Preference for the Predominant Stress Patterns of English Words," *Child Development* 64: 675–85, 1993.

On French four-day-olds discriminating French, see Mehler, J., Jusczyk, P., Lambertz, G., Halsted, N., Bertoncini, J., and Amiel-Tyson, C., "A Precursor to Language Acquisition in Young Infants," *Cognition* 29: 143–78, 1988.

38. Kuhl, P. S., Williams, K. A., Lacerda, F., Stevens, K., Lindblom, B., "Linguistic Experience Alters Phonetic Perception in Infants by Six Months of Age," *Science* 255: 606–608, 1992.

Mehler, J., and Christophe, A., "Maturation and Learning of Language in the First Year of Life." In Gazzaniga, M. S., ed., *The Cognitive Neurosciences* (Cambridge, Mass.: MIT Press, 1995), pp. 943–54. Jusczyk, P., and Hohne, E., "Infants' Memory for Spoken Words," *Science* 277: 1984–86, 1997.

39. See Stuart Sutherland, review of *In Other Words: The Science and Psychology of Second Language Acquisition,* Ellen Bialystok and Kenji Hakuts (New York: Basic Books, 1994), *Nature* 373: 30, Jan. 5, 1995. Also see Johnson, J., and Newport, E., "Critical Period Effects in Second Language Learning: The Influence of Maturational State on the Acquisition of English as a Second Language," *Cognitive Psychology* 21: 60–99, 1989.

40. Hart, B., and Risley, T., *Meaningful Differences in the Everyday Experience of Young American Children* (Baltimore: Paul H. Brookes, 1995).

41. Some children show marked acceleration in their expressive vocabulary around this age (fifteen to twenty months), a burst that may reflect a sudden insight into the idea that all things have names (cf. Baldwin, D. A., and Markham, E. M., "Establishing Word-Object Relationships: A First Step," *Child Development* 60: 381–98, 1989).

42. Keller, Helen, *The Story of My Life* (New York: Grosset and Dunlap, 1903), p. 22.

43. Ibid., p. 60.

44. Caplan, D., "The Cognitive Neuroscience of Syntactic Processing." In Gazzaniga, M. S., ed., *The Cognitive Neurosciences* (Cambridge, Mass.: MIT Press, 1995), pp. 871–80.

45. English listeners and readers consistently show a strong preference for interpreting the first prepositional phrase in sentences of this sort as specifying the destination. This results in a momentary confusion when they encounter the second preposition, in this case "in."

46. Tanenhaus, M. K., Spivey-Knowlton, M. J., Eberhard, K. M., Sedivy, J. C., "Integration of Visual and Linguistic Information in Spoken Language Comprehension," *Science* 268: 1632–34, 1995.

47. Petitto, L., and Marentette, P., "Babbling in the Manual Mode: Evidence for the Ontogeny of Language," *Science* 251: 1493–96, 1991.

48. Boothroyd, A., Geers, A. E., and Moog, J. S., "Practical Implications of Cochlear Implants in Children," *Ear and Hearing* (supplement) 12(4): 81s–89s, 1991.

    There are over 20 million people in the United States with hearing impairments severe enough to interfere with their comprehension of speech, but since most of them incurred their loss during adulthood, they do not have impaired language capacity.

49. Conrad, R., *The Deaf School Child: Language and Cognitive Function* (New York: Harper & Row, 1979); cited in Balkany, Thomas, "A Brief Perspective on Cochlear Implants," *New England Journal of Medicine* 328(4): 281–82, 1993. A recent survey by Gallaudet College that confirms poor English reading levels among sixteen- and seventeen-year-olds is cited in *The Washington Post Outlook,* March 10, 1996, C1.

50. For example, in one group of eighty adults who became profoundly deaf as adults, about 60 percent could distinguish some words and sentences after their implant, and some could hear on the phone—that is, without lipreading. Most patients could use their improved hearing to supplement their lip-reading skills. Cohen, N. L., Waltzman, S. B., Fisher, S. B., and the Department of Veterans Affairs Cochlear Implant Study Group, "A Prospective Randomized Study of Cochlear Implants," *The New England Journal of Medicine* 328(4): 233–37, 1993.

51. Staller, S. J., ed., "Multichannel Cochlear Implants in Children," *Ear and Hearing* (supplement) 12(4), August 1991.

52. Tye-Murray, N., Spencer, L., and Woodworth, G. G., "Acquisition of Speech by Children Who Have Prolonged Cochlear Implant Experience," *Journal of Speech and Hearing Research* 38: 327–37, 1995.

53. Barnet, A., and Lodge, A., "Diagnosis of Deafness in Infants with the Use of Computer-Averaged Electroencephalographic Responses to Sounds," *Journal of Pediatrics* 69: 753–58, 1966. For reviews, see Thomas, D. G., and Crow, C. D., "Development of Evoked Electrical Brain Activity in Infancy." In Dawson, G., and Fischer, K., eds., *Human Behavior and the Developing Brain* (New York: Guilford Press, 1994), pp. 207–31; and Salamy, A., "Maturation of the Auditory Brainstem Re-

sponse from Birth Through Early Childhood," *Journal of Clinical Neurophysiology* 1: 293–329, 1984.

54. Shepherd, Gordon M., *Neurobiology,* 3rd ed. (New York: Oxford University Press, 1994), p. 329.

3. PATHWAYS OF LANGUAGE

1. Bishop, D. V. M., North, T., and Donlan, C., "Genetic Basis of Specific Language Impairment: Evidence from a Twin Study," *Developmental Medicine and Child Neurology* 37: 56–71, 1995. For a review, see Pennington, B. F., "Genetics of Learning Disabilities," *Journal of Child Neurology* 10: 69–77, 1995. See also Rapin, I., and Allen, D., "Syndromes in Developmental Aphasia and Adult Aphasia." In Plum, F., ed., *Language, Communication, and the Brain* (New York: Raven Press, 1988), pp. 57–75.

2. Thompson, Lee A., "Genetic Contributions to Early Individual Differences." In Colombo, John, and Fagen, Jeffrey, eds. *Individual Differences in Infancy* (Hillsdale, N.J.: Lawrence Erlbaum, 1990), p. 60.

3. Gopnik, M., and Crago, M. B., "Familial Aggregation of a Developmental Language Disorder," *Cognition* 39: 1–50, 1991. Hurst, J. A., Baraister, M., Auger, E., Graham, F., and Norell, S., "An Extended Family with a Dominantly Inherited Speech Disorder," *Developmental Medicine and Child Neurology,* 32: 347–55, 1990. Fisher, S. E., Varga-Khadem, F., Watkins, K., Monaco, A., and Pembrey, M., "Localization of a Gene Implicated in a Severe Speech and Language Disorder," *Nature Genetics* 18: 168–70, Feb. 18, 1998.

   Affected family members also show impairments in coordination of speech and orofacial musculature (dyspraxia), and their verbal and full-scale IQs are somewhat lower than those of their normal relatives.

4. The phrase is J. P. Changeaux's. See *Neuronal Man* (New York: Pantheon, 1985).

5. Rogers, P. T., and Coleman, M., *Medical Care in Down Syndrome. A Preventive Medicine Approach* (New York: Marcel Dekker, 1992), p. 121.

6. Fisher, S. E., Varga-Khadem, F., Watkins, K., Monaco, A., and Pembrey, M., "Localization of a Gene Implicated in a Severe Speech and Language Disorder," *Nature Genetics* 18: 168–70, Feb. 18, 1998.

7. Tallal, P., Galaburda, A. M., Llinas, R. R., and Von Euler, C., *Temporal Information Processing in the Nervous System: Special Reference to Dyslexia and Dysphasia. Annals of the New York Academy of Sciences*

682: 27–47, 1993; Wright, B., Lombardino, L., King, W., Puranik, C., Leonard, C., and Merzenich, M. "Deficits in Auditory Temporal and Spectral Resolution in Language-Impaired Children," *Nature* 387: 176–78, 1997.

8. Tallal, P., Miller, S. L., Bedi, G., Byma, G., Wang, X., Nagarajan, S. S., Schreiner, C., Jenkins, W. M., and Merzenich, M. M., "Language Comprehension in Language-Learning Impaired Children Improved with Acoustically Modified Speech," *Science* 271: 81–84, 1996.

Merzenich, M. M., Jenkins, W. M., Johnston, P., Schreiner, C., Miller, S. L., and Tallal, P. "Temporal Processing Deficits of Language-Learning Impaired Children Ameliorated by Training," *Science* 271: 77–81, 1996. See also Chenausky, K., "Training Dyslexics First to Hear, Then to Read," *MIT Technology Review*, Aug.–Sept. 1997, 15–17. For a cautionary note, see Rice, M., "Evaluating New Training Programs for Language Impairment," *Journal of American Speech and Hearing Association*, Summer 1997, p. 13.

9. Benasich, A., and Tallal, P., "Auditory Temporal Processing Thresholds, Habituation, and Recognition Memory over the First Year," *Infant Behavior and Development* 19: 339–57, 1996.

10. Tallal, P., Galaburda, A. M., Llinas, R. R., and Von Euler, C., *Temporal Information Processing in the Nervous System: Special Reference to Dyslexia and Dysphasia*, pp. 70–82. *New York Academy of Sciences*, 682, 1993.

Galaburda, A., ed., *Dyslexia and Development. Neurobiological Aspects of Extraordinary Brains* (Cambridge, Mass.: Harvard University Press, 1993).

Farmer, M., and Klein, R., "The Evidence for a Temporal Processing Deficit Linked to Dyslexia: A Review," *Psychonomic Bulletin Review* 2: 460–93, 1995.

11. Blachman, B. A., "Getting Ready to Read: Learning How Print Maps to Speech." In Kavanagh, J. F., ed., *The Language Continuum: From Infancy to Literacy* (Timonium, Md.: York Press, 1991), pp. 2–20.

12. Kelly, J., "Hearing." In Kandel, E., Schwartz, J., and Jessell, T., eds., *Principles of Neural Science*, 3rd ed. (New York: Elsevier, 1991), p. 482.

13. For example, individual nerve fibers may have firing patterns that encode information both from the high frequency sound waves generated by vocal cord vibration and lower frequency modulations that are produced by mouth and tongue movement. "In this way the ear functions

like a demodulator in a radio to extract significant low frequency information from a high frequency carrier wave." See ibid. The quotation is from p. 491.

14. Shepherd, G. M., *Neurobiology*, 3rd ed. (New York: Oxford University Press, 1994), pp. 342–43.

15. Galaburda, A., and Livingstone, M., "Evidence for a Magnocellular Defect in Developmental Dyslexia." In Tallal, P., Galaburda, A. M., Llinas, R. R., and von Euler, C., eds., *Temporal Information Processing in the Nervous System. Annals of the N.Y. Academy of Sciences,* 682: 70–82, 1994. The cited text appears on p. 79.

16. Kelly, J., "Hearing." In Kandel, E., Schwartz, J., and Jessell, T., eds., *Principles of Neural Science,* 3rd ed. (New York: Elsevier, 1991), p. 497.

17. Shepherd, G. M., *Neurobiology,* 3rd ed. (New York: Oxford University Press, 1994), pp. 344–45.

18. Blumstein, S. E., "The Neurobiology of the Sound Structure of Language." In Gazzaniga, M. S., ed., *The Cognitive Neurosciences* (Cambridge, Mass.: MIT Press, 1995), pp. 916–27.

19. Shepherd, G. M., *Neurobiology,* 3rd ed. (New York: Oxford University Press, 1994), p. 677.

20. For all the senses, including hearing, there are small subcortical nerve fiber tracts that ascend without crossing the midline. In patients with unilateral injury to the contralateral pathway, hearing is supported by the ipsilateral (same-sided) ascending nerve fibers.

21. Sperry, R. W., "Lateral Specialization in the Surgically Separated Hemispheres." In Schmitt, F. O., and Worden, F. G., eds., *The Neurosciences: Third Study Program* (Cambridge, Mass.: MIT Press, 1974), pp. 5–19.

22. Caplan, D. "The Cognitive Neuroscience of Syntactic Processing." In Gazzaniga, M. S., ed., *The Cognitive Neurosciences* (Cambridge, Mass.: MIT Press, 1995), p. 874:

"Correlations between language impairments and lesion sites indicate that the association cortex in the region of the sylvian fissure is responsible for language processing. This region includes the pars triangularis and opercularis of the third frontal convolution (Broca's area, or Brodmann 45 and 44), the association cortex in the opercular area of the pre- and post-central gyri, the supramarginal and angular gyri of the parietal lobe (Brodmann area 39 and 40), the first temporal gyrus from the supramarginal gyrus to a point approximately lateral to Heschl's gyrus (Wernicke's area, or Brodmann 41 and 42), and possibly a portion of the adjacent second temporal gyrus. Language processing is restricted to this area in the left hemisphere in up to 98% of right-handed individuals and recruits or is exclusively based in the right hemisphere in up to a third of individuals who are ambidextrous or left-handed. The supplemental motor area and several subcortical gray matter structures (the caudate, putamen, parts of the thalamus) may play roles in language processing, but most language processing is cortically based." (See fig. 3-2, p. 66.)

23. Bellugi, U., Klima, E., S., and Poizner, H., "Sign Language and the Brain." In Plum, F., ed., *Language, Communication, and the Brain* (New York: Raven Press, 1988), pp. 39–56.

24. Ross, E., "Right Hemisphere's Role in Language, Affective Behavior, and Emotion," *Trends in Neuroscience* 7: 342–46, 1984; Brumback, R., Harper, C., Weinberg, W., "Nonverbal Learning Disabilities, Asperger's Syndrome, Pervasive Developmental Disorder—Should We Care?" Editorial, *Journal of Child Neurology* 11(6): 427–29, 1996.

25. Geschwind, N., and Levitsky, W., "Human Brain: Left-Right Asymmetries in Temporal Speech Region," *Science* 161: 186–87, 1968.

   Witelson, S. F., and Pallie, W., "Left Hemisphere Specialization for Language in the Newborn: Neuroanatomical Evidence of Asymmetry," *Brain* 96: 641–46, 1973.

   Certain nonhuman primate species are also reported to show right-left temporal anatomic asymmetries. See Gannon, P., Holloway, R., Broadfield, D., and Braun, A., "Asymmetry of Chimpanzee Planum Temporale: Humanlike Pattern of Wernicke's Brain Language Area Homolog." *Science* 279: 220–22, 1998.

26. On female right hemisphere language function, see Shaywitz, B., Shaywitz, S., Pugh, K., Constable, R., et al., "Sex Differences in the Functional Organization of the Brain for Language," *Nature* 373: 607–609, February 16, 1995.

   On male-female anatomic differences in language brain areas; see Harasty, J., Double, K., Halliday, G., Kril, J., and McRitchie, D., "Language-Associated Cortical Regions Are Proportionately Larger in the Female Brain," *Archives of Neurology* 54: 171–76, 1997.

27. Satz, P., Strauss, E., Wada, J., and Orsini, D. L., "Some Correlates of Intra- and Interhemispheric Speech Organization After Left Focal Brain Injury," *Neuropsychologia* 26(2): 345–50, 1988.

28. Elman, J., Bates, E., Johnson, M., Karmiloff-Smith, A., Parisi, D., and

Plunkett, K., *Rethinking Innateness* (Cambridge, Mass.: MIT Press, 1996); Vining, P., Freeman, J., Pillas, D., Uematsu, S., Carson, B., et al., "Why Would You Remove Half a Brain? The Outcome of 58 Children After Hemispherectomy—the Johns Hopkins Experience: 1968 to 1996," *Pediatrics* 100(2): 163–71, 1997; Vargha-Khadem, F., Carr, L., Isaacs, E., Brett, E., Adams, C., and Mishkin, M., "Onset of Speech After Left Hemispherectomy in a Nine-Year-Old Boy," *Brain* 120: 159–82, 1997.

29. The person having an MRI examination is positioned within a tunnel-like space surrounded by a powerful magnet. The magnet's field is strong enough to deflect the direction of spin of the nuclei of the two hydrogen atoms that (along with oxygen) constitute a water molecule. (Water in varying amounts is present in all body tissues.)

    During exposure to the magnet, the tissue being scanned is also briefly perturbed by controlled pulses of radio waves emitted by the scanner. The tissues absorb a small part of the radio-wave energy. As they return, between pulses, to their previous state in the magnetic field, the hydrogen nuclei of the water molecules in the tissues release radio-wave energy at a distinct frequency, which the MRI scanner picks up. The signal is used by a computer to construct an image. The more water there is in a tissue, the stronger the radio-wave signal; for this reason the signal from each type of tissue is distinctive.

    The magnetic field strengths and radio frequencies of the MRI can be manipulated to bring out details of different types of tissues, such as the white and gray matter of the brain, nerve fiber tracts, blood vessels, blood, and abnormal masses such as tumors. Successive planes of the brain are imaged. The computer can also produce three-dimensional pictures by combining images.

30. Barinaga, M., "The Anatomy of Learning," *Science* 274: 1612, 1996.

31. Barinaga, M., "New Imaging Methods Provide a Better View into the Brain," *Science* 276: 1974–76, 1997.

32. Hertz-Pannier, L., Gaillard, W., Mott, S., Cuenod, C., Bookheimer, S., Weinstein, S., Conry, J., Papero, P., Schiff, S., Le Bihan, D., and Theodore, W., "Noninvasive Assessment of Language Dominance in Children and Adolescents with Functional MRI: a Preliminary Study," *Neurology* 48: 1003–12, 1997.

33. Kim, K., Relkin, N., Lee, Kyoung-Min, and Hirsch, J., "Distinct Cortical Areas Associated with Native and Second Languages," *Nature* 388: 171–74, 1997.

34. Klein, D., Milner, B., Zatorre, R., Meyer, E., and Evans, A., "The

Neural Substrates Underlying Word Generation: A Bilingual Functional Imaging Study," *Proceedings of the National Academy of Sciences, U.S.A.* 92: 2899–2903, 1995.

35. Thomas, D., and Crow, C., "Development of Evoked Electrical Brain Activity in Infancy." In Dawson, G., and Fischer, K., eds., *Human Behavior and the Developing Brain* (New York: Guilford Press, 1994), pp. 207–31. See references in this article for changes in evoked responses with age.

36. Since human-brain evoked responses are recorded from the scalp, far from their source, and since they represent the average electrical activity from a large number of individual nerve cells, it is difficult to be sure of their precise origin. Another complication is that evoked activity in the direct pathway from receptor to cortex is often influenced by parallel or feedback circuitry; thus, a wave recorded from scalp electrodes is often an average of activity from several sources.

To ascertain what measures of brain activity in humans mean, whether they be evoked electrical potentials, blood flow, or MRI images, changes must be linked as closely as possible with real world events and behaviors. Parallel study in laboratory animals or in tissue cultures often can illuminate crucial issues. In animals brain functions can be studied using recordings from implanted electrodes that tap the activities of many neurons in a pathway or only one neuron, and these results correlated with the animal's behavior and neuroanatomical analyses.

37. Holcomb, P. J., Coffey, S. A., and Neville, H. J., "Visual and Auditory Sentence Processing: A Developmental Analysis Using Event-Related Brain Potentials," *Development Neuropsychology* 8(2 and 3): 203–41, 1992.

38. Experiments described in the text are summarized in Mills, D., Coffey-Corina, S., and Neville, H., "Variability in Cerebral Organization During Primary Language Acquisition." In Dawson, G., and Fischer, K., eds., *Human Behavior and the Developing Brain* (New York: Guilford Press, 1994), pp. 427–55. Our fig. 3-4 is adapted from fig. 13-3 on p. 438 of this article. Also see Neville, H., "Developmental Specificity in Neurocognitive Development in Humans." In Gazzaniga, M., *The Cognitive Neurosciences* (Cambridge, Mass.: MIT Press, 1995), pp. 219–31. Also see Molfese, D., and Molfese, V., "Short-Term and Long-Term Developmental Outcomes: The Use of Behavioral and Electrophysiological Measures in Early Infancy as Predictors." In Dawson, G., and Fischer, K., eds., *Human Behavior and the Developing Brain*, pp. 493–517.

These investigators and others find differences in evoked responses by stimulus type, but not necessarily the same differences. Many factors may account for differences in experimental results, including subjects' ages and individual differences and details of experimental methods.

39. Barnet, A. B., and Lodge, A., "Click Evoked EEG Response in Normal and Developmentally Retarded Infants," *Nature* 214: 252–55, 1967; Barnet, A. B., Ohlrich, E. S., and Shanks, B. L., "Evoked EEG Responses to Repetitive Stimulation in Normal and Down Syndrome Children," *Developmental Medicine and Child Neurology* 13: 321–29, 1971.

40. Pinker, S., "Introduction to Language." In Gazzaniga, M. S., ed., *The Cognitive Neurosciences* (Cambridge, Mass.: MIT Press, 1995), pp. 851–54. The cited text appears on p. 852.

4. HOW MUCH HELP DOES A BABY NEED?

1. On middle ear disease, see Merzenich, M. M., Jenkins, W. M., Johnston, P., Schreiner, C., Miller, S. L., and Tallal, P., "Temporal Processing Deficits of Language-Learning Impaired Children Ameliorated by Training," *Science* 271: 71–81, 1996. Page 77: ". . . or a child might generate a representation of phonetic information under early childhood conditions (for example, in the presence of middle ear disease) under which acoustic inputs are consistently muffled."

   Teele, D. W., Klein, J. O., Chase, C., Menyuk, P., Rosner, B., and the Greater Boston Otitis Media Study Group, "Otitis Media in Infancy and Intellectual Ability, School Achievement, Speech, and Language at Age 7 Years," *The Journal of Infectious Diseases* 162: 685–94, 1990.

   On iron deficiency; see Moffatt, M. E. K., Longstaffe, S., Besant, J., Dureski, C., "Prevention of Iron Deficiency and Psychomotor Decline in High-Risk Infants Through Use of Iron-Fortified Infant Formula: A Randomized Clinical Trial," *Journal of Pediatrics* 125: 527–33, 1994; Oski, F., "Iron Deficiency in Infancy and Childhood," *New England Journal of Medicine* 329(3): 190–93, 1993.

2. Behrman, R. E., Kliegman, Robert M., Nelson, Waldo E., and Vaughan, Victor C., III, *Nelson Textbook of Pediatrics*, 14th ed. (Philadelphia: W. B. Saunders, 1992), pp. 1788–89.

3. National Research Council, *Pesticides in the Diets of Infants and Children* (Washington, D.C.: National Academy Press, 1993).

   Chivian, E., McCally, M., Hu, H., and Haines, A., *Critical Condition: Human Health and the Environment* (Cambridge, Mass.: MIT Press, 1993).

4. Concerning the lack of certain nutrients—examples are iodine and folic acid—see Hetzel, Basil S., *The Story of Iodine Deficiency: An International Challenge in Nutrition* (New York: Oxford University Press, 1989). For the Centers for Disease Control recommendations for the use of folic acid to reduce the number of cases of spina bifida and other neural tube defects, see *Morbidity and Mortality Weekly Report* 41: 1–7, 1992.

5. Barnet, A. B., Weiss, I. P., Sotillo, M. V., Ohlrich, E. S., Shkurovich, Z. M., Cravioto, J., "Abnormal Auditory Evoked Potentials in Severely Malnourished Infants," *Science* 270: 450–52, 1978.

   Flinn, J. M., Barnet, A. B., Lydick, S., Lackner, J. "Infant Malnutrition Affects Cortical Auditory Evoked Potentials," *Perceptual and Motor Skills* 76: 1359–62, 1993.

6. Brown, J. L., and Pollitt, E. "Malnutrition, Poverty, and Mental Development," *Scientific American*, Feb. 1996, pp. 38–43.

7. Labeling children often has a profound, self-fulfilling effect on their lives. See, for example, Rosenthal, R., and Jacobson, L., *Pygmalion in the Classroom: Teacher Expectations and Pupil's Intellectual Development* (New York: Holt Rinehart and Winston, 1968).

8. Rutter, M., and Rutter, M., *Developing Minds: Challenge and Continuity Across the Life Span* (New York: Basic Books, 1993), pp. 32–34.

9. According to J. L. Brown, director of the Center on Hunger, Poverty and Nutrition at Tufts University, and E. Pollitt, of the University of California–Davis, "Globally, nearly 195 million children younger than five are malnourished." They also note that "in 1992 an estimated 12 million American children consumed diets that were significantly below the recommended allowances of nutrients established by the National Academy of Sciences." Brown, J. L., and Pollitt, E., "Malnutrition, Poverty and Intellectual Development," *Scientific American*, Feb. 1996, pp. 38–43.

   On rising child poverty in the United States, see *The State of America's Children Yearbook 1997* (Washington, D.C.: Children's Defense Fund, 1997), tables A2 and B1, pp. 92, 96–97.

10. Pinker, Steven, *The Language Instinct: How the Mind Creates Language* (New York: Morrow, 1994), p. 39.

11. Stromswold, K., "The Cognitive and Neural Bases of Language Acquisition." In Gazzaniga, M. S., ed., *The Cognitive Neurosciences* (Cambridge, Mass.: MIT Press, 1995), pp. 855–70; the cited text appears on p. 867.

12. Pinker, Steven, *The Language Instinct: How the Mind Creates Language* (New York: Morrow, 1994), p. 276.

13. Rymer, R., "A Silent Childhood," *New Yorker,* Apr. 13, 1992, pp. 41–81, and Apr. 20, 1992, pp. 43–77. Snow is quoted on p. 51 of the April 13 issue.

14. Chomsky, N., personal communication, June 27, 1997. See also Goldin-Meadows, Susan, "The Resilience of Recursion." In Gleitman, L., and Wanner, E., eds., *Language Acquisition: The State of the Art* (Cambridge, England: Cambridge University Press, 1982), pp. 51–77.

15. Examples (from the *Wall Street Journal*) cited in Hewlett, Sylvia Ann, *When the Bough Breaks: The Cost of Neglecting Our Children* (New York: HarperCollins, 1991), pp. 254–55.

16. Snow, C., Arlman-Rupp, A., Hassing, Y., Jobse, J., Joosten, J., and Vorster, J., "Mothers' Speech in Three Social Classes," *Journal of Psycholinguistic Research* 5(1): 2, 1976.

17. Snow, C. E., Perlmann, R., and Nathan, D., "Why Routines Are Different: Toward a Multiple-Factors Model of the Relation Between Input and Language Acquisition." In Nelson, K., and van Kleek, A., eds., *Children's Language,* vol. 6 (Hillsdale, N.J.: Erlbaum, 1987), p. 79.

18. Snow, Catherine E., "Social Interaction and Language Acquisition." In Dale, Philip S., and Ingram, David, eds., *Child Language: An International Perspective* (Baltimore: University Park Press, 1981), p. 197.

19. A child's seeking an emotional signal from a parent is called social referencing. See Emde, R. N., "The Infant's Relationship Experience: Developmental and Affective Aspects." In Sameroff, A. J., and Emde, R. N., *Relationship Disturbances in Early Childhood* (New York: Basic Books, 1993), p. 45.

20. Pinker, Steven. *The Language Instinct: How the Mind Creates Language* (New York: Morrow, 1994), p. 279.

21. Brody, L. R., and Hall, J. A., "Gender and Emotion." In Lewis, M., and Haviland, J. M., *Handbook of Emotions* (New York: Guilford Press, 1993), pp. 454–57. See also Berko-Gleason, J., "Sex Differences in Parent-Child Interaction." In Philips, S., Stelle, S., and Tanz, C., eds., *Language, Gender, and Sex in Comparative Perspective* (New York: Cambridge University Press, 1987), pp. 189–99.

22. Bruner, J., *Child's Talk: Learning to Use Language* (New York: Norton, 1983), pp. 45–63.

23. Snow, C. E., Perlmann, R., and Nathan, D., "Why Routines Are Different: Toward a Multiple-Factors Model of the Relation Between Input and Language Acquisition." In Nelson, K., and van Kleek, A., eds., *Children's Language* vol. 6 (Hillsdale, N.J.: Erlbaum, 1987), p. 93.

24. Weir, Ruth Hirsch, *Language in the Crib* (The Hague, Netherlands: Mouton, 1970), p. 19. Jakobson's comment is in his foreword to the book.

25. In chapter 10 we discuss research that indicates a relationship between quality of the child care setting and children's language development.

26. Boyer, E., *Ready to Learn: A Mandate for the Nation* (Princeton, N.J.: Princeton University Press, 1991).

27. See, for example, Louv, R., *Childhood's Future* (New York: Anchor Books, 1991), pp. 14–24.

28. Hart, B., and Risley, T. R., "American Parenting of Language-Learning Children: Persisting Differences in Family-Child Interactions Observed in Natural Home Environments," *Developmental Psychology* 28: 1096–1105, 1992. This research is further described and analyzed in Hart, B., and Risley, T., *Meaningful Differences in the Everyday Experience of Young American Children* (Baltimore: Paul Brookes, 1995). The study was discussed in another context in chapter 2.

29. Walker, D., Greenwood, C., Hart, B., and Carta, J., "Prediction of School Outcomes Based on Early Language Production and Socioeconomic Factors," *Child Development* 65: 606–21, 1994.

30. Recounted by Shirley Brice Heath in *Ways with Words: Language, Life, and Work in Communities and Classrooms* (New York: Cambridge University Press, 1983), p. 277.

31. Schieffelin, B., "Cross-cultural Perspective on the Transition: What Differences Do the Differences Make?" In Golinkoff, R., ed., *The Transition from Prelinguistic Communication: Issues and Implications* (Hillsdale, N.J.: Erlbaum, 1982); quoted in Warren, A. R., and McCloskey, L. A., "Pragmatics: Language in Social Contexts." In Berko-Gleason, J., ed., *The Development of Language*, 3rd ed. (New York: Macmillan, 1993), pp. 195–238.

32. Harkness, S., "A Cultural Model for the Acquisition of Language: Implications for the Innateness Debate," *Developmental Psychobiology* 23(7): 727–40, 1990.

33. Liberman, A. L., "In Speech Perception, Time Is Not What It Seems," *Annals of the New York Academy of Sciences* 682: 264–71, 1994. The syllabic-alphabetic principle came to the West by way of the Phoenicians and ancient Greeks. An alternative to writing symbols for sounds, invented in ancient Mesopotamia, is picture writing (logography). The pictures (icons) were probably at first quite representational and then, to make them faster to write and to convey unpicturable words, the icons became more abstract. Modern Chinese and Japanese have a lo-

gographic system but also use alphabetic notation. English is basically alphabetic but also uses logograms, such as "$" for "dollar sign," "13" for "thirteen," and "&" for "and." M. J. Adams (*Beginning to Read: Thinking and Learning About Print* [Cambridge, Mass.: MIT Press, 1994]), pp. 14–20, gives a brief history of writing with additional references.

34. McLane, Joan B., and McNamee, Gillian D., *Early Literacy* (Cambridge, Mass.: Harvard University Press, 1990).

    The quoted text is from McLane, J., and McNamee, G., "The Beginning of Literacy," *Zero to Three: Bulletin of National Center for Clinical Infant Programs* 12(1): 1–8, September 1991.

35. Lyon, G. E., "Research Initiatives in Learning Disabilities: Contributions from Scientists Supported by the National Institute of Child Health and Human Development," *Journal of Child Neurology* 10: 120–26, 1995.

    Stedman, L. C., and Kaestle, C. E., "Literacy and Reading Performance in the United States from 1880 to the Present," *Reading Research Quarterly* 22: 8–46, 1987.

36. Chomsky, Carol, "Stages in Language Development and Reading Exposure," *Harvard Educational Review* 42: 1–33, 1972.

37. Adams, M. J., *Beginning to Read: Thinking and Learning About Print* (Cambridge, Mass.: MIT Press, 1994), p. 85.

38. Purcell-Gates, V., *Other People's Words: The Cycle of Low Literacy* (Cambridge, Mass.: Harvard University Press, 1995). Purcell-Gates tells the story of Donny, a bright second-grader from an illiterate home and a culture in which print played little part, as he makes the slow and painful journey to literacy. Donny's family, who had moved to a big city, spoke "Appalachian" English, a dialect often mocked and depreciated by city dwellers. Many of Donny's teachers mistakenly felt that its use indicated deficient cognitive abilities, poor motivation, and devaluation of education.

39. Adams, M. J., *Beginning to Read: Thinking and Learning About Print* (Cambridge, Mass.: MIT Press, 1994), p. 86.

40. Quotes are from ibid., pp. 26–27.

41. The Commission on Reading is paraphrased in ibid., p. 26.

42. Heath, S. B., *Ways with Words* (Cambridge, England: Cambridge University Press, 1983).

43. Quote is from Heath, S. B., "What No Bedtime Story Means: Narrative Skills at Home and School," *Language in Society* 11(1): 49–76, 1982.

44. Heath, S. B., *Ways with Words* (Cambridge, England: Cambridge University Press, 1983), p. 349.
45. Ibid., pp. 80–81.
46. Ibid., p. 349.
47. Boyer, Ernest, *Ready to Learn: A Mandate for the Nation* (Princeton, N.J.: Princeton University Press, 1991).
48. Whitehurst, G., Falco, F., Lonigan, C., Fischel, J., DeBaryshe, B., Valdez-Menchaca, M., and Caulfield, M., "Accelerating Language Development Through Picturebook Reading," *Developmental Psychology* 24: 552–59, 1988.
49. The project is described in *Learning Readiness: Promising Strategies* (Washington, D.C.: U.S. Department of Health and Human Services, 1993).
50. *The Washington Post,* November 26, 1995, p. C4.

5. LANGUAGE OF THE HEART

1. Examples of child-rearing practices are from Kagan, Jerome, *The Nature of the Child* (1984; New York: Basic Books, 1994), p. 53.
2. Dwyer, T., Posonby, A. B., Newman, N. M., et al., "Prospective Cohort Study of Prone Sleeping Position and Sudden Infant Death Syndrome." *Lancet* 337: 1244–47, 1991; Mitchell, E., Brunt, J., and Everard, C., "Reduction in Mortality from Sudden Infant Death Syndrome in New Zealand, 1986–1992," *Archives of the Diseases of Children* 70: 291–94, 1994.
3. Watson, John B., *Psychological Care of Infant and Child* (New York: Norton, 1928), pp. 81–82.
4. Bowlby, John, *Attachment and Loss,* vol. 3 (New York: Basic Books, 1980), p. 442, is quoted in Sameroff, Arnold J., and Emde, Robert N., eds., *Relationship Disturbances in Early Childhood: A Developmental Approach* (New York: Basic Books, 1989), introduction: "Understanding Early Relationship Disturbances," p. 5.
5. Bowlby, John N., foreword. In Ainsworth, Mary, *Infancy in Uganda* (Baltimore: Johns Hopkins University Press, 1967), p. v. Quoted in Karen, R., *Becoming Attached: Unfolding the Mystery of the Infant-Mother Bond and Its Impact on Later Life* (New York: Warner Books, 1994), p. 4.
6. Suomi, Stephen J., "Influence of Attachment Theory on Ethological Studies of Biobehavioral Development in Nonhuman Primates." In

Goldberg, Susan; Muir, Roy; and Kerr, John, eds., *Attachment Theory: Social, Developmental, and Clinical Perspectives* (Hillsdale, N.J.: Analytic Press, 1995), pp. 185–86.

7. For reviews, see Belsky, J., Rosenberger, K., and Crnic, K., "The Origins of Attachment Security," and Main, Mary, "Recent Studies of Attachment." Both in Goldberg, Susan; Muir, Roy; and Kerr, John, eds., *Attachment Theory: Social, Developmental, and Clinical Perspectives* (Hillsdale, N.J.: Analytic Press, 1995).

8. Joan Riviere, quoted in Karen, R., *Becoming Attached: Unfolding the Mystery of the Infant-Mother Bond and Its Impact on Later Life* (New York: Warner Books, 1994), p. 45.

9. Ibid., p. 46. R. Karen quotes from an interview with John Bowlby, Jan. 14–15, 1989.

10. Gesell, Arnold, *Infancy and Human Growth* (New York: Macmillan, 1928). Quoted in ibid., p. 3. Gesell's most influential publication was *The First Five Years of Life*, with Amatruda, C. S., Ames, L. B., Castner, B. M., Halverson, H. M., Ilg, F. L., and Thompson, H. (New York: Harper and Brothers, 1940).

11. Scarr, S., "Developmental Theories for the 1990s: Development and Individual Differences," presidential address to the biennial meeting of the Society for Research in Child Development, April 1991. *Child Development* 63: 1–19, 1992. See also Gazzaniga, M., *Nature's Mind* (New York: Basic Books, 1992), p. 12, and Rowe, D., and Plomin, R., "The Importance of Nonshared (E1) Environmental Influences in Behavioral Development," *Developmental Psychology* 17(5): 517–31, 1981.

12. One such study of twins reared apart is Bouchard, T. J., Lykken, D. T., McGue, M., Segal, N. L., Tellegen, A., "Sources of Human Psychological Differences: The Minnesota Study of Twins Reared Apart," *Science* 250: 223–36, 1990. References to other twin studies can be found in the bibliography of this paper.

13. There are certain extremely rare instances in which monozygotic twins do not share a genetic trait and therefore differ in phenotype (appearance).

14. Sulloway, Frank, *Born to Rebel: Birth Order, Family Dynamics, and Creative Lives* (New York: Pantheon, 1996).

15. Plomin, R., and McClearn, G., eds., *Nature, Nurture, and Psychology* (Washington, D.C.: American Psychological Association, 1993).

16. Genesis 2:23 (New English Bible).

17. New parents' preoccupations, and the similarities of their thoughts and

behaviors to those of patients with obsessive-compulsive disorders, are reported in Leckman, J. F., and Mayes, L. C., "Maladies of Love: An Evolutionary Perspective on Some Forms of Obsessive-Compulsive Disorder. In Hann, D. M., Huffman, L., Lederhendler, I., Meinecke, D., eds., *Advancing Research in Developmental Plasticity: Integrating the Behavioral Science and Neuroscience of Mental Health* (Rockville, Md.: NIMH, U.S. Department of Health and Human Services; in press). The psychoanalyst Donald Winnicott called these feelings and behaviors "primary maternal preoccupation"; see Winnicott, D. W., *From Pediatrics to Psychoanalysis* (New York: Basic Books, 1958), chapter 14. They are paternal preoccupations as well.

18. For example, see Numan, M., and Sheehan, T., "Neuroanatomical Circuitry for Mammalian Maternal Behavior." In Carter, C. S., Lederhendler, I., and Kirkpatrick, B., eds., *The Integrative Neurobiology of Affiliation. Annals of the New York Academy of Sciences* 807: 101–25, 1997.

19. Presentation by Dr. James Leckman of Yale University Medical School at Children's Hospital Research Symposium, Washington, D.C., May 7, 1994.

20. Leckman, J. F., Goodman, W. K., North, W. G., et al., "The Role of Central Oxytocin in Obsessive-Compulsive Disorder and Related Normal Behavior," *Psychoneuroendocrinology* 19(8): 723–49, 1994.

21. Pedersen, C., "Oxytocin Control of Maternal Behavior: Regulation by Sex Steroids and Offspring Stimuli." In Carter, C. S., Lederhendler, I., and Kirkpatrick, B., *The Integrative Neurobiology of Affiliation. Annals of the New York Academy of Sciences* 808: 126–45, 1997.

On oxytocin receptors and paternal behavior: In one species of vole (voles are small mouselike rodents), mothers are the exclusive caregivers of their young. In another vole species, fathers participate equally in care of the young. Paternal oxytocin secretions differ in the two species. See Insel, T., and Shapiro, L., "Oxytocin Receptor Distribution Reflects Social Organization in Monogamous and Polygamous Voles," *Proceedings of the National Academy of Science, U.S.A.* 89: 5981–85, 1992.

22. Brown, J., Ye, H., Bronson, R., Dikkes, P., and Greenburg, M., "A Defect in Nurturing in Mice Lacking the Immediate Early Gene fosB," *Cell* 86: 297–309, 1996.

23. Fleming, A., Corter, C., and Steiner, M., "Sensory and Hormonal Control of Maternal Behavior in Rat and Human Mothers." In Pryce, C. R., Mar-

tin, R. D., and Skuse, D., eds., *Motherhood in Human and Nonhuman Primates: Biosocial Determinants* (New York: Karger, 1996), pp. 106–14.

24. Sarnyai, Z., and Kovacs, G. L., "Role of Oxytocin in the Neuroadaptation to Drugs of Abuse," *Psychoneuroendocrinology* 19: 85–117, 1993.

25. Quoted in Karen, R., *Becoming Attached: Unfolding the Mystery of the Infant-Mother Bond and Its Impact on Later Life* (New York: Warner Books, 1994), p. 13.

26. Bakwin, H., "Loneliness in Infants," *American Journal of Diseases of Children* 63: 30–40, 1942.

27. Dennis, W., "Causes of Retardation Among Institutional Children: Iran," *Genetic Psychology* 96: 47–59, 1960.

28. Spitz, R., "Hospitalism: An Inquiry into the Genesis of Psychiatric Conditions in Early Childhood," *The Psychoanalytic Study of the Child* 1: 53–74, 1945.

29. Skeels, H., and Skodak, H., "Studies of Environmental Stimulation: An Orphanage Preschool Project," *Studies in Child Welfare* (Des Moines: University of Iowa Press) 15(4): 1938.

30. Bowlby, J., *Maternal Care and Mental Health* (World Health Organization Monograph [Serial #2], 1951). Bowlby's report was translated into fourteen languages and sold 40,000 copies in the English-language edition alone.

    Robertson, J., *A Two-Year-Old Goes to Hospital* (film) (London: Tavistock Child Development Research Unit, 1953). Available through Penn State Audiovisual Services, University Park, Pa.

31. Sir Michael Rutter, a British child psychiatrist who is conducting research on 166 children adopted from Romanian orphanages by families in the United Kingdom, is quoted in *The Brown University Child and Adolescent Behavior Letter,* 12(6), June 1996. Rutter has found that infants adopted before they were six months of age were apparently normal at age four. They had gained an average of 50 I.Q. points and their weights were normal. Those adopted between the ages of six months and two and a half years also showed "impressive" gains, but there were continuing deficits in the group as a whole.

    In the group of 166 children, eleven (6.6 percent) had signs of autism. This is an extremely high incidence; in an unselected population autism occurs in only 15 out of every 10,000 individuals. See "What Is Autism?" Autism Society of America (http://www.autism-society.org/autism.html).

32. In his seminal paper "The Nature of the Child's Tie to His Mother," Bowlby cited Harlow's not-then-published study describing the profound distress of infant rhesus monkeys when they were removed from their mothers and isolated. The two papers are Harlow, H. F., "The Nature of Love," *American Psychologist* 13: 673–85, 1958; and Bowlby, J., "The Nature of the Child's Tie to His Mother," *International Journal of Psycho-Analysis* 39: 1–24, 1958.

33. On how social deprivation affects learning and emotional development, see Gluck, J. P., Harlow, H. F., and Schlitz, K. A., "Differential Effect of Early Enrichment and Deprivation on Learning in the Rhesus Monkey," *Journal of Comparative and Physiological Psychology* 84: 598–604, 1973.

34. Eric Kandel explains that the animal model of infant social isolation was developed accidentally. Wanting to raise a stock of sturdy and disease-free monkeys for their experimental psychological work, the Harlows separated the newborn monkeys from their mothers, fed them a special formula by remote control, and reared them with special hygienic precautions. Then they discovered the harm and sought to find therapies that could prevent it. Kandel, E. R., "Psychotherapy and the Single Synapse," *New England Journal of Medicine* 301(19): 1028–37, 1979.

35. Higley, J. D., Suomi, S., Linnoila, M., "CSF Monoamine Metabolite Concentrations Vary According to Age, Rearing, and Sex and Are Influenced by the Stressor of Social Separation in Rhesus Monkeys," *Psychopharmacology* 103: 551–56, 1991.

36. Suomi, S. J., "Influence of Attachment Theory on Ethological Studies of Biobehavioral Development in Nonhuman Primates." In Goldberg, S., Muir, R., and Kerr, J., *Attachment Theory: Social, Developmental, and Clinical Perspectives* (Hillsdale, N.J.: Analytic Press, 1995), pp. 185–201.

37. For summaries of this work and references, see Suomi, S. J., "Early Stress and Adult Emotional Reactivity in Rhesus Monkeys." In Bock, G. R., and Whelan, J., eds., *The Childhood Environment and Adult Disease* (Chichester, England: John Wiley & Sons, 1991), pp. 171–88; and Suomi, S., "Genetic and Maternal Contributions to Individual Differences in Rhesus Monkey Biobehavioral Development." In Krasnegor, N., Blass, E., Hofer, M., and Smotherman, W., eds., *Perinatal Development: A Psychobiological Perspective* (New York: Academic Press, 1987), pp. 397–420.

38. Both this quotation and the one in the following text are from Suomi, S. J., "Early Stress and Adult Emotional Reactivity in Rhesus Monkeys." In Bock, G. R., and Whelan, J., *The Childhood Environment and Adult Disease* (Chichester, England: John Wiley & Sons, 1991), pp. 171–88, p. 181.

39. Ainsworth, M., Blehar, M., Waters, E., and Wall, S., *Patterns of Attachment: A Psychological Study of the Strange Situation* (Hillsdale, N.J.: Erlbaum, 1978).

40. Bretherton, Inge, "The Origins of Attachment Theory." In Goldberg, S., Muir, R., and Kerr, J., eds., *Attachment Theory: Social, Developmental, and Clinical Perspectives* (Hillsdale, N.J.: Analytic Press, 1995), pp. 45–84.

41. The percentages of infants assigned to the various attachment classifications discussed in this section are from Appendix 2, "Patterns of Attachment in Infancy," Goldberg, S., Muir, R., and Kerr, J., eds., *Attachment Theory* (Hillsdale, N.J.: Analytic Press, 1995), p. 11.

42. For a summary of typical patterns of secure and insecure/anxious attachment see Karen, R., *Becoming Attached: Unfolding the Mystery of the Infant-Mother Bond and Its Impact on Later Life* (New York: Warner Books, 1994), Appendix, pp. 442–43.

43. Main, M., and Solomon, J., "Discovery of a New, Insecure–Disorganized/Disoriented Attachment Pattern." In Brazelton, T. B., and Yogman, M., eds., *Affective Development in Infancy* (Norwood, N.J.: Ablex, 1986), pp. 95–124.

   Main, M., and Hesse, E., "Parents' Unresolved Traumatic Experiences Are Related to Infant Disorganized Attachment Status: Is Frightened and/or Frightening Parental Behavior the Linking Mechanism?" In Greenburg, M., Cicchetti, D., and Cummings, E. M., eds., *Attachment in the Preschool Years* (Chicago: University of Chicago Press, 1990), pp. 161–82.

44. Goldsmith, H., and Alansky, J., "Maternal and Infant Temperamental Predictors of Attachment: A Meta-analytic Review," *Journal of Consulting and Clinical Psychology* 55: 805–16, 1987.

45. References on the relationships of attachment classification to development in later childhood can be found in Goldberg, S., Muir, R., and Kerr, J., eds., *Attachment Theory: Social, Developmental, and Clinical Perspectives* (Hillsdale, N.J.: Analytic Press, 1995), pp. 9–15. Also see Sroufe, L. A., *Emotional Development: The Organization of Emotional Life in the Early Years* (Cambridge, England: Cambridge University Press, 1996), pp. 172–91.

46. The Bielefeld-Regensburg research by Klaus Grossmann and Karin Grossmann is discussed in Karen, R., *Becoming Attached: Unfolding the Mystery of the Infant-Mother Bond and Its Impact on Later Life* (New York: Warner Books, 1994), pp. 261–66.

47. We are indebted to Mauricio Cortina for his stimulating paper "The Effects of Social Character on Parenting: Observation from Cross-cultural Studies on Attachment." Submitted for publication. See also Brazelton, T. Berry, and Cramer, Bertrand, *The Earliest Relationship: Parents, Infants, and the Drama of Early Attachment* (New York: Delacorte, 1990).

48. Fraiberg, S., Adelson, E., and Shapiro, V., "Ghosts in the Nursery: A Psychoanalytic Approach to the Problem of Impaired Infant-Mother Relationships," *Journal of the American Academy of Child Psychiatry* 14(3): 387–422, 1975.

49. Kagan, Jerome, *The Nature of the Child* (New York: Basic Books, 1994), pp. 64–72.

50. Interview with Jerome Kagan in Karen, R., *Becoming Attached: Unfolding the Mystery of the Infant-Mother Bond and Its Impact on Later Life* (New York: Warner Books, 1994), p. 253.

51. Kagan is quoted in ibid., p. 255.

52. The research of Jerome Kagan and his colleagues on temperament is described in Kagan's *Galen's Prophecy: Temperament in Human Nature* (New York: Basic Books, 1994). Daniel Goleman in *Emotional Intelligence* (New York: Bantam, 1995), pp. 215–28 gives an excellent summary of research in this area.

53. "Emboldening experiences" are discussed in Goleman, D., *Emotional Intelligence* (New York: Bantam Books, 1995), pp. 215–28.

54. For discussion of various schools of thought on temperament-attachment interrelationships, see Belsky, J., Rosenberger, K., and Crnic, K., "The Origins of Attachment Theory." In Goldberg, S., Muir, R., and Kerr, J., eds., *Attachment Theory: Social, Developmental, and Clinical Perspectives* (Hillsdale, N.J.: Analytic Press, 1995), pp. 156ff., and Sroufe, L. A., "Attachment Classification from the Perspective of Infant-Caregiver Relationships and Infant Temperament," *Child Development* 56: 1–14, 1985.

55. The infants in van den Boom's study, all firstborns with normal birthweights and neonatal medical examinations, were selected using the Brazelton Neonatal Behavioral Assessment Scale. Irritability, or a low threshold of expression of negative affect, is regarded by many psychologists as a temperamental dimension, but questions have been raised as

to whether irritability measured in the immediate neonatal period predicts irritability later in infancy (see Riese, M., "Neonatal Temperament in Monozygotic and Dizygotic Twin Pairs," *Child Development* 61: 1230–37, 1990). Van den Boom's subjects were tested at ten and fifteen days of age, when effects due to the babies' immediate postnatal state would be lessened. Van den Boom, D., "The Influence of Temperament and Mothering on Attachment and Exploration: An Experimental Manipulation of Sensitive Responsiveness Among Lower-Class Mothers with Irritable Infants," *Child Development* 65: 1457–77, 1994.

56. Chess, S., Thomas, A., and Birch, H., "Characteristics of the Individual Child's Behavioral Responses to the Environment," *American Journal of Orthopsychiatry* 29: 791–802, 1959. Stella Chess's influential work is discussed in Karen, R., *Becoming Attached: Unfolding the Mystery of the Infant-Mother Bond and Its Impact on Later Life* (New York: Warner Books, 1994), pp. 273–93.

57. Cortisol is a hormone produced by the adrenal cortex in response to stress. Its production is under the control of the pituitary gland, at the base of the brain. The pituitary is linked to brain centers that regulate metabolism and other essential body processes, and to centers for emotion. Cortisol level can be measured conveniently and with reasonable accuracy in saliva, which obviates the requirement for invasive blood or cerebrospinal fluid testing.

Experiments are described in Gunnar, Megan R., "Psychoendocrine Studies of Temperament and Stress." In Bates, J. E., and Wachs, T. D., eds., *Early Childhood: Expanding Current Models in Temperament: Individual Differences at the Interface of Biology and Behavior* (Washington, D.C.: American Psychological Association, 1994), pp. 175–98.

58. Kopp, C., "Antecedents of Self-regulation: A Developmental Perspective," *Developmental Psychology* 18: 199–214, 1982.

59. Schore, Allan N., *Affect Regulation and the Origin of the Self* (Hillsdale, N.J.: Erlbaum, 1994), p. xxx.

6. I AND THOU: EMOTIONAL RELATIONSHIP AND THE DISCOVERY OF SELF

1. Schanberg, S. M., and Field, T. M., "Sensory Deprivation, Stress, and Supplemental Stimulation in the Rat Pup and Preterm Human Neonate," *Child Development* 58: 1431–47, 1987.

2. Separation induces a whole range of physiological responses in both infant and mother, which Myron Hofer calls "hidden regulators." See Hofer, M., "Hidden Regulators: Implications for a New Understanding

of Attachment, Separation, and Loss." In Goldberg, S., Muir, R., and Kerr, J., eds., *Attachment Theory: Social, Developmental, and Clinical Perspectives* (Hillsdale, N.J.: Analytic Press, 1995), pp. 203–30.

3. On separation and pain, see MacLean, P., "Cerebral Evolution of Emotion." In Lewis, M., and Haviland, J. M., eds., *Handbook of Emotions* (New York: Guilford Press, 1993), p. 78.

   On the abolition of the separation cry, see MacLean, P. D., and Newman, J. D., "Role of Midline Frontolimbic Cortex in Production of the Isolation Call of Squirrel Monkeys," *Brain Research* 450: 111–23, 1988; cited in *Handbook of Emotions* (see above), p. 78. (Also see fig. 6-1, p. 146.)

4. Darwin, Charles, *The Expression of Emotions in Man and Animals* (1872; Chicago: University of Chicago Press, 1965), p. 1.

5. Ibid. He is quoted in LeDoux, J. E., *The Emotional Brain: The Mysterious Underpinnings of Emotional Life* (New York: Simon & Schuster, 1996), p. 111.

6. For example, see Ekman, Paul, and Davidson, Richard J., *The Nature of Emotion: Fundamental Questions* (New York: Oxford University Press, 1994).

7. Ekman, P., "Universals and Cultural Differences in Facial Expressions of Emotion." In Cole, J., ed., *Nebraska Symposium on Motivation* 19:207–83, 1972

8. Rosenstein, D., and Oster, H., "Differential Facial Responses to Four Basic Tastes in Newborns," *Child Development* 59: 1555–68, 1988.

9. For a discussion of definitions of emotions, see Solomon, R., "The Philosophy of Emotions." In Lewis, M., and Haviland, J. M., eds., *Handbook of Emotions* (New York: Guilford Press, 1993), pp. 3–87.

10. See White, Geoffrey M., "Emotions Inside Out: The Anthropology of Affect." In ibid., pp. 29–39.

11. Dyson, Freeman, *Disturbing the Universe* (New York: Harper & Row, 1979), p. 249.

12. Izard, C. E., *Human Emotions* (New York: Plenum Press, 1977).

13. Lewis, M., "The Emergence of Human Emotions." In Lewis, M., and Haviland, J. M., eds., *Handbook of Emotions* (New York: Guilford Press, 1993), pp. 223–35. The quotation is on p. 225.

14. Trevarthan, C., and Aitken, K. J., "Brain Development, Infant Communication, and Empathy Disorders: Intrinsic Factors in Child Mental Health," *Development and Psychopathology* 6: 597–633, 1994. Greenspan, S., with Benderly, B., *The Growth of the Mind* (Reading, Mass.: Addison-Wesley, 1997).

See also Damasio, Antonio, *Descartes' Error: Emotion, Reason, and the Human Brain* (New York: Putnam, 1994).

15. Stenberg, C. R., and Campos, J. J., "The Development of Anger Expressions in Infancy." In Stein, N. L., Leventhal, B., and Trabasso, T., eds., *Psychological and Biological Approaches to Emotion* (Hillsdale, N.J.: Erlbaum, 1990), pp. 247–82.

Experiments that use facial expressions as a response measure usually rely on observer assessment of movements of facial muscle groups: those of the brow, those around the eyes, and those around the mouth. Observation codes and interpretation are usually derived from the work of Carroll Izard or Paul Ekman—e.g., Izard, C., Fantauzzo, C., Castle, J., Haynes, M., Rayias, M., and Putnam, P., "The Ontogeny and Significance of Infants' Facial Expressions in the First 9 Months of Life," *Developmental Psychology* 31(6): 997–1013, 1995; and Ekman, P., "Facial Expression and Emotion," *American Psychologist* 48: 384–92, 1993.

16. Lewis, M., Sullivan, M. W., Ramsey, D., and Alessandri, S. M., "Individual Differences in Anger and Sad Expressions During Extinction: Antecedents and Consequences," *Infant Behavior and Development* 15, 443–52, 1992.

17. Brooks, J., and Lewis, M., "Infants' Responses to Strangers: Midget, Adult, and Child," *Child Development* 47: 323–32, 1976.

18. Margaret Mahler is quoted in Schore, A., *Affect Regulation and the Origin of the Self* (Hillsdale, N.J.: Erlbaum, 1994), p. 92.

19. Power, T., and Chapieski, M., "Childrearing and Impulse Control in Toddlers: A Naturalistic Investigation," *Developmental Psychology* 22: 271–75; Schore, A. N., "The Experience-Dependent Maturation of a Regulatory System in the Orbital Prefrontal Cortex and the Origin of Developmental Psychopathology," *Development and Psychopathology* 8: 59–87, 1996; the cited text is on p. 68.

20. Rozin, P., Haidt, J., and McCauley, C. R., "Disgust." In Lewis, M., and Haviland, J. M., eds., *Handbook of Emotions* (New York: Guilford Press, 1993), pp. 575–94.

21. James, William, *The Principles of Psychology*, vol. 2 (1890; New York: Dover, 1950), quoted in Damasio, A., *Descartes' Error: Emotion, Reason, and the Human Brain* (New York: Putnam, 1994), p. 129.

22. Kapp, B. S., Whalen, P. J., Supple, W. F., and Pascoe, J. P., "Amygdaloid Contributions to Conditioned Arousal and Sensory Information Process-

ing." In Aggleton, J. P., ed., *The Amygdala: Neurobiological Aspects of Emotion, Memory, and Mental Dysfunction* (New York: Wiley-Liss, 1992). Cited in LeDoux, J., *The Emotional Brain: The Mysterious Underpinnings of Emotional Life* (New York: Simon & Schuster, 1996), p. 149.

23. LeDoux has summarized his own and related research of others on fear in *The Emotional Brain* (New York: Simon & Schuster, 1996). The quotation is on p. 168.

24. Charles Darwin (*The Expression of Emotions in Man and Animals*, 1872) is quoted in ibid., p. 112.

25. Goleman, D., *Emotional Intelligence* (New York: Bantam, 1995), p. 13.

26. LeDoux, J., *The Emotional Brain* (New York: Simon & Schuster, 1996), pp. 252–61.

27. Scott, S., Young, A., Calder, A., Hellawell, D., Aggleton, J., and Johnson, M., "Impaired Auditory Recognition of Fear and Anger Following Bilateral Amygdala Lesions," *Nature* 385: 254–57, 1997; Young, A., Aggleton, J., Hellawell, D., Johnson, M., Broks, P., and Hanley, J., "Face Processing Impairments After Amygdalotomy," *Brain* 118: 15–24, 1995.

D.R.'s amygdalar lesions left her with other subtle but disabling shortfalls. She had problems in determining whether a spoken remark was a question or an exclamation; she had a hard time matching voice to speaker or interpreting another person's direction of gaze. The investigators propose that these abnormalities in the processing of socially important signals mean that the amygdala is a critical component of social cognition.

28. There is some disagreement as to which structures are included in the limbic system. Many anatomists include the entire neuronal circuitry that controls emotional behavior and motivational drives. See, for example, Guyton, A. C., and Hall, J. E., *Textbook of Medical Physiology*, 9th ed. (Philadelphia: W. B. Saunders), 1996. This textbook defines the limbic system to include both subcortical and cortical components. Subcortical structures include the hypothalamus, septum, paraolfactory area, epithalamus, anterior nucleus of the thalamus, the amygdala, and portions of the basal ganglia and hippocampus. Cortical components are in a band of cerebral cortex that surrounds subcortical limbic structures. These include the orbitofrontal area on the ventral surface of the frontal lobes (this area is also called the ventromedial cortex), the subcallosal gyrus, the cingulate gyrus, the parahippocampal gyrus, and the uncus. (See our fig. 6-1, p. 146.)

29. Shepherd, G. M., *Neurobiology,* 3rd ed. (New York: Oxford University Press, 1994), p. 515.

30. Ibid., p. 506.

31. Reichlin, Seymour, "Neuroendocrinology." In *Williams Textbook of Endocrinology,* 8th ed. (Philadelphia: Saunders, 1992).

32. Sapolsky, R., "Why Stress Is Bad for Your Brain," *Science* 273: 749–50, 1996; McEwen, B., and Sapolsky, R., "Stress and Cognitive Function," *Current Opinion in Neurobiology* 5: 205–16, 1995.

33. Panksepp, J., "Neurochemical Control of Moods and Emotions: Amino Acids to Neuropeptides." In Lewis, M., and Haviland, J. M., eds., *Handbook of Emotions* (New York: Guilford Press, 1993), p. 91.

34. Reichlin, S., "Neuroendocrine-Immune Interactions," *New England Journal of Medicine* 329(17): 1246–53, 1993; Glaser, R., and Kiecolt-Glaser, J., "Stress-Associated Depression in Cellular Immunity: Implications for Acquired Immune Deficiency Syndrome," *Brain, Behavior, and Immunity* 1(2): 107–12, 1987.

35. MacLean, P. D., *A Triune Concept of Brain and Behavior* (Toronto: University of Toronto Press, 1973).

36. The basal ganglia are affected in Huntington's disease, an early manifestation of which is patients' inability to remember, plan, and organize their daily routines. They seem content to sit and do nothing. MacLean, P. D., "Cerebral Evolution of Emotion." In Lewis, M., and Haviland, J. M., eds., *Handbook of Emotions* (New York: Guilford Press, 1993), p. 73.

37. See note 28, above, and fig. 6-1, p. 146, for the structures that constitute the limbic system.

38. MacLean, P. D., "Cerebral Evolution of Emotion." In Lewis, M., and Haviland, J. M., eds., *Handbook of Emotions* (New York: Guilford Press, 1993), pp. 67–83. MacLean calls nursing and maternal care, audiovocal communication for maintaining contact between mother and offspring, and play "the family triad." He postulates that the sense of parental responsibility that appeared with mammalian evolution may have generalized to become conscience, empathetic concern, and altruism.

39. The quotations are from ibid., p. 82.

40. Epstein, S., "Emotion and Self-theory." In Lewis, M., and Haviland, J. M., eds., *Handbook of Emotions* (New York: Guilford Press, 1993), p. 313.

41. James, William, *Psychology: The Briefer Course* (New York: Holt, 1907), p. 177.

42. Epstein, S., "Emotion and Self-theory." In Lewis, M., and Haviland, J. M., eds., *Handbook of Emotions* (New York: Guilford Press, 1993), p. 319.

43. Stern, Daniel N., *The Interpersonal World of the Infant* (New York: Basic Books, 1985), p. 5.

44. Emde, Robert N.; Biringen, Zeynep; Clyman, Robert B.; and Oppenheim, David, "The Moral Self of Infancy, Affective Core and Procedural Knowledge," *Developmental Review* 11: 252, 1991.

45. Sroufe, L. A., "Relationships, Self, and Individual Adaptation." In Sameroff, A. J., and Emde, R. N., *Relationship Disturbances in Early Childhood: A Developmental Approach* (New York: Basic Books, 1989), pp. 71–73.

46. Amsterdam, B., "Mirror Self-image Reactions Before Age Two," *Developmental Psychology* 5: 297–305, 1972.

47. George Herbert Mead is quoted in Sroufe, L. A., "Relationships, Self, and Individual Adaptation." In Sameroff, A. J., and Emde, R. N., *Relationship Disturbances in Early Childhood: A Developmental Approach* (New York: Basic Books, 1989), p. 70.

48. Sroufe, L. A., *Emotional Development: The Organization of Emotional Life in the Early Years* (New York: Cambridge University Press, 1996), p. 193.

49. Schore, Allan N., "The Experience-Dependent Maturation of a Regulatory System in the Orbital Prefrontal Cortex and the Origin of Developmental Psychopathology," *Development and Psychopathology* 8: 59–87, 1996; the quoted text appears on p. 61.

50. Tronick, E. Z., "Emotions and Emotional Communication in Infants," *American Psychologist* 44: 112–19, 1989. Our text paraphrases Tronick's analysis.

51. For a discussion of the uses of meditation to enhance parental awareness see Kabat-Zinn, Myla and Jon, *Everyday Blessings: The Inner Work of Mindful Parenting* (New York: Hyperion, 1997).

52. Family resource programs such as the Family Place teach parenting skills. Teaching aids include those developed by "Parents as Teachers" (Parents as Teachers National Center, 10176 Corporate Square Drive, Suite 230, St. Louis, MO 63132); Healthy Families America (332 N. Michigan Ave., 16th floor, Chicago, IL 60604); and HIPPY (Home Instruction Program for Preschool Youngsters). For a description, see Lombard, A., *Success Begins at Home: The Past, Present, and Future of*

the Home Instruction Program for Preschool Youngsters (Guilford, Conn.: Dushkin Publishing Group, 1994).

Information on parent education is also available at www.Zeroto three.org.

53. Louis Sander, a psychiatrist, notes the emergence of "the separate aware self." His theories are discussed in Sroufe, L. A., "Relationships, Self, and Individual Adaptation." In Sameroff, A. J., and Emde, R. N., *Relationship Disturbances in Early Childhood: A Developmental Approach* (New York: Basic Books, 1989), pp. 73–83.

54. Kierkegaard is quoted in ibid., p. 74.

55. Davidson, Richard J., and Fox, Nathan A., "Asymmetrical Brain Activity Discriminates Between Positive and Negative Affective Stimuli in Human Infants," *Science* 218: 1235–36, 1982.

Dawson, Geraldine, "Development of Emotional Expression and Emotion Regulation in Infancy: Contributions of the Frontal Lobe," and Davidson, Richard J., "Temperament, Affective Style, and Frontal Lobe Asymmetry." Both in Dawson, G., and Fischer, K. W., *Human Behavior and the Developing Brain* (New York: Guilford Press, 1994), pp. 346–79, 518–36.

56. George, M. S., Ketter, T. A., Parekh, P. I., Horwitz, B., Herscovitch, P., and Post, R. M., "Brain Activity During Transient Sadness and Happiness in Healthy Women," *American Journal of Psychiatry* 152(3): 341–51, March 1995.

57. Ibid. In the same issue, "Mapping Brain Activity Associated with Emotion" (editorial comment), pp. 327–29.

For a discussion of hemispheric specializations in emotion, see Tucker, D., "Developing Emotions and Cortical Networks." In Gunnar, M. R., and Nelson, C. A., eds., *Developmental Behavioral Neuroscience* 24 (Hillsdale, N.J.: Erlbaum, 1992), pp. 75–128.

58. Dawson, Geraldine; Klinger, Laura Gropher; Panagiotides, Heracles; Spieker, Susan; and Frey, Karin, "Infants of Mothers with Depressive Symptoms: Electroencephalographic and Behavioral Findings Related to Attachment Status," *Development and Psychopathology* 4: 67–80, 1992. Dawson's EEG research findings are summarized in Dawson, G., "Development of Emotional Expression and Emotion Regulation in Infancy: Contributions of the Frontal Lobe." In Dawson, G., and Fischer, K. W., eds., *Human Behavior and the Developing Brain* (New York: Guilford Press, 1994), pp. 346–79.

59. Emde, R. N., and Buchsbaum, H., "'Didn't You Hear My Mommy?' Autonomy *with* Connectedness in Moral Self-emergence." In Cicchetti, D., and Beeghly, M., eds., *The Self in Transition* (Chicago: University of Chicago Press, 1990), pp. 35–60.

60. Tucker, D. M., "Developing Emotions and Cortical Networks." In Gunnar, M. R., and Nelson, C. A., eds., *Developmental Behavioral Neuroscience 24* (Hillsdale, N.J.: Erlbaum, 1992), pp. 75–128.

61. Dunn, Judy, and Brown, Jane, "Relationships, Talk About Feelings, and the Development of Affect Regulation in Early Childhood." In Garber, Judy, and Dodge, Kenneth A., *The Development of Emotion Regulation and Dysregulation* (Cambridge, England: Cambridge University Press, 1991), p. 92.

62. Dunn, J., Bretherton, I., and Munn, P., "Conversations About Feelings Between Mothers and Their Young Children," *Developmental Psychology* 23: 132–39, 1987.

63. Dunn, J., and Brown, J., "Relationships, Talk About Feelings, and the Development of Affect Regulation in Early Childhood." In Garber, J., and Dodge, K., eds., *The Development of Emotion Regulation and Dysregulation* (Cambridge, England: Cambridge University Press, 1991), p. 99.

64. Ibid., pp. 102–105.

65. Damasio, Antonio R., *Descartes' Error: Emotion, Reason, and the Human Brain* (New York: Putnam, 1994), p. 245.

66. Damasio is quoted in Suplee, Curt, "Committee Without a Chairman: The Modular Theory of the Mind," *Washington Post*, December 19, 1994, p. A3.

67. Damasio, Antonio, *Descartes' Error* (New York: Putnam, 1994), pp. 177–78.

68. LeDoux, J., *The Emotional Brain: The Mysterious Underpinnings of Emotional Life* (New York: Simon & Schuster, 1996), p. 201.

69. For a review of research on forms of memory, see Squire, L. R., Knowlton, B., and Musen, G., "The Structure and Organization of Memory," *Annual Review of Psychology* 44: 453–95, 1993.

70. The fact that babies and young children have extraordinary capacity to remember and use vast quantities of new information of all kinds, but have no memories, or at best extremely fragmentary memories, of the events of their life as young children points to the multiplicity of memory systems of the brain. Also see LeDoux, J., *The Emotional Brain: The Mysterious Underpinnings of Emotional Life* (New York: Simon &

Schuster, 1996), pp. 205–206. Stress hormones have been shown to impair memory formation in the hippocampus. See, for example, McEwen, B., and Sapolsky, R., "Stress and Cognitive Functioning," *Current Opinion in Neurobiology* 5: 205–16, 1995.

71. Daniel Goleman paraphrases LeDoux's speculation about the psychological effects of early emotional memory in *Emotional Intelligence* (New York: Bantam, 1995), pp. 21–22.

7. EMPATHY, CONSCIENCE, AND MORAL DEVELOPMENT

1. Damon, William, *The Moral Child* (New York: Free Press, 1988), p. 18.

2. Hume, D., *A Treatise of Human Nature*. Quoted in Kohn, A., *The Brighter Side of Human Nature* (New York: Basic Books, 1990), p. 259.

3. Sagi, A., and Hoffman, M., "Empathic Distress in the Newborn," *Developmental Psychology* 12: 175–76, 1976.

4. Zahn-Waxler, Caroline, and Radke-Yarrow, Marian, "The Origins of Empathic Concern," *Motivation and Emotion* 14(2): 107–30, 1990.

5. For a study of twins at fourteen and twenty months of age, see Zahn-Waxler, C., Robinson, J. L., and Emde, R. N., "The Development of Empathy in Twins," *Developmental Psychology* 28(6): 1038–47, 1992.

   For a study of adults, see Rushton, J., Fulker, D., Neale, M., Nias, D., and Eysenck, H., "The Heritability of Individual Differences," *Journal of Personality and Social Psychology* 50: 1192–98, 1986.

6. For a discussion of the many ways empathy, sympathy, prosocial acts, and altruism are defined, see Eisenberg, N., and Miller, P., "The Relation of Empathy to Prosocial and Related Behaviors," *Psychological Bulletin* 101(1): 91–119, 1987.

   For an example of an observational study of young children, see Zahn-Waxler, C., Radke-Yarrow, M., Wagner, E., and Chapman, M., "Development of Concern for Others," *Developmental Psychology* 28(1): 126–36, 1992.

7. Murphy, Lois Barclay, "Sympathetic Behavior in Very Young Children," *Zero to Three* (bulletin of National Center for Clinical Infant Programs) 12(4): 1, Apr. 1992.

8. Rheingold, H. L., and Hay, D. F., "Prosocial Behavior of the Very Young." In Stent, Gunther S., ed., *Morality as a Biological Phenomenon* (Berkeley: University of California Press, 1980), pp. 106–12.

9. Hoffman, Martin L., "The Contribution of Empathy to Justice and Moral Judgment." In Eisenberg, Nancy, and Strayer, Janet, eds., *Empa-*

thy and Its Development (Cambridge, England: Cambridge University Press, 1987), pp. 47–80, 51.

10. Angela and José were observed at the Family Place.

The development of empathy is described in Zahn-Waxler, C., and Radke-Yarrow, M., The Origins of Empathic Concern," *Motivation and Emotion* 14(2): 107–30, 1990.

11. Eisenberg, N., and Fabes, R., "Emotion, Regulation, and the Development of Social Competence." In Clark, M. S., ed., *Emotion and Social Behavior,* vol. 14 (Newbury Park, Calif.: Sage, 1992), pp. 119–50.

12. See Eisenberg, N., Fabes, R., Murphy, B., Karbon, M., Maszk, P., Smith, M., O'Boyle, C., and Suh, K., "The Relations of Emotionality and Regulation to Dispositional and Situational Empathy-Related Responding," *Journal of Personality and Social Psychology* 66: 776–97, 1994; Fabes, Richard A., et al., "Socialization of Children's Vicarious Emotional Responding and Prosocial Behavior: Relations with Mothers' Perceptions of Children's Emotional Reactivity," *Developmental Psychology* 30(1): 44–55, 1994.

13. Hay, D. F., "Prosocial Development," *Journal of Child Psychology and Psychiatry* 35: 29–71, 1994. Hay, who is on the faculty of social and political science at Cambridge University, gives a helpful review of this topic.

14. Ibid.

15. "A prince must learn how not to be good." This quotation from Machiavelli serves as the epigraph of Dale Hay's review of children's prosocial development, ibid. Also see Coles, R., *The Moral Intelligence of Children* (New York: Random House, 1997). Coles reminds us that children learn how to be good and how not to be good under the tutelage, conscious and unconscious, of adults, especially parents. He also describes how parents sometimes allow their little princes and princesses to become spoiled tyrants.

16. The example is from Angier, Natalie, "Empathy Unfolds Slowly in a Child," *New York Times,* May 9, 1995, p. C6. Children develop a "theory of mind" as they mature. A younger child cannot imagine that what he knows is not known by another, or that what he sees cannot be seen by another. Julian, on the telephone at two years of age, points to the object about which he is talking and says, "*You* know!" But at five he knows he must describe or name the object in order to be understood by the person at the other end of the line.

17. The follow-up study (Koestner, R., Franz, C., and Weinberger, J., "The

Family Origins of Empathic Concern: A 26-Year Longitudinal Study," *Journal of Personality and Social Psychology* 58[4]: 709–17, 1990), uses data collected by Sears, R., Maccoby, E., and Levin, H., in 1951–52 and published in *Patterns of Child-rearing* (Evanston, Ill.: Row Peterson, 1957). These data are archived in the Henry A. Murray Research Center, Cambridge, Mass.

18. See Koestner et al., cited in the preceding note, for a list of the test measures and a discussion of their validity.

19. For a discussion see the following reviews: Zahn-Waxler, C., and Radke-Yarrow, M., "The Origins of Empathic Concern," *Motivation and Emotion* 14(2): 107–30, 1990; Eisenberg, N., and Miller, P., "The Relation of Empathy to Prosocial and Related Behaviors," *Psychological Bulletin* 101(1): 91–119, 1987.

20. Winnicott, D. W., *The Family and Individual Development* (London: Tavistock, 1965). Quoted in Sameroff, A., and Emde, R. N., *Relationship Disturbances in Early Childhood* (New York: Basic Books, 1989), p. 34.

    On the blend of social and biological codes, see the Sameroff and Emde article just cited, p. 28. See also Bronfenbrenner, Urie, *The Ecology of Human Development* (Cambridge, Mass.: Harvard University Press, 1979).

21. Plato is discussed in Postman, Neil, *The Disappearance of Childhood* (New York: Delacorte, 1990), p. 8.

22. Cooley is quoted in Kohn, Alfie, *The Brighter Side of Human Nature: Altruism and Empathy in Everyday Life* (New York: Basic Books, 1990), epigraph. The quotation from Mencius is on p. 63.

23. Jeremiah 17:9.

24. Darwin is quoted and paraphrased in Kohn, Alfie, *The Brighter Side of Human Nature: Altruism and Empathy in Everyday Life* (New York: Basic Books, 1990), p. 219. Also see Jerome Kagan's comments in *The Nature of the Child* (New York: Basic Books, 1994), pp. 124–34.

25. See, for example, Dawkins, Richard, *The Selfish Gene* (New York: Oxford University Press, 1976).

26. Philip Hallie tells the story of a French village that sheltered its Jewish residents during World War II and saved their lives. *Lest Innocent Blood Be Shed: The Story of the Village of Le Chambon and How Goodness Happened There* (New York: Harper, 1976, 1985).

    On risk-loving rescuers, see London, P., "The Rescuers: Motivational Hypotheses About Christians Who Saved Jews from the Nazis." In Macaulay, J. R., and Berkowitz, L., eds., *Altruism and Helping Behavior* (New York: Academic Press, 1970).

27. Jencks, Christopher, "Varieties of Altruism." In Mansbridge, Jane J., ed., *Beyond Self-Interest* (Chicago: University of Chicago Press, 1990), pp. 53–67; Smith, Adam, *The Theory of Moral Sentiments* (1759; Oxford, England: Clarendon Press, 1976).

28. Miller, R. E., Murphy, J. V., and Mirsky, I. A., "Relevance of Facial Expression and Posture as Cues in Communication of Affect Between Monkeys," *Archives of General Psychiatry* 1: 480–88, 1959.

   Brothers, Leslie, "A Biological Perspective on Empathy," *American Journal of Psychiatry* 146(1): 10–19, Jan. 1989.

29. Brothers, L., Ring, B., and Kling, A., "Response of Neurons in the Macaque Amygdala to Complex Social Stimuli," *Behavioral Brain Research* 41: 199–213, 1990.

   Hasselmo, M. E., Rolls, E. T., and Baylis, G. C., "The Role of Expression and Identity in the Face-Selective Responses of Neurons in the Temporal Visual Cortex of the Monkey," *Behavioral Brain Research* 32: 203–18, 1989.

30. Allman, John, and Brothers, Leslie, "Faces, Fear, and the Amygdala," *Nature* 372: 613–14, Dec. 15, 1994; Adolphs, R., Tranel, D., Damasio, H., and Damasio, A., "Impaired Recognition of Emotion in Facial Expressions Following Bilateral Damage to the Human Amygdala," *Nature* 372: 669–72, 1994; Scott, S., Young, A., Calder, A., Hellawell, D., Aggleton, J., and Johnson, M., "Impaired Auditory Recognition of Fear and Anger Following Bilateral Amygdala Lesions," *Nature* 385: 254–57, 1997. Also see chapter 3, note 23 for additional references.

31. Brothers, Leslie, "A Biological Perspective on Empathy," *American Journal of Psychiatry* 146(1): 10–19, Jan. 1989.

32. Hoffman is quoted in Angier, Natalie, "Scientists Mull Role of Empathy in Man and Beast," *New York Times,* May 9, 1995, p. C1.

33. Our discussion of early emotional foundations of morality is based on Emde, Robert N.; Biringen, Zeynep; Clyman, Robert B.; and Oppenheim, David, "The Moral Self of Infancy: Affective Core and Procedural Knowledge," *Developmental Review* 11: 251–70, 1991. Also see Greenspan, S., with Benderly, B., *The Growth of the Mind* (Reading, Mass.: Addison-Wesley, 1997).

34. Hume, David, *A Treatise of Human Nature* (1739–40; Hammondsworth, England: Penguin, 1969).

35. Piaget, Jean, *The Moral Judgment of the Child* (New York: Free Press, 1965), p. 27.

36. Kohlberg is cited in Schweder, R. A., Mahapatra, M., and Miller, J. G.,

"Culture and Moral Development." In Kagan, Jerome, and Lamb, Sharon, eds., *The Emergence of Morality in Young Children* (Chicago: University of Chicago Press, 1987), p. 5.

37. Kagan, Jerome, introduction to Kagan, Jerome, and Lamb, Sharon, eds., *The Emergence of Morality in Young Children* (Chicago: University of Chicago Press, 1987). The discussion in this section follows Kagan's work here and in *The Nature of the Child* (New York: Basic Books, 1994).

38. See Kagan, Jerome, *The Second Year: The Emergence of Self-Awareness* (Cambridge, Mass.: Harvard University Press, 1981).

39. These examples are found in Kagan, Jerome, *The Nature of the Child* (New York: Basic Books, 1994), p. 126.

40. Emde, R. N., and Buchsbaum, H. K., "'Didn't You Hear My Mommy?' Autonomy *with* Connectedness in Moral Self-emergence." In Ciccheti, D., and Beeghly, M., eds., *The Self in Transition: Infancy to Childhood* (Chicago: University of Chicago Press, 1990), pp. 35–60.

41. Damon, W., *The Moral Child* (New York: Free Press, 1988), p. 85.

42. Kagan, Jerome, *The Nature of the Child* (New York: Basic Books, 1994), p. 117.

43. Damasio, A., *Decartes' Error* (New York: Putnam, 1994), pp. 34–51.

44. Ibid., Figure 4-1, p. 55.

   The brain areas involved in patients like Elliot are the ventral (orbital) and medial sectors of the frontal lobes. Dorsolateral sectors of the lobes are not affected. Patients with ventromedial damage also cannot guide their behavior with the help of an informed guess based on previous experience. Damasio and colleagues contrast such patients with normal persons in Bechara, A., Damasio, H., Tranel, D., and Damasio, A., "Deciding Advantageously Before Knowing the Advantageous Strategy," *Science* 275: 1293–95, 1997.

   When, in addition to ventral and medial sectors, dorsolateral frontal areas are damaged, there are additional deficits in attention and working memory. Ibid., p. 61.

   Damage in limbic-system structures and in right somatosensory cortical locations also can cause deficits in rational decision making and emotion. See ibid., pp. 52–79. Also see our fig. 6-1, p. 146.

45. Emde, R. N., "Development Terminable and Interminable. I. Innate and Motivational Factors from Infancy," *International Journal of Psychoanalysis* 69: 23–42, 1988.

   Emde, R. N., and Buchsbaum, H. K., "'Didn't You Hear My Mommy?' Autonomy *with* Connectedness in Moral Self-emergence." In

Ciccheti, D., and Beeghly, M., eds., *The Self in Transition: Infancy to Childhood* (Chicago: University of Chicago Press, 1990), pp. 35–60.

46. Piaget, J., *The Moral Judgment of the Child* (New York: Free Press, 1965), p. 136.

47. See Mrazek, P. J., and Haggerty, R. J., eds., *Reducing Risks for Mental Disorders* (Washington, D.C.: National Academy Press, 1994), p. 172.

48. Authoritative and authoritarian patterns were delineated by Diana Baumrind in Baumrind, D., "Child-Care Patterns Anteceding Three Patterns of Preschool Behavior," *Genetic Psychology Monographs* 75: 43–88, 1967, and Baumrind, D., "Current Patterns of Parental Authority," *Developmental Psychology Monographs* 4: 1–103, 1971.

49. Kochanska, Grazyna; DeVet, Katherine; Goldman, Marguerita; Murray, Kathleen; and Putman, Samuel P., "Maternal Reports of Conscience Development and Temperament in Young Children," *Child Development* 65: 852–68, 1994. Kochanska, G., "Socialization and Temperament in the Development of Guilt and Conscience," *Child Development* 62: 1369–92, 1991; Kochanska, G., "Toward a Synthesis of Parental Socialization and Child Temperament in Early Development of Conscience," *Child Development* 64: 325–47, 1993.

50. Lewis, Michael, "Self-conscious Emotions: Embarrassment, Pride, Shame, and Guilt." In Lewis, M., and Haviland, J. M., eds., *Handbook of Emotions* (New York: Guilford Press, 1993), pp. 563–73; the cited material appears on p. 569.

51. Darwin is quoted in ibid., p. 564.

52. Sroufe, L. A., *Emotional Development. The Organization of Emotional Life in the Early Years* (Cambridge, England: Cambridge University Press, 1996), p. 202.

8. CHILDREN'S ANGER AND ADULT VIOLENCE

1. Lewis, M., "The Emergence of Human Emotions." In Lewis, M., and Haviland, J. M., eds., *Handbook of Emotions* (New York: Guilford Press, 1993), pp. 223–35; the quoted text is on p. 233.

2. Lewis, Michael, and Ramsay, Douglas S., "Developmental Change in Infants' Responses to Stress," *Child Development* 66: 657–70, 1995.

3. See Bowlby, J., *Attachment, Separation and Loss*, vol. 2 (New York: Basic Books, 1973).

4. Potegal, M., Kosorok, M., and Davidson, R., "The Time Course of Angry Behavior in the Temper Tantrums of Young Children." In Ferris, C., and Grisso, T., *Understanding Aggressive Behavior in Children. Annals*

of the New York Academy of Sciences 794: 31–45, 1996; Kopp, C., "Emotional Distress and Control in Young Children," *New Directions for Child Development* 55: 41–56, 1992.

5. For references concerning the psychological processes important in the organization and regulation of emotions in individuals (such as conditioning, priming, sensitization, and attributional biases), see Pervin, L., "Affect and Personality." In Lewis, M., and Haviland, J. M., eds., *Handbook of Emotions* (New York: Guilford Press, 1993), pp. 301–11. Pervin makes the point that links between emotions as well as patterns in their relationships are quite idiosyncratic. Jealousy is linked to love by one person and hate by another; anger can be associated with fear, resentment, sorrow, or glee—with pleasure or pain—or with a blend of these and other emotions. Cultural factors also greatly influence the mix.

6. Goodenough, F., *Anger in Young Children* (Minneapolis: University of Minnesota Press, 1931).

7. Ibid.; Radke-Yarrow, M., and Kochanska, G., "Anger in Young Children." In Stein, N., Leventhal, B., and Trabasso, T., eds., *Psychological and Biological Approaches to Emotion* (Hillsdale, N.J.: Erlbaum, 1990), pp. 297–310.

8. The psychiatrist James Gilligan interviewed a large number of prison inmates who had committed serious violent crimes and found that many had been "chronically humiliated." See Weissbourd, R., *The Vulnerable Child* (Reading, Mass.: Addison-Wesley, 1996), p. 87.

9. For a discussion of the relationship of shame to inhibition of expressions of anger, see Schore, A. N., *Affect Regulation and the Origin of the Self: The Neurobiology of Emotional Development* (Hillsdale, N.J.: Erlbaum, 1994), pp. 339–47.

   On angry mothers and angry children, see Crockenberg, S., "Infant Irritability, Mother Responsiveness, and Social Support Influences on the Security of Mother-Infant Attachment," *Child Development* 52: 857–65, 1981. Our summary of this research follows Lewis, M., and Haviland, J. M., *Handbook of Emotions* (New York: Guilford Press, 1993), p. 540.

   On "inhibited-wary children," see Rubin, K., Coplan, R., Fox, N., and Calkins, S., "Emotionality, Emotion Regulation, and Preschoolers' Social Adaptation," *Development and Psychopathology* 7: 49–62, 1995.

10. Cummings, E., "Toddlers' Reactions to Maternal Anger," *Merrill-Palmer Quarterly* 31: 361–73, 1985; also see the discussion and refer-

ences in Lewis, M., and Haviland, J. M., *Handbook of Emotions* (New York: Guilford Press, 1993), pp. 543–44.

11. Hay, D., and Ross, H., "The Social Nature of Early Conflict," *Child Development* 53: 105–13, 1982.

12. Radke-Yarrow, M., and Kochanska, G., "Anger in Young Children." In Stein, N. L., Leventhal, B., and Trabasso, T., eds., *Psychological and Biological Approaches to Emotion* (Hillsdale, N.J.: Erlbaum, 1990), pp. 297–310; Fabes, R., and Eisenberg, N., "Young Children's Coping with Interpersonal Anger," *Child Development* 63: 116–28, 1992; Stein, N. L., Trabasso, T., Liwag, M., "The Representation and Organization of Emotional Experience: Unfolding the Emotion Episode." In Lewis, M., and Haviland, J. M., eds., *Handbook of Emotions* (New York: Guilford Press, 1993), pp. 279–300.

13. Lemerise, E., and Dodge, K., "The Development of Anger and Hostile Interactions." In *Handbook of Emotions* (see preceding note), pp. 541–42.

14. Fabes, R., and Eisenberg, N., "Young Children's Emotional Arousal and Anger/Aggressive Behaviors." In Fraczek, A., and Zumkley, H., eds., *Socialization and Aggression* (Berlin: Springer-Verlag, 1992), pp. 85–102.

15. Offord, D., Boyle, M., Racine, Y., Fleming, J., Cadman, D., Blum, H., Byrne, C., Links, P., Lipman, E., and Macmillan, H., "Outcome, Prognosis and Risk in a Longitudinal Follow-up Study," *Journal of the American Academy of Child and Adolescent Psychiatry* 31(5): 916–23, 1992; White, J., Moffitt, T., Earls, F., and Silva, P., "How Early Can We Tell? Predictors of Childhood Conduct Disorder and Adolescent Delinquency," *Criminology* 24(4): 507–33, 1990.

16. Loeber, R., and Dishion, T., "Early Predictors of Male Delinquency: A Review," *Psychological Bulletin* 93: 68–99, 1983.

17. For a review of studies linking child maltreatment, family discord, and adult crime in later years, see Mrazek, P. J., and Haggerty, R. J., eds., *Reducing Risks for Mental Disorders* (Washington, D.C.: National Academy Press, 1994), pp. 176–78.

18. See Greenspan, Stanley, *The Challenging Child* (Reading, Mass.: Addison-Wesley, 1995); Shaw, D., and Bell, R., "Parental Contributors to Antisocial Behavior," *Journal of Abnormal Child Psychology* 21(5): 493–518, 1993; Lepper, M. R., "Social Control Processes, Attributions of Motivation, and the Internalization of Social Values." In Higgins, E. T., Rubble, D. N., and Hartup, W. W., eds., *Social Cognition and So-*

cial Behavior: Developmental Perspectives (Cambridge, England: Cambridge University Press, 1982), pp. 294–332.

This section also draws on Lemerise, E., and Dodge, K., "The Development of Anger and Hostile Interactions." In Lewis, M., and Haviland, J. M., eds., *Handbook of Emotions* (New York: Guilford Press, 1993), pp. 537–46.

19. For follow-up studies, see Erickson, M., Sroufe, L. A., Egeland, B., "The Relationship Between Quality of Attachment and Behavior Problems in Preschool in a High-Risk Sample." In Bretherton, I., and Waters, E., eds., *Growing Points of Attachment Theory and Research.* Monographs of the Society for Research in Child Development 50 (209): 147–67, 1985. See also: Renken, B., Egeland, B., Marvinney, D., Mangersdorf, S., and Sroufe, A. L., "Early Childhood Antecedents of Aggression and Passive Withdrawal in Early Elementary School," *Journal of Personality* 57: 257–81, 1989; Lyons-Ruth, K., Alpern, L., and Repacholi, B., "Disorganized Infant Attachment Classification and Maternal Psychosocial Problems as Predictors of Hostile-Aggressive Behavior in the Preschool Classroom," *Child Development* 64: 572–85, 1993.

20. Bowlby, J., "Forty-four Juvenile Thieves: Their Characters and Home Life," *International Journal of Psycho-analysis* 25: 107–27, 1944; see also Karen, R., *Becoming Attached: Unfolding the Mystery of the Infant-Mother Bond and Its Impact on Later Life* (New York: Warner Books, 1994), pp. 48–60.

21. Quinton, D., and Rutter, M., *Parental Breakdown: The Making and Breaking of Intergenerational Links* (Aldershot, England: Gower Publishing, 1988).

22. Shaw, D., and Bell, R., "Developmental Theories of Parental Contributors to Antisocial Behavior," *Journal of Abnormal Child Psychology* 21(5): 493–518, 1993; Zeanah, C., "Psychopathology in Infancy," *Journal of Child Psychology and Psychiatry* 28: 81–99, 1997; Hashima, P., and Amato, P., "Poverty, Social Support, and Parental Behavior," *Child Development* 65: 394–403, 1994; Minde, K., "Aggression in Preschoolers: Its Relation to Socialization," *Journal of the American Academy of Child and Adolescent Psychiatry* 31(5): 853–62, Sept. 1992.

23. Sroufe, L. A., Cooper, R., and DeHart, G., *Child Development: Its Nature and Course*, 2nd ed. (New York: McGraw-Hill, 1992). Cited in Karen, R., *Becoming Attached: Unfolding the Mystery of the Infant-*

Mother Bond and Its Impact on Later Life (New York: Warner Books, 1994), p. 204.

24. Mrazek, P. J., and Haggerty, R. J., eds., *Reducing Risks for Mental Disorders: Frontiers for Preventive Intervention Research* (Washington, D.C.: National Academy Press, 1994), p. 82; Loeber, R., and Schmaling, K., "Empirical Evidence for Overt and Covert Patterns of Antisocial Conduct Problems: A Meta-analysis," *Journal of Abnormal Child Psychology* 13(2): 337–52, 1985; Coie, J., Terry, R., Lenox, K. F., Lochman, J., and Hyman, C., "Childhood Peer Rejection and Aggression as Predictors of Stable Patterns of Adolescent Disorder," *Development and Psychopathology* 7: 697–713, 1995.

25. The quotation is from Mrazek and Haggerty, *Reducing Risks for Mental Disorders* (see preceding note). Their conclusion is based on the research of Offord, D. R., et al., *The Ontario Child Health Study*. These epidemiological studies were published from 1987 to 1992. Citations for the studies are given in Mrazek and Haggerty, p. 124.

Also see Weiss, C., and Hechtman, L., *Hyperactive Children Grown Up* (New York: Guilford Press, 1986); Hinshaw, S., Lahey, B., and Hart, E., "Issues of Taxonomy and Comorbidity in the Development of Conduct Disorder," *Development and Psychopathology* 5: 36, 1993.

26. See Shoda, Yuichi; Mischel, Walter; and Peake, Philip K., "Predicting Adolescent Cognitive and Self-Regulatory Competencies from Preschool Delay of Gratification," *Developmental Psychology* 26(6): 978–86, 1990.

Mischel's research is summarized in Goleman, Daniel, *Emotional Intelligence* (New York: Bantam Books, 1995), pp. 80–83. The quoted summary statement about the boys' personalities is Goleman's.

27. Block, J., "On the Relation Between I.Q., Impulsivity, and Delinquency," *Journal of Abnormal Psychology* 104: 395–98, 1995; White, J., Moffitt, T., Capsi, A., Bartusch, D., Needles, D., and Stouthamer-Loeber, M., "Measuring Impulsivity and Examining Its Relation to Delinquency," *Journal of Abnormal Psychology* 103: 192–205, 1994.

28. Parent education ("parenting") classes are becoming more widely attended. The Family Place and other family resource centers use a parent education curriculum, home visits, and counseling, all designed to help parents deal constructively with their children's oppositional behaviors. Daniel Goleman, in his 1995 book *Emotional Intelligence* (New York: Bantam Books), describes a variety of courses designed to promote

"emotional literacy" (see the chapter entitled "Schooling the Emotions," pp. 261–87). Also see Grossman, D., Neckerman, H., Koepsell, T., Liu, P., Asher, K., Beland, K., Frey, K., and Rivara, F., "Effectiveness of a Violence Prevention Curriculum Among Children in Elementary School," *Journal of the American Medical Association* 277(20): 1605–11, 1997.

29. Zahn-Waxler, C., "Warriors and Worriers: Gender and Psychopathology," *Development and Psychopathology* 5: 79–89, 1993; Zoccolillo, M., "Gender and the Development of Conduct Disorder," *Development and Psychopathology* 5: 65–78, 1993.

30. Richters, J. E., "Disordered Views of Aggressive Children: A Late Twentieth Century Perspective." In Ferris, C. F., and Grisso, T., eds., *Understanding Aggressive Behavior in Children. Annals of the New York Academy of Science* 794: 208–23, 1996.

31. Research comparing delinquent and nondelinquent eleven-year-old boys found that children with high levels of lead in their bones—evidence of early chronic exposure—are at increased risk of delinquency. See Needleman, H., Riess, J., Tobin, M., Biesecker, G., and Greenhouse, J., "Bone Lead Levels and Delinquent Behavior," *Journal of the American Medical Association* 275: 363–69, 1996. Also see the editorial by Terrie Moffitt, "Measuring Children's Antisocial Behaviors," in the same issue, pp. 403–404. For an overview, see Denno, D., *Biology and Violence* (New York: Cambridge University Press, 1990).

32. Anderson, E., "The Code of the Streets," *The Atlantic Monthly,* May 1994, pp. 81–92.

33. See, for example, McCord, J., and Tremblay, R., eds., *Preventing Antisocial Behavior: Interventions from Birth Through Adolescence* (New York: Guilford Press, 1992).

34. On autonomic underarousal, see Raine, A., "Autonomic Nervous System Factors Underlying Disinhibited, Antisocial, and Violent Behavior." In Ferris, C., and Grisso, T., eds., *Understanding Aggressive Behavior in Children. Annals of the New York Academy of Sciences* 794: 46–59, 1996.

On cortisol and sex hormones, see Simon, N., et al., "Development and Expression of Hormonal Systems Regulating Aggression," and Susman, E., et al., "Gonadal and Adrenal Hormones: Developmental Transitions and Aggressive Behavior." Both in Ferris and Grisso, pp. 8–30.

On serotonin, see Ferris, C., and Grisso, T., "Serotonin, Stress, and Impulsivity." In *Understanding Aggressive Behavior in Children,* pp. 82–103.

35. Forgatch, Marion S., Presentation at the American Society of Criminol-

ogy, November 1994. Cited in Gibbs, W., "Seeking the Criminal Element," *Scientific American,* Mar. 1995, p. 102.

36. Price, B., Daffner, K., Stowe, R., and Mesulam, M., "The Comportmental Learning Disabilities of Early Frontal Lobe Damage," *Brain* 113: 1383–93, 1990. One patient's injuries were due to a car accident that caused skull fractures and sudural bleeding; the other had suffered birth trauma.

37. Studies of Vietnam war veterans, murderers on death row, and neglected children are described in Gladwell, M., "Damaged," *The New Yorker,* Feb. 24–Mar. 3, 1997, pp. 132–47.

38. See discussion of the National Incidence Study of Child Abuse and Neglect in *The State of America's Children: Yearbook 1997* (Washington, D.C.: Children's Defense Fund), pp. 51–52.

39. Kaufman, J., and Zigler, E., "Do Abused Children Become Abusive Parents?" *American Journal of Orthopsychiatry* 57(2): 186–92, 1987; Simons, Ronald L.; Wu, Chyi-In; Johnson, Christine; and Conger, Rand D., "A Test of Various Perspectives on the Intergenerational Transmission of Domestic Violence," *Criminology* 33(1): 141–72, 1995.

For a review of studies of abuse, see Hemenway, David; Solnick, Sara; and Carter, Jennifer, "Child-Rearing Violence," *Child Abuse and Neglect* 18(12): 1011–20, 1994.

40. Widom, C., and Maxfield, M., "A Prospective Examination of Risk for Violence Among Abused and Neglected Children." In Ferris, C., and Grisso, T., eds., *Understanding Aggressive Behavior in Children. Annals of the New York Academy of Sciences* 794: 224–35, 1996. ("Neglect cases were those in which a court found a child to have no proper parental care or guardianship. . . . They reflected the court's judgment that parents' deficiencies in child care were beyond those found acceptable by community and professional standards at the time." "Involuntary neglect" was not included.)

41. Ibid., p. 234. Citations for the studies mentioned are on pp. 236–37.

42. A discussion of possible consequences of depression is in Weissbourd, R., *The Vulnerable Child* (Reading, Mass.: Addison-Wesley, 1996), p. 73. For the percentages of depressed mothers, see Parker, S., Greer, S., Zuckerman, B., "Double Jeopardy: The Impact of Poverty on Early Child Development," *Pediatric Clinics of North America* 35(6): 1233, Dec. 1988; cited in Weissbourd, p. 250. Most depressed parents neither abuse nor neglect their children, but the risk of such behavior rises with depression.

Also see Baumrind, D., "The Social Context of Child Maltreatment," *Family Relations* 43: 360–68, 1994.

43. Olds, D., Eckenrode, J., Henderson, C., Kitzman, H., Powers, J., Cole, R., Sidora, K., Morris, P., Pettitt, L., and Luckey, D., "Long-term Effects of Home Visitation on Maternal Life Course and Child Abuse and Neglect," *Journal of the American Medical Association* 278(8): 637–43, 1997.

44. Tracy, P. E., Wolfgang, M. E., and Figlio, R. M., *Delinquency Careers in Two Birth Cohorts* (New York: Plenum Press, 1990).

45. Wiesel, Torsten N., "Genetics and Behavior," *Science* 264: 1647, 1994.

46. Yudofsky is quoted in Gibbs, W. Wayt, "Seeking the Criminal Element," *Scientific American,* Mar. 1995, pp. 100–107. The quotation is on p. 101.

47. Quoted in Angier, Natalie, "Elementary, Dr. Watson. The Neurotransmitters Did It," *New York Times,* Jan. 23, 1994, p. C1.

48. Butterfield, Fox, "Studies Find a Family Link to Criminality," *New York Times,* Jan. 31, 1992, p. A1.

49. Wright, L., "Double Mystery," *The New Yorker,* Aug. 7, 1995, pp. 45–62. The quotation appears on p. 57.

50. Rutter, M., and Rutter, M., *Developing Minds: Challenge and Continuity Across the Life Span* (New York: Basic Books, 1993), p. 50.

51. The Sentencing Project, Washington, D.C., personal communication, June 25, 1997.

52. Fredericson, Emil, and Birnbaum-Barnet, Ann, "Competitive Fighting Between Mice With Different Hereditary Backgrounds," *Journal of Genetic Psychology* 85: 271–80, 1954.

53. De Kloet, E., Korte, S., Rots, N., and Kruk, M., "Stress Hormones, Genotype, and Brain Organization: Implications for Aggression." In Ferris, C., and Grisso, T., eds., *Understanding Aggressive Behavior in Children. Annals of the New York Academy of Sciences* 794: 179–91, 1996. The serotonergic receptor studied was 5-HT1A.

54. Saudou, F., Amara, D., Dierich, A., LeMeur, M., Ramboz, S., Segu, A., Buhot, M.-C., and Hen, R., "Enhanced Aggressive Behavior in Mice Lacking 5-HT1B Receptor," *Science* 265: 1875–78, 1994.

55. Oosting, R., Stark, K., Ramboz, S., Castanon, N., and Hen, R., "Targeting Aggressive Behavior: Constitutive, Inducible, and Tissue-Specific Knockouts." In Takahashi, J. S., *What's Wrong With My Mouse? New Interplays Between Mouse Genetics and Behavior* (Washington, D.C.: Society for Neuroscience, 1996), pp. 50–58.

56. Ibid.

57. De Kloet, E., Korte, S., Rots, N., and Kruk, M., "Stress Hormones, Genotype, and Brain Organization: Implications for Aggression." In Ferris, C., and Grisso, T., eds., *Understanding Aggressive Behavior in Children. Annals of the New York Academy of Sciences* 794: 179–91, 1996. See, especially, pp. 183–85.

58. Hofer, M., "Hidden Regulators in Attachment and Loss." In Goldberg, S., Muir, R., and Kerr, J., eds., *Attachment Theory: Social, Developmental, and Clinical Perspectives* (Hillsdale, N.J.: Analytic Press, 1995), pp. 203–30.

59. Handling during a rat's first week of life also causes an increase in circulating thyroid hormones. These hormones have pervasive effects throughout the developing central nervous system. One such effect involves regulation of central serotonin metabolism. Both handling and thyroid hormones increase serotonin stimulation and turnover in the hippocampus of the neonatal rat. Serotonin in the neonatal animal increases glucocorticoid receptor density in the hippocampus, and the effect is persistent. These receptors serve to decrease stress responses. See Francis, D., Diorio, J., LaPlante, P., Weaver, S., Seckl, J., and Meaney, M., "The Role of Early Environmental Events in Regulating Neuroendocrine Development: Moms, Pups, Stress, and Glucocorticoid Receptors." In Ferris, C., and Grisso, T., eds., *Understanding Aggressive Behavior in Children. Annals of the New York Academy of Sciences* 794: 136–52, 1996. See especially pp. 142–47.

60. In Norway rats, which are used in many of these experiments, mothers naturally show stable individual differences in the amount of licking and grooming they give their pups, and also in the time intervals between bouts of licking and grooming. Differences in maternal care can also be induced if the experimenter removes newborn pups from their mother for fifteen minutes a day for a few weeks. Such handling approximately doubles the mother's rate of licking and grooming each time the pups are returned to her. (It is thought to be this increase in maternal care, rather than the human handling, which decreases infants' stress responses.) See Sapolsky, R., "The Importance of a Well-Groomed Child," *Science* 277: 1620–21, 1997.

61. Francis, D., Diorio, J., LaPlante, P., Weaver, S., Seckl, J., and Meaney, M., "The Role of Early Environmental Events in Regulating Neuroendocrine Development: Moms, Pups, Stress, and Glucocorticoid Receptors." In Ferris, C., and Grisso, T., eds., *Understanding Aggressive*

Behavior in Children. Annals of the New York Academy of Sciences 794: 136–52, 1996; Liu, D., Diorio, J., Tannenbaum, B., Caldji, C., Francis, D., Freedman, A., Sharma, S., Pearson, D., Plotsky, P., and Meaney, M., "Maternal Care, Hippocampal Glucocorticoid Receptors, and Hypothalamic-Pituitary-Adrenal Responses to Stress," *Science* 227: 1659–62, 1997; Sapolsky, R., "The Importance of a Well-Groomed Child," *Science* 277: 1620–21, 1997.

62. Judith Havemann, *Washington Post,* Feb. 7, 1997, p. 1A.

63. Personal communication, Feb. 6, 1993, Dept. of Neurosurgery, Children's National Medical Center, Washington, D.C. The quotation is from Behrman, R., and Kliegman, R., eds., *Nelson's Textbook of Pediatrics,* 14th ed. (Philadelphia: Saunders, 1992), p. 80.

64. Guyer, B., Strobino, D. M., Ventura, S. J., MacDorman, M., and Martin, J. A., "Annual Summary of Vital Statistics—1995," *Pediatrics* 98(6): 1015, Dec. 1996.

65. Prothrow-Stith, Deborah, "Eye for an Eye: The Fight Against Adolescent Violence," *Harvard Medical Alumni Bulletin,* Spring 1988, p. 40. Also see Prothrow-Stith, D., and Weissman, M., *Deadly Consequences: How Violence Is Destroying Our Teenage Population, and a Plan to Begin Solving the Problem* (New York: HarperCollins, 1993).

66. Statistics presented by Brian R. Flay, director, Prevention Research Center University of Chicago, at annual meeting of the Society for Adolescent Medicine, Chicago, March 19, 1993.

Wright, Joseph L., "Youth and Adolescent Violence: A Public Health Emergency." Grand Rounds, Children's National Medical Center, Washington, D.C., November 16, 1994.

67. Oatley, Keith, "Social Construction in Emotions." In Lewis, M., and Haviland, J. M., *Handbook of Emotions* (New York: Guilford Press, 1993), pp. 341–51.

68. Quoted in Goleman, Daniel, *Emotional Intelligence* (New York: Bantam Books, 1995), p. 311.

69. Garbarino, James, *Raising Children in a Socially Toxic Environment* (San Francisco: Jossey-Bass, 1995).

70. The quotations in this paragraph are from the Summary Report of the American Psychological Association Commission on Violence and Youth, *Violence and Youth* (Washington, D.C.: APA, 1993), p. 33.

71. "TV Getting a Closer Look as a Contributor to Real Violence," *New York Times,* Dec. 14, 1994, p. D20.

72. Richters, John E., and Martinez, Pedro, "The NIMH Community Violence Project: Children as Victims of and Witnesses to Violence," *Psychiatry* 56: 7–21, Feb. 1993.

73. Osofsky, J., Wewers, S., Hann, D., and Flick, A., "Chronic Community Violence: What Is Happening to Our Children?" *Psychiatry* 56: 36–45, Feb. 1993.

74. Emde, Robert N., "The Horror! The Horror! Reflections on Our Culture of Violence and Its Implications for Early Development and Morality," *Psychiatry* 56: 119–23, 1993.

75. Dodge, K. A., and Somberg, D. R., "Hostile Attributional Biases Among Aggressive Boys Are Exacerbated Under Conditions of Threats to Self," *Child Development* 58: 213–24, 1987.

76. Cummings, E. Mark; Simpson, Kelly S.; and Wilson, Amy, "Children's Responses to Interadult Anger as a Function of Information About Resolution," *Developmental Psychology* 29(6): 978–85, 1993.

77. Crockenberg, Susan, "How Children Learn to Resolve Conflicts in Families," *Zero to Three*, Apr. 1992, pp. 11–13; Crockenberg, S., and Litman, C., "Autonomy as Competence in Two-Year-Olds: Maternal Correlates of Child Compliance, Defiance, and Self-assertion," *Developmental Psychology* 26: 961–71, 1992.

78. Yoshikawa, Hirokazu, "Long-term Effects of Early Childhood Programs on Social Outcomes and Delinquency." In *The Future of Children* (Los Altos, Calif.: Center for the Future of Children, 1995), pp. 51–75.

79. For return on investment, see Schweinhart, L. J., Barnes, H. V., and Weikart, D. P., *Significant Benefits: The High/Scope Perry Preschool Study Through Age 27* (Ypsilanti, Mich.: High/Scope Press, 1997). See also Butterfield, Fox, "Intervening Early Costs Less than '3-Strikes' Laws, Study Says," *New York Times*, June 23, 1996, p. A24.

80. Butterfield, Fox, "Most Efforts to Stop Crime Fall Far Short, Study Finds," *New York Times*, Apr. 16, 1997, p. A1. L. W. Sherman, chair of the Dept. of Criminology and Criminal Justice at the University of Maryland, is lead author of this study, "Preventing Crime: What Works, What Doesn't, What's Promising," which can be found at www.ncjrs.org.

 For a discussion of delinquency-prevention programs beginning in early childhood, see Yoshikawa, H., "Long-term Effects of Early Childhood Programs on Social Outcomes and Delinquency." In *The Future of Children: Long-Term Outcomes of Early Childhood Programs* (Los Altos, Calif.: Center for the Future of Children, 1995), pp. 51–75.

Large ongoing longitudinal studies documenting the course from childhood through adulthood of aggressive behaviors, and trials of prevention methods, include the Project on Human Development in Chicago Neighborhoods and the Seattle Social Development Project.

Also see McCord, J., and Tremblay, R., eds., *Preventing Antisocial Behavior: Interventions from Birth Through Adolescence* (New York: Guilford Press, 1992).

81. Sampson, R. J., Raudenbush, S. W., and Earls, F., "Neighborhoods and Violent Crime: A Multilevel Study of Collective Efficacy," *Science* 277: 918–23, Aug. 15, 1997. The data reported are from the Project on Human Development in Chicago Neighborhoods. Felton Earls, the principal investigator, outlines the questions and methodologies of this very large study in an article entitled "Not Fear, Not Quarantine, but Science: Preparation for a Decade of Research to Advance Knowledge About Causes and Control of Violence in Youths," *Journal of Adolescent Health* 12: 619–29, 1991.

"Collective efficacy" refers to the capacity of a neighborhood to achieve common goals. Positive influences include home ownership and long residential tenure. Negative influences include concentrated poverty and racial segregation, which often lead, according to the researchers, to an immobilizing perception of powerlessness.

9. BEATING THE ODDS

1. The study and its findings are described in detail in four books and a number of articles and monographs. The books are Werner, E. E., Bierman, J. M., and French, F. E., *The Children of Kauai* (Honolulu: University of Hawaii Press, 1971); Werner, E. E., and Smith, R. S., *Kauai's Children Come of Age* (Honolulu: University of Hawaii Press, 1977); Werner, E. E., and Smith, R. S., *Vulnerable but Invincible: A Longitudinal Study of Resilient Children and Youth* (New York: McGraw-Hill, 1989); and Werner, E. E., and Smith, R. S., *Overcoming the Odds: High-Risk Children from Birth to Adulthood* (Ithaca, N.Y.: Cornell University Press, 1992). At the thirty-two-year follow-up (the most recent book-length report), 505 of the original 837 individuals were studied.

2. Werner, E., and Smith, R., *Overcoming the Odds: High-Risk Children from Birth to Adulthood* (Ithaca, N.Y.: Cornell University Press, 1992), p. 2.

3. For references, see Schorr, L., *Within Our Reach: Breaking the Cycle of Disadvantage* (New York: Doubleday, 1988), pp. 25–28.

4. Werner, E., and Smith, R., *Overcoming the Odds: High-Risk Children from Birth to Adulthood* (Ithaca, N.Y.: Cornell University Press, 1992), p. 56.

5. Quotations in the preceding paragraphs are from Werner, Emmy, "Risk, Resilience and Recovery," *Development and Psychopathology* 5: 497–515, 1993.

6. The studies referred to in this paragraph are discussed in Werner, E., and Smith, R., *Overcoming the Odds: High-Risk Children from Birth to Adulthood* (Ithaca, N.Y.: Cornell University Press, 1992), pp. 5–13.

7. On the problems of apparently resilient children, see Luthar, S. S., Doernberger, C. H., and Zigler, E., "Resilience Is Not a Unidimensional Construct: Insights from a Prospective Study of Inner-City Adolescents," *Development and Psychopathology* 5: 703–17, 1993.

8. Zimrin, H., "A Profile of Survival," *Child Abuse and Neglect* 10: 339–49, 1986; reviewed in Garmezy, Norman, "Children in Poverty: Resilience Despite Risk," *Psychiatry* 56: 127–36, 1993.

9. Dennis is not his real name. He gave us permission to tell his story. Except for our own children's and grandchildren's, all names of individuals in the examples and anecdotes in this book have been changed.

10. Centerwall, Brandon S., "Race, Socioeconomic Status, and Domestic Homicide," *Journal of the American Medical Association* 273(22): 1755–58, June 14, 1995.

11. Bane, M. J., et al., "Childhood Poverty and Disadvantage." Unpublished paper, John F. Kennedy School of Government, 1991; cited in Weissbourd, R., *The Vulnerable Child* (Reading, Mass.: Addison-Wesley, 1996), p. 23.

12. Egeland, B., Carlson, E., and Sroufe, L. A., "Resilience as Process," *Development and Psychopathology* 5: 517–28, 1993.

13. For a profile of risk factors facing children in the fifty largest U.S. cities, see *Kids Count Data Book* (Baltimore: Annie E. Casey Foundation, 1997).

14. Rutter, M., and Rutter, M., *Developing Minds: Challenge and Continuity Across the Life Span* (New York: Basic Books, 1993). Garmezy, Norman, "Children in Poverty: Resilience Despite Risk," *Psychiatry* 56: 127–36, Feb. 1993. Sameroff, A. J., Seifer, R., Barocas, R., Zax, M., and Greenspan, S., "Intelligence Quotients of 4-Year-Old Children: Social-Environmental Risk Factors," *Pediatrics* 79: 343–50, 1987.

15. Van der Kolk, B. A., and Fisler, R. E., "Child Abuse and Neglect and Loss of Self-regulation," *Bulletin of the Menninger Clinic* 58(2): Spring 1994.

   For a review of studies on the effect of parental mental health problems on children's conduct disorders, see Mrazek, P. J., and Haggerty, R. J., eds., *Reducing Risks for Mental Disorders* (Washington, D.C.: National Academy Press, 1994), pp. 175–79.

16. Baumrind, Diana, "The Social Context of Child Maltreatment," *Family Relations* 43: 361, 1994.

17. Rende, R., and Plomin, R., "Families at Risk for Psychopathology: Who Becomes Affected and Why?" *Development and Psychopathology* 5: 529–40, 1993.

18. Rutter, M., "Nature, Nurture, and Psychopathology: A New Look at an Old Topic," *Development and Psychopathology* 3: 125–36, 1991.

19. Sroufe, L. A., "Psychopathology as an Outcome of Development," *Development and Psychopathology* 9: 251–68, 1997.

20. See Rende, R., and Plomin, R., "Families at Risk for Psychopathology: Who Becomes Affected and Why?" *Development and Psychopathology* 5: 529–40, 1993.

21. Wilson, William Julius, *The Truly Disadvantaged* (Chicago: University of Chicago Press, 1987).

22. Rutter, M., "Psychosocial Resilience and Protective Mechanisms," *American Journal of Orthopsychiatry* 57: 316–31, 1987.

23. The breakdowns by age are based on 1993 figures. The average cost is $4,300 for each child enrolled. Ninety-five percent of enrolled children are from families with incomes below the poverty line. Currie, Janet, and Thomas, Duncan, "Does Head Start Make a Difference?" *American Economic Review* 85(3): 341–64, June 1995

24. Report of the Advisory Committee on Head Start Quality and Expansion, *Creating a 21st Century Head Start* (Washington, D.C.: U.S. Department of Health and Human Services, 1993).

25. For Head Start evaluations, see Consortium for Longitudinal Studies, *As the Twig Is Bent . . . Lasting Effects of Preschool Programs* (Hillsdale, N.J.: Erlbaum, 1984); and Gomby, Deanna; Larner, M.; Stevenson, C.; Lewitt, E.; and Behrman, R., "Long-term Outcomes of Early Childhood Programs: Analysis and Recommendations," *The Future of Children* 5(3): 6–24, 1995. See also articles by W. Steven Barnett and by Hirokazu Yoshikawa on long-term effects of early childhood programs

on school outcomes, social outcomes, and delinquency, in the same issue.

26. Report of the Advisory Committee on Head Start Quality and Expansion, *Creating a 21st Century Head Start* (Washington, D.C.: U.S. Department of Health and Human Services, 1993).

27. Currie, J., and Duncan, T., "Does Head Start Make a Difference?" *American Economic Review* 85(3): 341–64, June 1995.

28. Lamb, Michael E., "Nonparental Child Care: Context, Quality, Correlates, and Consequences." In Sigel, I. E., and Renninger, K. A., eds., *Child Psychology in Practice* (New York: Wiley, 1998), pp. 73–133.

29. Campbell, F., and Ramey, C., "Effects of Early Intervention on Intellectual and Academic Achievement: A Follow-up Study of Children from Low-Income Families," *Child Development* 65: 684–98, 1994; Landesman, S., and Ramey, C., "Developmental Psychology and Mental Retardation: Integrating Scientific Principles with Treatment Practices," *American Psychologist* 44(2): 409–15, 1989.

    The quotation is from an interview of Craig Ramey in Russell, Christine, "Early Help Improves Learning Ability," *Washington Post* (Health Section), Feb. 13, 1996, p. 7.

30. Blair, C., Ramey, C., and Hardin, M., "Early Intervention for Low Birth Weight Premature Infants: Participation and Intellectual Development," *American Journal of Mental Retardation* 99(5): 542–54, 1995.

31. McCarton, C., Brooks-Gunn, J., Wallace, I., Bauer, C., et al., "Results at Age 8 Years of Early Intervention for Low-Birth-Weight Premature Infants: The Infant Health and Development Program," *Journal of the American Medical Association* 277(2): 126–32, 1997.

32. Ramey, C., and Ramey, S. L., "Early Experience and Early Intervention," *American Psychologist*, in press.

33. For more information on the Early Head Start evaluation, contact the Research, Demonstration, and Evaluation Branch, Administration on Children, Youth, and Families, 2411 Mary Switzer Bldg., 330 C St. SW, Washington, D.C. 20201.

34. Barnett, W. Steven, "Long-term Effects of Early Childhood Programs on Cognitive and School Outcomes," *The Future of Children* 5(3): 25–50, Winter 1995. The quotation is from p. 43.

35. Solnit, A., Foreword. In Provence, S., and Naylor, A., eds., *Working with Disadvantaged Parents and Their Children: Scientific and Practice Issues* (New Haven, Conn.: Yale University Press, 1983), pp. vii–ix.

36. The Family Place and other family resource programs are described more fully in Weissbourd, Bernice, "Family Support Programs." In Zeanah, C., ed., *Handbook of Infant Mental Health* (New York: Guilford Press, 1993), pp. 402–13. For more information, write the Family Resource Coalition of America, 20 N. Wacker Dr., Chicago, IL 60606.

In her book *Common Purpose: Strengthening Families and Neighborhoods to Rebuild America* (New York: Doubleday, 1997), Lisbeth Schorr discusses how small successes such as Family Place can be sustained and expanded. She points to the need to tame bureaucracies, redirect public funds, create new public-private partnerships, affirm effective programs, and give teachers, counselors, and others on the front line the flexibility they need to do their jobs. Schorr makes a point that is critical for citizens and policymakers to understand: no single element can do the job our children need—not parents or a model program, not housing or economic development or better policing, not even a better school system. Schorr shows how some communities are putting together programs that work and are transforming entire neighborhoods.

10. CARING FOR CHILDREN

1. On young children and divorce, see Shiono, P., and Quinn, L, "Epidemiology of Divorce." In Behrman, R., series ed., *The Future of Children: Children and Divorce* 4(1): 18, Spring 1994.

On unmarried mothers, see Furstenberg, F., "History and Current Status of Divorce in the United States." In Behrman, R., series ed., *The Future of Children: Children and Divorce* 4(1): 32, Spring 1994.

On teenage parenthood, see Testa, M. F., introduction to Rosenheim, M. K., and Testa, M. F., eds., *Early Parenthood and Coming of Age in the 1990's* (New Brunswick, N.J.: Rutgers University Press, 1992), p. 6; Hayes, C. D., Palmer, J. L., and Zastow, M. J., eds., *Who Cares for America's Children? Child Care Policy for the 1990s* (Washington, D.C.: National Academy Press, 1990), pp. 16–39.

On the birthrate among adolescents, see Children's Defense Fund, *The State of America's Children: Yearbook 1997* (Washington, D.C.: Children's Defense Fund, 1997), p. 81.

2. On percentages of preschool children in child care centers, by the age of the child, from 1965 to 1993, see graph based on census data in Hofferth, S., "Child Care in the United States Today." In *The Future of Children: Financing Child Care* 6(2), Summer–Fall 1996, p. 46.

3. Children's Defense Fund, *The State of America's Children: Yearbook 1997* (Washington, D.C.: Children's Defense Fund, 1997), Table B3, p. 99.

4. On child support awards and lack of enforcement, see Teachman, J., and Paasch, K., "Financial Impact of Divorce on Children and Their Families." In *The Future of Children: Children and Divorce* 4(1): 73, Spring 1994 (1989 figures); Children's Defense Fund, *The State of America's Children: Yearbook 1997* (Washington, D.C.: Children's Defense Fund, 1997), p. 99.

   On the income of female-headed households with preschool children, see Stanfield, Rochelle L., "When a Penny Saved Is a Dollar Spent," *National Journal,* Apr. 29, 1995, p. 1059.

5. West, J., Wright, D., and Hausken, E. G., *Child Care and Early Education Program Participation of Infants, Toddlers and Preschoolers* (Washington, D.C.: U.S. Department of Education, 1995); cited in Hofferth, Sandra L., "Child Care in the United States Today," *The Future of Children* 6(2): 44, Summer–Fall 1996. The David and Lucile Packard Foundation. See also Casper, L. M., "Who's Minding Our Preschoolers?" *Current Population Reports* (Washington, D.C.: U.S. Bureau of the Census, pamphlet P70-53, 1996). Quoted in Szanton, Eleanor Stokes, "Infant/Toddler Care and Education." In Seefeldt, Carol, and Galper, Alice, eds., *Continuing Issues in Early Childhood Education,* 2nd ed. (New York: Merrill/Prentice Hall, 1997), pp. 62–86.

6. National Child Care Information Center, citing U.S. Department of Education survey, "Child Care and Early Education Program Participation of Infants, Toddlers, and Preschoolers," which uses 1995 data. Personal communication, Dec. 12, 1997.

7. NICHD Early Child Care Research Network, "Child Care During the First Year of Life," *Merrill-Palmer Quarterly* 43(3): 340–60, 1997.

   The NICHD sample includes a higher proportion of nonmaternal child care (over 80 percent) than that reported from some other studies.

8. Lamb, Michael, E., "Nonparental Child Care: Context, Quality, Correlates, and Consequences." In Sigel, I. E., and Renninger, K. A., eds., *Child Psychology in Practice* (New York: Wiley, 1998), pp. 73–133.

9. Clarke-Stewart, K. A., Allhusen, V. D., and Clements, D. C., "Nonparental Caregiving." In Bornstein, M. H., ed., *Handbook of Parenting,* vol. 3 (Mahwah, N.J.: Erlbaum, 1995), pp. 151–76. The cited text appears on p. 155.

10. Spock, B., and Rothenberg, M., *Baby and Child Care: 40th Anniversary Edition* (New York: Pocket Books, 1985); Leach, P., *Your Baby and Child* (New York: Knopf, 1989).

    Bowlby is quoted in Karen, R., *Becoming Attached: Unfolding the Mystery of the Infant-Mother Bond and Its Impact on Later Life* (New York: Warner Books, 1994), p. 325.

11. Scarr, Sandra, *Mother Care/Other Care* (New York: Basic Books, 1984), p. 100.

12. On policymakers and children under three years of age, see Kammerman S., and Kahn, A., "Innovations in Toddler Care and Family Support Services: An International Overview," *Child Welfare* 74(6): 1281–1300, 1995.

13. Results from a number of studies are given in Clarke-Stewart, K., Allhusen, V. D., and Clements, D. C., "Nonparental Caregiving." In Bornstein, M. H., ed., *Handbook of Parenting*, vol. 3 (Mahwah, N.J.: Erlbaum, 1995), pp. 151–76. The quotation is from this article.

14. Broberg, A. G., Wessels, H., Lamb, M. E., and Hwang, C. P., "Effects of Day Care on the Development of Cognitive Abilities in 8-Year-Olds: A Longitudinal Study," *Developmental Psychology* 33(1): 62–69, 1997.

15. For a comprehensive review and analysis of these studies, see Lamb, Michael E., "Nonparental Child Care: Context, Quality, Correlates, and Consequences." In Sigel, I. E., and Renninger, K. E., eds., *Child Psychology in Practice* (New York: Wiley, 1998), pp. 73–133.

16. Belsky, Jay, "Developmental Risks Associated with Infant Day Care: Attachment Insecurity, Noncompliance, and Aggression?" In Chehrazi, Shala S., ed., *Psychosocial Issues in Day Care* (Washington, D.C.: American Psychiatric Press, 1990), p. 59.

17. NICHD Early Child Care Research Network, "Child Care During the First Year of Life," *Merrill-Palmer Quarterly* 43(3): 340–60, 1997.

18. NICHD Early Child Care Research Network, "Mother-Child Interactions and Cognitive Outcomes Associated with Early Child Care: Results of the NICHD Study." Poster symposium presented at the Society for Research in Child Development, Washington, D.C., April 1997. See also "Infant Child Care and Attachment Security: Results of the NICHD Study of Early Child Care," *Child Development* 68: 860–79, 1997.

19. U.S. General Accounting Office, *Welfare to Work: Child Care Assistance Limited; Welfare Reform May Expand Needs*. Catalogue item GAO/HEHS-95-220, Sept. 1995.

20. Cited in Lamb, Michael E., "Nonparental Child Care: Context, Quality, Correlates, and Consequences." In Sigel, I. E., and Renninger, K. A., eds., *Child Psychology in Practice* (New York: Wiley, 1998), pp. 73–133.

21. Zigler, Edward F., and Freedman, Johanna, "Psychological-Developmental Implications of Current Patterns on Early Child Care." In Chehrazi, S. S., ed., *Psychosocial Issues in Day Care* (Washington, D.C.: American Psychiatric Press, 1990), p. 5.

22. Helburn, S., *Cost, Quality and Outcomes in Child Care Centers: Technical Report* (Denver: University of Colorado, 1995). The states in which the study was conducted were California, Colorado, Connecticut, and North Carolina.

23. Quoted in Goodman, Ellen, "Who Will Take Care of the Children?" *Washington Post,* Feb. 11, 1995.

24. Kontos, S., Howes, C., Shinn, M., and Galinsky, E., *Quality in Family Child Care and Relative Care* (New York: Teachers College Press, 1994), p. 2; Helburn, S., and Howes, C., "Child Care Cost and Quality." In Behrman, R., series ed. *The Future of Children: Financing Child Care* 6(2): 62–82, Summer–Fall 1996.

25. Cited in Gormley, William T., Jr., and Peters, B. Guy, "National Styles of Regulation: Child Care in Three Countries," *Policy Sciences* 25: 384–85, 1992.

26. Quoted in Louv, R., *Childhood's Future* (New York: Doubleday, 1990), p. 100.

27. On staff turnover, wage decline, and the low priority given women's work and child care, see Helburn, S., and Howes, C., "Child Care Cost and Quality," *The Future of Children* 6(2): 68, 75, 80, Summer–Fall 1996. See also "Financing Child Care: Analysis and Recommendations" in the same issue, p. 10.

    On lack of benefits: U.S. General Accounting Office report, *Early Childhood Programs* (Feb. 1995), p. 25.

    On kennel attendants and grocery baggers, see Stanfield, Rochelle L., "When a Penny Saved Is a Dollar Spent," *National Journal,* Apr. 4, 1995, p. 1059.

28. Friedman, S. "Assessing the Child Care Environment." Presentation for Conference for State Officials, Feb. 7, 1997. Also see Friedman, S., and Amadeo, J., "Assessing the Child Care Environment and Experience." In Friedman, S., and Wachs, T., eds., *Assessment of the Environment Across the Lifespan* (Washington, D.C.: American Psychological Association Press, 1997).

29. Casper, Lynne M., "What Does It Cost to Mind Our Preschoolers?" (Washington, D.C.: U.S. Bureau of the Census, pamphlet P70-52, Sept. 1995); 1993 figures.

30. Sylvia Ann Hewlett cites references for this contention in *Child Neglect in Rich Nations* (New York: UNICEF, 1993), pp. 6, 7. The finding that parental time has been reduced by ten to twelve hours a week is in Fuchs, Victor R., *Women's Quest for Economic Equality* (Cambridge, Mass.: Harvard University Press, 1988), p. 111, and is cited in Hewlett, p. 6.

31. Zick, C., and Bryant, W., "A New Look at Parents' Time Spent in Child Care: Primary and Secondary Time Use," *Social Science Research* 25: 1–21, 1996. The data analyzed are from the 1977–78 Eleven State Time Use Survey. Bulletin VP 1–2, Blacksburg, Va., Virginia Agricultural Experiment Station, 1981. Maternal employment averaged sixteen hours per week.

32. The *Wall Street Journal* survey is cited in Hewlett, Sylvia Ann, *Child Neglect in Rich Nations* (New York: UNICEF, 1993), p. 7.

33. Szanton, E., "Infant/Toddler Care and Education." In Seefeldt, C., and Galper, A., eds., *Continuing Issues in Early Childhood Education*, 2nd ed. (New York: Merrill/Prentice Hall, 1997), pp. 62–86.

34. Gerson, Kathleen, "A Few Good Men: Overcoming the Barriers to Involved Fatherhood," *American Prospect* 16: 78–90, Winter 1994.

35. Hochschild, A., *The Second Shift: Working Parents and the Revolution at Home* (New York: Viking, 1989). Statistics on father time at home are in the appendix. Also see Hochschild, A., *The Time Bind* (New York: Metropolitan, 1997).

SELECTED
BIBLIOGRAPHY

Adams, Marilyn Jager. *Beginning to Read: Thinking and Learning About Print.* Cambridge, Mass.: MIT Press, 1994.

Allman, John, and Leslie Brothers. "Faces, Fear and the Amygdala." *Nature* 372: 613–14, 1994.

American Psychological Association Commission on Violence and Youth. *Violence and Youth.* Washington, D.C.: APA, 1993.

Bakwin, Harry H. "Loneliness in Infants." *American Journal of Diseases of Children* 63: 30–40, 1942.

Balkany, T. "A Brief Perspective on Cochlear Implants." *The New England Journal of Medicine* 328: 281–82, 1993.

Bates, Elizabeth, and Virginia A. Marchman. "What Is and Is Not Universal in Language Acquisition." In F. Plum, ed., *Language, Communication, and the Brain.* New York: Raven Press, 1988.

Baumrind, Diana. "Child-Care Patterns Anteceding Three Patterns of Preschool Behavior." *Genetic Psychology Monographs* 75: 43–88, 1967.

———. "The Social Context of Child Maltreatment." *Family Relations* 43: 360–67, 1994.

Behrman, Richard R., series ed. *The Future of Children.* Vol. 3(3), *Home Visiting,* Winter 1993; vol. 4(1), *Children and Divorce,* Spring 1994; vol. 5(3), *Long-Term Outcomes of Early Childhood Programs,* Winter 1995; vol. 6(2), *Financing Child Care,* Summer–Fall 1996. Los Altos, Calif.: Center for the Future of Children.

Berg, Paul, and Maxine Singer. *Dealing with Genes: The Language of Heredity.* Mill Valley, Calif.: University Science Books, 1992.

Berko-Gleason, Jean. "Sex Differences in Parent-Child Interaction." In S. U. Philips, S. Steele, and C. Tanz, eds., *Language, Gender, and Sex in Comparative Perspective.* New York: Cambridge University Press, 1987.

Blumstein, Sheila E. "The Neurobiology of the Sound Structure of Language." In M. S. Gazzaniga, ed., *The Cognitive Neurosciences.* Cambridge, Mass.: MIT Press, 1995.

Bouchard, T. J., D. T. Lykken, M. McGue, N. L. Segal, and A. Tellegen. "Sources of Human Psychological Differences: The Minnesota Study of Twins Reared Apart." *Science* 250: 223–36, 1990.

Bowlby, John. *Maternal Care and Mental Health.* Geneva: World Health Organization Monograph Series, no. 2, 1951.

———. *Attachment.* New York: Basic Books, 1969.

Boyer, Ernest. *Ready to Learn: A Mandate for the Nation.* Princeton, N.J.: Princeton University Press, 1991.

Brazelton, T. Berry, and Bertrand Cramer. *The Earliest Relationship: Parents, Infants, and the Drama of Early Attachment.* New York: Delacorte, 1990.

Brothers, Leslie L. "A Biological Perspective on Empathy." *American Journal of Psychiatry* 146: 10–18, 1989.

Brown, J., H. Ye, R. Bronson, P. Dikkes, and M. Greenberg. "A Defect in Nurturing in Mice Lacking the Immediate Early Gene fosB." *Cell* 86: 297–309, 1996.

Brown, J. Larry, and Ernesto Pollitt. "Malnutrition, Poverty and Mental Development." *Scientific American,* Feb. 1996, pp. 38–43.

Bruner, Jerome. *Child's Talk: Learning to Use Language.* New York: Norton, 1983.

Campbell, Frances, and Craig Ramey. "Effects of Early Intervention on Intellectual and Academic Achievement: A Follow-up Study of Children from Low-Income Families." *Child Development* 65: 684–98, 1994.

Caplan, David. "The Cognitive Neuroscience of Syntactic Processing." In M. S., Gazzaniga, ed., *The Cognitive Neurosciences.* Cambridge, Mass.: MIT Press, 1995.

Chivian E., M. McCally, H. Hu, and A. Haines. *Critical Condition: Human Health and the Environment.* Cambridge, Mass.: MIT Press, 1993.

Chomsky, Noam. *Rules and Representations.* New York: Columbia University Press, 1980.

Christophe, A., E. Dupoux, and J. Mehler. "Do Infants Perceive Word

Boundaries? An Empirical Study of the Bootstrapping of Lexical Acquisition." *Journal of the Acoustical Society of America* 95: 1570–80, 1994.

Clinton, Hillary Rodham. *It Takes a Village and Other Lessons Children Teach Us.* New York: Simon & Schuster, 1996.

Coie, J., R. Terry, K. F. Lenox, J. Lochman, and C. Hyman. "Childhood Peer Rejection and Aggression as Predictors of Stable Patterns of Adolescent Disorder." *Development and Psychopathology* 7: 697–713, 1995.

Coles, Robert. *The Moral Intelligence of Children.* New York: Random House, 1997.

Conel, J. L. *Postnatal Development of the Human Cerebral Cortex.* Cambridge, Mass.: Harvard University Press, 1939 and 1959.

Corina, D. P., J. Vaid, and U. Bellugi. "The Linguistic Basis of Left Hemisphere Specialization." *Science* 255: 1258–60, 1992.

Curtiss, Susan. *Genie: A Psycholinguistic Study of a Modern-Day "Wild Child."* New York: Academic Press, 1977.

———. "The Independence and Task-Specificity of Language." In M. Bornstein and J. Bruner, eds., *Interaction in Human Development.* Hillsdale, N.J.: Erlbaum, 1989.

Damasio, Antonio. *Descartes' Error: Emotion, Reason, and the Human Brain.* New York: Putnam, 1994.

Darwin, Charles. "A Biographical Sketch of an Infant." Originally published in *Mind*, pp. 285–94, July 1877. Reprinted in supplement no. 24 to *Developmental Medicine and Child Neurology* 13:5, 1971.

Davidson, Richard, and Nathan Fox. "Asymmetrical Brain Activity Discriminates Between Positive and Negative Affective Stimuli in Human Infants. *Science* 218: 1235–36, 1982.

Dawson, Geraldine, and Kurt W. Fischer, eds. *Human Behavior and the Developing Brain.* New York: Guilford Press, 1994.

DeCasper, A. J., J. Lecanuet, M. Busnel, C. Granier-Deferre, and R. Maugeais. "Fetal Reactions to Recurrent Maternal Speech." *Infant Behavior and Development* 17: 159–64, 1994.

Degler, Carl. *In Search of Human Nature.* New York: Oxford University Press, 1991.

Dodge, Kenneth, and D. Somberg. "Hostile Attributional Biases Among Aggressive Boys Are Exacerbated Under Conditions of Threats to Self." *Child Development* 58: 213–24, 1987.

Egeland, B., E. Carlson, and L. A. Sroufe. "Resilience as Process." *Development and Psychopathology* 5: 517–28, 1993.

Eimas, P. D., and J. L. Miller. "Organization in the Perception of Speech by Young Infants." *Psychological Science* 3: 340–45, 1992.

Eisenberg, Nancy, and P. A. Miller. "The Relation of Empathy to Prosocial and Related Behaviors." *Psychological Bulletin* 101(1): 91–119, 1987.

Ekman, Paul. "Facial Expression and Emotion." *American Psychologist* 48: 384–92, 1993.

Ekman, Paul, and Richard Davidson. *The Nature of Emotion: Fundamental Questions.* Oxford, England: Oxford University Press, 1994.

Emde, R., Z. Biringen, R. Clyman, and D. Oppenheim. "The Moral Self of Infancy: Affective Core and Procedural Knowledge." *Developmental Review* 11: 251–70, 1991.

Fenson, L., P. S. Dale, J. S. Reznick, E. Bates, D. J. Thal, and S. J. Pethick. "Variability in Early Communicative Development." *Monographs of the Society for Research in Child Development* 59: 163–89, 1994.

Fernald, Anne. "Approval and Disapproval: Infant Responsiveness to Vocal Affect in Familiar and Unfamiliar Languages." *Child Development* 64: 657–74, 1993.

Ferris, Craig F., and Thomas Grisso, eds. *Understanding Aggressive Behavior in Children. Annals of the New York Academy of Science* 794: 208–23, 1996.

Fisher, S. E., F. Varga-Khadem, K. Watkins, A. Monaco, and M. Pembrey. "Localization of a Gene Implicated in a Severe Speech and Language Disorder." *Nature Genetics* 18: 168–70, 1998.

Fraiberg, Selma, Edna Adelson, and Vivian Shapiro. "Ghosts in the Nursery: A Psychoanalytic Approach to the Problem of Impaired Infant-Mother Relationships." *Journal of the American Academy of Child Psychiatry* 14(3): 387–422, 1975.

Fromkin, Victoria A. "The State of Brain/Language Research." In F. Plum, ed., *Language, Communication, and the Brain.* New York: Raven Press, 1988.

Garber, Judy, and Kenneth Dodge, eds. *The Development of Emotion Regulation and Dysregulation.* Cambridge, Mass.: Cambridge University Press, 1991.

Gazzaniga, Michael S., ed. *The Cognitive Neurosciences.* Cambridge, Mass.: MIT Press, 1995.

Geschwind, Norman, and W. Levitsky. "Human Brain: Left-Right Asymmetries in Temporal Speech Region." *Science* 161: 186–87, 1968.

Goldberg, Susan, Roy Muir, and John Kerr, eds. *Attachment Theory: Social, Developmental, and Clinical Perspectives.* Hillsdale, N.J.: Analytic Press, 1995.

Goleman, Daniel. *Emotional Intelligence: Why It Can Matter More Than IQ.* New York: Bantam Books, 1995.

Gopnik, Myra, and Martha B. Crago. "Familial Aggregation of a Developmental Language Disorder." *Cognition* 39: 1–50, 1991.

Greenspan, Stanley, with J. Salmon. *The Challenging Child.* Reading, Mass.: Addison-Wesley, 1995.

Greenspan, Stanley, with Beryl Benderly. *The Growth of the Mind.* Reading, Mass: Addison-Wesley, 1997.

Guyton, Arthur C., and John E. Hall. *Textbook of Medical Physiology,* 9th ed. Philadelphia: W. B. Saunders, 1996.

Harkness, Sara. "A Cultural Model for the Acquisition of Language: Implications for the Innateness Debate." *Developmental Psychobiology* 23(7): 727–40, 1990.

Hart, Betty, and Todd R. Risley. *Meaningful Differences in the Everyday Experiences of Young American Children.* Baltimore: P. H. Brookes, 1995.

Hay, Dale F. "Prosocial Development." *Journal of Child Psychology and Psychiatry* 35(1): 29–71, 1994.

Heath, Shirley Brice. *Ways with Words: Language, Life, and Work in Communities and Classrooms.* New York: Cambridge University Press, 1983.

Hewlett, Sylvia Ann. *When the Bough Breaks: The Cost of Neglecting Our Children.* New York: HarperCollins, 1991.

Hochschild, Arlie. *The Second Shift: Working Parents and the Revolution at Home.* New York: Viking, 1989.

Hofer, Myron. "Hidden Regulators: Implications for a New Understanding of Attachment, Separation, and Loss." In S. Goldberg, R. Kerr, and J. Muir, eds., *Attachment Theory: Social and Developmental Perspectives.* Hillsdale, N.J.: Analytic Press, 1995.

Holcomb, P. J., S. A. Coffey, and H. J. Neville. "Visual and Auditory Sentence Processing: A Developmental Analysis Using Event-Related Brain Potentials." *Developmental Neuropsychology* 8(2 and 3): 203–41, 1992.

Huttenlocher, Peter R. "Morphometric Study of Human Cerebral Cortex Development." *Neuropsychologia* 28(6): 517–27, 1990.

Izard, Carroll E. *Human Emotions.* New York: Plenum Press, 1977.

Johnson, J., and E. Newport. "Critical Period Effects in Second Language Learning: The Influence of Maturational State on the Acquisition of English as a Second Language." *Cognitive Psychology* 21: 60–99, 1989.

Jusczyk, Peter W., A. Cutler, and N. J. Redanz. "Infants' Preference for the Predominant Stress Patterns of English Words." *Child Development* 64: 675–85, 1993.

Kagan, Jerome. *Galen's Prophecy: Temperament in Human Nature*. New York: Basic Books, 1994.

————. *The Nature of the Child*. New York: Basic Books, 1994.

Kagan, Jerome, and Sharon Lamb. *The Emergence of Morality in Young Children*. Chicago: University of Chicago Press, 1987.

Kandel, Eric, James Schwartz, and Thomas Jessell. *Principles of Neural Science*, 3rd ed. New York: Elsevier, 1991.

Karen, Robert. *Becoming Attached: Unfolding the Mystery of the Infant-Mother Bond and Its Impact on Later Life*. New York: Warner Books, 1994.

Keller, Helen. *The Story of My Life*. New York: Grosset & Dunlap, 1905.

Kochanska, Grazyna. "Toward a Synthesis of Parental Socialization and Child Temperament in Early Development of Conscience." *Child Development* 64: 325–47, 1993.

Koestner, R., C. Franz, and J. Weinberger. "The Family Origins of Empathic Concern: A 26-Year Longitudinal Study." *Journal of Personality and Social Psychology* 58(4): 709–17, 1990.

Kohn, Alfie. *The Brighter Side of Human Nature: Altruism and Empathy in Everyday Life*. New York: Basic Books, 1990.

Kopp, Claire B. "Antecedents of Self-Regulation: A Developmental Perspective." *Developmental Psychology* 18(2): 199–214, 1982.

Kuhl, P. K., K. A. Williams, F. Lacerda, K. N. Stevens, and B. Lindblom. "Linguistic Experience Alters Phonetic Perception in Infants by Six Months of Age." *Science* 255: 606–8, 1992.

Lamb, Michael E., "Nonparental Child Care: Context, Quality, Correlates, and Consequences." In I. E. Sigel and K. A. Renninger, eds., *Child Psychology in Practice*. New York: Wiley, 1998.

LeDoux, Joseph E. *The Emotional Brain: The Mysterious Underpinnings of Emotional Life*. New York: Simon & Schuster, 1996.

Lewis, Michael, and Jeannette M. Haviland. *Handbook of Emotions*. New York: Guilford Press, 1993.

Liu, D., J. Diorio, B. Tannenbaum, C. Caldji, D. Francis, A. Freedman, S. Sharma, D. Pearson, P. Plotsky, and M. Meaney. "Maternal Care, Hippocampal Glucocorticoid Receptors, and Hypothalamic-Pituitary-Adrenal Responses to Stress." *Science* 277: 1659–62, 1997.

Louv, Richard. *Childhood's Future*. New York: Doubleday, 1990.

McCarton, C., J. Brooks-Gunn, I. Wallace, C. Bauer, et al. "Results at Age 8 Years of Early Intervention for Low-Birth-Weight Premature Infants." *Journal of the American Medical Association* 277(2): 126–32, 1997.

McEwen, Bruce, and Robert Sapolsky. "Stress and Cognitive Function." *Current Opinion in Neurobiology* 5: 205–16, 1995.

Mehler, Jacques, and Anne Christophe. "Maturation and Learning of Language in the First Year of Life." In M. S. Gazzaniga, ed., *The Cognitive Neurosciences*. Cambridge, Mass.: MIT Press, 1995.

Merzenich, M. M., W. M. Jenkins, P. Johnston, C. Schreiner, S. L. Miller, and P. Tallal. "Temporal Processing Deficits of Language-Learning Impaired Children Ameliorated by Training." *Science* 271: 77–81, 1996.

Mills, Debra, Sharon Coffey, and Helen Neville. "Language Acquisition and Cerebral Specialization in 20-Month-Old Infants." *Journal of Cognitive Neuroscience* 5(3): 326–42, 1993.

Mrazek, Patricia, and Robert Haggerty, eds. *Reducing Risks for Mental Disorders*. Washington, D.C.: National Academy Press, 1994.

Nelson, Phillip. "Palimpsest or Tabula Rasa: Developmental Biology of the Brain," *Journal of the American Academy of Psychoanalysis* 21: 525–37, 1993.

Neville, Helen, J. "Developmental Specificity in Neurocognitive Development in Humans." In M. S. Gazzaniga, ed., *The Cognitive Neurosciences*. Cambridge, Mass.: MIT Press, 1995.

NICHD Early Child Care Research Network. "Child Care in the First Year of Life." *Merrill-Palmer Quarterly* 43(3): 340–60, 1997.

Ojemann, George A. "Cortical Organization of Language." *The Journal of Neuroscience* 11(8): 2281–87, August 1991.

Pedersen, Cort. "Oxytocin Control of Maternal Behavior: Regulation by Sex Steroids and Offspring Stimuli." In C. S. Carter, I. Lederhendler, and B. Kirkpatrick. *The Integrative Neurobiology of Affiliation. Annals of the New York Academy of Sciences* 808: 126–45, 1997.

Pinker, Steven. *The Language Instinct: How the Mind Creates Language*. New York: Morrow, 1994.

Plomin, Robert, and Gerald McClearn, eds. *Nature, Nurture, and Psychology*. Washington, D.C.: American Psychological Association, 1993.

Plum, Fred, ed. *Language, Communication, and the Brain*. New York: Raven Press, 1988.

Purcell-Gates, Victoria. *Other People's Words: The Cycle of Low Literacy*. Cambridge, Mass.: Harvard University Press, 1995.

Rakic, Pasko. "Specification of Cerebral Cortical Areas." *Science* 241: 170–76, 1988.

Ramey, Craig, and Sharon L. Ramey. "Early Experience and Early Intervention." *American Psychologist,* in press.

Rubin, K. H., R. J. Coplan, N. A. Fox, and S. D. Calkins. "Emotionality, Emotion Regulation, and Preschoolers' Social Adaptation." *Development and Psychopathology* 7: 49–62, 1995.

Rutter, Michael, and Marjorie Rutter. *Developing Minds: Challenge and Continuity Across the Life Span.* New York: Basic Books, 1993.

Sameroff, Arnold J., and Robert N. Emde. *Relationship Disturbances in Early Childhood: A Developmental Approach.* New York: Basic Books, 1989.

Satz, P., E. Strauss, J. Wada, and D. L. Orsini. "Some Correlates of Intra- and Interhemispheric Speech Organization After Left Focal Brain Injury." *Neuropsychologia.* 26(2): 345–50, 1988.

Schanberg, S. M., and Tiffany M. Field. "Sensory Deprivation, Stress, and Supplemental Stimulation in the Rat Pup and Preterm Human Neonate." *Child Development* 58: 1431–47, 1987.

Schore, Allan N. *Affect Regulation and the Origin of the Self: The Neurobiology of Emotional Development.* Hillsdale, N.J.: Erlbaum, 1994.

Schorr, Lisbeth. *Common Purpose: Strengthening Families and Neighborhoods to Rebuild America.* New York: Doubleday, 1997.

Schweinhart, L. J., H. V. Barnes, and D. P. Weikart. *Significant Benefits: The High/Scope Perry Preschool Study Through Age 27.* Ypsilanti, Mich.: High/Scope Press, 1997.

Shepherd, Gordon M. *Neurobiology,* 3rd ed. New York: Oxford University Press, 1994.

Shinn, Millicent W. *The Biography of a Baby.* Originally published, New York: Houghton Mifflin, 1900. Reprinted by Arno Press in the series *Classics in Child Development,* 1975.

Snow, Catherine E., Rivka Perlmann, and Debra Nathan. "Why Routines Are Different: Toward a Multiple-Factors Model of the Relation Between Input and Language Acquisition." In K. Nelson and A. van Kleek, eds., *Children's Language,* vol. 6. Hillsdale, N.J.: Erlbaum, 1987.

Sperry, Roger W. "Lateral Specialization in the Surgically Separated Hemispheres." In F. O. Schmitt and F. G. Worden, eds., *The Neurosciences: Third Study Program.* Cambridge, Mass.: MIT Press, 1974.

Spitz, René. "Hospitalism: An Inquiry into the Genesis of Psychiatric Conditions in Early Childhood." *The Psychoanalytic Study of the Child* 1: 53–74, 1945.

Sroufe, L. Allen. *Emotional Development: The Organization of Emotional Life in the Early Years.* Cambridge, England: Cambridge University Press, 1996.

Stern, Daniel N. *The Interpersonal World of the Infant.* New York: Basic Books, 1985.

Suomi, Stephen J. "Genetic and Maternal Contributions to Individual Differences in Rhesus Monkey Biobehavioral Development." In N. Krasnegor, E. Blass, M. Hofer, and W. Smotherman, eds., *Perinatal Development: A Psychobiological Perspective.* New York: Academic Press, 1987.

———. "Early Stress and Adult Emotional Reactivity in Rhesus Monkeys." In G. R. Bock and J. Whelan, eds., *The Childhood Environment and Adult Disease.* Chichester, England: John Wiley & Sons, 1991.

Super, Charles M. S., and Sara Harkness. "The Developmental Niche: A Conceptualization at the Interface of Child and Culture." *International Journal of Behavioral Development* 9: 545–69, 1986.

Tallal, P., S. L. Miller, G. Bedi, G. Byma, X. Wang, S. S. Nagarajan, C. Schreiner, W. M. Jenkins, and M. M. Merzenich. "Language Comprehension in Language-Learning Impaired Children Improved with Acoustically Modified Speech." *Science* 271: 81–84, 1996.

Tanenhaus, M. K., M. J. Spivey-Knowlton, K. M. Eberhard, and J. C. Sedivy. "Integration of Visual and Linguistic Information in Spoken Language Comprehension." *Science* 268: 1632–34, 1995.

Thomas, David G., and C. Donel Crow. "Development of Evoked Electrical Brain Activity in Infancy." In G. Dawson and K. W. Fischer, eds., *Human Behavior and the Developing Brain.* New York: Guilford Press, 1994.

Tomarken, A. J., R. J. Davidson, R. E. Wheeler, and R. C. Doss. "Individual Differences in Anterior Brain Asymmetry and Fundamental Dimensions of Emotion." *Journal of Personality and Social Psychology* 62: 676–87, 1992.

Trevarthen, C., and K. J. Aitken. "Brain Development, Infant Communication, and Empathy Disorders: Intrinsic Factors in Child Mental Health." *Development and Psychopathology* 6: 597–633, 1994.

Tronick, E., H. Als, L. Adamson, S. Wise, and T. B. Brazelton. "The Infant's Response to Entrapment Between Contradictory Messages in Face-to-Face Interaction." *Journal of Child Psychiatry* 17: 1–13, 1978.

Tucker, Don M. "Developing Emotions and Cortical Networks." In M. R. Gunnar and C. A. Nelson, eds., *Developmental Behavioral Neuroscience* 24. Hillsdale, N.J.: Erlbaum, 1992.

Tye-Murray, N., L. Spencer, and G. G. Woodworth. "Acquisition of Speech by Children Who Have Prolonged Cochlear Implant Experience." *Journal of Speech and Hearing Research* 38: 327–37, April 1995.

Walker, D., C. Greenwood, B. Hart, and J. Carta. "Prediction of School Outcomes Based on Early Language Production and Socioeconomic Factors." *Child Development* 65: 606–21, 1994.

Walsh, C., and C. Cepko. "Widespread Dispersion of Neuronal Clones Across Functional Regions of the Cerebral Cortex." *Science* 255: 434–40, 1992.

Weinberger, J. "The Family Origins of Empathic Concern: A 26-Year Longitudinal Study." *Journal of Personality and Social Psychology* 58: 709–19, 1990.

Weir, Ruth H. *Language in the Crib.* The Hague, Netherlands: Mouton & Co., 1970.

Weissbourd, Bernice. "Family Support Programs." In C. Zeanah, ed., *Handbook of Infant Mental Health.* New York: Guilford Press, 1993.

Weissbourd, Richard. *The Vulnerable Child: What Really Hurts America's Children and What We Can Do About It.* Reading, Mass.: Addison-Wesley, 1996.

Werner, Emmy, and Ruth Smith. *Overcoming the Odds: High Risk Children from Birth to Adulthood.* Ithaca, N.Y.: Cornell University Press, 1992.

Witelson, S. F., and W. Pallie. "Left Hemisphere Specialization for Language in the Newborn: Neuroanatomical Evidence of Asymmetry." *Brain* 96: 641–46, 1973.

Zahn-Waxler, Caroline, and Marian Radke-Yarrow. "The Origins of Empathic Concern." *Motivation and Emotion* 14: 107–29, 1990.

INDEX

Page numbers in *italics* refer to illustrations.